W9-BSN-725

THE AUTHENTIC WILD WEST

THE GUNFIGHTERS

THE AUTHENTIC WILD WEST

THE GUNFIGHTERS

JAMES D. HORAN

GRAMERCY BOOKS
New York • Avenel

FOR

Cattle Gert and our beloved little bravos:
Christopher Gary, Brian Burgers, Jeffrey Peter, and Stephanie Peters

This 1994 edition is published by Gramercy Books,
distributed by Random House Value Publishing, Inc.,
40 Engelhard Avenue, Avenel, New Jersey 07001.

Random House
New York • Toronto • London • Sydney • Auckland

Printed and bound in the United States of America

Designed by Ruth Smerechniak

Library of Congress Cataloging-in-Publication Data
Horan, James David
The Gunfighters: The authentic wild West.
Bibliography: p.
1. Crime and criminals—The West. 2. The West—
Biography. I. Title.
F594.H79 978'.02'0922 [B] 76-10758
ISBN 0-517-11855-6

8 7 6 5 4 3 2 1

ACKNOWLEDGMENTS

The efforts and courtesy of many people helped to make this book possible and it is a pleasure to acknowledge their kindness and contributions. They include:

American Philosophical Society, Philadelphia, Carl F. Miller, Assistant Manuscript Librarian; Arizona Historical Society, Margaret S. Bret Harte, Research Librarian; The University of Arizona Library, Mrs. Lynn M. Cresson, Special Collections, Donald M. Powell, Head, Special Collections; Library of the Boston Athenaeum, Ann L. Wadsworth, Reference Department; The Bancroft Library, University of California, Berkeley, Peter E. Hanff, Coordinator, Technical Services, Miss Estelle Rebec, Head, Manuscript Division, William M. Roberts, Reference Librarian; California Historical Society, Lee L. Burtis, Librarian, Photograph Department; California State Library, Greg Swalley, J. E. Reynolds, Van Nuys, California; Newspaper Staff of the Chicago Public Library and the Research Staff of the Chicago Historical Society; Diana Haskell, Curator of Modern Mss., The Newberry Library, Chicago; The State Historical Society of Colorado, Ms. Alice L. Sharp, Reference Librarian, Documentary Resources, and Mrs. Catherine T. Engel, Reference Librarian, Documentary Resources; Denver Public Library, Western History Department, Eleanor M. Gehres; Connecticut State Library, Eunice Gillman, Reference Librarian, Archives, History and Genealogy Unit; Melancthon W. Jacobus, Curator of Prints, The Connecticut Historical Society; Gus Johnson, photographer, Windsor, Connecticut; The Huntington Library, San Marino, California, Mrs. Valerie Franco, Assistant Curator, Western Manuscripts; Indiana Historical Society (William Henry Smith Memorial), Mrs. Leona T. Alig, Manuscripts Librarian; Indiana State Library, Ms. Jean E. Singleton, Reference Librarian, Indiana Division; Jersey City Library, Jersey City, New Jersey, Bruce Brandt, Research Department and the Staff of the Fine Arts Division, Joslyn Art Museum, Omaha, Nebraska, Ms. Mildred Goosman, Curator, Western Collections; Kansas State Historical Society, Eugene D. Decker, Archivist; Mrs. Edwin M. Johnson, McClung Historical Collection, Knoxville County Library; The Library of Congress, William Matheson, Chief, Reference Department, Rare Book and Special Collections Division, Bernard A. Bernier, Jr., Head, Reference Section, Serial Division;

Foreign and Commonwealth Office, Mrs. G. W. Arney, London; Los Angeles Public Library, Edith W. Johnson, Library Assistant, General Reading Services, Charles A. Lush, Senior Librarian, James Vale, Library Assistant; Jackson County, Missouri, Historical Society, Mrs. Donald B. Erlich, Director of Archives; Montana Historical Society, Mrs. Harriett C. Meloy, Librarian, Ms. Lory Morrow, Photo-Archivist; Robert E. Miller, Helena, Ms. Dorothy Johnson, Missoula, and E. E. MacGilvra, Butte, Montana; Minnesota Historical Society, Janet Moosbrugger, Reference Librarian; The State Historical Society of Missouri, Mrs. Billie Mojonnier, Newspaper Library, Mrs. Lynn M. Roberts, Secretary, Pat Weiner, Reference Librarian, Mrs. Winifred Stufflebam, Newspaper Library, Carole Sue Warmbrodt DeLaite, Newspaper Library; University of Missouri Library, Western Historical Manuscript Collection, Nancy C. Prewitt, Assistant Director, Nancy Lankford, Manuscripts Reference Head; New Mexico State Records Center and Archives, James H. Purdy, Historian; New Mexico Highlands University, Las Vegas, V. C. Roybal, Reference Librarian, R. Anaya, Assistant Reference Librarian; Museum of New Mexico, Arthur H. Olivas, Photographic Archivist, Stephany Eger, Librarian; Old Lincoln County Memorial Commission, Molly Madden; National Archives, Elaine C. Everly, Navy and Old Army Branch, Military Archives Division, C. George Younkin, Chief, Archives Branch, M. M. Johnson, Legislative, Judicial and Fiscal Branch Civil Archives Division, Richard S. Maxwell, Civil Archives Division, William B. Fraley, Acting Assistant Director, General Archives Division, Milton O. Gustafson, Chief, Diplomatic Branch, Civil Archives Division, Michael Goldman, Natural Resources Branch, Civil Archives Division, Mark G. Eckhoff, Chief, Legislative, Judicial and Fiscal Branch, Robert Svenningsen, Chief, Archives Branch, Katherine F. Gould, Acting Head, Reference Section, Serial Division; Nebraska State Historical Society, Mrs. Ann Reinert, Librarian; The R. W. Norton Art Gallery, Shreveport, Louisiana, Jerry M. Bloomer, Secretary-Registrar;

National Collection of Fine Arts, Andrea Brown, Office of Photographic Services; Oklahoma State Historical Society, Mary Lee Ervin, Genealogist; The Paine Art Center and Arboretum, Oshkosh, Wisconsin, Kathy L. Nitkowski, Secretary-Registrar; Robert Rockwell, The Rockwell Gallery, Corning, New York; South Dakota Department of Educational and Cultural Affairs, Historical Resource Center, Ms. Denise Ramse; Shelburne Museum, Shelburne, Vermont, Sterling D. Emerson, Director; Smithsonian Institution, James A. Steed, Assistant Archivist, Ms. Paula J. Richardson, Museum Specialist, National Anthropological Archives; County Clerk's Office, Travis County, Texas, Mrs. Deloris Hastings, Deputy, Probate Division, Doris Shropshire, County Clerk; Fort Worth, Texas Public Library, Patricia Chadwell, Head, Southwestern Collection; The Museum of Fine Arts, Houston, Neal von Hedemann, Registrar's Aide; Amon Carter Museum of Western Art, Fort Worth, Texas, Mrs. Nancy G. Wynne, Librarian; Chester V. Kielman, Librarian-Archivist, Barker Texas History Center, The University of Texas at Austin; The Wenatchee Daily World, Wenatchee, Washington, Sheila Graves, Newsroom; The Washington State Historical Society, Frank L. Green, Librarian; West Point Museum, Michael J. McAfee, Museum Curator; Wyoming State Archives and Historical Department, John C. Paige, Research Historian, Historical Research and Publications Division, Teresa Matthews, Curator of Photography, William H. Barton, Research Historian and Historical Research and Publications Division, Laura Hayes, Curator, Photographic Section; Paula West, Photographic Section.

A special note of appreciation must be given to Dr. Louis Moloney, Librarian, Hugh Black, Chief Reference Librarian and the staff of the Southwest Texas State University Library, San Marcos, Texas; Dr. Alfred Taylor, Head, The Journalism Department, and Michael Diehl, Geronimo, Texas, for their united effort in getting me copies of the rare and fragile John Wesley Hardin letters and photographs; Alvin J. Lucke, Havre, Montana, for allowing me to use his collection of photographs of Kid Curry and his times; Ms. Claire Kuehn, Archivist-Librarian, Panhandle-Plains Historical Museum, Canyon, Texas, for Deluvina Maxwell's memories of Billy the Kid as told to J. Evetts Haley and Father Blaine Burkey, Center for Research, Thomas More Prep, Hays City, Kansas, for his material on Wild Bill Hickok.

A note of thanks is due the late Mrs. Zoe Tilghman, Frank Dimaio and Lowell Spence for their reminiscences, photographs, letters, and so on, and to the late Percy Seibert and Victor Hampton for their material on Butch Cassidy, The Sundance Kid, and Etta Place in Bolivia.

And above all to Gertrude who made this long and arduous journey with me into the Wild West, carefully typed this huge manuscript and saved me from numerous errors.

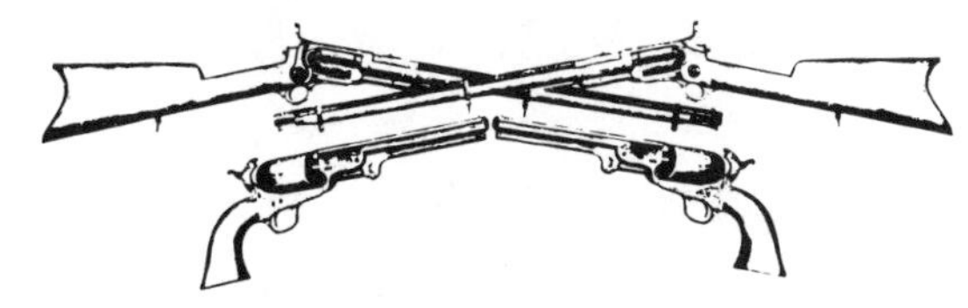

CONTENTS

INTRODUCTION: DAY OF THE GUNFIGHTER 1

BILLY THE KID 9

WILD BILL HICKOK 81

BEN THOMPSON 123

JOHN WESLEY HARDIN 155

KID CURRY AND THE LOGANS OF MONTANA 187

TOM HORN 221

HARRY TRACY 255

NOTES 287

BIBLIOGRAPHY 302

INDEX 309

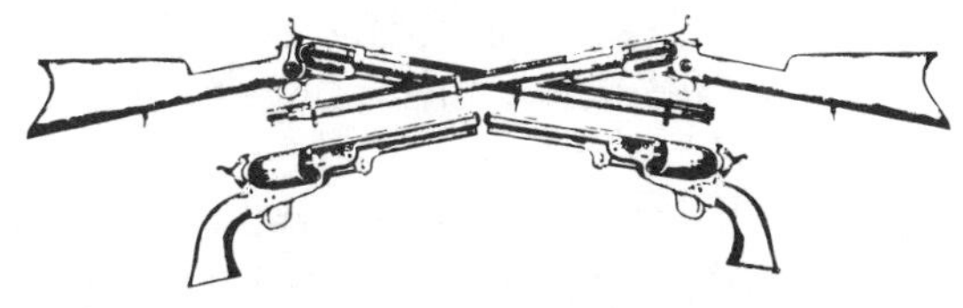

INTRODUCTION
DAY OF THE GUNFIGHTER

THE MIDDAY SUN BAKES THE RAW TRAIL'S END COW TOWN. The rutted street bordered by frame houses is deserted, even the benches on the drover's hotel porch are empty. There is a menacing stillness, a sense of suppressed violence about to explode.

Suddenly the gunfighter appears. He is tall, tanned to the color of old saddle leather. Under the rim of his sombrero his blue eyes are cold, steady. Holsters with six-shooters are tied to his thighs with buckskin thongs. He advances slowly down the street, hands casually hanging at his sides.

Men and women peer anxiously from doorways and windows. In the livery a horse, waiting to be shod, snorts impatiently. A hot breeze toys with the dust. Somewhere a door slams.

Then another man appears. There is an arrogance in his walk. Like the gunfighter he wears guns. He approaches, stops. For a long moment they take each other's measure in the taut silence. Almost as if someone had given a signal, the hands of both men flash to the butts of their guns. The stillness is shattered by the roar of single-action Colt .45s. The gunfighter continues to stand erect, untouched while his opponent slowly crumples. The town erupts, men and women pouring out into the street, some looking with awe at the gunfighter who calmly, almost sadly, holsters his gun and walks away while others bend over the man who was dead before his body hit the ground.

This trite, ritualized scene has been played countless times in books, songs, ballads, on television, and in movies, always with the gunfighter as the central character.

He is one of our nation's most popular folklore figures, more popular than Washington's Continentals, Lee's cavalrymen, troopers of the Indian Fighting Army, mountain men, explorers, miners, loggers, prizefighters, and rivermen.

His specific crimes or acts of violence are largely forgotten, but the romantic pageantry remains. Perhaps evil is more interesting than goodness.

In reality the gunfighter lived in the Wild West from about the time of the founding of the cow towns after the end of the Civil War to the 1880s. By the turn of the century the few survivors were frontier anachronisms unable to cope with a more sophisticated society. They were finally done in by barbed wire, the telephone, and a more effective form of law enforcement which, ironically, they had helped to establish.

Richard Fox's pink *Police Gazette* first molded their image. Its circulation was enormous; it has been estimated that the male half of the population of the latter part of the nineteenth century read the *Gazette* in cow camps, saloons, barbershops, bordellos, pool halls, gambling houses, and livery stables. The paper passed from hand to hand until it literally fell apart.

Fox's editors quickly recognized the inherent drama of the gunfighter. In every story he was handsome, a superb horseman, a skilled marksman who provided the oppressed with life, liberty, and an opportunity to pursue happiness.

His motivation for entering a life of danger and self-destruction was usually a false arrest, a father killed by corrupt lawmen in the pay of a mortgage holder, or the most popular version—a southern cavalier, a patriot of the Confederacy, who had been driven into outlawry by his ruthless enemies in the North.

Frank Leslie's Weekly and *Harper's*, while generally more factual and less garish, also focused on the Wild West, assigning special correspondents like Theodore Davis, a superb Civil War artist. Writers sent back stories of wild stagecoach rides, Indian attacks, buffalo hunts, cattle drives, railroading, the trials and tribulations of homesteaders—and interviews and sketches of gunfighters.

Together with the *Gazette*, many frontier newspapers, and Beadle's dime novels, they helped to make the bloodletters romantic figures, majestic in their bearing, Lochinvars of the cow towns.

The saga of Wild Bill Hickok is an excellent example of how they turned an obscure stock tender into an imperishable American hero. When Colonel George Ward Nichols of *Harper's New Monthly Magazine*, who had fought with Sherman during the Civil War, met the handsome Hickok on the frontier, he was completely lost, swallowing Wild Bill's outrageous lies of how he had killed a band of desperados at the Rock Creek Overland Stage Depot in Nebraska. The tall tale was believed by generations; it wasn't until 1927 when George W. Hansen's article in the *Nebraska History Magazine* exposed the fraud and revealed how Hickok had cold-bloodedly killed two unarmed men and watched while a third was beaten to death with a hoe.

In contrast, Billy the Kid, known across the world as one of the leading actors in the Wild West, was portrayed as an adenoidal moronic killer. A cache of extant, little known official documents in Washington, D.C., reveals the incredible role he played as leader of a group of ranchers fighting a powerful frontier ring of corrupt officials.

Who were these men? Where did they come from? Were they all illiterate, psychotic killers? What is the truth of their lives and their legendary exploits?

Ironically you can find some of the answers in their own writings. Some wrote their autobiographies or assisted their biographers; others supplied material for newspaper feature stories or serials; nearly all had been interviewed by reporters, not only from frontier newspapers but from New York City papers. They also wrote letters to editors, complaining that the news accounts of their time portrayed them inaccurately.

Despite the horrors of Huntsville prison, John Wesley Hardin read law, emerged a lawyer, and wrote his autobiography. Ben Thompson, who, Bat Masterson claimed, had no peer in the fast draw, was elected marshal of Austin, made that community one of the safest in Texas, and spent a great deal of time with his biographer, a respected judge.

Billy the Kid's letters to New Mexico's territorial governor, Lew Wallace—the author of *Ben Hur*—and his affidavit to Washington agent Frank Warner Angel (sent to investigate official corruption in the Territory) are impressive proof he was not illiterate.

Tom Horn, who hired his gun to the cattle barons, finished his autobiography just before he was executed.

Their accounts are difficult to find. Many of their books were published by local newspapers or job shops as paperbacks. They were sold in small quantities by "candy butchers" on trains and quickly disappeared. Some issues of frontier newspapers are not even in the Library of Congress or state historical societies and can only be found in smaller regional or private collections.

The gunfighters all had enormous egos. Harvey Logan, the deadly Kid Curry of the Wild Bunch, wrote to a friend in Montana that after he escaped from the Knoxville jail in 1901 his exploits would "outshine" those of Harry Tracy, another gunfighter and killer then being hunted in the Northwest.

Wild Bill Hickok preened like a peacock, strutting in Fifth Avenue fashion about the cow towns and rough army posts. Harry Tracy, while he admitted that newspapermen were more to be feared than the bullets of the posses, usually advised his victims to notify the nearest sheriff so photographers could take their pictures and mention his name. Tom Horn bitterly excoriated the "yellow journals" of his day for convicting him in the press but never refused an interview and posed gladly for visiting photographers while he waited execution.

They lived and died by the gun. Single-action Colt .45s, fashioned to a hair-trigger response, oiled and polished daily like a favorite deadly toy, sawed-off shotguns, rifles, derringers, army and navy Colts—were all used. Confrontations took place in saloons, alleys, streets, and other public places.

Curiously, several of these cold, calculating killers were among the best lawmen in the Wild West. Only a thin, almost invisible line separated them from the posts of marshal and sheriff. Their expertise with guns was badly needed as the wild cow towns flourished after the Civil War by rushing beef to the East. For the killer to cross the line was simple: the harassed, perhaps terrified town council, after quickly voting to hire the gunfighter, gave him their blessing and a tin star. They knew he had the raw courage to wade into a mob of drunken armed young Texans fresh from a long drive. Gamblers were also intimidated and prevented from cheating the cowhands—unless they had made an "arrangement."

"He [Wild Bill Hickok] broke up all the unfair gambling, made professional gamblers move their tables into the light and when they became drunk stopped the games," Joseph G. McCoy, mayor of Abilene recalled. He had hired Hickok in 1871 for $150 a month and 25 percent of all imposed fines. Wild Bill was charged by Abilene's town council to be "industrious and vigilant" in bringing offenders to justice and to control or prevent all "affrays, riots and breaches of peace." Any vagrant, drunk, "or former Confederate soldier" caught carrying a pistol, bowie knife, dirk or deadly weapon was fined $100 or three months in jail.

The town fathers were also aware that the gunfighter's reputation as a man killer would be enough to make any would-be desperado turn around and ride off. As the old rustler's jingle went:

> "When we turned our sixes loose, we let the sheriff know,
> It took a joe dandy to bring us back from Mexico!"

The gunfighter's fame, however, made his life a prize. A hasty killing was often then a premium on the only sort of life insurance he could carry. He had to be quick to strike and ready to do so at the slightest provocation or forfeit his rank and fame—and perhaps his life.

"Fair play is a jewel," King Fisher of Texas once said, "but I don't care for jewelry."

Was the gunfighter a coward or a valiant? The question can be safely answered only by saying that sometimes he was one and sometimes the other.

While being held in a frontier jail for trial on charges of murder, one said:

"It's all right to talk about courage but courage is a mighty peculiar thing, and nobody's got it with him all the time. Take me on a sunshiny day, full of good grub and with a couple of drinks under my belt, I'd stand up to a regiment and take my chances; but take me on before daybreak in the rain, hungry and cold, and I'd run from one Greaser if he was hunting me . . ."

The bravest of them had their moments of weakness. It was said there were times when Wild Bill Hickok went to sleep "as nervous as an old maid peering under her bed for intruders." He would spread the floor with newspapers, to be awakened by the rustling. He personally inspected all doors and windows and refused to lie in line with a window. A light sleeper, he was up a dozen times at night. Charles Michelson, who knew many of the gunfighters and badmen of the Wild West, described in *Munsey's Magazine* of 1901 how Wild Bill entered a room:

"He would never enter a place and walk up the middle of the floor, or turn his back to the door. His mode of entry was to step swiftly across the threshold of a room and move to one side so that nobody who saw him enter could shoot him from the outside. Next, standing close to the wall, he would survey the room, noting every person in it. Then he would make his way along the wall to the bar or wherever he desired to go. It may be noted that this was caution made necessary by the knowledge that many men would assassinate him at the first opportunity . . ."

They were not all cavaliers of myth.

Kid Curry patiently waited all night to ambush Jim Winters, the Montana stockman who had killed his younger brother, Johnny. Tracy cold-bloodedly murdered the guards he had held as hostages. Wild Bill, firing from behind a curtain, killed the unarmed McCanles at the Rock Creek stage station. Ben Thompson tried to talk the teen-age John Wesley Hardin into killing Hickok when he was sheriff of Abilene. Billy the Kid gunned down the guards in his famous escape from the Lincoln jail.

Yet, these dangerous men who lived by their own codes were capable of incongruous acts of kindness, generosity, and loyalty. Tom Horn could have saved his life by naming the cattle barons who had hired him to kill rustlers, homesteaders, small ranchers, and sheepherders, but he greeted the offer with contempt. Lips sealed, he went to the gallows.

Billy the Kid, a wandering, homeless orphan, supported the maverick young ranchers fighting the powerful, corrupt Santa Fe Ring, although he knew his life could have been easier, more affluent, if he had pledged his gun to the other side.

In the last moments of his life, the wounded Kid Curry committed suicide rather than be a burden to his companions as a posse closed in.

The indomitable Tracy was trapped because he lingered to help a farmer build his barn.

They all had an extraordinary attraction for women. To the bored, restless frontier women, imprisoned in remote farmhouses, log cabins, ranches, and puritanical eighteenth-century towns, the gunfighter was a romantic hero in contrast to the bone-tired, dull, hardworking men who surrounded them. In their wretched loneliness these women often created fantasy in which the gunfighter in jail, on the dodge, or just passing through had come to rescue them.

The wives of the farmers who willingly prepared meals for Harry Tracy remembered him as "a gentleman . . . very soft spoken and courteous." Kid Curry dazzled the matrons of Knoxville to such a degree that the sheriff was forced to cut off the flow of packages of flowers, love letters, and "fine foods" that crowded his cell. One may have assisted him to escape.

An attractive schoolteacher desperately tried to save Horn from hanging, and Hickok lived with a succession of tarts, finally marrying a high-wire artist and equestrian, who is credited with inventing the two-ring circus.

Yet, some had loving wives and children, owned property, and were regarded with respect, admiration, and affection by people in their communities. Ben Thompson's estate disclosed he was a man of some affluence; his funeral cortege was one of the longest in Austin's history. For months after his death, Texas newspapers editorially demanded that prosecutors start grand jury probes to determine if he had been cut down by hidden assassins.

In El Paso, John Wesley Hardin was a respected lawyer with a good practice until he was shot from behind by a lawman who himself had once been a desperado and wanted man.

In our time, Hollywood's films and television's electronic tube have become the modern mythmakers of the West. After the movies emerged from Coney Island peep shows, the West became the most popular and profitable subject. The plots were simple, a weeping heroine and stalwart gunfighter, upholding law and order, played their roles against the cattle town facade built in Fort Lee, New Jersey. By the Great Depression, westerns were Hollywood's bread and butter items. In the 1950s gunfighters were seen almost every night on television, fanning the hammers of their guns in the backlot streets. Apparently no one told the producers that the guns of the West were mostly inaccurate and in reality any man slamming his hand down on a heavy Colt .45 would have been a candidate for the local Boot Hill.

From this endless flow of silly fiction we have come to regard the gunfighter of the Wild West as a flawless fighting machine, walking down the street at high noon to kill an enemy in an awesome display of his fast draw. Such is not the case. Some, as Meredith said, were caught in the "incredible imbroglio of comedy."

What of New Mexico's Governor Lew Wallace who indignantly wrote to Secretary of the Interior Carl Schurz that the jailed Billy the Kid was being serenaded by groups of citizens who stood outside the outlaw's cell window?

What of Kid Curry who hurled himself through a rear door of a saloon to escape a posse only to fall into a deep railroad gulch?

What of the frontier editor who received an indignant note from Wild Bill Hickok insisting he was very much alive and had not been killed in a gunfight?

What of Ben Thompson, whom Bat Masterson called the West's premier gunslinger, denouncing the villain of *East Lynn*, firing his six-shooter at the actors and laughing as the theatre emptied? The shots were blanks.

But not all is comedy. Billy the Kid coolly called out a greeting and killed the guard Olinger as he escaped from jail. Tracy shot the guards from the wall of the Oregon Penitentiary and Tom Horn, who boasted murder was his business, cut down a sheepherder's fourteen-year-old son . . .

It is not my intent to destroy legends here; many times the truth is more exciting, more romantic. Conveying the authentic rather than mere debunking is the point of this book. In the case of the gunfighter, myth and legend have always had an incestuous relationship with fact and reality. The broadest truth about these strange, violent figures is that even well before the turn of the century they had been isolated as anarchic men of action in a nation slowly but steadily moving toward regimentation in lawful and orderly communities.

More than twenty years ago, in an effort to find the truth behind the legends of these magnetic men, I started to gather material on their lives: official documents and photographs, contemporary newspaper and magazine articles. A second volume about outlaws and lawmen is now in preparation. Fortunately, when I began my research, men and women were still living who knew some of the gunfighters, badmen, and outlaws, and could convey what life was like on the frontier, in the rowdy cow towns, cow camps, on the plains, and on a cattle drive. I taped their memories and to the best of my ability independently confirmed their stories. Some at my request wrote their recollections. It was a moving experience to read the laboriously written letter from one while on my desk was his faded wanted poster.

One finds this appeal of the gunfighter of America's Wild West is now worldwide. Outside Paris, in a replica of a western cow town, famous gunfights are played and replayed by aficionados. In Italy their lives and times are discussed by some with as much gravity as the current political crisis. In London a group issues a scholarly publication. From a tiny village near the Arctic Circle a correspondent sends a thoughtful letter, detailing the relationship between Billy the Kid and the Santa Fe Ring.

Yet, for all this international attention and magnification, an examination of their lives yields the commonplace conclusion that crime does not pay. They were men of evil, ruthless killers who could scorn fair play and shoot from ambush. Ironically, therefore, they helped to develop the very forces that destroyed them. Certainly the killings they committed—even in the name of law and order—did point up the corruption of some sheriffs and marshals and the cowardice of others and finally awakened the frontier communities to seek out better men to protect them.

The gunfighters—saints and sinners—are a vital part of the history of the western frontier. Unfortunately, the saints are often tarnished while the sinners blaze on in the ballads and myths of a nation. Nonetheless, giving the devil his due and perhaps jostling the angels in the process, we admire their shared vitality, enormous self-confidence, courage, gusto, individuality, and irrepressible independence—the archetypal American character.

JAMES D. HORAN
The Notch, 1976

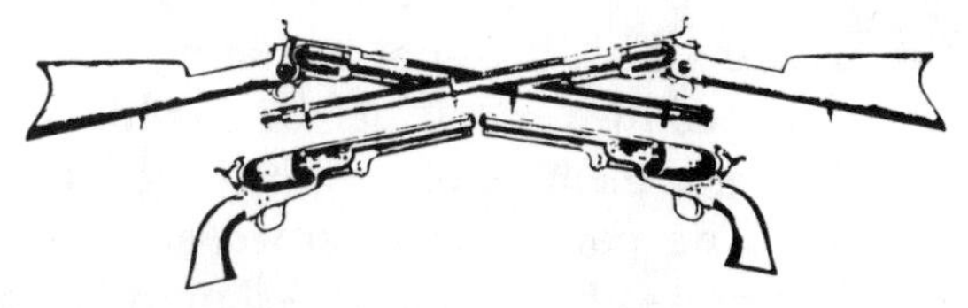

BILLY THE KID

A DECADE AFTER THE CIVIL WAR THE TRAGEDY OF BILLY THE Kid was played out in the beautiful New Mexico river valleys whose names ring like Spanish chapel bells: Ruidoso, Tularosa, Hondo, Bonito, Pecos, and the Ponasco. Ballads, books, films, and ballet have been written on his life. He is one of the world's favorite legends—a merry-eyed youth, the Robin Hood of the American southwestern frontier whose deadly skill with a six-shooter protects the oppressed ranchers against the evil cattle barons.

In the past, reminiscences of octogenarians and sparse accounts in yellowing newspapers supplied a flimsy framework of his life but a "secret history," an extant cache of little known official documents in government depositories, reveals the real Billy the Kid and the role he played in the most savage political and economic range war in the history of the American West.[1]

The portrait that emerges of him from the thousands of pages of affidavits, reports, trial transcripts, his letters, and his testimony is neither the mythical Robin Hood nor the stereotyped adenoidal moron and pathological killer.

Rather Billy appears as a disturbed, lonely young man, honest, loyal to his friends, dedicated to his beliefs, and betrayed by our institutions and the corrupt, ambitious, and compromising politicians of his time. He also kept a part of himself so hidden that it has never been touched by any document, newspaper article, or memories of those who knew him. Billy the Kid bared his soul to no man.

The existing records also shatter the myth that "he killed a man for every year of his life—not including Mexicans and Indians." The total is nearer four some killed in self-defense, in his celebrated escape from the Lincoln County jail or as a member of a vigilante group.

The popularly accepted account of the Kid's life is based on information supplied by Marshall Ashmun Upton, better known as Ash Upton, a veteran newspaperman, who had started on the *New York Herald* and drifted to the New Mexico frontier where he became a newspaper editor, railroad conductor, storekeeper, and unofficial postmaster.

He gained literary immortality by ghosting for Sheriff Pat Garrett, *The Authentic Life of Billy the Kid, the Noted Desperado of the Southwest, Whose Deeds of Daring and Blood Made His Name a Terror, in New Mexico, Arizona, and Northern Mexico.* The book, printed in 1882, sold for $1.25; today an original copy is valued in the hundreds of dollars by collectors. Ironically, Garrett and Upton sold their slow-moving stock of books for twenty-five cents a copy; the buyer took them away in a wheelbarrow.[2]

Upton's usually inaccurate account, source of countless volumes and articles written on Billy the Kid, included the one indisputable fact that Billy the Kid was born in New York City.

What he did not know—or had deliberately ignored—was that Billy the Kid's real name was Henry McCarty, that his father, Michael, had died when he was a child, and his mother, Catharine McCarty, moved west with him and his younger brother, Joseph. The long journey of this tiny family from New York City to the sparsely settled Civil War frontier is documented in yellowing land claims, mortgages, city directories, and the brittle pages of forgotten newspapers.[3]

What emerges is not the accepted version of an impoverished widow burdened with two small children living a hand-to-mouth existence in the raw towns of the Middle Border before she finally married William Henry Antrim. Rather, the attractive Widow McCarty appears to have been an aggressive, independent businesswoman who supported herself and her family by dealing in real estate and operating hotels, boardinghouses, and laundries, services always needed in the frontier communities.[4]

Indianapolis was one of their first stops after leaving New York. When interviewed for the city directory she described herself as the widow of Michael and the head of a family of two boys.

In 1865, the year of Appomattox, she met Antrim, then twenty-three and a driver for an Indianapolis express company. Antrim, born in Huntsville, Madison County, Indiana, on December 1, 1842, was the son of a merchant and hotel owner in Anderson. In 1862 he enlisted as a private in Company 1 of the Fifty-fourth Indiana Infantry but was given a medical discharge after serving three months.

More than a century later it cannot be determined how the attractive young widow and express company driver met. A city map of the period shows the McCarty residence was only a short distance from the express company's office; did they become acquainted through the delivery of a package, a chance meeting on the street, through mutual friends . . . ?[5]

The generally accepted daguerreotype or tintype of Catherine McCarty Antrim, mother of Billy the Kid. *Courtesy Division of Manuscripts, University of Oklahoma*

William Antrim, stepfather of Billy the Kid. *Courtesy Museum of New Mexico*

They had a curious romance. For more than six years Antrim courted his widow-sweetheart, following her from Indiana to the rough Kansas frontier town of Wichita, but could not get her to the altar.

In Wichita, then a cluster of shacks on the east bank of the Little Arkansas, she established the City Laundry. It is evident she was recognized as a businesswoman in the community when the editor of the *Wichita Tribune* urged that "those who wish their linen clean" patronize Mrs. McCarty's laundry.

Land records reveal Antrim contributed to the improvements of the log cabin where the McCartys—and probably Antrim—lived. As he stated in an affidavit to the land receiver in the United States Land Office in Augusta, Kansas, on March 25, 1871, he built the 12- by 14-foot house, "1 story, highboard roof, 1 door and 2 windows," and had seven acres under cultivation with a hedgerow extending 640 rods and seven feet wide "with posts and rails for further fencing." He also included a 12-foot well and "57 fruit trees set and growing," along with a six by eight "outdoor cellar covered with earth and timbers."

The house was located in the Osage trust territory and Antrim's affidavit was filed to support the widow's claim to the land. The cost was $1.25 an acre and she paid $200 in cash.

The McCartys lived in Wichita for about a year with twelve-year-old Henry —in a few years to be the notorious Billy the Kid—doing the usual chores of a boy on the frontier, probably running out with his younger brother, Joe, to cheer and wave at the Eldorado-Wichita stage as it pounded past the little log cabin. Billy and Joe worked in the laundry and watched the life of the bustling little town move along Main Street. There were the usual gunfights, saloon brawls, and the occasional groups of shabby Indians to thrill any youngster who had grown up in the teeming tenements of New York City and the more sedate and sophisticated Indianapolis.

Then in the late spring of 1871 Mrs. McCarty abruptly stopped dealing in real estate and began selling her properties. The reason was her health; a physician had told her she had tuberculosis, a death warrant in those days, and he undoubtedly urged her to try the therapy of the time, move to a high dry climate.[7]

Printed at the TIMES Office, Eldorado, Kansas.

LAND OFFICE, Augusta, Kansas, March 25 **1871.**

In the matter of the application of Catharine McCarty *of* Sedgwick *County, Kansas, to purchase the* North West *Quarter of Section No.* 12 *in Township No.* 27. *South, in Range No.* 1 *East, under the provisions of the Joint Resolution of Congress approved April 10, 1869, for the disposal of the lands ceded by the Osage Indians under the Second Article of the Treaty of September 29, 1865.*

Personally appeared the said Catharine McCarty *and offered proof in support of* ~~his~~ her *application, as follows, viz:* William Antrim *of lawful age being duly sworn, deposes and says: I have known* Catharine McCarty *for* 6 *years last past; that she is* a single woman over the age twenty one years the head of a family *consisting of* two children *a citizen of the United States, and a bona fide settler upon the foregoing described land, which she seeks to purchase, having settled thereon about the* 10 *day of* August *1870; on or about the* 10. *day of* August *1870 he built a house upon said lands,* 12 *by* 14 *feet* 1 *story high* board *roof* 1 *door* & 2 *window,* *SHe moved into said house with* her family & Effects *on or about the* 4th *day of* March *A. D. 1871, and has resided in said house and upon said land to the present time, and that he has made the following additional improvements on said land:* She has about 7 acres Enclosed & in Cultivation She has Osage Hedge Row about 7 ft wide She has Posts & Rails on ground for further fencing She has a Well 12 ft deep. She has 51 fruit & forest trees Set & growing She has an out door Cellar 6 x 8 ft covered with Earth & timber I estimate the Value of Improvements at from $250 to $300 dollars

Wm H Antrim

Sworn to & Subscribed before me this 25th of March 1871

W A Shannon Register

Indiah Daily of lawful age being by me first duly sworn according to Law deposes & Says I have Known Catharine McCarty for the [illegible] months last past & Know of my own personal Knowledge

The application of Mrs. Catherine McCarty, mother of Billy the Kid, for Osage Trust Lands in Kansas. This is the supporting affidavit of William H. Antrim, who later became Billy's stepfather. Mrs. McCarty paid the total sum of $200 in cash for her section. The application and other documents confirm the young outlaw's name was Henry McCarty and he and his mother and younger brother, Joe, moved from New York City to Indianapolis where she met Antrim. *Courtesy National Archives*

Also, March 1st
1873, Mr. William H. Antrim and Mrs. Catherine
McCarty, both of Santa Fé, New Mexico.
Witnesses, Harry Edwards, Henry McCarty,
Joseph McCarty, Mrs. A. R. McFarland
and Miss Katie McFarland. Given under my
hand and seal, the day and date above written,
D. F. McFarland, First
Pastor of Pres. Church Santa Fe
New Mexico,

A copy of the civil marriage record of Catherine McCarty and William H. Antrim. They were married March 1, 1873, in the First Presbyterian Church of Santa Fe. Henry McCarty (Billy the Kid) and his brother Joseph were witnesses. By this time Billy's mother knew she was dying of tuberculosis. She died the following year. *Courtesy New Mexico State Records Center and Archives*

There is some evidence Antrim, the widow, and her two sons first settled in Denver, New Orleans, then finally Silver City, New Mexico. The still attractive widow who apparently knew she was dying finally agreed to marry Antrim. On March 1, 1873, according to extant records, they were married in the First Presbyterian Church of Santa Fe; Henry, then fourteen, and Joseph were among the witnesses.

Once again she opened a boardinghouse while Antrim worked in the mines. A year later she was dead. It had been a bitter year for the future outlaw as he watched his mother, then thirty-four, slowly dying from "galloping consumption," as they called it. Billy's close friend, Chauncey I. Truesdell, whose mother nursed Mrs. Antrim, recalled how Billy was constantly at his mother's side for the four months she was confined to bed, holding her tightly when she was shaken by deep racking coughs.

The funeral was held from the Antrim's home on Main Street with Mrs. Truesdell, a few friends, Antrim, Billy, and Joe riding in the carriages behind the hearse to the tiny cemetery on the outskirts of town.

Watching his mother die apparently did something to Billy. The pleasant, smiling youngster refused to attend the frontier school; monte and poker chips were now taking the place of school books. Antrim tried to keep his family together but Billy was becoming uncontrollable; he eagerly accepted Mrs. Truesdell's offer to take in his stepson.

The Truesdells operated the Star Hotel in Silver City and for a year Billy worked for his keep, waiting on tables and doing kitchen chores.

Many years later when she was asked about Billy, the frail, silver-haired Mrs. Truesdell quietly rocked for a few minutes, then told the interviewer that of all the boys who had worked in her frontier hotel, Billy had been the only one who had never stolen anything. He was polite, worked hard, and obeyed any order. He never really was a bad boy, she said, only a little wild after he got under the influence of an older small town thief named "Sombrero Jack," so called because he wore a large Mexican hat.[8]

Billy quickly adopted Mrs. Truesdell as a mother image and it is evident she cared for him deeply, constantly warning him that his association with the Silver City toughs would only lead him into trouble.

Billy charmed her as he would many women. He was about five foot eight

A

ACT OF FEBRUARY 6, 1907.

DECLARATION FOR PENSION.

THE PENSION CERTIFICATE SHOULD NOT BE FORWARDED WITH THE APPLICATION.

State of New Mexico }
County of Socorro } ss.

On this second day of March, A. D., one thousand nine hundred and seven personally appeared before me, a Notary Public within and for the county and State aforesaid, William H. Antrim, who, being duly sworn according to law, declares that he is 64 years of age, and a resident of Mogollon county of Socorro, state of New Mexico and that he is the identical person who was ENROLLED at Indianapolis Indiana under the name of William H. Antrim, on the ——— day of April, 1862 as a private, in Co. I 54th Regt Indiana Vols. (Here state rank, and company and regiment in the Army, or vessels if in Navy.)

in the service of the United States, in the Civil (State name of war, Civil or Mexican.) war, and was HONORABLY DISCHARGED at Indianapolis Ind on the ——— day of July or August, 1862 that he also served No other service (Here give a complete statement of all other services, if any.)

that he was not employed in the military or naval service of the United States otherwise than as stated above. That his personal description at enlistment was as follows: Height, five feet 10 1/2 inches; complexion, fair; color of eyes blue; color of hair, light; that his occupation was farmer; that he was born December 1st, 1842 at Huntsville, Madison Co. Indiana,

That his several places of residence since leaving the service have been as follows: Indianapolis Ind to 1869, Wichita Kans to 1872, Silver City N. Mex to 1880, Mogollon N. Mex to present. (State date of each change, as nearly as possible.)

That he is a pensioner, ~~That he has heretofore applied for pension~~ Holding Pension Certificate No 977482 (If a pensioner, the certificate number only need be given. If not, give the number of the former application, if one was made.)

That he makes this declaration for the purpose of being placed on the pension roll of the United States under the provisions of the act of February 6, 1907, and he hereby appoints Henry D. Phillips, of Washington, D. C., his true and lawful attorney to prosecute his claim with power of substitution and revocation.

That his post-office address is Mogollon county of Socorro, State of New Mexico.

William H. Antrim
(Claimant's signature in full.)

Attest: (1) Charles N. Mimms
(2) George F. Williams

Also personally appeared Charles N. Mimms, residing in Mogollon N. Mex and George F. Williams, residing in Mogollon N. Mex, persons whom I certify to be respectable and entitled to credit, and who, being by me duly sworn, say that they were present and saw William H. Antrim, the claimant, sign his name [or make his mark] to the foregoing declaration; that they have every reason to believe, from the appearance of the claimant and their acquaintance with him of 30 years and 7 years, respectively, that he is the identical person he represents himself to be, and that they have no interest in the prosecution of this claim.

Charles N. Mimms
George F. Williams
Signatures of witnesses

SUBSCRIBED and sworn to before me this 2d day of March A. D. 1907 and I hereby certify that the contents of the above declaration, etc., were fully made known and explained to the applicant and witnesses before, swearing, including the words that he has heretofore applied for pension, erased, and the words ———, added; and that I have no interest, direct or indirect in the prosecution of this claim.

L. S.

C. H. Kirkpatrick
Signature.
Notary Public
Official character.

U. ... MAR 14 1907 ... OFFICE

Valid.

E.C.P., Law.

William Antrim's application for a pension. In it he stated that Billy's mother "was married to McCarty, date not known, died in New York City." He added: "My wife had two boys, one died in the eighties [Billy the Kid] and the other I have not heard from in fourteen years." He was referring to Billy's brother, Joseph, a Denver gambler, who reportedly died about 1930. *Courtesy National Archives*

Billy the Kid. The fading tintype was taken in Lincoln County when he was about nineteen. The itinerant photographer was ready to pack his gear when Billy ran out and had his picture taken. *The James D. Horan Civil War and Western Americana Collection*

inches, slender with wavy light hair. The traditional faded tintype taken hastily one day in Fort Sumner unfortunately shows him to be a bucktoothed moron leaning on a rifle. Actually two upper teeth protruded slightly but did not disfigure his face. He had an easy smile, a sense of humor, and was well liked in the town. He also had startling blue eyes that some men recalled would dance when he laughed; others told how they became cold and full of menace before he went for his gun.

After the Truesdells sold their hotel Billy went to live with a Mrs. Brown. In September 1875, the *Grant County Herald* reported he had been arrested and sent to jail to await action by the grand jury on a charge of "stealing clothes from Charley Sun and Sam Chung, celestials, sans cue sans Joss sticks." His codefendant was Sombrero Jack, who had actually taken the clothes and given them to Billy to hide. The loot was discovered by Mrs. Brown who notified Sheriff Harvey H. Whitehall, who arrested Billy. Sombrero Jack had fled.

Early one morning Billy knocked on Mrs. Truesdell's door. When she opened it he whispered he was on the run; he had escaped from jail by climbing up the chimney. She fed him, gave him money from her savings, and put him on the stage to Globe, Arizona. She never saw him again.

Where young Henry McCarty got the name William H. Bonney is still a mystery. In 1902 Sheriff Whitehall, who had arrested him for the first time, claimed Billy had changed his name to Bonney "in order to keep the stigma of disgrace from his family," which seems logical in view of the reverence he had for his mother's memory.

Truesdell, his boyhood friend, also said he had "never heard the name of Bonney until after he became notorious. After Henry left town some people who knew him said he called himself Bill Bonney. It was the same boy all right, they knew him well . . ."[9]

Three years later Billy appeared in Grant City, an incongruous figure in store shoes and pants and a six-shooter stuck in his belt as he mingled with the frontiersmen, miners, and cowboys in George Adkins's saloon. He had now gained the nickname of "Kid."

He killed his first man in Grant City. On August 17, 1877, he shot E. P. Cahill, who the *Arizona Daily Citizen* reported had made a deathbed statement that "he had some trouble with Antrim during which the shooting was done."

A coroner's jury's verdict called the killing "criminal and unjustifiable and Henry Antrim, alias Kid, is guilty thereof."

As always with the events in Billy the Kid's life, there is another side.

Half a century later an old army scout, Gus Gildea, told the *Citizen* what had actually happened that day.[10]

Billy the Kid Kills His First Man

It was in the fall of '77 when I first met Billy the Kid. He was an easy going, likeable youth still in his teens. I was scouting at Fort Grant then, when Billy came to town dressed like a "country jake" with store pants on and shoes instead of boots. He wore a six-shooter stuck in his trousers.

The blacksmith frequented George Adkins' saloon. He was called "Windy" because he was forever blowing about first one thing, then another. I don't recall the rest of his name. Shortly after the Kid came to Fort Grant Windy started abusing him.

He would throw Billy on the floor, ruffle his hair, slap his face and humiliate him before the men in the saloon.

Yes, the Kid was rather slender, with blue eyes and fair hair. The blacksmith was a large man with a gruff voice and blustering manner.

Billy the Kid, then Henry McCarty Antrim, killed his first man on August 17, 1877, near Camp Grant, Arizona. The brief item in the *Arizona Citizen* mistakenly had his first name as "Austin" and failed to note that the bullying blacksmith was beating Billy, a slender teen-ager. *Courtesy Arizona Historical Society*

AUSTIN ANTRIM shot F. P. Cahill near Camp Grant on the 17th instant, and the latter died on the 18th. Cahill made a statement before death to the effect that he had some trouble with Antrim during which the shooting was done. Bad names were applied each to the other. Deceased has a sister—Margaret Flanegan in Cambridge, Mass., and another—Kate Conlon in San Francisco. He was born in Galway, Ireland, and was aged about 32. The coroner's jury found that the shooting "was criminal and unjustifiable, and that "Henry Antrim alias Kid, is guilty thereof." The inquest was held by M. L. Wood, J. P., and the jurors were M. McDowell, Geo. Teague, T. McCleary, B. E. Norton, Jas. L. Hunt and D. H. Smith.

One day he threw the youth to the floor. Pinned his arms down with his knees and started slapping his face.

"You are hurting me. Let me up!" cried the Kid.

"I want to hurt you. That's why I got you down," was the reply.

People in the saloon watched the two on the floor. Billy's right arm was free from the elbow down. He started working his hand around and finally managed to grasp his .45.

Suddenly silence reigned in the room. The blacksmith evidently felt the gun in his side for he straightened sharply. There was a deafening roar. Windy slumped to one side and the Kid squirmed free and ran to the door and vaulted into the saddle of John Murphy's racing pony and left for Fort Grant.

When I came to town the next day from Hookers ranch where I was working, Murphy was storming and cursing the Kid, calling him a horse thief, murderer and similar names. I told him he would get his horse back, for the Kid was no thief.

In about a week one of Murphy's friends rode into town on Cashaw, Murphy's horse, saying the Kid had asked him to return the animal to the owner.

The teen-age killer now became a wanderer, drifting among the cow camps on the New Mexico-Arizona frontier, stopping for a time in mining camps and towns to gamble, drink, and work at odd jobs. He finally made his way into New Mexico's Lincoln County, the nation's largest county, 150 miles east and west and 170 miles north and south.[11]

And there began the legend of Billy the Kid . . .

Billy's first stop was at the cow camp of Jimmy Dolan, who controlled Lincoln County's powerful Murphy & Co. Whether Dolan was present is not known but after an argument with Billy Morton, the outfit's foreman, the Kid packed his gear and rode off.

Some weeks later he stopped at the Coe ranch in the beautiful valley of the Rio Ruidoso, ten miles below Lincoln and the Rio Bonito. George Coe, about Billy's age, never forgot him. They became close friends and from Coe and his cousin Frank, the Kid first learned of the growing hate and bitterness in the county that the Coes predicted would soon explode into a shooting war.[12]

As Coe explained, the cattle king of Lincoln County was John Chisum, a former Texas cowboy whose ranch was one of the largest in the West. More than 60,000 head grazed on the open land, and his army of hands, most of them fast with a gun, was ready to drive off any homesteader or small rancher who dared trespass on the king's domain.

It was a familiar tale repeated in many parts of the West of the cattle baron who had hacked an empire from the wild lands, fought off the Indians, rustlers, and outlaws, and now in his middle years was determined to bar the outside world—even the tin stars and United States marshals with their official papers and documents.[13]

But when Billy arrived, the Lincoln County frontier was slowly changing, the king's domain was being challenged by the growing number of smaller ranchers like the Coes, and there was the smell of death in the thin desert air.

The second combatant in this growing war was L. G. Murphy & Co., called "The Company," run by the deadly Jimmy Dolan and Jimmy Riley in league with Jesse Evans's outlaws. Even the powerful Chisum appeared helpless against the Murphy combination. In addition to its hired guns, "The Company" had the protection of the Santa Fe Ring, a seemingly invincible group of corrupt politicians that controlled prosecuting attorneys, judges, sheriffs, and deputies, along with the profitable army and Indian agency contracts. A hundred years later the power and corruption in the Territory appears incredible; even Washington seemed unable to crush it.

Head of the ring was Tom Catron, Santa Fe's prosecuting attorney and one of the most powerful politicians on the frontier; in Mesilla, seat of Dona Ana County, the ring was represented by Colonel William L. Rynerson, a giant Tennesseean who had fought on the Rio Grande for the Union.

The Murphy mercantile firm was headed by Major Lawrence G. Murphy, an immigrant Irishman who had enlisted in Kit Carson's famous New Mexico Volunteers. After Appomattox he joined forces with Lieutenant Colonel Emil Fritz, a German soldier of fortune, and the two built a stone store at Fort Stanton. When the army paid them $8,000 for the store and its supplies, the partners built a bigger headquarters known as "The House" in the western part of Lincoln County.

Jimmy Dolan, like Murphy, was an Irish immigrant. Before he enlisted he had worked in a dry-goods store back east. Following his discharge at Fort Stanton, he was hired as a clerk in Murphy's store. He was bright, efficient, and knew how to keep account books. As the years passed he became indispensable to Murphy; by 1877 he controlled the firm's many enterprises in the cattle country.

Jimmy Riley, another aggressive young Irishman, bought his way into Murphy's firm with a $6,000 investment and helped Dolan boss the business and the cow camps.

About the time the Kid arrived at the Coe ranch, Lieutenant Colonel Fritz, Murphy's partner, died in Stuttgart, Germany, leaving a $10,000 insurance policy to his sister and brother who had settled on the Rio Bonito, eight miles from Lincoln. The policy would have a strange effect on the Kid's destiny.

At the Coe ranch Billy also met Dick Brewer, undisputed leader of the small ranchers who were fighting Chisum's land monopoly.[14] Sitting around the

German-born Lieutenant Colonel Emil Fritz who, with Major L. G. Murphy of Kit Carson's First New Mexico Volunteers, built a store at Fort Stanton, in western Lincoln County. When the army paid them $8,000 for the post, they established a larger store, known as "The House," in the west end of Lincoln County. Fritz died in Germany in 1874. His $10,000 life insurance policy strangely affected the life of Billy the Kid. *Courtesy Museum of New Mexico, John G. Meem Collection*

large, rough-hewn table in the Coe's main house, the Kid heard Brewer describe how he and his fellow ranchers had been victimized by Murphy's high rate credit system. Brewer also disclosed that two new faces had appeared in the county within the last year: Alexander A. McSween, an attorney with offices in Lincoln, and John Tunstall, an Englishman who had established a ranch at the headwaters of the Rio Feliz (Felix) and had opened a store in Lincoln to compete with the Murphy mercantile business. Many of the small ranchers had transferred their accounts to Tunstall, who had a reputation for honesty and fairness. As a result, Murphy's business, heavily mortgaged to Tom Catron, head of the Santa Fe Ring, was in financial difficulties.

Jesse (Jessie) Evans's gunmen had threatened several of the ranchers, Brewer revealed, and there had been some near confrontations. The volatile county was near bursting into flame. It is believed Brewer, who was Tunstall's foreman, introduced the Kid to the Englishman who immediately hired the eighteen-year-old drifter. Many years later Frank Coe recalled:

"Tunstall saw the boy was quick to learn and not afraid of anything . . . he made Billy a present of a good horse, saddle and a new gun . . . my, but the boy was proud . . . said it was the first time in his life he had ever had anything given to him . . ."

In Silver City Billy had adopted Mrs. Truesdell, the kindly boardinghouse owner as a surrogate mother; the cultured Englishman from a different world now became a father image.

Frank Coe also saw an example of Billy's skill with a six-shooter. One day the Kid met Coe to help him cut oats on the Brewer ranch. As they rode through the valley, Billy pointed to a row of cowbirds sitting on a branch. As Frank said, he never saw Billy draw but he did see the birds tumble off their perch.[15]

As in all tragedies, the peculiar knack that brings success also brings ruination . . .

Alexander McSween, lawyer and leader with John Tunstall of the opposition against the corrupt ring of New Mexico officials. With Billy the Kid, he played a leading role in the Battle of Lincoln. Following Billy during the retreat from his burning home, he was shot and killed. *Courtesy Special Collections, University of Arizona Library*

John Tunstall, the cultured, wealthy Englishman who was brutally murdered during the Lincoln County War. *Courtesy Museum of New Mexico*

The John Tunstall store in Lincoln. *Courtesy Special Collections, University of Arizona Library*

During the long winter nights the Kid was delighted when Frank played the violin and would "jig alone and cut amusing capers about the little room."

While he was lighthearted, "always joking and full of tricks," the Coes also noticed the Kid at times could be moody, withdrawn, and thoughtful.

He was slight in build but the Coes were amazed at his strength. At the Tunstall ranch he seemed happy, contented, and proud when he was asked by his employer to accompany him to Lincoln.

On one of these trips the Kid met McSween, the Lincoln lawyer and partner in Tunstall's combination store and bank.

Billy could understand Tunstall who, for all his funny accent and a library valued at $3,000, was also familiar with horses and cattle and loved the majestic country of the Feliz, but McSween made him uncomfortable. The lawyer was a townsman, frail, round-shouldered, with dark hair, smoldering dark eyes, and a deep, rolling voice that sounded like a preacher's when he spoke of the evils of Murphy, Dolan, Riley, their hired gunmen, and the corrupt men who headed the Santa Fe Ring.

McSween, a graduate of Saint Louis University, had first practiced in Kansas but chronic asthma brought him to the arid plains of New Mexico and finally Lincoln. He had led Tunstall to the county, warned the Englishman that Dolan and Murphy were trying to sell him untitled land, then advised him to buy the Rio Feliz ranch.

McSween was retained by the late Lieutenant Colonel Fritz's brother and sister to collect the $10,000 insurance policy. During the winter of 1877 McSween traveled to New York to collect the money and made side trips to Kansas, combining the Fritz family business with transactions he was doing for John Chisum.[16]

During his absence Jimmy Dolan persuaded the Fritz relatives to sue McSween for failing to turn over the money, although the lawyer had made it clear he was still trying to determine if there were additional heirs in Germany who might lay claim to the policy.

Significantly, Tom Catron's firm, Catron & Thornton of Santa Fe, was retained by the Fritz family in their action against McSween.

During the winter of 1877 and 1878, the Dolan-Murphy-Riley group instituted a series of legal maneuvers against McSween, aided by the political power of the Santa Fe Ring. Christmas saw the lines drawn in Lincoln County: McSween-Tunstall against Murphy & Co., its junior partners, Dolan and Riley, aided by Jesse Evans's band of outlaws and Lincoln County's sheriff, William Brady, who admitted to McSween in a moment of frustration, "Murphy controls me."

Billy, now known as the Kid, gradually emerged as leader of the hands on Tunstall's ranch. It was the day of the gun and not only the Englishman's riders but also those who worked the range for Dolan and Murphy had seen or had heard about the boy's extraordinary skill with a six-shooter.

Billy was still the lighthearted youngster George Coe had first met, but now there was also a tense alertness about him. He still laughed a lot and delighted in dancing with the Mexican girls at the neighborhood *baile*, but his friends noticed the blue eyes could suddenly become cold and hostile when strangers approached the Tunstall spread or when he escorted his employer on the long ride to Lincoln.

In February the Murphy group made its first move. Billy Mathews, deputized by Sheriff Brady, and the Jesse Evans gang, all sworn in as a "sheriff's posse," rode to the Tunstall ranch. A few days before, Brady, armed with a writ of attachment, had confiscated McSween's private and personal property. Now with another writ Mathews and his gang attempted to take over Tunstall's cattle and horse herds on the tenuous charge that Tunstall was McSween's business partner.

Mathews and his men found the ranch "forted up" with Billy warning them they were ready to shoot it out. Mathews retreated but promised to return.[17]

That afternoon Bob Widenmann, Tunstall's friend who sometimes tended his steers, rode to Lincoln to warn Tunstall.

The following morning the Englishman returned to his ranch and ordered Billy and the others to leave; rather than risk their lives he had decided to turn over his cattle and horse herd to the sheriff's posse and seek redress in the courts.

Billy urged him to go back to Lincoln and let them defend his ranch and property but Tunstall was adamant; he had faith in America's democracy and laws, he told the angry boy; all the steers and horses in the West weren't worth a man's life. The next day they headed back to Lincoln: Tunstall, Billy, his best friend, the half-Cherokee Fred Waite, Dick Brewer, Bob Widenmann, and John Middleton, a young cowboy. They had with them nine horses, all personal property and not included in the writ of attachment.

Unknown to them Dolan, with another large "sheriff's posse," arrived at the Tunstall ranch a short time later. When Tunstall's old cook, Godfrey (George) Gauss, told him his boss had left for Lincoln, Mathews selected a dozen riders under the leadership of Billy Morton, Dolan's new camp foreman, to bring back the horses.

The light was purpling when Morton's posse caught up with Tunstall's party on the desolate mountain trail. Billy, in the rear, pulled up short at the sound of rifle fire. When he looked back he saw thirteen men outlined on the crest of a small rise. Suddenly with shouts and cries they started galloping down the road. Billy shouted a warning. All of them scattered, riding hard to reach a small hill dotted with boulders where the Kid later said "we could make a stand."

When they reached the hill's peak they were dismayed to find Tunstall who —Middleton later testified was "excited and confused"—had remained behind and riders were surrounding him. There were shots and moments later the soft-spoken Englishman who had hoped to find a "new life," as he called it, in the American West, was dead and the Lincoln County War had begun.

The framework of the events of that day have been told many times but only the lean, stark surviving accounts of those who were there, including Billy, tell the real story.

The genesis of these documents was Carl Schurz, Lincoln's friend and secretary of the interior under President Hayes. Infuriated by Territorial Governor

Sam Axtell's partisan support of the Dolan-Murphy clan and the Santa Fe Ring, and impressed by the chilling visit of Sir Edward Thornton, Great Britain's minister to Washington, who demanded that Tunstall's killers be brought to justice, Schurz proposed to the president that a confidential agent be sent to Lincoln to obtain the facts.

When he received White House approval, Schurz assigned Frank Warner Angel, an assistant United States attorney in New York City, to investigate Tunstall's murder and the rapidly spreading violence in Lincoln County. He would then return to Washington and make his report to Schurz, who would turn over his findings and recommendations to the president.

Three weeks after Tunstall was buried outside his store, Angel arrived in Lincoln. The first witnesses he contacted were McSween and Billy the Kid.

McSween's 22,000 word statement, a major portion of the more than 100,000 words of testimony and supporting documents obtained by Angel, is one of the most important documents in southwestern frontier history. The lawyer detailed for Angel the causes and effects of the Lincoln County War, named names, times, and places, and turned over to the Washington agent many confidential documents that helped support his accusations.

McSween knew the affidavit was his death warrant; in a few months he would be shot to death in the bloody Battle of Lincoln. Billy, who fought at his side, escaped to bring the war to the enemy.

Following are the highlights from McSween's affidavit, notarized by Frank Warner Angel, March 1, 1878.[18]

Events Leading to the Murder of John Tunstall

I have given the subject of what has caused the trouble in Lincoln County considerable attention and study, and have inquired and talked to a great number of persons as to the case which has produced the present state of affairs, which resulted in the death of John H. Tunstall and as to the general lawlessness which exists in the said county.

From this examination and inquiry of the matter, I am informed that Lawrence G. Murphy and Emil Fritz, doing business under the style of L. G. Murphy & Co., had the monopoly for the sale of merchandise in this County and used their powers to oppress and grind out all they could from the farmers and ranchers and forced those who opposed them to leave the county.

For instance, the farmers and ranchers would buy merchandise of them at exorbitant prices and were compelled to turn in their products to payment thereof at prices that suited Murphy & Co. If a man refused to do so, they were subjected to litigation and the whole judicial machinery was used to accomplish that object, the result of these proceedings were that L. G. Murphy & Co. were absolute monarchs of Lincoln County and rule their subjects with an oppressive iron heel.

This state of affairs has existed for some time, at least ten years, and was carried out by L. G. Murphy & Co. L. G. Murphy, in carrying out their schemes, would drive out a settler who had opposed them or who would not follow their beck and call, and without a particle of right title or claim would take possession of such person's real estate and claim that it belonged to them, and then rent it to some other person who had been led to believe it legally belonged to them. If such person found out afterwards that he had no right title or interest in the property and refused to pay them for the rental thereof, a system of persecution would then be instituted which resulted in the opposing party leaving the county.

This rule of Murphy & Co. continued until the matter was precipitated by the killing of John H. Tunstall. In order to support their monarchy, L. G. Murphy, J. J. Dolan and J. H. Riley have surrounded themselves with and are employing the most desperate characters in the country. Affairs were carried out with such a high hand after the deponent came to this county, that Murphy, desiring to regain lost power and obtain control over the people, organized a vigilante committee ostensibly to put down horse stealing but really as after facts show, to kill persons who were opposed to him.

Among other persons [than Tunstall] he named to me who he intended to have the Vigilante Committee kill, were Honorable J. B. Patron [speaker of the New Mexico Territorial Assembly], Richard M. Brewer [leader of the smaller ranchers opposed to John Chisum] and he had informed me, that inasmuch as I opposed him I would have to leave the county or be killed.

Deponent further states that he discountenanced these measures and used his influence to prevent that state of affairs, wishing rather that the courts be resorted to and the people would stand by and see the laws be enforced. He further states that the people were determined to throw off the burden of Murphy & Co. who had found that the power to influence courts, juries and even to kill persons was being lost. This rendered them more desperate and compelled them to resort to more desperate measures which culminated in the death of John Tunstall.

Deponent has heard L. G. Murphy assert that he controlled not only the courts and juries but that he could cause the death of any person who opposed him. Deponent verily believes that as far as the courts are concerned they were used to work out his schemes and revenge.

In November 1876, John H. Tunstall came to the county for the purpose, as he said, of going into the stock raising business and took steps to secure four thousand acres of land for that purpose and then invested $2,000 in this business of stock raising and in merchandise for a store which he operated in Lincoln.

At this time the firm of J. J. Dolan & Co. composed of J. J. Dolan and John H. Riley seemed to be friends of his, and knowing that he had considerable wealth to invest, they tried to have him as far away from Lincoln as they could, and also to get his money so he would be financially crippled. For that purpose they tried to have him purchase the L. G. Murphy Ranch at Fairview, about thirty-five miles from Lincoln. Knowing that I was a friend of Tunstall they tried to induce me to use my influence with Tunstall to have him buy (this property) and if I would induce Tunstall to buy it, that they would give me five thousand dollars.

I informed Tunstall of this affair and told him that they had no government title to the land and Tunstall refused to buy it. This was the beginning of the enmity of Murphy, Dolan and Riley against Tunstall.

During the month of August 1877, horses were stolen from Tunstall and myself by Jesse Evans and Tom Hill, the said Evans and Hill admitted to me and others they had stolen the horses.

At our insistence [McSween and Tunstall] they were afterwards arrested at Bockwith's [ranch] at Seven Rivers by Sheriff [William] Brady and lodged in jail at Lincoln under an indictment for stealing the said horses. On or about November 1877 I was informed by J. B. Patron that Evans, Baker, Hill and Davis [all members of the Evans gang of outlaws] had filed off their shackles and cut the logs in their cell and were ready to make their escape.

I told Mr. Patron to inform Sheriff Brady who was acting as the jailer, which he did so. Patron subsequently informed me Brady, Patron and D. P. Shields [McSween's brother-in-law and law partner] and we went and examined the said prisoners at the jail and found Patron's statement to be correct. The sheriff, however, took no precautionary steps to better secure their confinement.

A few days later Brady, intoxicated, came into Tunstall's store and charged Tunstall with helping the prisoners escape. Tunstall told him, "You know their shackles are filed and there are holes cut in the logs of their cell and you have taken no pains to secure them and now you dare to accuse me—who have aided in their arrest and whose life has been threatened by them—with assisting them to escape?"

Sheriff Brady then put his hand on his revolver as though he was going to draw it but I stepped in between them and said:

"It ill becomes you as a peace officer to violate the law."

Brady replied to Tunstall: "I won't shoot you now but you haven't long to run . . . I ain't always going to be sheriff," and then he left.

A day or two after the prisoners made their escape. Upon hearing of their escape J. B. Patron, John Tunstall and this deponent went to the jail and found several sacks in which rocks, weighing twenty to twenty-five pounds, were tied along with augers and files. Upon further investigation I discovered that no one had been left in charge of the prisoners and not even the doors had been locked.

I have been told that the augers and files had been placed in goods brought to the store of J. J. Dolan and one of his employees had delivered them to the men in the jail.

I am also informed that the escaped prisoners went to Tunstall's ranch and took horses, saddles and guns by force.

When I went to Sheriff Brady and offered to raise a posse of twenty men to go and recapture the escaped prisoners, Brady replied:

"I arrested them once and I will be d--- if I'm going to do it again. Hereafter I am going to look after Brady's interests."

He declined my offer. Subsequently some of the escaped prisoners were seen in Brady's company at the J. J. Dolan's store but I have been informed by George Washington [McSween's employee] that Brady did not arrest them.

McSween then discussed a letter Tunstall had written to the *Mesilla Independent,* January 27, 1878, charging Sheriff Brady, who was also the county's tax collector, with turning territorial money over to Dolan and Riley to help their tottering mercantile company. McSween and Tunstall based their charge on a check the lawyer had given Brady. It had been endorsed by the sheriff to Dolan. McSween also described for Angel the complicated insurance policy suit filed against him by the heirs of Lieutenant Colonel Emil Fritz, Murphy's deceased partner.

The Murphy-Dolan group at the time of Angel's arrival had also used their political influence to have Sheriff Brady appointed as administrator of the Fritz estate.

On my return to Lincoln I found that J. H. Riley was exceedingly angry and was trying to create trouble. He had broken into my office, destroyed some of my furniture, grossly insulted my wife and vowed that he would run me out of the county.

On or about the 5th day of February, 1878, I started for Lincoln [from Las Vegas] with Deputy Sheriff A. P. Barrier, D. P. Shields [his brother-in-law], J. B. Wilson [the local justice of the peace] and John Tunstall. On the evening of the same day we camped at St. Augustine [ranch], and shortly after Jesse Evans, Frank Baker, Long, alias "Rivers", all notorious outlaws, came into our camp and inquired if we had passed J. J. Dolan on the road. Whereupon D. P. Shields said that we had not . . . then Baker said they had always found "Jimmie", meaning J. J. Dolan, very punctual in their engagements with them. He said Dolan had made an appointment with them to meet them here and he was sure he would come.

It was a notorious fact that this Evans, Baker and Rivers and others had determined to take J. H. Tunstall's and my life, owing to our activities in having them arrested for horse stealing.

On the morning of the 6th, February 1878, Dolan reached St. Augustine. About 8 or 9 o'clock while Tunstall, Shields, Wilson and myself were eating breakfast at our camping site on the east end of the St. Augustine corral, I saw J. J. Dolan, and Jesse Evans going into a westernly direction, thus hiding themselves from us by the southeast corner of the corral.

In a few minutes Dolan and Evans came around the corner of the corral. Dolan drew his Winchester carbine, pointed it at Tunstall and asked:

"Are you ready to fight?"

"Are you asking me to fight a duel?" Tunstall asked.

Dolan replied: "You G--- D--- coward, I want you to fight and settle our differences."

Then Dolan drew his six-shooter cocked on Mr. Tunstall three times. Mr. Barrier placed himself between or in line with Evans and Dolan and saved the lives of Tunstall and myself. When Dolan was leaving he said to Tunstall:

"You won't fight this morning, you G-- D--- coward but I'll get you soon."

After he had gone off about twenty yards he returned and said:

"When you write the *Independent* again, say that I am with 'The Boys.' "

The term "The Boys" being used at Lincoln and in the neighborhood to denote notorious thieves, outlaws and murderers, such as Evans, Baker, Hill and Davis. And the reason he had mentioned the *Independent* was because Mr. Tunstall had written that letter charging Brady, the sheriff, with having turned Territorial tax money over to Dolan.

McSween then described how Sheriff Brady, Dolan, and Murphy rode into Lincoln with the writ of attachment.

They made the occasion a merriment and J. H. Riley said he had swept out the jail the night before so he could say he had cleaned out the cell for McSween. Then Brady told several persons that McSween and Tunstall had charged him with being a defaulter of Territorial funds but he was going to prove he was a no defaulter when it came to taking McSween's and Tunstall's goods.

On the 17th of February, 1878, Brady not only attached my personal property but my real, together with the property of John H. Tunstall [in the store] even pictures of the family and also a notarial seal belonging to D. P. Shields. The sheriff was ordered to attach property valued at $8,000 but he took property valued at $40,000. We were then informed that J. B. Mathews [foreman for Dolan's and Murphy's ranch], with Baker, Evans, Hill and Davis, sworn and deputized as a sheriff's posse, were to go to Tunstall's ranch and confiscate his stock of cattle and horses. Robert Widenmann came in from Tunstall's ranch and told us what had taken place, that he had told Mathews if he came back in a day or two he would "round up" the cattle and horses.

Widenmann told us that he was satisfied. Mathews, Evans and the others were prepared to raise a large force and come and take the cattle and horses by force, and that Baker had gone down to Dolan's and Murphy's new camp to raise all the men he could and meet Mathews with his posse at Turkey Springs, a few miles from Tunstall's ranch.

In my presence Tunstall was informed by George Washington [McSween's employee] that Murphy, Riley, Dolan and others had raised a band of forty-three men and Riley had told Washington that now there was no use of McSween and Tunstall trying to get away, that they had us completely in their power, that they could not be beat as they had the District Attorney [meaning Rynerson, prosecutor of Dona Ana County] and all the power in Santa Fe to back them. That they planned to send in two Mexicans to make a sham roundup to draw the cowboys from Tunstall's house, then the balance of the posse was to take possession of the house and "get" Tunstall's men.

Upon receiving this information, Tunstall concluded to go to his ranch and to order his men to allow Mathews and his posse to take the property and that he would seek the remedy in the courts. He left Lincoln on the night of the 16th, he said it was his intention to take this remedy. That was the last time I saw Tunstall alive . . .

I have been informed by John Middleton, W. Bonney, called "The Kid", R. A. Widenmann, Fred Waite and Henry Brown, that Mr. Tunstall reached his cattle ranch on the night of the 17th and commanded them to leave the ranch and come to Lincoln which they did. William McCloskey [killed] informed me that Tunstall sent him to get Martin Merz [a neighboring rancher], a good cattle man, to come to the ranch and turn over the cattle to Deputy Sheriff J. B. Mathews and his posse who were then at Turkey Springs, numbering forty-three men, and to inform him [Mathews] that the cattle were properly tallied and that he, Tunstall, would seek his remedy at law, that he would not sacrifice the life of one of his men for all the cattle, for they would all be killed if they remained on the ranch.

McCloskey also informed me that he not only delivered that verbal message to Mathews and added (to Mathews) that Tunstall would offer no resistance to the taking of the property although some of it belonged to me.

On the night of the 18th of February, I was informed by W. Bonney that J. H. Tunstall was murdered on the road to Lincoln about twenty miles from his cattle ranch . . .

During the time he was in Lincoln County, Frank Warner Angel interviewed thirty-five participants in what he officially called "a war," obtained a sworn notarized statement from each one, and collected twenty-one exhibits.

The New York lawyer, moving about the hostile, dangerous territory, conducted an impressive nonpartisan investigation, collecting information not only from members of the McSween-Tunstall faction and those who were members or allied to the Murphy-Dolan-Riley group, but also the army command that had been drawn into the affair by Washington's orders to help the civilian law enforcement officers keep the peace and prevent violence.

The eyewitness accounts of the Tunstall killing highlight the hundreds of pages Angel wrote for Schurz and President Hayes. The stark statements Washington's confidential agent collected from Billy the Kid, John Middleton, Tunstall's cowboy, who heard the Englishman's last words, and Samuel R. Perry, a member of the deadly "sheriff's posse" who murdered the unarmed man, paint a vivid grim picture of what actually took place in the gathering dusk on that lonely trail.[19]

Statement of William H. Bonney, Known as "the Kid"

On the 13th of February, 1878, J. B. Mathews who claimed to be a deputy sheriff, came to the Tunstall ranch in the company of Jesse Evans, Frank Baker, Tom Hill and Rivers, all known outlaws who had been confined in the Lincoln County jail and had succeeded in making their escape; John Hurley, George Hinman, Roberts [Shotgun Roberts], an Indian and Ponciacho, who I believe is the murderer of Bennito Cruz. The Governor of the Territory had offered a $500 reward for the arrest of the murderer of Cruz.

Prior to the arrival of Mathews and his posse, having heard they were going to round up all the cattle and drive them off and kill those persons who were at the ranch, we had cut portholes in the walls of the house and filled sacks with earth, so that should we be attacked or our murder attempted, we could defend ourselves.

This course was considered necessary because the sheriff's posse was composed of murderers, outlaws and desperate characters, none of whom had any interest or stake in the County.

When Mathews came to within 50 yards of the house we called out to him to stop, advance alone and state his business. Mathews said he had come to attach the cattle and property of A. A. McSween. We told Mathews that McSween did not have any cattle or property on the Tunstall ranch but that if he had they could take it.

Mathews then said he though some of the cattle belonging to R. Brewer [Tunstall's neighboring rancher and foreman] were on Tunstall's place and some belonged to McSween. Then Brewer told Mathews if he wanted to round up his cattle he would help him. Mathews replied he would go back to Lincoln and get further instructions [from Sheriff William Brady] and if he came back to the ranch he would come back with one man. Mathews and his posse were then invited to come into the house and get something to eat.

Robert Widenmann told Richard Brewer and the others who were inside the ranch that he was going to arrest Baker, Jesse Evans and Tom Hill [Widenmann, a deputy U.S. marshal had warrants for the trio], but Brewer told Widenmann that the arrest could not be made because if it was made at the ranch, all of us would be killed by the sheriff's posse.

When Mathews and his men approached the house, Evans advanced upon Widenmann, swinging his gun and catching it, cocked and pointed it directly at Widenmann.

"Are you hunting for me?" Evans asked.

"If I was looking for you, you would find it out," Widenmann said.

"Do you have a warrant for me?" Evans asked.

"That's my business," answered Widenmann.

"If you ever come to arrest me," Evans said, "you'll be the first man I intend to shoot at."

"That's all right," Widenmann told him, "two can play at that game."

During the talking, Frank Baker stood near Widenmann swinging his pistol on his finger, cocking it and pointing it at Widenmann. With me at this time were R. Brewer, John Middleton, G. Gauss, R. A. Widenmann, Henry Brown, F. Waite, William McCloskey.

After eating, Mathews started for Lincoln with John Hurley, the rest of the party or posse saying they were going to the Rio Penasco.

I started for Lincoln with R. Widenmann, F. Waite and arrived at Lincoln on the same evening. We left Lincoln the next day, February 14, in company of the same persons, having heard that Mathews was going back to the ranch with a large party of men to take the cattle.

I arrived at the ranch with Widenmann and Waite, the same day. Waite took the road for Lincoln, the rest of the party taking the trail with the horses. When we had traveled about thirty miles, John Middleton and I were riding in the rear of the party and just upon reaching the brow of a hill we saw a large party coming toward us from the rear at full speed. Middleton and I rode forward to warn the balance of the party. We had barely reached Brewer and Widenmann who were some 200 or 300 yards to the left of the trail when the attacking party cleared the brow of the hill and began firing at us. With Widenmann and Brewer I rode over the hill toward another hill which was covered with large rocks and trees so we could defend ourselves and make a stand.

But the attacking party, undoubtedly seeing Tunstall, left off pursuing us to turn back to the canon in which the trail was. Shortly afterwards we heard two separate and distinct shots. The remark was made by Middleton that they, the attacking party, must have killed Tunstall. Middleton, in the meantime, had joined me, Widenmann and Brewer. I then rode to Lincoln with Brewer, Middleton, Widenmann and Waite, stopping on the Rio Ruidoso in order to get men to look for the body of Tunstall.

Neither I or any member of the party fired either rifle or pistol and none of us fired a shot.

Statement of John Middleton, Who Was with John Tunstall When He Was Murdered

On the morning of the 18th, Tunstall, myself, Widenmann, Brewer, Bonney and Waite left for Lincoln, Waite taking the main road with the wagon, the others taking the trail. About thirty miles from the ranch we scattered for the purpose of hunting some turkeys. While so doing we heard yelling and saw a large crowd of men coming over the hill, firing as they were coming.

Tunstall and I were on the side of a hill, about 700 yards from some horses we were bringing from the Rio Feliz ranch to Lincoln, belonging to Tunstall, Widenmann, Bonney, Brewer and myself. The horses numbered nine. If they [the posse] wanted the horses they could easily have got them without coming within 700 yards of us. Not one of us who I have named fired a shot. We decided to escape to save our lives. I was within 30 steps of Tunstall when we heard the shooting first. I sang out to Tunstall to follow me. He was on a good horse. He appeared to be very much excited and confused. I kept saying to him:

"For God's sakes follow me."

His last words were: "What John? What John?"

Then with the exception of Tunstall we made an effort to join each other.

Territory of New Mexico }
County of Lincoln }

William H. Bonney being duly sworn, deposes and says, that he is a resident of said County, that on the 11th day of February A.D. 1878 he in company with Robt. A. Widenmann and Fred. T. Waite went to the ranch of J. H. Tunstall on the Rio Feliz, that he and said Fred. T. Waite at the time intended to go to the Rio Penasco to take up a ranch, for the purpose of farming. That the cattle on the ranch of said J. H. Tunstall were throughout the County of Lincoln known to be the property of said Tunstall; that on the 13th of February A.D. 1878 one J. B. Mathews claiming to be Deputy Sheriff came to the ranch of said J. H. Tunstall in company with Jesse Evans, Frank Baker, Tom Hill and Rivera, known outlaws who had been confined in the Lincoln County jail and had succeeded in making their escape, John Hurley, George Hindman, Roberts and an Indian and Ponceano, the latter said to be the murderer of Benito Cruz, for the arrest of the murderers of whom (Benito Cruz) the Governor of this Territory offers a reward of $500.— Before the arrival of said J. B. Mathews, deputy Sheriff and his posse, having been informed that said deputy Sheriff and posse were going to round up all the cattle and drive them off and kill the persons at the ranch, the persons at the ranch cut portholes into the walls of the house and filled sacks with earth, so that they, the persons at the ranch, should they be attacked or their murder attempted, could defend

Billy the Kid's dramatic, eyewitness account of the killing of John Tunstall, which he dictated to Frank Warner Angel, the Washington agent sent by Secretary of the Interior Schurz, with presidential approval, to investigate Tunstall's death and widespread official corruption. The affidavit is signed by the Kid. *Courtesy National Archives*

themselves, this course being thought necessary as the sheriffs posse was composed of murderers, outlaws and desperate characters none of whom had any interest at stake in the County, nor being residents of said County. That said Mathews when within about 50 yards of the house was called to to stop and advance alone and state his business, that said Mathews after arriving at the ranch said that he had come to attach the cattle and property of A. A. McSwein, that said Mathews was informed that A. A. McSwein had no cattle or property there, but that if he had he, said Mathews could take it. That said Mathews said that he thought some of the cattle belonging to R. M. Brewer, whose cattle were also at the ranch of J. H. Tunstall, belonged to A. A. McSwein, that said Mathews was told by said Brewer that he, Mathews, could round up the cattle and that he, Brewer, would help him. That said Mathews said, that he would go back to Lincoln to get new instructions and if he came back to the ranch he would come back with one man. That said Mathews and his posse were then invited by R. M. Brewer to come to the house and get something to eat.

Deponent further says that Robert A. Widenmann told R. M. Brewer and the others at the ranch, that he was going to arrest Frank Baker, Jesse Evans and Tom Hill, said Widenmann having warrants for them. That said Widenmann was told by Brewer and the others at the ranch that the arrest could not be made because if it was made they, all the persons at the ranch would be killed and murdered by J. J. Dolan & Co. and their party. That Jesse Evans advanced upon said Widenmann, said Evans swinging his gun and catching it cocked and pointed directly at said Widenmann. That said Jesse Evans asked said Widenmann whether he, Widenmann, was hunting for him, Evans, to which Widenmann answered, that if he was looking for him, he, Evans would find it out. Evans also asked Widenmann whether he had a warrant for him, Widenmann answered that that was his (Widenmann's) business. Evans told Widenmann, that if he ever came to arrest him (Evans) he, Evans would pick Widenmann as the first man to shoot at, to which Widenmann answered that that was all right, that two could play at that game. That during the talking Frank Baker stood near said Widenmann, swinging his pistol on his finger, catching it full cocked & pointed at said Widenmann. — The persons at the ranch were R. M. Brewer, John Middleton, G. Gauss, McCarty, R. A. Widenmann, Henry Brown, F. T. Waite, Wm. McCloskey and this deponent. J. B. Mathews, after eating started for Lincoln with John Hurley and Ponce and the rest of the party or posse saying they were going to the Rio Peñasco. Deponent started for Lincoln with Robt. A. Widenmann and F. T. Waite and arrived at Lincoln the same evening and again left Lincoln on the next day, February the 14th in company with the above named persons, having heard that said Mathews was going back to the ranch of said J. H. Tunstall with a large party of men to take the cattle and deponent and Widenmann and Waite arrived at said ranch the same day. — Deponent states that on the road to Lincoln he heard said Mathews ask said

Widenmann whether any resistance would be offered if Mathews returned to take the cattle, to which said Widenmann, answered that no resistance would be offered if the cattle were left at the ranch but if an attempt was made to drive the cattle to the Indian Agency and kill them for beef as he, said Mathews had been heard to say would be done, he said, Widenmann would do all in his power to prevent this.

Deponent further says, that on the night of the 17th of February A.D. 1878 J. H. Tunstall arrived at the ranch and informed all the persons there, that reliable information had reached him that J. B. Mathews was gathering a large party of outlaws and desperadoes as a posse and that said posse was coming to the ranch, the mexicans in the party to gather up the cattle and the balance of the posse to kill the persons at the ranch. It was thereupon decided that all persons at the ranch excepting G. Gauss, were to leave and Wm McCloskey was that night sent to the Rio Peñasco to inform the posse who were camped there, that they could come over and round up the cattle, count them and leave a man there to take care of them and that Mr Tunstall would also leave a man there to help round up and count the cattle and help ~~them~~ to take care of them, and said McCloskey was also ordered to go to Martin Martz, who had left Tunstalls ranch when deponent, Widenmann and Waite returned to the town of Lincoln on the 13th of February, and ask him said Martz to come to the ranch of said Tunstall and aid the sheriffs posse in rounding up and counting the cattle and to stay at the ranch and take care of the cattle.

Deponent left the ranch of said Tunstall in company

with J.H. Tunstall, R.A. Widenmann, R.M. Brewer, John Middleton and F.T. Waite, said Tunstall, Widenmann, Brewer, Middleton and deponent driving the loose horses, Waite driving the wagon. Said Waite took the road for Lincoln with the wagon, the rest of the party taking the trail with the horses. Deponent says that all the horses which he and party were driving, excepting 3 had been released by sheriff Brady at Lincoln that one of these 3 horses belonged to R.M. Brewer, and another was traded by Brewer to Tunstall for one of the released horses.—

Deponent further says, that when he and party had travelled to within about 30 miles from the Rio Ruidoso he and John Middleton were riding in the rear of the balance of the party and just upon reaching the brow of a hill they saw a large party of men coming towards them from the rear at full speed and that he and Middleton at once rode forward to inform the balance of the party of the fact. Deponent had not more than barely reached Brewer and Widenmann who were some 200 or 300 yards to the left of the trail when the attacking party cleared the brow of the hill and commenced firing at him, Widenmann and Brewer. Deponent Widenmann and Brewer rode over a hill towards another which was covered with large rocks and trees and in order to defend themselves and make a stand. But the attacking party, undoubtedly seeing Tunstall, left off pursuing deponent and the two with him and turned back to the cañon in which the trail was. Shortly afterwards we heard two or three separate and distinct shots and the remark was then made by Middleton that they, the attacking

party pursued and [illegible] killed Tunstall. Middleton had
in the meantime joined deponent and Widenmann
and Brewer. Deponent then made the best of his way
to Lincoln in company with Robt. A. Widenmann,
Brewer, Waite and Middleton stopping on the
Rio Ruidoso in order to get men to look for the
body of J. H. Tunstall.
Deponent further says, that neither he nor any
of the party fired off either rifle or pistol and that
neither he nor the parties with him fired a shot.

William H. Bonney

Sworn and subscribed to before me this eighth
day of June A.D. 1878.

John B. Wilson

Justice of the Peace

George Hindman, Jesse Evans, Frank Baker were the only ones I can remember who were in the posse who murdered Tunstall.

I have been informed by Tom Green who was in that posse, that Jesse Evans shot Tunstall first in the breast. Tunstall before this had surrendered his pistol, the only weapon he had, to William Morton [deceased]. When Tunstall received the first shot in the breast he turned and fell on his face. Morton then fired at Tunstall from his own pistol, the ball entering the back of his head. Morton then fired another shot out of Tunstall's pistol at Tunstall's horse, killing it.

[Samuel R.] Perry then proposed that they carry Tunstall's corpse and lay it out by the side of his dead horse which was done. I later saw the corpse of Tunstall at the house of Alexander McSween in Lincoln and attended his burial on February 22, 1878.

Statement of Samuel R. Perry,
a Member of the Sheriff's Posse Who Killed John H. Tunstall on February 18, 1878

I was one of the posse that went to attach Tunstall's property. I reside on the Pecos at Seven Rivers and I have been employed by Dolan and Riley. On or about the 10th day of February, 1878, I was informed that William S. Morton had been deputized by J. B. Mathews and that papers had been brought to Mathews by Jac [sic] Rivers. I was on or about the said day summoned to join the posse.

On the night of the same day I left for the Penasco at Pauls Ranch, the place where the whole posse was to meet. We arrived there on the night of the 17th. The next morning we started for Tunstall's ranch on the Feliz. On our way we met Henry Brown [a friend of Billy the Kid]. He did not say there would or would not be any resistance. He did say there was no one there. [William] McCloskey was at Pauls before we started. I did not hear him say anything about resistance or no resistance. He might have said something out of my hearing.

We arrived at the Feliz on the morning of the 18th. We found there Martin Metz [Mertz] who was in charge of the cattle. [He was either there before or came before we left, I am not positive] and a cook by the name of [George] Gauss.

We inquired for the horses and they told us they had gone but they did not know where they had gone; they had left about daylight and thought they had gone to Lincoln but did not know for sure.

Mathews then gave the attachment papers to Billy Morton and told him to take some men and attach the horses. Morton selected Robert W. Beckwith, Wallace Olinger, Sam Perry, Charley [Dutch Charley] Kruling, Thomas Cockrane, Thomas Green, P. Gallogos, John Hurley, Charles Marshall, Manuel—Kit, Ramon Montoya, George Hindman, Frank Baker, Jesse Evans, Thomas Hill.

The three latter were not called upon, they volunteered saying they had a horse among the horses Tunstall had taken away and that they wished to go after it. I do not remember if there was any objections made by anyone to them accompanying us but J. J. Dolan said to either Mathews or Morton, that they [Baker, Evans, and Hill] better not go.

Either Baker, Evans or Hill replied that a person had a right to go for their property or something to that effect. I am positive Dolan did not come with us.

We started after the horses, myself, Hindman and George Marshall having tired horses, brought up in the rear. We had gone about 30 miles when Manuel appeared in front of us, beckoning to us to come on.

We rode on and when we were about a half mile from our party who were ahead and had overtaken Tunstall's property and party, Hindman said, "I heard a shot."

I replied, "I guess not, it was a horse stumbled."

Then he said, "I heard another."

When we reached the top of the hill, we saw some of our party rounding up the horses. When we reached the horses, Morton came up and said,

"Tunstall was killed."

I said, "It could not be for I don't believe Tunstall is here."

He said he had followed after Tunstall, where upon Tunstall turned and came riding up to him. Then Morton started to read him the warrant, whereupon Tunstall drew his pistol and fired two shots at him. Before Tunstall had fired, Jesse Evans called out to him to throw up his hands and he would not be hurt.

Tunstall disregarded this and fired as I have set forth, whereupon he [Morton], Jesse Evans and Tom Hill fired at him. The result of the firing was that Tunstall and his horse were killed.

After the above statement had been made to me, Evans and more of our party being present, I went up to the place where Tunstall was laying. I found him lying on his face, his horse was close beside him, their heads being in the same direction. The horse was still alive but nearly dead. Tom Hill, thereupon to put the horse out of misery, shot him with his [Hill's] carbine.

I then took his [Tunstall's] blankets and myself, Tom Green, Wallace Olinger,

George Hindman and Charley Kruling, laid him out by the side of his horse. We did not see his hat nor did anyone put it under his horse's head.

Tom Hill had Tunstall's revolver which he had found eight or ten feet from where the horse fell. Tom Hill handed it to Montoya and Montoya handed it to me and I placed it at the side of Tunstall. I did not examine the pistol. Tunstall's face was bruised by the fall but his head was not mutilated by any members of our party.

We thereupon returned to the Feliz with the horses. We found Dolan at the camp about 500 yards from Tunstall's house. I am sure and positive that Dolan was not with our party that went out after Tunstall's property.

After our return to the ranch I either heard Baker, Evans or Hill say the death of Tunstall was a small loss and he ought to have been killed or something to that effect.

While I was laying out Tunstall I heard three shots. I am not positive I inquired what they were shooting about, but said they were shooting at that tree.

There was some talk about this time that either Hill, Morton or Evans had fired off Tunstall's pistol. I thought it strange they were shooting at a mark. I did not think it was an appropriate time to be shooting at a mark. I do not know who was shooting at a mark, I was busy laying Tunstall out.

Statement of John Wallace Olinger, a Member of the Sheriff's Posse

Angel found Olinger in Dona Ana and read him Perry's statement. Olinger agreed the facts were correct. However, when Angel discovered Olinger had also heard Hill firing the two shots from Tunstall's revolver, he had him make a separate affidavit.

> I heard two shots fired. I heard the shots before I examined the [Tunstall's] revolver. I think Hill fired those shots. I thought at the time that Tunstall's party might be firing at us, then I thought the shots were fired to collect our party.

From the statements it is evident that after murdering Tunstall, Evans, Hill, and Morton had fired two shots from the dead man's pistol to support their claim he fired twice at them after they demanded he surrender his weapons and turn over the nine horses.

Tunstall's four-man party—the half-breed Waite was driving the wagon on the lower road—was clearly outnumbered; as Middleton told Angel, the posse could have easily taken the horses without gunfire.

Widenmann, who appears older and better educated than the others, also disclosed to Angel he had "been informed" that Morton, Hill, and Evans had "promised" to kill the Englishman before the day was over.

On the basis of the evidence Angel collected, he had clearly established a prima facie case of premeditated murder.

But the legality of the case did not interest Billy the Kid; the man he admired and respected had been gunned down like a rabid coyote. Nothing in his young life, not even his mother's death, would move him more than the brutal scene on that mountain trail. Tunstall's death had a tragic influence on Billy's brief remaining years. He was nineteen.

After Mathews's "sheriff's posse" had ridden off, Billy proposed Widenmann and the others circle the area and ride to Lincoln to notify McSween of Tunstall's murder. Meanwhile he would head for the Coe ranch on the Ruidoso to get someone to bring in the body.

Billy reached the Coe ranch late that night. Frank Coe never forgot the boy's tight face and glittering eyes.

"They killed Mr. Tunstall," he said hoarsely. "They shot him down like a dog . . . he's over in Sanchez Canyon . . ."

The stunned Coe listened as the Kid told the story. He refused to sit down but paced up and down the room describing the events of that afternoon.[20]

Finally, when he had ended the story, he stared into space for a moment, then in a bitter voice swore he would kill every man who had any connection with the killing of Tunstall—even Sheriff Brady who wasn't there but had sent the murderers out with fraudulent tin badges . . .

At Billy's suggestion Frank Coe paid an old Mexican sheepherder to bring in the corpse. The next day the sheepman arrived at a neighboring ranch; Tunstall's body, torn and lacerated by the ride through the thorny brush, was put in a wagon and removed to Lincoln.

News of Tunstall's murder spread like a grass fire and men and women streamed across Lincoln's dusty plaza to the store. McSween told them the time had now come to fight the Murphy-Dolan-Riley-Santa Fe group, there was no longer any law left in the land so they must supply it.

In the large adobe room, shadows wavering on the stark walls in the lantern light, McSween recounted the robberies, beatings, and killings they had suffered.

Suddenly, about midnight, the door flew open and a drunken Jimmy Riley, Murphy's junior partner, staggered into the room. Glassy-eyed and swaying, he made his way to the table to face McSween. At the lawyer's order he emptied his pockets and handed his six-shooter over to George Washington, the McSween cook and handyman, to prove he had come in good faith to make a peaceful agreement.

The Kid had his gun drawn and was ready as Washington told Frank Warner Angel "to do in Riley" but McSween pushed his way between the drunken, cursing man and the grim-faced boy. He then escorted Riley to the door, pushed him out, and urged him to get riding, his life wasn't worth a bent horseshoe nail in that room.

Someone examined the things Riley had dumped from his pockets; one was a small memorandum book. The entries proved shocking; Riley had listed in code the names of the men involved in furnishing stolen beef to the Murphy-Dolan-Riley organization.[21]

The next morning Dr. Taylor E. Ealy, a medical missionary who lived with McSween, and Fort Stanton's post surgeon, Dr. D. M. Appel, performed a postmortem on Tunstall's body.

Dr. Appel's official report, which he turned over to Angel, described in detail the path of the two fatal wounds. Tunstall's skull, he said, had been fractured from the fall because "his skull was thin from venereal disease."

The two bullets, he decided, had caused instant death.

Before Tunstall was buried, the outraged residents of the county formed what was called "The Regulators." The group had a quasi-official blessing because Dick Brewer, Tunstall's foreman and fellow rancher, had been deputized by Lincoln's justice of the peace, John B. Wilson. In reality, both the Regulators and Mathews's "sheriff's posse" were little more than vigilantes.

Wilson issued warrants for Evans and the others, charging them with murder, and demanded that Sheriff Brady bring them into Lincoln. When Brady ignored his orders, Wilson gave the warrants to Antonio Martinez, a Lincoln constable. In his affidavit to Angel, Martinez told how he had deputized Billy and the half-Cherokee, Fred Waite, to accompany him but upon their arrival at the Dolan ranch, Sheriff Brady had immediately placed them under arrest "for disturbing the peace." Dolan and his gang disarmed the Kid and Waite but later released Martinez.[22]

The Kid demanded that he be let go to attend Tunstall's funeral services but Brady refused. On Friday afternoon, after the Englishman had been buried outside his store, Brady released Billy and Waite. They rode to Lincoln to meet the ranchers and townspeople who were still lingering after attending the funeral.

When they gathered about him, Billy described what had happened. The following morning with Billy riding stirrup-to-stirrup with Dick Brewer, the Regulators rode out of Lincoln to find and arrest Billy Morton and Frank Baker.

They found them in the rough country below the lower Penasco. After a brief exchange of shots, the Kid ran down Morton's horse and took him prisoner; Brewer and the others captured Frank Baker.

They camped out that night after Brewer received word by a rider that Jimmy Dolan was raising a large force to storm Lincoln and release the prisoners. On the morning of March 8, 1878, Morton, who knew those stonefaced men would never let him reach Lincoln alive, wrote a moving letter to a lawyer-cousin in Virginia, begging him to look into his death because "I have heard we are not to be taken alive to that place [Lincoln]."

The letter was prophetic; on March 8, Ash Upton, who later ghostwrote Pat Garrett's autobiography, advised the *Mesilla Independent* that Morton had "suddenly snatched" a pistol from the holster of William McCloskey, a member of the posse, and killed him. He then broke free and followed by Baker tried to escape.

"They were quickly overtaken and killed," Upton added. When word of the latest killings reached Governor Sam Axtell, a Dolan-Murphy partisan, he revoked Wilson's commission as a justice of the peace, nullifying Dick Brewer's deputy status; the Regulators were now officially described to be lawless vigilantes.

Sheriff Brady and a posse, aided by troops of the Ninth Cavalry, combed the hills for Brewer, the Kid, and Waite who seemed to be Brady's principal targets. On Monday, April 8, the Kid, leading a small group of the Regulators, slipped into Lincoln and took refuge at Tunstall's store. When he heard Brady and George Hindman were coming into town, the Kid and several others took up posts behind the gate at the east end of the Tunstall store. Sheriff Brady and Hindman left the Wortley Hotel and casually started down the street. There was a burst of gunfire from behind the gate, Brady spun around and was dead before he hit the ground. Hindman was hit as he ran but reached cover. Mathews, the leader of the Tunstall death posse, heard the shots and, as the Kid emerged from behind the gate, fired, his bullet creasing Billy's side. In an exchange of shots, the Kid and Fred Waite made their way to the corral, mounted and rode for San Patricio, several miles away.

Three days after the shooting of Brady and Hindman, the Kid led a band of the Regulators on a wide sweep of the western desolate section of the county, looking for other members of Mathews's posse.

At the home and sawmill of Dr. Joseph H. Blazer on the Mescalero Apache Reservation, they found Andrew (Buckshot) Roberts, the crippled buffalo hunter who had been a member of the "sheriff's posse." Billy undoubtedly recalled Roberts shouting to Mathews that morning at the Tunstall ranch:

"Why talk? Let's pitch in and fight and kill them all."

Charlie Bowdre shouted for Roberts to surrender. The buffalo hunter's reply was a rifle shot that tore off Bowdre's gun belt and shattered George Coe's hand but Bowdre's bullet hit Roberts in the lower stomach. Roberts managed to get off another shot severely wounding Frank Middleton, John's brother, then made his way into Blazer's house.

Holding his gaping wound with one hand, Roberts dragged a heavy buffalo gun he had found to the window where he propped up a mattress. The Regulators now had spread out to surround the sawmill with Dick Brewer covering the far end of the building. Minutes passed. Suddenly the tense silence was shattered by a booming shot. The Kid and Waite squirmed around the mill to find Brewer with the top of his head blown off. Inside the dying Roberts was crying: "I killed the son of a bitch! I killed him!"

The Kid wanted to storm the mill and kill Roberts but the others pointed out that Roberts was surely dying, Middleton had been shot through the lungs, and Coe had lost his trigger finger; both men needed medical attention. Billy reluctantly agreed. Middleton was helped onto his horse and with two men holding him upright in the saddle they made their way to Lincoln.

That afternoon when Blazer returned to his mill he found Roberts dead, the buffalo gun lying beside him.

A few days later a coroner's jury charged "William Antrim, alias the Kid" with killing Roberts, although Bowdre had shot the hunter. Acting Sheriff George Peppin immediately announced the Kid would soon be in custody but from his hideout in the hills Billy sent back a mocking challenge to come and get him.[23]

Meanwhile the Lincoln County grand jury dismissed charges against McSween that he had embezzled Lieutenant Colonel Fritz's, $10,000 insurance policy. This was good news to Billy and the Regulators but it was still evident that Murphy & Company had powerful friends in Santa Fe.

As Antonio Martinez, the Lincoln constable, told Frank Warner Angel in his affidavit, he had overheard Colonel Rynerson, the prosecutor, tell Jimmy Dolan:

"Don't give up, Jimmy! Stick to that McSween crowd. I will aid you all I can and give you twenty men. Stick to the fight. This is the only way we can win . . ."[24]

In April 1878, Billy and the Regulators continued to seek out the Murphy-Dolan-Riley riders in the desolate areas of Lincoln County. "Doc" Scurlock, who legend insists was a former medical student, was now the accepted leader with Billy, the youngest, second in command. Once they raided Dolan's cow camp on the Pecos and drove off a herd of horses. On another occasion they traded shots across Lincoln's plaza with Dolan's men but no one was wounded.

The harassment by the Regulators, the increasing hostility of the county residents, and the illness of old Colonel Murphy finally forced Dolan to publish a public notice that Murphy & Company had suspended business. Tom Catron, head of the Santa Fe Ring who held the mortgage, took over the mercantile firm and appointed his young brother-in-law, Edgar Walz, as manager of the store and all his enterprises in Lincoln County—including his share of Dolan's herds of cattle and horses.

Catron, a tough, pioneering lawyer, decided that Billy the Kid was not only the chief troublemaker in the county, but was also responsible for the money he had lost in backing Murphy's company and for the horses stolen from Dolan's cow camp. He wrote a letter to Governor Sam Axtell demanding troops be brought into Lincoln to restore order.

Then to add to Lincoln's complex political picture, the county commissioners appointed a new sheriff, John Copeland, an honest but inefficient peace officer; George Peppin remained as his deputy.

On May 18, Governor Axtell shocked the residents of Lincoln County by issuing an official proclamation—undoubtedly at Catron's urging—removing Copeland and appointing Peppin sheriff.[25]

Now Catron not only had his own peace officer ruling Lincoln County but in Peppin he had a friend of Dolan, Murphy, and Riley—the Kid's bitterest enemies. All that spring and early summer, Billy, the Regulators, and Peppin's posse, sought out each other in the barren hills or along the lonely trails. At Fritz Spring, ten miles from Lincoln, three of the Kid's friends were ambushed by Peppin and his men: Frank McNab was killed, Ab Sanders badly wounded, and Frank Coe taken prisoner.

Then on the morning of July 11, 1879, Billy and the Regulators joined forces in Lincoln with a large band of Mexicans under his old friend Martin (Chaves) Chavez.

Under a new federal law United States troops were forbidden to interfere in domestic law enforcement matters; now it would be a final showdown between the Murphy-Dolan-Riley-Peppin forces and the McSween and Tunstall group.

While Chavez took over the Montano building, Billy and his riders joined McSween in his house. He had a new rider, Tom O'Folliard, a young Texan, who would follow him almost to the end of the trail . . .[26]

Peppin immediately accepted the challenge. He deputized a new gang of outlaws and desperados led by John Kinney, a notorious horse thief and rustler, as another "sheriff's posse" and rode into Lincoln. Only a few weeks before, Kinney's gang had invaded San Patricio, taking over the entire town, insulting women, terrorizing shopkeepers and shattering glass windows with their gunfire. Peppin ignored the complaints of the outraged citizens.

With Peppin was Bob Beckwith, young son of a Pecos rancher, who had written an enthusiastic letter to his sister how he and the posse had been hunting "for them [Billy and the Regulators] like Indians."

In a few days he would be dead.

Peppin, worried that he might be outgunned and outgeneraled, sent a message to Fort Stanton's new commander, Colonel N. A. M. Dudley, demanding that troops be sent into Lincoln.

There had been jubilation in the county when Dudley had replaced Colonel George A. Purington, an incredibly insensitive and stupid officer who antagonized Lincoln's citizens with his open approval of the Murphy-Dolan group.

However, it soon became clear that Dudley, like Purington, favored the politically influential Murphy-Dolan and Riley forces. In fact, as McSween later discovered, Dudley had been defended in a court-martial by Catron's Santa Fe law firm.

Dudley was typical of the post-Civil War Indian fighting army officers who protected the far-flung western frontier with dedication, personal courage, and too few men and supplies. On the debit side, he was hard drinking, ambitious, and viewed civilians with a career officer's contempt. He had known Catron before he reached Stanton and undoubtedly had been advised by the Santa Fe politician to rely on Murphy-Dolan and Riley for advice and guidance.

His initial meeting with McSween had been abrasive; the ramrod straight officer with the fierce moustache quickly dismissed the dumpy man in a baggy store suit as a troublemaker and his followers, such as "the Kid" as he called him, as outlaws and killers.

It was all black and white for Dudley: Murphy-Dolan-Riley, and Sheriff Peppin were the stalwarts of the law; McSween and "his nest of scoundrels" were dangerous meddlers challenging tradition and authority by violence.

Although he had been warned by the War Department of the new law, which barred the army from interfering in the problems of local law enforcement, Dudley led a column of thirty or more troopers of the Ninth Cavalry into Lincoln. At his side was the despised Purington. But what stunned the residents were the "cannon" and Gatling gun that rumbled across Lincoln's plaza directly behind Dudley.[27]

McSween, Billy, and the others peered through the portholes hacked out of the adobe walls, watching the column make its way down the street to halt at the Wortley Hotel where Dudley held a conference with Sheriff Peppin.

Dudley's first official act was to warn Chaves that if any of his troops were fired upon, he would order the Montano building shelled.

When Chaves pointed out to Dudley he had posted his troops directly in the line of fire and it was impossible not to fire at least over their heads, Dudley simply repeated his warning and walked away.

After a conference with Billy and McSween, Chaves withdrew his men from Lincoln. As he later testified, Dudley's howitzer—"the cannon"—and Gatling gun would have wiped out his followers in minutes.

Dudley also convened a three-man panel that quickly decided McSween was guilty of firing at one of his men. A warrant was issued for the lawyer's arrest and Peppin's men marched up to the shuttered windows to serve it.

"My God, we have warrants for you people!" McSween shouted, as he

Tom O'Folliard, Billy the Kid's closest friend, who was killed during the gunfight at Fort Sumner, December 19, 1880. *Courtesy Special Collections, University of Arizona Library*

A rare photograph of Susan McSween, heroine of the Battle of Lincoln and a friend of Billy the Kid. *Courtesy Special Collections, University of Arizona Library*

warned them to get back to the hotel. Dudley also posted three soldiers outside the McSween house. When McSween wrote a note demanding to know why the military was guarding his house, Dudley replied it was "his business" and warned the lawyer, as he had told Chaves, that shots fired over the heads of his men would be answered by cannon fire. As the hours passed, McSween sent another note delivered by his courageous twelve-year-old daughter advising Dudley they had legal warrants for the arrest of Peppin and his gang for murder and larceny but the colonel dictated a terse reply he wasn't interested and denied he had soldiers surrounding the lawyer's house.

Sunday, July 14, 1878, when Billy the Kid and his Regulators joined McSween in his house, until the following Friday when Colonel Dudley moved into town, the Battle of Lincoln was confined to sporadic firing; one of Sheriff Peppin's men was killed and a few of the Regulators slightly wounded.

Incredible as it seems, Dudley made camp a short distance away, sharing drinks with Peppin, Dolan, Riley, John Kinney, the outlaw leader, and other members of the "sheriff's posse," some of whom were fugitives from charges of murder, horse stealing, and rustling.

From the testimony of witnesses, it appeared Susan McSween was a petite, attractive iron butterfly. At the peak of the battle she stormed down the street into Dudley's tent, demanding that he escort her husband and the others in the house to the fort to wait while word was sent to Washington informing Frank Warner Angel and the White House of what was happening.

Dudley listened and as one witness recalled: "He had no regard for her. He told his orderly to get her out of his camp."

On Friday, as dusk was thickening, Andrew I. Boyle and Jack Long, known as "Rivers," both Peppin's deputies, set fire to the rear door of the McSween house. Billy and the others tried to put out the flames but the brisk evening wind fanned the blaze that fed on the sunbaked floorboards and framework.

The rooms filled with smoke; it was almost impossible to see. Again Mrs. McSween, coughing and red-eyed, swept out of the house, crying to Peppin's sharpshooters perched on the surrounding rooftops that now was their chance to shoot down a woman. There was only silence as she made her way to the colonel's tent.

The pompous officer, his face flushed a deep red from anger and whiskey, again ordered his men to escort her back to her burning house. It was, as she recalled, a nightmare.

The house was in flames when she returned; Billy, she said, urged her to leave with the children. She wrapped a shawl around her head, brought up her two girls to kiss their father, then for a long moment before they parted for the last time, McSween and his wife clung to each other.

Legend insists she played "Home Sweet Home" and "The Star Spangled Banner" on an organ in those last hours of the battle. Years later she denounced it as a fool's tale. The testimony of Doctor Ealy, the missionary, shows he had a small organ in his nearby house which Dudley agreed to let him remove to the street after his house, adjacent to McSween's caught fire. That was the only musical instrument in the area.

When darkness fell Billy, now the accepted leader, sketched their final plans: They would make a run for it from the rear door, firing as they headed for the gate and corral. His goal was to get McSween on a horse and away to the hills where they would be joined by Chaves and his men.

Cylinders were spun, bullets jammed home, cartridge belts tightened. The small band, faces blackened by soot and coughing from the thick smoke, waited tensely as the Kid peered through a porthole.

In his affidavit to Frank Warner Angel, Billy said that when the door was opened they all ran out, silhouetted by the glare of the burning buildings which, as he recalled, "made it almost light as day."

Billy told Angel that as he plunged through the billowing smoke he saw three troopers firing at him from the nearby Tunstall building. Directly in front of him, McSween was hit with five bullets and died. Harvey Morris, a young law student who had been reading law in McSween's office, staggered and died on his feet. Billy, bullets whistling about him, reached the gate and escaped to the Bonito River.[28]

After he had made his escape to the Bonito, Billy was joined by Tom O'Folliard, and other riders. They ran along the banks of the river until they had cleared the town and found the trail that led to the valley of the Ruidoso.

They slept like dead men in the hills that night. Fred Waite, Charlie Bowdre, Doc Scurlock, and John Middleton, still weak from the wound inflicted by Buckshot Roberts during the fight at Blazer's Mill, met them a few days later with horses, rifles, ammunition, and food.

When he received word from friends in Lincoln that Dudley had a patrol searching the hills for them, Billy led his ragtag band to Fort Sumner on the

Pecos, west of the Canadian River country. Here the Kid had many friends among the Mexicans in the area who would feed and shelter them. There was also work on nearby ranches.

He promised they would return to Lincoln and take care of their old enemies, Murphy & Company . . .

Frank Warner Angel, Washington's undercover agent, who did not "have his wings clipped" while conducting an investigation of the Lincoln County War, as one frontier newspaper predicted, was busy that summer of 1878, "arranging and indexing" the affidavits and depositions he had gathered. It had been "a very difficult and dangerous mission" for Angel, a New York tenderfoot, who had crisscrossed sprawling Lincoln County by buckboard and on horseback interviewing members of both the McSween-Tunstall and Murphy-Dolan clans.

He had met Billy the Kid who escorted him to the ranches of the Coes on the Ruidoso and to the hideouts of his riders. Here is a marvelous picture of the tough young gunfighters and rustlers dictating their statements, then laboriously signing them with Angel's pen under the eyes of their young leader.

It was inevitable that Angel's identity and mission would become known; Tom Catron, head of the Santa Fe Ring and his henchman Colonel Rynerson, had ruled their frontier empire for too many years to be threatened by a young eastern lawyer, even though he represented faraway Washington. One can only guess what type of "obstacles," as Angel called them, were "thrown in my path."

The prosecutor returned East in early August 1878. Using his private law office at 62 Liberty Street as a base, he began preparing a report on the Tunstall killing and the incredible corruption he had uncovered in the Territory of New Mexico.

He first sent a list of thirty-one "interrogatories" to Governor Samuel Beach Axtell to answer and return within thirty days.[29] Angel had skillfully prepared the questions based on the evidence he had collected, including a charge the governor had accepted a $2,000 bribe.

The "interrogatories" stunned Axtell. They were received at the "Governor's Palace," an ancient adobe building, on a Sunday; the next morning Axtell sent an angry reply to Angel, demanding to know the identity of his accusers and protesting the thirty-day time limit.[30]

Angel immediately replied, expressing "surprise" that Axtell objected to being investigated:

"I have found certain parts of this territory in a terrible and deplorable state —someone is responsible for the same, and with a view to try and discover if you were responsible for the same, I prepared and forwarded the interrogatories to you without the least personal feeling against you . . ."

Angel informed Axtell that the questions were based on affidavits he had obtained from "various citizens," but refused to disclose their identities. As to the time limit of thirty days, Angel tersely informed Axtell: "If I were the accused party I should not want, desire or wish twenty-four hours to answer same . . ."

The following week Angel sent copies of Axtell's letters to Secretary Schurz with the wry observation, "As you can see we did not part the best of friends on his part."

Angel's final report on Axtell was a devastating condemnation of his official conduct. It consisted of twelve charges of misconduct, official corruption, and partisanship in the Lincoln County War. Angel wrote:

"I found Lincoln County convulsed by an internal war. I enquired the cause. Someone was responsible for the bloodshed in that County. I found two parties in the field—one headed by Murphy, Dolan and Riley, the other by McSween. Both had done many things contrary to the law—both were violating the law. McSween I firmly believe acted conscientiously—Murphy, Dolan and Riley for revenge and personal gain.

"The Governor came and heard the Murphy, Dolan and Riley side but refused to hear the people who were with McSween or the citizens of the county and acted strictly in advancing the Murphy and Dolan and Riley party.

"Unlawful acts followed, instead of peace and quiet which could have been accomplished if the Governor had acted as he should have done and listened patiently to both sides. The opportunity presented itself to him to have quieted and stopped the trouble in Lincoln County—but by his partisan action he allowed it to pass and the continuations of that trouble that exist to this day in Lincoln County are chargeable to him. He was a partisan, either through corruption or weakness . . ."

Angel also revealed he had uncovered evidence that Axtell had borrowed $1,800 from Riley in May 1876 and, "although it is alleged Axtell repaid the money in September, his action lays him open to suspicion that his friendship with Murphy, Dolan and Riley was stronger than his duty to his people and the government he represented."

Angel severely criticized Axtell for removing the local justice of the peace, J. B. Wilson, and John Copeland, appointed as sheriff after Brady's murder, and replacing Copeland with G. W. Peppin, who he described as "one of the leaders of the Murphy, Dolan, Riley party who comes from Mesilla accompanied by John Kinney and his murderous outfit of outlaws, as a bodyguard to assist him in enforcing law and order." He added:

"Again we have an unusual number of murders, robbery, accompanied by arson, and after Kinney and his party have accomplished their mission of murdering McSween and robbing and stealing all they can, they retire on their laurels and return from whence they came, and Sheriff Peppin, without the confidence of the people or even confidence in himself, returns to Fort Stanton at which place he is under the care and protection of the soldiers . . ."

Angel summed up his long report by strongly recommending Axtell be removed from office.[31]

In September the Department of Interior forwarded copies of Angel's report to Governor Axtell. Now the first cracks appeared in the foundation of the Santa Fe Ring. At a conference between Axtell and Tom Catron, it was decided that Colonel William L. Rynerson, territorial district attorney, Third District, Catron's hatchet man and bitter enemy of Billy the Kid, had to be sent to New York to see Frank Warner Angel.

The meeting took place in Angel's Liberty Street office in early September.

Angel, in a letter to Secretary Schurz, briefly mentions the visit, pointing out to Schurz that Rynerson was Axtell's appointee, "a strong partisan whose conduct in the Lincoln trouble is open to censure . . ."

Although a copy of the charges had been forwarded to Axtell, Rynerson demanded to know "the grounds" on which Angel had recommended the removal of the governor. Angel shrugged off the request; it was out of his hands, he told Rynerson; everything now rested with Secretary Schurz, the Department of the Interior, and President Hayes. Rynerson undoubtedly told Angel he was going over his head to Washington, because the New Yorker warned the interior secretary: "I presume he will soon pay you a visit."[32]

Catron, Rynerson, and the other members of the Santa Fe Ring applied a great deal of political pressure on Washington; petitions signed by hundreds of New Mexico citizens were forwarded to the White House but Carl Schurz, after reviewing Angel's report, evidence, and recommendation, was determined to remove Axtell. He had little difficulty in getting President Hayes to approve Angel's recommendation. On or about September 1, 1878, a presidential order directed Secretary Schurz to suspend Axtell from the governor's office and remove him if he refused to accept his suspension.

His successor would be Lew Wallace, Civil War hero, author, prominent Republican party politician, and Hayes's counsel in the disputed Tallahassee, Florida, election returns. A board made up of two Republicans and one Democrat decided that Florida's vote in the Electoral College belonged to the Republicans.

When he was in Washington to attend Hayes's inauguration, the president-elect asked him what embassy post he would like; Wallace replied he preferred Rome, Spain, Brazil, or Mexico—in that order. There was no presidential appointment and Wallace was bitterly disappointed when the offer came to be New Mexico's new governor. He was at first inclined to refuse the offer but then accepted the post that paid $2,400 a year. Wallace not only needed money but his political sense told him that if New Mexico became a state he could be elected by the legislature to the United States Senate.

It was also an opportunity for him to finish his new biblical novel. He had been doing a great deal of research in the Library of Congress and had told friends he was very enthusiastic over the book's potential sales.

Before he left for New Mexico Wallace met Angel and read his reports and affidavits. The New York prosecutor viewed the McSween party as the most trustworthy in violent Lincoln County and he may have given Wallace the name of Billy the Kid as an influential leader who should be contacted.

Wallace also conferred with Secretary of War George W. McCrary about using troops if violence erupted in the county and discussed with Secretary Schurz the legality of the White House issuing a presidential proclamation, calling on all citizens to end hostilities. When Wallace raised the question of his power to grant a general amnesty to the territorial lawbreakers, the issue was debated at a cabinet meeting with President Hayes; the decision was that Wallace had the authority to grant amnesty and pardons, fines and forfeitures against the laws of the Territory.

Wallace arrived in New Mexico in late September 1878. He had stayed over-

Interior Department

In the matter of the investigation of the charges against S. B. Axtel Governor of New Mexico

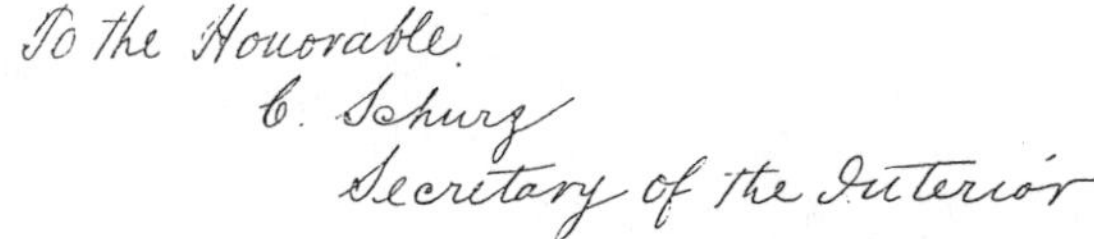

To the Honorable
C. Schurz
Secretary of the Interior

—In compliance with your request made at the time I made my first report herein I herewith make my supplemental and final report as to the charges against said S. B. Axtel. Since making said report I have found no reason for changing the same—but on the contrary believe as I did then that the best interests of New Mexico demanded the removal of S. B. Axtel as Governor . . . I determined to see with my own eyes and hear with my own ears I traveled over most of the Territory I visited almost every important town and talked with the principal citizens thereof.—

—I was met by every opposition possible by the United States civil officials and every obstacle thrown in my way by them to prevent a full and complete examination—

—I found an universal complaint against the administration of affairs in the Territory.

I found Lincoln County convulsed by an internal war. I enquired the cause. Some one was responsible for the blood shed in that County, I found two parties in the field one headed by Murphy Dolan and Riley—the other lead by McSween—both had done many things contrary to law—both were violating the law.—McSween I firmly believe acted conscientious—Murphy Dolan & Riley for revenge and personal gain. The Governor came heard the Murphy Dolan and Riley side, refused to hear the people who were with McSween or the residents of the County and acted strictly in advancing the Murphy Dolan and Riley party—Murder and unlawful acts followed instead of peace and quiet which could have been accomplished if the Governor had acted as he should have done and listened patiently to both sides. The opportunity presented itself to him to have quieted and stopped the trouble in Lincoln Co.—by his partizan action he allowed it to pass and the continuations of the troubles that exist to day in Lincoln County are chargeable to him. He was a partizan either through corruption or weakness and charge first and second have been sustained—

Frank Warner Angel's final report to Secretary of the Interior Carl Schurz, listing charges against New Mexico Territorial Governor Samuel Beach Axtell. President Hayes followed Angel's recommendation that Axtell be removed and appointed Lew Wallace. Shortly after he arrived in New Mexico, Wallace met with Billy the Kid, who earlier had assisted Angel. *Courtesy National Archives*

— It is seldom that history states more corruption, fraud, mismanagement, plots and murders, than New Mexico, has been the Theatre under the administration of Governor Axtell —
— I transmit herewith the testimony herein —
— All of which is respectfully submitted —
— Dated Washington Oct 3 1878 —
Frank Warner Angel
Special agent
Department Interior

General Lew Wallace, author of the famous novel *Ben Hur,* who was appointed territorial governor of New Mexico, after Washington's secret agent, Frank Warner Angel, uncovered the corruption there. In a dramatic meeting on the frontier, Wallace promised Billy the Kid amnesty if he would aid the government's investigation. *Photo by Mathew Brady, The James D. Horan Civil War and Western Americana Collection*

night in Cimarron with Frank W. Springer, a young attorney who had worked with Angel, and went on to Santa Fe by buckboard. There was no welcoming committee and after crawling into bed in the Governor's Palace, Wallace may have had second thoughts about his appointment. As he wrote his wife, the trip over the narrow rocky roads had been torturous. He called the buckboard "a deadlier instrument of torture [that] was never used in the days of Torquenado . . ."

Wallace had the disagreeable task of informing Axtell he had been suspended but the chief executive was a gracious man who wished him well. He was sworn in and became governor of the Territory of New Mexico at 3:15 P.M., September 30, 1878.[33]

A courier brought Billy the news at Fort Sumner that President Hayes had issued a proclamation and the Territory had a new governor; the Kid, a realist, shrugged off the announcement and warned his friends to wait and see what the new politician had to offer. Other things were more important: the weekly dances, the new girls, and the horse races.

It was about this time in Sumner that Billy met Pat Garrett, the bartender for Beaver Smith's combination saloon and gambling hall. They became friends, sharing drinks, the gambling tables, and the girls. They made a curious pair: Garrett, six foot four, slender with long arms, thin bony face, deep-set brown eyes, and a handlebar moustache; Billy the Kid, five eight and a hundred and thirty pounds. A native of Chambers County, Alabama, Garrett was ten years older than Billy.

In Santa Fe that fall, Wallace was greeted with reports of new violence. John Kinney's outlaws and professional gunmen had been replaced by a larger and more vicious band led by John Selman, a Texas rustler and gunfighter, who had made his way to New Mexico a few hoofbeats away from a vigilante committee.

The large ranches supplied steers to be rustled and herds of horses to be stolen. Later Selman's band tried to hold up a mercantile store in Lincoln but were driven off. They next selected a store at the junction of the Bonito and Ruidoso. But their latest outrage was the murder of four young Mexican boys who had refused to turn over their father's horses to the gang. One was retarded, the oldest was fourteen. As a rancher later testified, the Murphy-Dolan-Riley and McSween feud had developed into a war between outlaws and honest citizens.

One man wrote:

"The general feeling in the country is that everyone will have to abandon their property . . . travel is dangerous . . . strangers are challenged by whatever party until their relations are given . . ."

That fall the Regulators began breaking up. John Middleton, still bothered by the bullet wound in his lungs, and Henry Brown moved north to Kansas. Fred Waite begged Billy to come home with him to the Indian Nations but Billy shrugged. Lincoln was the only home he knew and he wanted to stay there. Maybe the new governor . . .

With Waite and Brown gone, Billy and his latest recruit Tom O'Folliard rode back to Lincoln, first saying good-bye to Pat Garrett, still tending bar, and Doc Scurlock and Charlie Bowdre working at a nearby ranch.

In Santa Fe the newly appointed Governor Wallace had many visitors: Jimmy Dolan, briefly dropping his role as leader of the murdering sheriff's posse for that of a concerned merchant; Colonel Dudley, who raged about the outlaws and desperados in the county; Riley, the slender young Irishman who was anxious about the $6,000 he had invested in Murphy & Co.; and Sheriff Peppin who told him it was impossible to keep law and order in the county without arms and men.

But Wallace also had other visitors: Mrs. McSween, the bitter widow who described Dudley's outrageous performance at the Battle of Lincoln, how her husband and John Tunstall had fought the losing battle against the corruption in high places and how the Murphy Company had cheated and terrorized the small ranchers for many years. With her was Houston J. Chapman, a one-armed lawyer and partner of Ira E. Leonard in a Las Vegas law firm. Both were young idealist attorneys who had known and admired the older McSween. Chapman and Leonard had agreed to carry on McSween's fight against crime and corruption in Lincoln County.[34]

In a letter to Secretary Schurz, Chapman had denounced Dudley, Tom Catron, and the Santa Fe Ring, and charged Dudley was "responsible for the murder of Alexander McSween." He also requested a military guard be placed around the home of Mrs. McSween to protect her and her children. Washington passed this on to General Edward Hatch, commanding the Missouri District, who foolishly sent Chapman's letters and demands to Dudley at Fort Stanton. Like McSween, Chapman became a doomed man.

By the President of the United States of America.

A Proclamation.

Whereas it is provided in the laws of the United States that whenever, by reason of unlawful obstructions, combinations or assemblages of persons, or rebellion against the authority of the Government of the United States, it shall become impracticable, in the judgment of the President, to enforce by the ordinary course of judicial proceedings the laws of the United States within any State or Territory, it shall be lawful for the President to call forth the militia of any or all the States and to employ such parts of the land and naval forces of the United States as he may deem necessary to enforce the faithful execution of the laws of the United States, or to suppress such rebellion, in whatever State or Territory thereof the laws of the United States may be forcibly opposed or the execution thereof forcibly obstructed;

And whereas it has been made to appear to me that by reason of unlawful combinations and assemblages of persons in arms, it has become impracticable to enforce, by the ordinary course of judicial proceedings, the laws of the United States within the Territory of New Mexico, and especially within Lincoln County therein; and that the laws of the United States have been therein forcibly opposed and the execution thereof forcibly resisted;

And whereas the laws of the United States require that whenever it may be necessary, in the judgment of the President, to use the military force for the purpose of enforcing the faithful execution of the laws of the United States, he shall forthwith, by proclamation, command such insurgents to disperse and retire peaceably to their respective abodes, within a limited time:

Now, therefore, I, Rutherford B. Hayes, President of the United States do hereby admonish all good citizens of the United States, and especially of the Territory of New Mexico against aiding, countenancing, abetting or taking part in such unlawful proceedings, and I do hereby warn all persons engaged in or connected with said obstruction of the laws, to disperse and retire peaceably to their respective abodes on or before noon of the thirteenth day of October instant.

In witness whereof I have hereunto set my hand and caused the seal of the United States to be affixed.

Done at the city of Washington this seventh day of October in the year of our Lord eighteen hundred and seventy-eight, and of the Independence of the United States the one hundred and third.

R B Hayes

By the President.

F. W. Seward
Acting Secretary of State.

The proclamation by President Rutherford B. Hayes, October 7, 1878, in which he gave the warring factions in the Lincoln County War six days to disperse. *Courtesy National Archives*

When Wallace proclaimed a territorial amnesty in November 1878 for crimes committed since February 1878, including army officers, Dudley wrote a blistering, insulting letter to the new governor, declining the pardon that he claimed "is for a crime never committed." His letter was endorsed by five of Stanton's officers. Instead of bringing peace to the community, Wallace had intensified the feuds.

A new incident flared up in December when Dudley dispatched a young officer, Second Lieutenant J. H. French, to look for fugitives supposedly hiding in the McSween home in Lincoln. French, who was drunk, broke into the house as the widow, Chapman, and Captain Saturino Baca, a friend of McSween's, were eating. French, who apparently knew about Chapman's charges against his commanding officer, overturned furniture and cursed the one-armed lawyer, the widow, and Baca as "scoundrels and friends of desperadoes."[35]

On February 18, 1879, as Lincoln held its breath, Billy and Tom O'Folliard casually rode down the town's main street to the local saloon. An intermediary for the Dolan-Murphy-Riley gang had made peace overtures to the Kid, with the proposal he ride into town and talk to Jesse Evans and Jimmy Dolan.

The Kid and O'Folliard met with Dolan, Evans, and several other riders in the saloon. Present was Catron's brother-in-law, Edgar Walz, who may have made the arrangements. With Evans and Dolan was Bill Campbell, a singularly vicious gunman who had recently joined the gang.

Evidently a truce was concluded at the meeting. Late that evening the Kid and O'Folliard left the saloon with Evans, Dolan, and Campbell, as Chapman, Mrs. McSween's lawyer, was crossing the plaza.

"Who are you and where are you going?" Campbell snarled.

"I'm attending to my business," the lawyer calmly replied.

"Maybe we can make you talk differently, lawyer," Campbell said.

Chapman refused to be bulldozed by the drunken gunfighter.

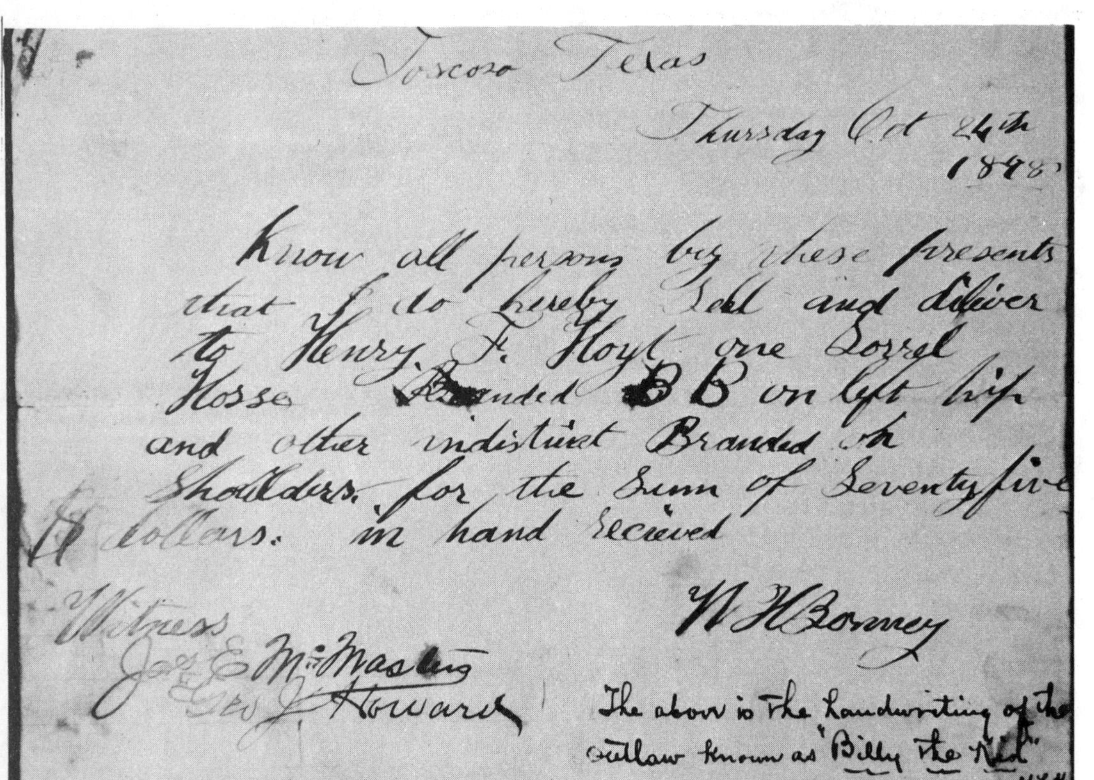

Toscoso Texas

Thursday Oct 24th
1878

Know all persons by these presents that I do hereby Sell and deliver to Henry F. Hoyt one Sorrel Hosse Branded BB on left hip and other indistinct Branded on Shoulders, for the Sum of Seventyfive $ dollars. in hand received

W H Bonney

Witness
Jas. E. McMasters
Geo J. Howard

The above is the handwriting of the outlaw known as "Billy the Kid" H.F.H.

Billy the Kid's bill of sale for his horse. *Courtesy Panhandle-Plains Historical Museum, Canyon, Texas*

"You cannot scare me, boys," he said. "I know you and it's no use. You have tried that before."

"Then I'll settle you," Campbell said and drawing his six-shooter fired at Chapman, the ball entering the lawyer's chest. As he fell, Dolan fired two more shots into the dying man. Then as a witness reported: "They set fire to the body. It is thought they soaked his clothes with whiskey to make them burn."

Eyewitnesses reported that Billy tried to leave but Evans drew his pistol and made the Kid and Tom O'Folliard watch them murder the one-armed man and set fire to his body.

The Kid and Tom were outnumbered. When Dolan and Evans "invited" them into the saloon they had no choice but to accept. Leaning against the bar Campbell swore: "I promised my God and General Dudley that I'd kill Chapman and I've done it . . ."

Over glasses of whiskey someone pointed out that Chapman had been unarmed; Campbell urged young Walz to go outside and put a six-shooter in the dead man's hand. When Walz begged off, Billy said he would do it. Dolan shouted that was a good idea and handed Billy a gun. The Kid, followed by Tom, went out, hurrying past the smoldering pile of charred rags and seared flesh, and ran to the corral and their horses.

The following morning Dolan and his riders rode into Lincoln to pack the hearing room where the coroner's inquest was held. "The Dolan party was in the town all armed and the people were so bulldozed no evidence could be brought up," *Las Cruces Thirty Four* reported. The verdict: death at the hands of persons unknown.

Governor Wallace was infuriated when Lincoln's new sheriff—conspicuous

H. J. Chapman, the one-armed attorney for Mrs. McSween, announced his intention in *Thirty-Four,* the territorial New Mexico newspaper, of going to Washington and making charges against Colonel Dudley, commander of the troops during the Battle of Lincoln. *Courtesy New Mexico Highlands University*

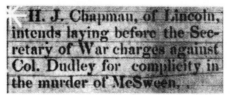

H. J. Chapman, of Lincoln, intends laying before the Secretary of War charges against Col. Dudley for complicity in the murder of McSween.

A letter written to the editor of *Thirty-Four,* giving an eyewitness account of the brutal murder of Chapman which the gang forced Billy the Kid to watch. *Courtesy New Mexico Highlands University*

When they met, one of the Dolan party asked "who are you and where are you going?" Chapman answered and told them he was attending to his business. He was told to talk differently or they would make him. He answered, raising a bandage from his face, "You cannot scare me, boys. I know you and it's no use. You have tried that before." "Then" said Campbell "I'll settle you," and fired his pistol, the ball going in at the breast and coming out at the back. As he fell Dolan shot him with his Winchester. They then set fire to his body. It is thought they soaked his clothes with whiskey to make them burn.

When they first met, "Kid" tried to get away and ran around an angle in the lane wall, but Evans held the other fast and made him look on during the whole affair. Next day a coroner's jury was held, but the Dolan party was in town armed and the people were so bulldozed no evidence could be brought out.

BILLY THE KID.

$500 REWARD.

I will pay $500 reward to any person or persons who will capture William Bonny, alias The Kid, and deliver him to any sheriff of New Mexico. Satisfactory proofs of identity will be required.

LEW. WALLACE,
Governor of New Mexico.

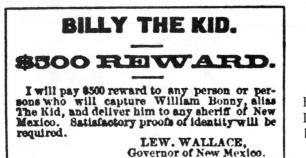

Billy the Kid wanted poster ordered by Governor Lew Wallace. *The James D. Horan Civil War and Western Americana Collection*

by his absence during the murder of Chapman and the inquest—telegraphed him the news. But it was Chapman's law partner, Ira E. Leonard, who carried the fight to the Murphy-Dolan-Riley and Santa Fe Ring. His angry letters to Wallace and Secretary of the Interior Schurz disclosed that on the morning of the day Chapman was murdered he had warned his partner "to be careful and more discreet in his conduct—or he would have trouble." Chapman replied he could expect only trouble from Dudley and his Lieutenant French.

In his letter to Wallace, Leonard disclosed he was on his way to Lincoln to appear in court to produce "proof as strong as the holy writ" that both officers were implicated in the deaths of McSween and Chapman.

Leonard's letter prompted Wallace to visit Lincoln. As the governor later recalled, he was shocked to find how terror and violence had paralyzed the county. He returned to Santa Fe and wrote to General Hatch, asking that he remove Dudley at once and arrest Dolan, Evans, and Campbell for murder.

An informer from Lincoln brought Billy the news in his hideout along with a warning that Wallace had sent out troops to pick him up as a witness against Dudley. What was more disturbing was the $500 reward Wallace had offered for the capture of the Kid.

In March Billy, weary of being hunted, wrote to Governor Wallace offering to come in and discuss his surrender. The simply written letter with few errors is impressive proof Billy the Kid was far from the legendary bucktoothed moron.[37]

*Billy the Kid's Letter to Territorial Governor of New Mexico Lew Wallace, March 1879**

TO HIS EXCELLENCY THE GOVERNOR,
GEN. LEW WALLACE.
DEAR SIR:

I have heard that you will give one thousand dollars for my body which I can understand it means alive as a witness. I know it is as a witness against those that murdered Mr. Chapman. if it was so that I could appear at court, I could give the desired information but I have indictments against me for things that happened in the late Lincoln County War and am afraid to give up because my enemies would kill me. the day Mr. Chapman was murdered I was in Lincoln, as the request of Good Citizens to meet Mr. J. J. Dolan to meet as friends. as to be able to leave aside our arms and go to Work. I was present when Mr. Chapman was murdered and knew who did it and if it were not for those indictments I would have made it clear before now. If it is in your power to annul those indictments I hope you will do so as to give me a chance to explain. Please send me an answer telling me what you can do. You can send Answer by bearer.

*Billy's punctuation has been followed.

I have no Wish to fight anymore indeed I have not raised an arm since your Proclamation. as to my Character I refer to any of the Citizens for the Majority of them are my Friends and have been helping me all they could. I am called Kid Antrim but Antrim is my stepfather's name.

Waiting for an answer, I remain,
Your Obedient servant,
W. H. Bonney

A few days later Governor Wallace sent his answer "by bearer" to Billy in the hills.

Governor Wallace's Reply to Billy the Kid, March 15, 1879

LINCOLN, MARCH 15, 1879

W. H. BONNEY:

Come to the house of old Squire Wilson, (not the lawyer) at nine (9) O'clock Monday night alone. I don't mean his office but his residence. Follow along the foot of the mountain south of the town, come in on that side and knock on the east door. I have authority to exempt you from prosecution, if you will testify to what you say you know.

The object of the meeting at Squire Wilson's is to arrange the matter in a way to make your life safe. To do that the utmost secrecy is to be used. So come alone. Don't tell anybody—not a living soul—where you are coming or the object. If you could trust Jesse Evans you can trust me.

Lew Wallace.

Monday night was the 17th and Billy made his way alone along the base of the Capitan Mountains to Squire Wilson's house.

Wallace, who would always remember that meeting, sat at a table with Wilson, who knew and liked the Kid, in a room on the east side of the adobe building. A coal oil lamp cast wavering shadows on the wall. Promptly at nine o'clock there was a knock at the door.

"Come in," Wallace called out.

The door opened and Billy stepped inside.

"I was sent to meet Governor Wallace at nine o'clock," he said to Wilson. "Is he here?"

Wallace, a well-built man with a dark spade beard, rose and motioned Billy to an empty chair.

"I am Governor Wallace," he said.

"Your note gave me promise of utmost protection," Billy pointed out.

"Yes, I have been true to my promise," the governor replied. "This man here, whom of course you know, and I are the only ones in the house."

Billy slowly lowered the Winchester he was cradling in one arm and advanced to the table where he shook hands with Wallace and Wilson.

It was one of the most dramatic and romantic meetings in frontier history: the boy outlaw and the prominent Civil War general. Billy the Kid and Wallace, the man who had been Lincoln's friend, who had saved Washington from capture by Jubal Early's troops, who had investigated the shocking conditions at Andersonville, and who had served on the jury that tried the Lincoln conspirators, studied each other in the dim light as the night wind moaned about the eaves.

They talked for more than an hour with Wallace urging Billy to testify before the grand jury as a people's witness so they could convict Chapman's murderers. In return he promised a complete pardon.

For Billy a pardon meant many things: to be able to wander about the Bonito and Ruidoso valleys, living the free life, drifting from cow camp to ranch, stopping off at the little Mexican villages to whirl the pretty girls about in a wild fandango, caring not for tomorrow only for today, and never more to sleep under a bush with a Winchester while playing hare and hounds with the sheriff's posse and bounty hunters eager to collect that $500 reward . . .

But the Kid pointed out to Wallace that the Dolan-Murphy-Riley Santa Fe forces still controlled the Territory; if he turned state's evidence he could be dead within hours.

Wallace assured him he had the power and men to protect him.

The Kid finally accepted Wallace's plan; after a planned arrest, he would be taken before a grand jury. Following his appearance as a witness in a trial against Campbell, Evans, and the others, the indictment for the Brady murder would be dismissed. As the governor promised, he would go "scot-free."

Billy said he would think it over and left. Two days later Jesse Evans and Bill Campbell easily escaped from the Fort Stanton guardhouse. The Kid sent a letter to Squire Wilson, asking him to talk to Wallace and find out if the deal was still firm; Wilson's brief note assured him it was.

On March 21, 1879, Billy allowed himself to be "captured" by Sheriff Kimbrell and a posse; Tom O'Folliard insisted he go along.

Billy made himself at home in jail with friends constantly visiting him. The amazed Wallace reported to Secretary Schurz that one night he heard music and went outside to find musicians "actually serenading" the Kid in jail.[38]

Billy kept his promise to Wallace. On March 23, 1879, he gave the governor a long detailed statement, outlining the rustling activities in the county and revealing the names of those who bought stolen cattle. In April he testified before the Lincoln County grand jury.

Ira E. Leonard, Chapman's former law partner, had volunteered to act as Billy's counsel while Wallace set up a special headquarters at Fort Stanton to direct personally the hunt for Campbell and Evans and round up the rustling and horse-stealing gangs named by the Kid. The outlaws retaliated, once unsuccessfully, trying to assassinate Wallace as he rode from the fort to Lincoln and threatening District Judge Bristol with death if he accepted the grand jury's findings and indictments.[39] Bristol appealed to Wallace, who assigned him a guard of soldiers. In his quarters Colonel Dudley wrote letters to the War Department denouncing the governor and the "desperate characters" advising him.

Curiously, a few days before the court started its first session in Lincoln, Wallace left for a long, leisurely trip to Santa Fe; as he explained, he had to meet his wife. The leg-ironed Kid, instinctively uneasy, took his seat on the hard bench in the dusty old courtroom to grin at the glaring Colonel W. L. Rynerson, who had suddenly appeared as prosecutor.

Statements by Kid, made Sunday night March 23. 1879

1. There is a cattle trail beginning about 5 miles above Yellow Lake in a cañon, running a little west of north to Cienega del Macho (mule spring) and continuing around the point of the Capitan mountain down toward Carrisozo in the direction of the Rio Grande. Frank Wheeler, Jake Owens and Dutch Chris are supposed to have used this trail taking a bunch of cattle over. Vansickle told K. so. They stopped and killed two beeves for Sam Corbett — hush money to Vansickle to whom they gave the beeves. Vansickle also said the Owens-Wheeler outfit including "Chris" had been using the trail for about a year; but that lately their horses had given out, and of 140 head which they started with they had only got through with 40. That now they were going to the Reservation to make a raid on the Indian horses to work on.

The Rustlers.

The "Rustlers" Kid says, were organized in Fort Stanton. Before they organized as "Rustlers" they had been with Peppin's posse. They came from Texas. Owens was conspicuous amongst them. They were organized before the burning of McSween's house, and after that they went on their first trip down the country as far as the Coe's ranche and thence to the Felix, where they took the Tunstall cattle. From the Felix they went to the Pecos, where some of them deserted, Owens amongst them. (Martin, known to Sam Corbett,) was in charge of the Tunstall cattle, and was taken prisoner, and saw them kill one of their own party. On the same trip they burnt Lola Wise's house, and took some horses. [illegible] at the time was ranching at the house. On this trip they moved behind a body of soldiers, one Company, and a Company of Navajo Scouts. They moved in sight of the soldiers, taking horses, insulting women. Gregorio Trujillo, (Jose Perea) Juan Trujillo, Jose M. Gutierrez, Pancho Sanchez, Santos Tafoya, are witnesses against them. They stopped on Pecos at Seven Rivers. Collins, now at Silver city, was one of the outfit — nick-named the Prowler by the cow boys. At Seven Rivers there joined them Gus. Gildey (wanted at San Antonio for killing Mexicans) Gildey is carrying the mail now from Stockton to Seven Rivers — James Irvin and Reese Gobly, (rumored that their bodies were found in a drift down the Pecos) — Rustling Bob (found dead in the Pecos, killed by his own party) — John Selman (whereabouts unknown) Came to Roswell while Carroll was there —

The R's stayed at Seven Rivers," which they left on their second trip via the Berenda, for Fort Stanton. On their return back they killed Chaves boys and the Crazy boy, Lorenzo and the Sanchez boy, 14 yrs. old. They also committed many robberies. They broke up after reaching the Pecos, promising to return when some more horses got fat.

Notes made by Governor Lew Wallace after his dramatic night meeting with Billy the Kid. *Courtesy William N. Wallace and the Indiana Historical Society, William Henry Smith Memorial Library*

Rynerson had barely spoken when Billy realized he had been betrayed by the establishment; the giant Tennesseean's booming voice filled the small room as he asked the court to grant his application for a change of venue from Lincoln County to Dona Ana, where he intended to hold the trial of William H. Bonney, charged with the murder of Sheriff William Brady. No jury in Lincoln would ever convict the Kid; Dona Ana was controlled by Rynerson. Bristol quickly approved the application and Billy was escorted back to his cell under Rynerson's mocking smile.[40]

Tom O'Folliard, who had been acquitted of a flimsy rustling charge by a Lincoln County jury, which had only taken minutes to render its verdict, urged Billy to break out but the Kid shook his head. Washington had finally ordered a court of inquiry to investigate Dudley's conduct at the Battle of Lincoln and Billy was to be one of the principal witnesses; as he told Tom, he intended to even the score with his old army enemy from the witness stand.

Billy and numerous other witnesses, including Governor Wallace, testified at Dudley's trial. The more than 1,300 pages of testimony prove beyond a doubt that the hard-drinking career officer had acted outrageously during the violent days at Lincoln and was indirectly responsible for the murder of McSween. Billy's testimony, confirmed by other eyewitnesses, described Dudley's defiance of Washington's orders when he led his detachment into Lincoln and posted soldiers about the McSween house so it was impossible for them to return the fire of the fraudulent "sheriff's posse." Billy pointed out to the court of inquiry that soldiers had fired what Dudley himself called "a volley," which might have killed young Harvey Morris, the law student, and the Mexicans who had followed him as he ran from the burning McSween house.

A century later it is shocking to discover General W. T. Sherman's letter denouncing the inquiry and its witnesses as besmirching the "honor of a distinguished army officer."

After several days the court of inquiry dismissed all charges against Dudley. It was the old army game of protecting its own.

Leonard, Chapman's law partner who had pushed the inquiry and became the chief complainant against Dudley, wrote a protesting letter to Secretary Schurz. One can visualize the short, stocky German liberal and reformer slamming down the letter as he wondered aloud whether the War Department or the country's elected officials were running the government.

In his Santa Fe Palace, Wallace, also stunned by the court of inquiry's verdict, had received other setbacks: Jimmy Dolan with Colonel Rynerson's help had won an easy acquittal of Chapman's murder in a trial—not held at Lincoln where a jury would have quickly sentenced him to the hangman's noose—but at Socorro where the judges were friendly. Even Jesse Evans and the vicious Bill Campbell had easily avoided the patrol of troopers from Stanton to escape to Texas.

Wallace had scored one small victory: General Hatch, defying General Sherman and the chiefs of staff, transferred Dudley to Fort Union. The controversial officer had won acquittal but this move ended his career on the frontier.

Billy now had enough of the establishment's law and order; on a warm June night in 1879 he slipped the handcuffs over his slender wrists and simply walked out of jail. Faithful Tom O'Folliard and Doc Scurlock had the horses ready and they trotted out of Lincoln headed for the distant friendly hills.

That summer the Kid, O'Folliard, and Scurlock made their headquarters in Beaver Smith's saloon at Fort Sumner, drifting along the Pecos, working on ranches, gambling, racing horses, and taking part in any dance they could find. When Billy returned to Sumner, Deluvina, a Navajo slave the Maxwell family had bought many years ago for $10, cooked a meal and mothered him. The old woman worshipped and worried over the Kid like a fat, wrinkled copper-skinned grandmother.

When Billy first arrived at Sumner, Pete Maxwell, only surviving son of Lucian B. Maxwell, onetime owner of the famous Maxwell land grant, had told him his friend Pat Garrett was working the ranches along the Ruidoso.

In January 1880, Billy claimed his next victim, Joe Grant, a young tough who had sworn to kill him. The Kid tried to cajole Grant out of a fight in Jose Valdez's saloon but the drunken young gunslinger fired at him. The shot missed and Billy drew. In seconds Grant was dead.

The *Las Vegas Gazette*, no friend of the outlaw, published a terse account.[41]

Billy the Kid Kills Joe Grant

> One day [the] Kid and his gang of followers, then composed of Charley Bowdrie, Tom Follard [*sic*] and Charley Thomas called for their mail and while looking through it, Bowdrie incidentally remarked to Mr. Rudolph, the postmaster, that another man had turned up his toes at Fort Sumner.
>
> Upon being asked who it was, he replied that Joe Grant had been killed a short time before by Billy the Kid. Rudolph asked Billy what occasioned the trouble and he remarked:
>
> "Oh, nothing—it was a game of two and I got there first."
>
> The daring young rascal seemed to enjoy the telling as well as the killing. But he will not run at large on the plains seeking victims any longer. His career probably will be checked by a halter.

In April Billy was still wandering, stopping off at the small towns to gamble or race horses but always returning to Sumner. That spring he met Jim Greathouse, owner of a small freighting company forty miles from White Oaks, who in turn introduced him to Dave Rudabaugh, wanted by railroad detectives and lynch mobs in Missouri where he had given Jesse James competition in robbing stagecoaches, banks and trains. Rudabaugh's latest exploit was masterminding a jail delivery of John Joshua Webb, another notorious gunman. After he and his companions had killed the jailer, Rudabaugh was stunned to find Webb refused to leave his cell. As the angry Webb explained, a pardon was on its way from Governor Wallace. Rudabaugh then made his way south to find refuge with his old friend Jim Greathouse. Before the Kid left White Oaks, Rudabaugh and two other young gunslingers, Billy Wilson and Tom Pickett, had joined him, Tom O'Folliard, and Doc Scurlock.[42]

That summer Pat Garrett, who had bought a small ranch with his savings, was appointed deputy sheriff of Lincoln County. In the fall election he was elected sheriff. He would take office in January 1881, but in the interim, through the influence of Tom Catron, he was appointed deputy United States marshal. If Catron's power in the Territory was slowly declining, he could trace it to the troubles in Lincoln County; he never forgot that one of his chief enemies there was Billy the Kid . . . as a federal marshal Garrett could cross county lines in a hunt for Billy . . .[43]

Catron was also instrumental in the appointment of Robert (Bob) Olinger as Garrett's deputy; Catron didn't have to urge this new officer to hunt down the Kid—Olinger had been the best friend of Bob Beckwith, killed during the last minutes of the Battle of Lincoln when Billy had led the desperate escape from the McSween house.

Billy's friends at Sumner, including Pete Maxwell and the faithful Deluvina, urged him to leave the Territory for Old Mexico; they knew ultimately there had to be a confrontation between Garrett and the Kid. But Billy spent the winter at Sumner; he seemed unable to leave. In Lincoln, Garrett ignored Catron's urging to go after the Kid; he seemed reluctant to ride to Sumner.

The final act of the frontier tragedy had begun.

In the fall of 1880, Billy, Dave Rudabaugh, and Billy Wilson narrowly escaped capture by a White Oaks posse. During the pursuit the Kid and Wilson had their horses shot from under them but after riding double with Rudabaugh and walking, they finally reached the Greathouse freighting building. The posse trailed them there and a siege began.

Fort Sumner
Dec 12th 1880

Gov. Lew Wallace

Dear Sir
I noticed in the Las Vegas Gazette a piece which stated that, "Billy" the "Kid," the name by which I am known in the Country was the Captain of a Band of Outlaws who hold Forth at the Portales. There is no such Organization in Existence. So the Gentleman must have drawn very heavily on his Imagination. My business at the White Oaks the time I was waylaid and my horse killed was to See Judge Leonard who has my Case in hand. he had written to me to Come up, that he thought he could get Everything Straightened up I did not find him at the Oaks & Should have gone to Lincoln if I had met with no accident. After mine and Billie Wilsons horses

12-12-18

2

were killed we both made our way to a Station, forty miles from the Oaks kept by Mr Greathouse. When I got up next morning The house was Surrounded by an outfit led by one Carlyle, Who came into the house and Demanded a Surrender. I asked for their Papers and they had none. So I Concluded it amounted to nothing more than a mob and told Carlyle that he would have to Stay in the house and lead the way out that night. Soon after a note was brought in Stating that if Carlyle did not Come out inside of five minutes they would Kill the Station Keeper (Greathouse) who had left the house and was with them. in a Short time a Shot was fired on the outside and Carlyle thinking Greathouse was killed jumped through the window. breaking the Sash as he went and was killed by his own Party they thinking it was me trying to make my Escape. the Party then withdrew.

They returned the next day and burned an old [illegible] house and Greathouses also

When their leader, Jimmy Carlyle, was killed, the manhunters withdrew. In the evening Billy, Rudabaugh, and Wilson found new horses and escaped.

On November 30, the *Las Vegas Gazette* charged Billy had gone to the Greathouse company to sell a stolen horse herd. The inaccuracy of the article infuriated the young outlaw who sent a letter to Governor Wallace denying the story, insisting he had been making his living at gambling since leaving Lincoln.[44]

Billy the Kid's Letter to Governor Lew Wallace, December 12, 1880

GOV. LEW WALLACE
Dear Sir:

I noticed in the *Las Vegas Gazette* a piece which stated that Billy "The Kid", the name by which I am known in this country, was the Captian of a band of outlaws who held forth the Portales. There is no such Organization in Existence. So the Gentlemen must have drawn very heavily on their Imagination.

My business at White Oaks the time I was waylaid and my horse shot, was to see Judge [Ira E.] Leonard who has my case in hand. he had written to me to come up, that he thought he could get Everything Straightened Up. I did not find him at the Oaks & should have gone to Lincoln if I had met with no accident. After mine and Billie Wilsons' horses were killed we both made our way to a Station, forty miles from the White Oaks, kept by Mr. Greathouse. When I got up next morning the house was surrounded by an outfit led by one Carlyle, who came into the house and demanded a Surrender. So I concluded it to be nothing more than a mob and told Carlyle he would have to stay in the house and lead the way out

3 12-12-1880

I made my way to this Place afoot and During my absence Deputy Sheriff Garrett Acting under Chisums orders went to the Portales and found Nothing. on his way back he went by Mr Yerbys ranch and took a pair of mules of mine which I had left with Mr Bowdre who is in Charge of mr Yerbys cattle. he (Garrett) Claimed that they were stolen and even if they were not he had a right to Confiscate any Outlaws property.

I have been at Sumner Since I left Lincoln making my living Gambling the mules were bought by me the truth of which I can prove by the best Citizens around Sumner J. S. Chisum is the man who got me into Trouble and was benifited Thousands by it and is now doing all he can against me There is no Doubt but what there is a great deal of Stealing going on in the Territory. and a great deal of the Property is taken across the Plains as it is a good outlet but so far as my being

4 12-12-1880

at the head of a Band there is nothing of it in Several Instances I have recovered Stolen Property when there was no Chance to get an Officer to do it.

one instance for Hugo Zuber Postoffice Puerto De Luna. another for Pablo Analla Same Place.

if Some impartial Party were to investigate this matter they would find it far Different from the impression put out by Chisum and his Tools.

Yours Respect
William Bonney

Billy the Kid's letter to Governor Lew Wallace, denying that he was an outlaw leader and explaining the role he played in the gun battle of White Oaks. *Courtesy William N. Wallace and the Indiana Historical Society, William Henry Smith Memorial Library*

that night. Soon after a note was brought in stating that if Carlyle did not come out outside of five minutes they would Kill the Station Keeper [Greathouse] who had left the house and was with them. in a short time a shot was fired on the outside and Carlyle thinking Greathouse had been killed, he jumped through the window, breaking the sash as he went and was killed by his own Party, they thinking it was me trying to make my Escape. the Party then withdrew.

they returned the next day and burned an old man named Spencer's house and Greathouse's also. I made my way to this place [Fort Sumner] afoot and during my absence Deputy Sheriff Garrett acting under [John] Chisum's orders went to the Portales and found Nothing. on his way back he went to Mr. Yerby's ranch and took a pair of mules of mine which I had left with Mr. [Charles] Bowdre who is in Charge of mr. Yerby's cattle. he [Garrett] claimed they were stolen and Even if they were he had not a right to confiscate any outlaws property.

I have been at Sumner since I left Lincoln making my living by Gambling. the mules were bought by me the truth by which I can prove by the best Citizens around Sumner. J. S. Chisum is the man who got me into trouble, and was benefited Thousands by it and is now doing all he can against me. There is no doubt but what there is a great deal of Stealing going on in the Territory, and a Great deal of Property is taken across the Plains as it is a good outlet but so far as my being at the head of a Band there is nothing of it. Several Instances I have recovered Stolen Property when there was no chance to get an Officer to do it.

one instance for Hugo Zuber Postoffice Puerto de Luna, another for Pablo Analla Same Place. if Some impartial Party were to investigate this matter they would find it far Different from the impression put out by Chisum and his Tools.

Yours Respect.
William Bonney

Garrett, joined by Frank Steward, T. W. Garrard, and several tough Texas gunfighters and stockmen's detectives hired by ranchers determined to wipe out the rustling gangs, finally moved against the Kid and his gang during the winter of 1880, the bitterest in the history of the Territory.

The posse fought blizzards, deep snow, and searing winds, hoping to surprise the Kid and his riders at Fort Sumner. But the native grapevine warned Billy, who escaped.

Garrett and his men continued to wait at the old fort. On December 19 as the last light was fading Billy led his men into Sumner to get supplies.

The *Las Vegas Gazette*, which had closely followed the manhunt, later gathered the dramatic details of what happened that day and the capture of Billy and his men at Stinking Springs from Garrett, Steward, and Garrard.[45]

The Capture of Billy the Kid at Stinking Springs

On the 19th Tom O'Folliard, Tom Pickett, the Kid, [Dave] Rudabaugh, Charley Bowdre and Billy Wilson, riding two and two, came into Fort Sumner as the light was fading.

Garrett and his men had just returned and when the six came around the northeast corner of the hospital building, Garrett, who was in advance, called out to them to halt.

O'Folliard and Pickett were in the front. O'Folliard reached for his six shooter but was not quick enough for Garrett who shot first, bringing him down. The other five put spurs to their horses and escaped under heavy fire.

Pools of blood were discovered and it was first thought Pickett was wounded but only O'Folliard was shot beside a horse.

The night was so foggy the Kid and his men got away easily. They made Bazil's [a ranch owned by M. S. Bazil] and Rudabaugh's horse was found to be badly shot through the entrails and it is a wonder that it did not die on the way.

Rudabaugh and one of the others doubled up and they made off as fast as they could.

Tom O'Folliard lived only two hours after being shot.

Word was brought to Garrett at Sumner that the crowd was hanging around Bazil's and Frank Yerby's ranch and Wednesday night sixteen men under command of Garrett set out for Bazil's, ten miles east of Sumner. They arrived there about midnight and learned that the Kid, Rudabaugh, Wilson, Pickett and Bowdre had been there during the afternoon but had ridden away again. About three or four inches of snow was on the ground and the moon being out, it was easy to follow their trail.

Following it up to about three o'clock they came to an old deserted house at Stinking Springs four miles away where they found the men. They divided up into several parties and keeping guard on the house, lay down to wait until daybreak.

The house is built of stone with a door and window on one side. It is situated six or seven steps from the arroyo, on the top of a hill.

Just at daybreak Charley Bowdre came to the door and stepped out. He had on a hat like what the Kid was wearing and he was mistaken for him. The Kid had repeatedly given out that he would never surrender even though a six-shooter was placed to his head, that it wasn't thought worth while to give him a chance to surrender.

Someone fired and Bowdre staggered and then braced himself up for a moment against the door-post [and] stepped into the house. He told his companions he was badly wounded and could not help them anyway and wanted to go out, calling to the men outside, the situation was explained.

Bowdre stepped out again and started forward to give himself up when he reeled a little and said: "I wish—" and while making an effort to express his desire, he fell dead close by where one of the besiegers was lying concealed.

Quiet prevailed all day, the besiegers were determined to stay until they carried out the outlaws dead or alive. The outlaws had two horses in the house with them and about four o'clock were discovered trying to drag in a third. They had his head and shoulders just inside the door when Garrett brought it down and it fell on the doorstop blocking up the entrance to the house. Two other horses were tied outside the house, and the besiegers amused themselves by shooting at their helters and succeeded in cutting them loose.

The intention of the gang was to get the third horse inside the house and then all four were to make a break on horseback. But they were forced to give up their plan as the body of the dead horse was a blockade against them.

A consultation was held and Rudabaugh, Wilson and Pickett voted to surrender much to the disgust of the Kid who kicked and kicked but it was of no avail. He branded the others as cowards but was unable to dissuade them from their project to surrender.

Finally, some of the attacking party saw a rag being twirled about the end of a stick stuck through the door which was mistrusted to be a flag of truce. Remembering the fate of poor Carlyle at Greathouse's, Garrett said that two could play at the game and let the crowd amuse themselves by waving the stick.

He called out to them to know what they wanted and Rudabaugh announced they wanted to surrender. They had not counted on such an easy capture and felt that the desperadoes were playing some game. But in response to the call "come out then", Rudabaugh advanced and talked to some of the men.

He offered to surrender conditionally, provided the party would take them to Santa Fe, and everything being arranged he returned to the house again. A short time only elapsed before they all filed out and gave themselves up.

They were mounted with some of their captors and rode to Bazil's house, sending back a team for the guns and the outfits the gang had left in the house. The two horses which had been stabled in the house belonged to the Kid and Wilson and the former made a present of his to Frank Stewart.

The Kid's animal is a beautiful bay mare which he has always trusted to take him out of a tight place and has shared his love in common with his guns.

Stewart now has the pleasure of owning the fleetest horse in the Territory, for it is said by many who have had an opportunity for judging that there is not another such animal in the Territory.

The party spent the night at Bazil's where Rudabaugh and the Kid were chained together. The body of Bowdre was taken to the house and it was found he had been shot through the right breast, the ball coming out in the neck.

Just after sunrise, Friday morning, the party set out for Sumner with the body of Bowdre, and leaving that came on toward Vegas with a guard of nine men keeping watch over the prisoners who were placed in Mr. Bazil's wagon.

They reached Gerhardt's ranch about ten o'clock that night and remained there all night setting out the next morning again. Arriving at Puerta de Luna Saturday night about sundown they stopped long enough to change horses and chain Pickett and Wilson together who until that time had not been bound. Here four of the guards left them and the rest traveling all that night, and on the way the lock fastening the chain binding Wilson and Pickett was broken but a sharp lookout was kept on them.

They took breakfast at Mr. Hayes's yesterday morning about ten o'clock and then came right through.

Before he was taken to Santa Fe, Billy gave the *Las Vegas Gazette* reporter an exclusive interview. Now under the gay desperado role, there was a note of bitterness, disillusionment with those in command of law and order, justice, and fair play. The Kid now realized he had been betrayed and was a scapegoat.

The *Gazette*'s anonymous reporter entered the cellblock as Mike Cosgrove, "the mail contractor who had often met the boys while on business down the Pecos," was delivering four new suits for the Kid, Wilson, Pickett, and Rudabaugh.

"I want the boys to go away in style," he explained.

The reporter then waited until the local blacksmith removed their shackles. Wilson was glum and uncommunicative, but the Kid was "laughing, joking and chatting" with the crowd of curious, jamming the jail hoping to catch a glimpse of "the best known man in New Mexico," as the *Gazette* described him.[46]

Billy the Kid's Interview with the Las Vegas Gazette

"You appear to take it easy," the reporter said.

"Yes. What's the sense of looking on the gloomy side of everything? The laugh's on me this time." He looked around the cell. "Is the jail at Santa Fe any better than this?"

This seemed to trouble him considerably, for, as he explained: "This is a terrible place to put a fellow in." He put the same question to anyone who came near him and when he learned that there was nothing better in store for him, he shrugged his shoulders and said something about putting up with what he had to.

He was the attraction of the show and as he stood there, lightly kicking the toes of his boots on the stone pavement to keep his feet warm, one would scarcely mistrust that he was the hero of the "Forty Thieves" romance which this newspaper had been running in serial form for six weeks or more.

"There was a big crowd gazing at me, wasn't there?" he explained, then smilingly continued, "well, perhaps some of them will think me half man now, everybody seems to think I was some kind of animal."

He did look human indeed but there was nothing mannish in his appearance, he looked and acted like a mere boy. He is about five feet eight or nine inches in height, slightly built and lithe, weighing about 140, with the traditional silky fuzz on his upper lip, clear blue eyes, with a roguish snap about them, light hair and complexion. He is in all, quite a handsome looking fellow, the only imperfection being two teeth, slightly protruding like squirrel's teeth and he has agreeable and winning ways. A cloud came over his face when he made some allusion to his being the hero of fabulous yarns, and something like indignation was expressed when he said our EXTRA misrepresented him when he said he called his associates cowards . . .

"I never said such a thing . . . I know they ain't cowards . . ."

Billy Wilson was glum and sober but from underneath his broad-brimmed hat we saw a face that a by me [sic] mean, bad look. He is light complexioned, light haired, gray bluish gray eyes, is a little stouter than Bonney and far quieter. He appeared shamed and not in very good spirits.

A final blow of the hammer and the last rivet on the bracelets and they clanked to the pavements.

Bonney straightened up, then rubbing his wrists where the sharp edged iron had chafed them, said:

"I don't suppose you fellows believe it but this is the first time I ever had bracelets on. But many another better fellow has had them on too."

With Wilson he walked to the little hole in the wall to the place which is no "cell" or place of confinement. Just before entering he turned and looked back and exclaimed: "They say a fool for luck, and a poor man for children—Garrett takes them all in."

United States Marshal J. F. Morrissey of Santa Fe, on his arrival in Las Vegas, learned that Rudabaugh had confessed to a stagecoach robbery in August and to a November 1879 train robbery. Because mail had been taken, a federal charge was lodged against him.

Rudabaugh was no sniveling, frightened young outlaw; in fact, he was cool, calculating, and shrewd. He had confessed to the federal charge to avoid trial in San Miguel for the murder of Deputy Sheriff Antonio Lino Valdez. He had shot and killed the deputy in April 1880, during his bungled jail delivery of John J. Webb, the murderer who refused to leave his cell.

When the news swept the city that Rudabaugh would be taken to Santa Fe instead of being tried by a San Miguel county jury, armed men began gathering. As the *Gazette* reported:

"There are rumors in the city that the captured at Stinking Springs would be taken from the jail and lynched."

Garrett and Steward immediately took up guard outside the cell where the Kid and his men were locked. The mood of the citizens, the *Gazette* said, was at "boiling point," but when a spokesman for the Mexican community appeared at the jail insisting Rudabaugh had to remain and stand trial for the murder of Valdez, Steward told him:

"That makes no difference. We gave all four our word that we would take them to Santa Fe and go they shall."

Hilario Romero, the local sheriff, then telegraphed Governor Wallace demanding an order restraining Garrett, Steward, and the other members of the posse guarding the jail from removing the prisoners but Wallace ignored his plea.

In the morning Romero "sent his deputies every which way, commanding the attendance of various citizens to be at the depot."

At train time Garrett and Steward rushed the chained Billy and Rudabaugh to the depot and helped them into the smoker of the Santa Fe train. Suddenly the stationmaster announced a delay and the cars were sidetracked.

As the angry armed mob swept across the plaza to surround the train, Billy the Kid casually leaned out the car window and continued his interview with the *Gazette* reporter:

Billy the Kid's Interview at the Las Vegas Depot

I don't blame you for writing of me as you have. You had to believe other stories but then I don't know as anyone would believe anything good of me anyway. I wasn't the leader of my gang, I was for Billy all the time. About that Portales business, I owned the ranche with Charlie Bowdre. I took it up and was holding it because I knew that sometime a stage would run by there and I wanted to keep it for a station. But I found that there were certain men who wouldn't let me live in the country and so I was going to leave. We had all our grub in the house when they took us in and we were going to a place about six miles away in the morning to cook it and then "light" out.

I haven't stolen any stock. I made my living by gambling but that was the only way I could live. They wouldn't let me settle down; if they had I wouldn't be here today and then he held up his left hand with the bracelet. [John] Chisum got me into all this trouble and then wouldn't let me get out. I went up to Lincoln to stand my trial on the warrant that was out for me, but the Territory took a change of venue to Dona Ana and I knew that I had no show, and so I "skinned" out.

When I went up to White Oaks the last time, I went there to consult with a lawyer, who had sent for me to come up. But I knew I couldn't stay there either.

The conversation then drifted to the question of the final round-up of the party. Billy's story is the same that was given in our EXTRA, issued at midnight last Sunday.

> If it hadn't been for the dead horse in the doorway I wouldn't be here today, I would have ridden out on my bay mare and taken my chances of escaping. But I couldn't ride over that [the dead horse] for she would have jumped back and I would have got it in the head. We could have staid in the house but there wouldn't have been anything gained by that for they would have starved us out. I thought it was better to come out and get a good square meal—don't you?

The prospects of a fight with the mob exhilarated him and he bitterly bemoaned being chained.

"If I only had my Winchester I'd lick the whole crowd," was his comment on the attacking party. He sighed and sighed again for a chance to take a hand in the fight, and the burden of his desire was to be set free to fight on the side of his captors as soon as he should smell powder.

Albert E. Hyde, a young magazine writer who happened to be in Las Vegas at the time, left an excellent eyewitness account of that tense morning when Garrett and Steward faced the lynch mob and Billy the Kid begged to be given a Winchester "to lick the whole crowd."[47]

Billy the Kid and Pat Garrett Face the Mob at the Las Vegas Depot

> I was lounging on the veranda of the Grand View Hotel one afternoon when a man on a horse covered with foam galloped past. He shouted to Dr. Sutfin, the proprietor, as he rode by: "Garrett's got the Kid and three of the gang. He's bringing 'em in to Vegas."
>
> In half an hour, Oldtown, usually peaceful and quiet in the afternoon, was seething with excitement.
>
> The news of the capture of the Kid spread like a prairie fire. People began at once to line up on each side of the road by which Garrett would enter the town. As it terminated in the street in front of the Grand View, I merely moved my position from the veranda to the adobe fence which inclosed the yard.
>
> The news was not generally believed. The capture of Billy the Kid alive was simply beyond belief. A rumor, however, was sufficient to turn the entire populace to curious expectancy.

Santa Fe, as Billy the Kid knew it. After his capture the young outlaw was brought here by Pat Garrett. *Photo by Henry Brown, The James D. Horan Civil War and Western Americana Collection*

It was a beautiful afternoon, and the elevation of the Grand View afforded a wide range of vision across the plains, stretching to the blue line of distant hills.

As the hours passed, the crowds began to grow more impatient and distrustful. All had become skeptical, when from our point of vantage we discerned a cloud of dust in the southwest. When the cause of it advanced close enough for the people to descry a wagon outfit accompanied by mounted men, a mighty shout went up. The good news was indeed true. Billy the Kid was a prisoner, and Pat Garrett was a hero.

As the wagon, pulled by four mules, approached, we saw four men sitting in the bed, two on a side, facing each other. The Kid, whom Dr. Sutfin had known in his cow-boy days and instantly recognized, was on the hotel side of the wagon, chained to a fierce-looking, dark-bearded man, who kept his slouch-hat pulled well down over his eyes, and who looked neither to the right nor to the left. This was the daring and dangerous Dave Rudabaugh, who, among many other crimes, had killed the Mexican jailer at Las Vegas a short time before, making good his escape along with the companions he released. He feared recognition, as well he might, for the Mexican population thirsted for his blood. The other two prisoners were Pickett and Wilson, prominent members of the Kid's gang.

Billy the Kid was in a joyous mood. He was a short, slender, beardless young man. The marked peculiarity of his face was a pointed chin and a short upper lip which exposed the large front teeth and gave a chronic grin to his expression. He wore his hat pushed far back, and jocularly greeted the crowd. Recognizing Dr. Sutfin, he called: "Hello, doc! Thought I jes drop in an' see how you fellers in Vegas air behavin' yerselves."

Heavily armed deputies rode on each side of the wagon, with two bringing up the rear. Garrett rode in front. The large crowd evidently surprised and annoyed him. Fearing for the safety of Rudabaugh, he turned and gave a low order to the muledriver, who instantly whipped up his team, and a run was made across the plaza to the jail.

Garrett heard enough during the next few hours to convince him that an attempt would be made to lynch Rudabaugh. He promptly increased his force to thirty men, who guarded the jail that night. In the meantime he planned to take the prisoners next day to Santa Fé for safe-keeping. Not a suspicion of this move was allowed to get out.

Just before train-time Garrett dressed the men in plain clothes. He waited until the train was due, and then placed the prisoners in a closed carriage and drove rapidly to the depot. He placed his men in the smoking-car, and but for the accident of a delayed north-bound train his ruse would have been entirely successful. Las Vegas was the meeting-point, and the south-bound train had received orders to side-track. The Kid was still chained to Rudabaugh, and as they brushed past me on the platform I had a good look at the wild animal, and met the gaze of a pair of round, cold gray eyes.

Now this cruel, slender, boyish-looking man sat in the smoker of the south-bound train, handcuffed to Rudabaugh and chained to the seat. When the train backed in on the siding, I and a companion started back to the hotel. We had gone only a few yards when we heard men shouting, and soon met crowds of Mexicans armed with Winchesters running in our direction. It flashed upon me at once that Garrett's move was known, and that a mob was coming to take Rudabaugh.

Opposite the side-track on which the passenger-train stood, and only fifty feet away, was another siding holding several empty freight-cars. I suggested to my friend that we occupy the top of one of the cars. We could not have selected a better place. Our position commanded an excellent view of the interior of the smoker, and we could observe every movement of its occupants.

The moment Garrett was informed of the approaching danger, he requested the passengers to leave the train and seek a place of safety, which advice they were not slow to follow. Fearing that Rudabaugh might be shot from the outside, he unchained him from the Kid and moved him across the aisle, pulling down the lattice-shade. Walking up and down the car from door to door, his Winchester across his arm, Garrett calmly awaited developments.

We could see Rudabaugh through the window at which the Kid still sat, but he was not visible to those standing on the ground. He leaned back against the window-shade, quietly puffing a cigar. He did not appear to be disturbed by the thought that his life hung in the balance, and that a horrible death awaited him should the mob succeed in its purpose. His expression was that of a man absolutely indifferent to his fate.

The mob arrived and assembled between the freight-cars and the passenger-train. Two men with Winchesters were stationed at the engine. The leaders, three in number, mounted the steps of the smoker and demanded admittance. This was promptly refused, and the men were ordered off the car. They came back to the main body and demanded the prisoner Rudabaugh.

"I have reason to believe that these prisoners are not safe here," replied Garrett, "and I am taking them to Santa Fe, where they can be more securely guarded."

This explanation failed to satisfy the crowd.

"Take the other prisoner to Santa Fe," replied their spokesman, "but give Rudabaugh to us. His crime was committed here against one of our own people, and you have no right to remove him."

Slowly Garrett replied: "I have risked my life to bring these men to justice alive, and I will risk it again to protect them, for this is my sworn duty. I solemnly warn you that an attempt to take them from me will fail, unless you kill me first."

During this exciting colloquy, Billy the Kid, with his head thrust out of the window, was an amused listener. Unable to restrain himself, he began in rapid Greaser Spanish to tell the crowd what he thought of them, and judging from the interpretation of my friend, his regard for them and their forebears was not of a complimentary kind. He turned rapidly to Garrett, and said: "Pat, take these things off [holding up his manacled hands], give me a couple of guns, and turn me loose in that crowd of Greasers. If you will do that I'll walk right back in here and hold out my hands for the bracelets."

Wise old Garrett said nothing, but shook his head.

The spokesmen of the Mexicans, after considerable discussion among themselves, changed the form of their demand. They wanted Rudabaugh returned to the Las Vegas jail.

Garrett refused to yield the point.

Then there was a cry of rage. Some one yelled "Look out!" and there was instantly a hurried scattering of the mob.

The Mexicans hastily sought cover. They dropped behind piles of cross-ties, the trucks of the freight-cars, and other shelter, and then the ugly muzzles of guns covered the smoking-car from all directions.

We thought the battle was squarely on, and quickly flattened ourselves on the top of the car, expecting every minute to hear the roar of guns; but seconds passed, and not a shot disturbed the stillness. Venturing a look into the car, we

> saw Garrett, his face pale but sternly set, his hand upon the lever of his rifle, waiting grimly the first shot. Rudabaugh had not moved his position, but was chewing viciously at the stump of his cigar. The Kid, still begging Garrett to turn him loose temporarily, seemed perfectly wild to get actively into the excitement. He was in his element, but for the first time in his life his hands were tied, and the novelty of the situation galled him.
>
> Gradually the Mexicans came out and assembled for another parley. Twice more was this stirring scene repeated.
>
> Garrett began to weary, and at last declared that at the first shot he would arm the prisoners. This settled it. A compromise was quickly arranged. Garrett proposed that two citizens, representing the Mexicans of Las Vegas, accompany him to see that he turned the prisoners over to the proper authorities at Santa Fé.
>
> Amid the cheers of belated passengers and white spectators, the train, held up for an hour, pulled out from the station. The coolness, nerve, and resource of Pat Garrett had saved the day.

Billy sent four letters from his Santa Fe cell to Wallace reminding him of his promise and asking for an interview. But the governor ignored the letters; *Ben Hur* was now a best seller and the trials and tribulations of a young outlaw were no longer important. In fact, Wallace probably never gave the Kid a second thought when he left Santa Fe on the day Billy arrived; he was on his way to Washington to exchange the shabby governor's palace for the more glamorous quarters in Turkey as United States minister.[48]

Billy was finally tried, convicted, and sentenced to hang in Mesilla by his old enemy, Justice Warren Bristol. Two years before in his confidential reports to Secretary of Interior Carl Schurz, Frank Warner Angel had pointed out Bristol's suspicious friendships with the Santa Fe Ring leaders. Dona Ana County was the home ground for former prosecutor Rynerson and his friend the sheriff had hand-picked the jury; it was a legal lynch mob.

Billy was broke. He didn't have the $50 for court fees, which could have won him a new trial. He was also afraid of lynching in this hostile county ruled by the Santa Fe Ring.

As he told the *Mesilla News* editor: "If mob law is going to rule, better dismiss judges, sheriffs, etc. and let all take chances alike."

Billy was finally sent back to Lincoln to await his execution on May 13, 1881.

But as Billy told Garrett's deputy, the taunting Bob Olinger: "There's many a slip twixt the cup and the lip . . ."

On Thursday, April 18, Billy the Kid escaped from his cell on the second floor of the old Murphy-Dolan store in Lincoln, used by the county commissioners as a jail.

From the first day Garrett had insisted that the Kid had to be leg-ironed and handcuffed; his jailers were Olinger and J. W. Bell. Billy killed Bell with a six-shooter his friends had hidden in the privy, then killed Olinger with a shotgun blast. He found the key to his cuffs in Bell's pocket and forced the old janitor, George Gauss, who had been Tunstall's cook, to throw him a miner's pickax. When he freed one leg iron, he tied the other chain to his belt.

No 506

To the Sheriff of Lincoln County, New Mexico, Greeting:

At the March term, A.D. 1881, of the District Court for the Third Judicial District of New Mexico, held at La Mesilla in the county of Doña Ana, William Bonny, alias Kid, alias William Antrim, was duly convicted of the crime of Murder in the First degree; and on the fifteenth day of said term, the same being the thirteenth day of April, A.D. 1881, the judgment and sentence of said court were pronounced against the said William Bonny, alias Kid, alias William Antrim, upon said conviction according to law: whereby the said William Bonny, alias Kid, alias William Antrim, was adjudged and sentenced to be hanged by the neck until dead, by the Sheriff of the said county of Lincoln, within said county.

Therefore, you, the Sheriff of the said county of Lincoln, are hereby commanded that on Friday, the thirteenth day of May, A.D. 1881, pursuant to the said judgment and sentence of the said court, you take the said William Bonny, alias Kid, alias William Antrim, from the county jail of the county of Lincoln where he is now confined, to some safe and convenient place within the said County, and there, between the hours of ten o'clock, A.M., and three o'clock, P.M., of said day, you hang the said William Bonny, alias Kid, alias William Antrim by the neck until he is dead. And make due return of your acts hereunder.

Done at Santa Fé in the Territory of New Mexico, this 30th day of April, A.D. 1881.

Witness my hand and the great seal of the Territory.

Lew. Wallace,
Governor New Mexico.

By the Governor
W. G. Ritch
Secretary
N.M.

The execution order for Billy the Kid, issued and signed by Governor Lew Wallace and delivered to Sheriff Pat Garrett. *Courtesy New Mexico State Records Center and Archives*

Territory
vs
Wm Bonny, alias
Kid
Death Warrant

New Mexico, May 24th 1881
I hereby certify that the within warrant was not served owing to the fact that the within named prisoner escaped before the time set for serving said warrant.

Pat F. Garrett
Sheriff
Lincoln County
New Mexico

FILED
JUN 3 1881
W. G. RITCH

Pat Garrett's death warrant for Billy the Kid which, as he explains, was not served because the Kid had escaped. *Courtesy New Mexico State Records Center and Archives*

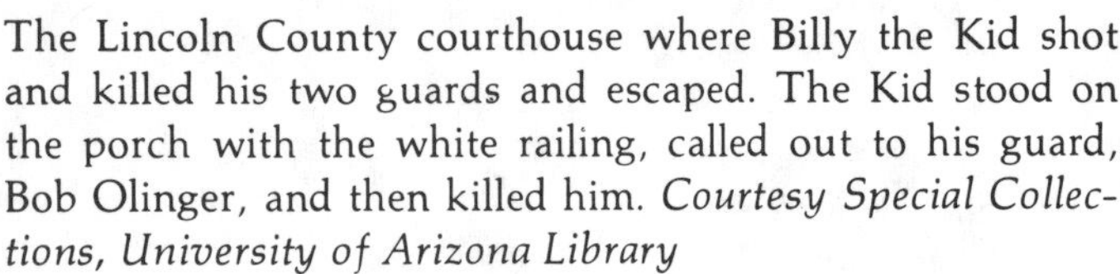
The Lincoln County courthouse where Billy the Kid shot and killed his two guards and escaped. The Kid stood on the porch with the white railing, called out to his guard, Bob Olinger, and then killed him. *Courtesy Special Collections, University of Arizona Library*

Bob Olinger, killed by Billy the Kid during his escape from the Lincoln County courthouse. *Courtesy Special Collections, University of Arizona Library*

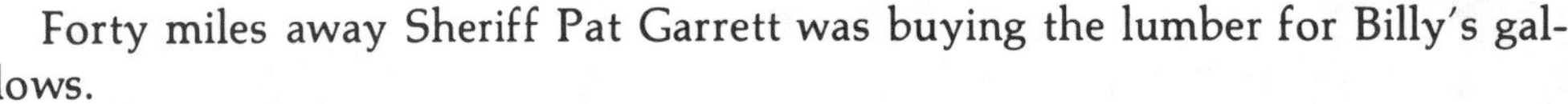
Forty miles away Sheriff Pat Garrett was buying the lumber for Billy's gallows.

Several years later Gauss wrote his own account of that day for the *Lincoln County Leader*.[49]

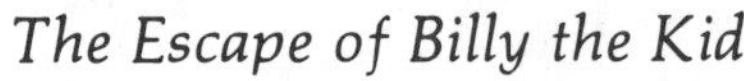

The Escape of Billy the Kid

I came out of my room whence I had gone to light my pipe, and was crossing the yard behind the courthouse when I heard a shot fired, then a tussle upstairs in the courthouse, someone hurrying downstairs, and Deputy Sheriff Bell emerging from the door, running towards me.

When I arrived at the garden gate, leading to the street in front of the court house, I saw the other deputy sheriff, Ollinger, coming out of the hotel opposite, with four or five county prisoners where they had taken their dinner. I called to him to come quick. He did so, leaving his prisoners in front of the hotel. When he had come close up to me I told him I had left Bell laying dead behind me in the yard, and before he could reply he was struck by a well directed shot from the window above us and fell dead at my feet.

I ran for my life to reach my room and safety, and Billy the Kid called out to me: "Don't run, I wouldn't hurt you. I'm alone and master, not only of the courthouse but also of the town, for I will allow nobody to come near me. You go," he said "and saddle one of Judge [Ira E.] Leonard's horses and I will clear out as soon as I can have the shackles loosened from my legs."

With a little prospecting pick I had thrown to him through the window he was working for at least an hour, and he came to the conclusion to await a better chance, tie one shackle to his waist belt and start. I had saddled a small skittish pony belonging to Billy Burt, as there was no other horse available, and had also by Billy's command, tied a pair of red blankets behind the saddle.

I came near forgetting to say that whilst I was busy saddling and Billy was trying to get his shackles off, Mr. Sam Wortley [owner of the hotel] appeared at the gate leading from the garden where he had been at work, and that when he saw the two sheriffs lying dead he did not know whether to go in or retreat, but on the assurance of Billy the Kid that he would not hurt him, he went in and made himself generally useful.

When Billy went downstairs at last, on passing the body of Bell he said:

"I'm sorry I had to kill him but I couldn't help it."

On passing the body of Ollinger, he gave him a tip of his boot saying:

"You're not going to round me up again."

We went out together to where I had tied the pony, and he told me to tell the owner, Billy Burt, that he would send it back the next day. I, for my part, didn't believe in such a promise, but sure enough the pony arrived safe and sound, trailing a long lariat, at the courthouse in Lincoln.

And so, Billy the Kid started out that evening, after he had shaken hands with everybody around and after having a little difficulty in mounting on account of the shackle on his leg, he went on his way rejoicing.

Who will blame Billy the Kid for killing his two guards at the time of his escape from Lincoln whilst he himself was to be hanged the week following? This is the only murder I knew Billy ever committing. I did not blame him then—I do not blame him now. Life is sweet . . .

Billy soon found friends like Ygenio Salazar, who had played dead to survive the Battle of Lincoln, to feed him and knock off the remaining leg iron. He was given a fine bay mare and he rode to Fort Sumner, the only refuge left.

After he returned to Lincoln, Pat Garrett appeared strangely indecisive, almost reluctant to raise a posse and hunt down the Kid. Days passed. In Sumner, Billy was once again the lighthearted *caballero* who charmed the Mexican girls, raced his bay mare, and played monte.

Fifty years ago Paulita Maxwell, daughter of the famous landowners of New Mexico, remembered for Walter Noble Burns, one of Billy's biographers, how the Kid was the attraction at Sumner's weekly dances.

"His record as a heart breaker was quite a formidable one," she said, "like a sailor he had a sweetheart in every port of call. In every *Placeta* in the Pecos some little Senorita was proud to be known as his *querida* . . . even after he escaped from Lincoln he came to the weekly dances . . . he loved to dance, spoke fluent Spanish and was well liked."

Although the Mexicans protected him, Billy's friends again urged him to escape to Old Mexico while he had the chance and give up the confrontation to which he was committing himself. Wise old Deluvina tried in many ways to make life for him seem more logical, more natural than death, by feeding him elaborate meals and urging the girls to dance and sing for him.

When she begged him to flee across the border he told her in Spanish he had to stay.

Why? He shrugged. Billy knew what he had to do but never knew the reason why . . .

In May 1881, Pat Garrett hired John Poe, a lean, taciturn Kentuckian, as a deputy. He had cleaned up Fort Griffin, as wild in its day as Abilene or Dodge, then joined the Canadian River Cattle Association as a stockman's detective. He resigned his U.S. deputy marshal's post when Garrett offered him the job as deputy sheriff of Lincoln County.[50]

Poe began a methodical cleanup of rustlers and horse thieves, trailing some into Arizona where he took them at gunpoint. In July, when he stopped off at White Oaks, a barroom derelict whom he had befriended told him a strange story: he had been sleeping off a drunk in a livery stable when he heard two men discussing Billy the Kid and how he was still living at Fort Sumner.

Poe was stunned; both he and Garrett assumed that by this time Billy was safe in Mexico. He missed Garrett in Lincoln but finally found him at his ranch on the Pecos. Pat was skeptical and reluctantly agreed to ride with Poe and Roswell Deputy Sheriff Thomas L. (Tip) McKinney to Sumner.

It is difficult to explain Garrett's strange lethargy. Perhaps he was bored with his job and yearned for the rancher's life he loved. Then again he might have been secretly jubilant that Billy had made his escape—it is clear he was uneasy when Poe gave him the news.

Pat Garrett, Billy's friend of those wonderful lazy days when the only crisis was a bad poker hand in Beaver Smith's saloon, now rode slowly along the trail toward Fort Sumner where Billy the Kid almost fatalistically waited for their meeting . . .

Garrett's account of how he killed Billy the Kid on that warm July evening in 1881, written by the unreliable Ash Upton, has been the standard version, but Poe's account, not as well known, is vivid and precise. Published in a London magazine shortly after World War I, Poe gives a step-by-step account of the killing of the West's greatest legend.[51]

The Killing of Billy the Kid

After a few hours spent in Roswell arranging for the trip, we started about sundown, riding out of town in a different direction from that which we intended to travel later, as it was absolutely necessary to keep the public in ignorance of our plans if anything were to be accomplished. After we were well out of the settlements we changed our course and rode in the direction of Fort Sumner until about midnight, when we stopped, picketed our horses and slept on our saddle blankets for the remainder of the night. The next day we rode some fifty or fifty-five miles, halting late in the evening at a point in the sand hills some five or six miles out from Fort Sumner, where we again picketed our horses and slept until morning.

It was then agreed that, as I was not known in Fort Sumner, while the other two men were, Garrett having a year or two previously resided there, I should ride into the place with the object of reconnoitering the ground and gathering such information as was possible that might aid us in our purpose, while the other two men were to remain out of sight in the sand hills for the day, and in case of

The trio of lawmen who hunted Billy the Kid and his riders. *Left:* Pat Garrett, who killed the outlaw. *Right:* John W. Poe, who accompanied Garrett and later succeeded Garrett as sheriff. *Center:* James Brent, who aided Garrett in suppressing the lawlessness in Lincoln County in 1877-1881. This photograph was taken in 1883 or 1884. *The James D. Horan Civil War and Western Americana Collection*

A rare and original tintype of Billy the Kid. It was found in 1936 in a family album once owned by a rancher from Silver City, New Mexico, where Billy spent his formative years. *Courtesy The Oregonian*

my failure to return to them before night, they were to meet me after darkness came on at a certain point agreed on, some four miles out of Fort Sumner.

In pursuance of this plan I next morning left my companions and rode into town, where I arrived about ten o'clock. Fort Sumner at that time had a population of only some two or three hundred people, nearly all of whom were natives or Mexicans, there being perhaps not more than one or two dozen Americans in the place, a majority of whom were tough or undesirable characters, in sympathy with "The Kid," while the remainder stood in terror of him.

When I entered the town I noticed that I was being watched from every side, and soon after I had stopped and hitched my horse in front of a store which had a saloon annex, a number of men gathered around and began to question me as to where I was from, where bound, etc. I answered with as plausible a yarn as I was able, telling them I was from White Oaks, where I had been engaged in mining, and was on my way to the Panhandle, where I had formerly lived. This story seemed to allay their suspicions to some extent, and I was invited to join in a social drink at the saloon, which I did, being very careful that I absorbed but a very small portion of the liquor. This operation was repeated several times, as was the custom in those days, after which I went to a nearby restaurant for something to eat. After I had eaten a square meal I loitered about the village for some three hours, chatting casually with people I met, in the hope of learning something definite as to whether or not "The Kid" was there, but was unable to learn anything further than that the people with whom I conversed were still suspicious of me, and it was plain that many of them were on the alert, expecting something to happen—in fact, there was a very tense situation in Fort Sumner on that day, as "The Kid" was at that very time hiding in one of the native's houses there, and if the object of my visit had become known, I would have stood no chance for my life whatever.

It was understood when I left my companions in the morning that in case of my being unable to learn any definite information in Fort Sumner, I was to go to the ranch of a Mr. Rudolph (an acquaintance and supposed friend of Garrett's) whose ranch was located some seven miles north of Fort Sumner at a place called "Sunnyside," with the purpose of securing from him, if possible, some information as to the whereabouts of the man we were after. Accordingly I started from Fort Sumner about the middle of the afternoon for Rudolph's ranch, arriving there some time before night. I found Mr. Rudolph at home, presented the letter of introduction which Garrett had given me, and told him that I wished to stop overnight with him. After reading the letter he said that Garrett was a very good friend of his, and that he would be very glad to furnish me with accommodations for the night; invited me into his house, took charge of my horse, etc. After supper was over I engaged in conversation with him, discussing the conditions in the country generally, and after some little time I led up to the escape of "Billy the Kid" from Lincoln, and remarked that I had heard a report that "The Kid" was hiding in or about Fort Sumner. Upon my making this remark, the old gentleman showed plainly that he was getting nervous; said he had heard that such a report was about, but did not believe it, as "The Kid" was, in his opinion, too shrewd to be caught lingering in that part of the country with a price on his head and knowing that the officers of the law were diligently seeking him. By this time I was pretty well convinced that Mr. Rudolph was naturally well-intentioned, but like so many others, was in almost mortal terror of "The Kid," and on account of this fear was very reluctant to say anything whatever about him. I then told him plainly the object of our errand—that I had come to him with the express purpose of learning, if possible, where "The Kid" could be found; that we believed he was hiding in or near Fort Sumner, and that Garrett, the sheriff, expected that he (Rudolph) would be able to put us on the right trail. Upon my making this statement, Mr. Rudolph apparently became more nervous and excited than ever, and reiterated his reasons for believing that "The Kid" was not in that part of the country, and showed plainly—so it seemed to me—that he was not only embarrassed but alarmed. The truth was, we afterward learned, that he was well aware of the fact that "The Kid" was then, and had been for some time, hiding about Fort Sumner, but his dread of "The Kid" caused him to make misleading statements while withholding facts.

Darkness was now approaching and I said to Mr. Rudolph that, inasmuch as myself and my horse were by this time pretty well rested, having had a good feed, I had changed my mind, and instead of stopping overnight with him, would saddle up and ride during the cool of the evening to meet my companions. This I accordingly did, much, I thought, to the relief of Rudolph. I rode directly to the point where I had agreed to meet my companions, and, strange to say, as I approached the point from one direction, they came into view from the other, so that we did not have to wait for each other. This proved to be a night of strange happenings with us, however, all the way through. We here held a consultation as to what further course we should pursue. I had spent the day in endeavoring to learn something definite of the whereabouts of the man we wanted, but without success, save that from the actions of the people I had met at Fort Sumner, together with Mr. Rudolph's nervous and excited manner, I was more firmly convinced than ever that our man was in that vicinity.

Garrett seemed to have but little confidence in our being able to accomplish the object of our trip, but said that he knew the location of a certain house occupied by a woman in Fort Sumner which "The Kid" had formerly frequented, and that if he was in or about Fort Sumner he would most likely be found entering or leaving this house some time during the night, and proposed that we go into a grove of trees near the town, conceal our horses, then station ourselves in the peach orchard at the rear of the house and keep watch on who might come or go. This course was agreed on, and we entered the peach orchard about nine o'clock that night, stationing ourselves in the gloom or shadow of the peach trees, as the moon was shining very brightly. We kept up a fruitless watch here until some time after eleven o'clock, when Garrett stated that he believed we were on a cold trail; that he had had very little faith in our being able to accomplish anything when we started on the trip; and proposed that we leave the town without letting anyone know that we had been there in search for "The Kid."

I then proposed that before leaving we should go to the residence of Peter Maxwell, a man who, up to that time, I had never seen, but who by reputation I knew to be a man of wealth and influence, and who by reason of his being a leading citizen and having large property interests should, according to my reasoning, be glad to furnish such information as he might have to aid us in ridding the country of a man who was looked upon as a scourge and curse by all law-abiding people.

Garrett agreed to this, and thereupon led us from the orchard by circuitous bypaths to Maxwell's residence, which was a building formerly used as officers' quarters during the days when a garrison of troops had been maintained at the fort. Upon our arriving at the residence (a very long, one-story adobe, standing end to and flush with the street, having a porch on the south side, which was the direction from which we approached; the premises all being enclosed by a paling fence, one side of which ran parallel to and along the edge of the street up to and across the end of the porch to the corner of the building), Garrett said to me: "This is Maxwell's room in this corner. You fellows wait here while I go in and talk with him," and thereupon stepped onto the porch and entered Maxwell's room through the open door (left open on account of the extremely warm weather), while McKinney and myself stopped on the outside, McKinney squatting on the outside of the fence and I sitting on the edge of the porch in the small open gateway leading from the street onto the porch.

It should be mentioned here that up to this moment I had never seen "Billy the Kid" nor Maxwell, which fact, in view of the events transpiring immediately afterward, placed me at an extreme disadvantage.

It was probably not more than 30 seconds after Garrett had entered Maxwell's room when my attention was attracted from where I sat in the little gateway, to a man approaching me on the inside of and along the fence, some forty or fifty steps away. I observed that he was only partially dressed, and was both bare-headed and bare-footed—or rather, had only socks on his feet, and it seemed to me that he was fastening his trousers as he came toward me at a very brisk walk.

As Maxwell's was the one place in Fort Sumner that I had considered above suspicion of harboring "The Kid," I was entirely off my guard, the thought coming into my mind that the man approaching was either Maxwell or some guest of his who might have been staying there. He came on until he was almost within arm's length of where I sat before he saw me, as I was partially concealed from his view by the post of the gate. Upon his seeing me he covered me with his six-shooter as quick as lightning, sprang onto the porch, calling out in Spanish, "Quien es?" (Who is it?), at the same time backing away from me toward a door through which Garrett only a few seconds before had passed, repeating his query, "Who is it?" in Spanish several times. At this I stood up and advanced toward him, telling him not to be alarmed; that he should not be hurt, and still without the least suspicion that this was the very man we were looking for. As I moved toward him trying to reassure him, he backed up into the doorway of Maxwell's room, where he halted for a moment, his body concealed by the thick adobe wall at the side of the doorway, from whence he put his head out and asked in Spanish for the fourth or fifth time who I was. I was within a few feet of him when he disappeared into the room. After this, and until after the shooting, I was unable to see what took place on account of the darkness of the room but plainly heard what was said on the inside. An instant after the man left the door I heard a voice inquire in a sharp tone: "Pete, who are those fellows on the outside?" An instant later a shot was fired in the room, followed immediately by what everyone within hearing distance thought was two other shots. However, there were only two shots fired, the third report, as we learned afterward, being caused by the rebound of the second bullet which had struck the adobe wall and rebounded against the headboard of a wooden bedstead.

I heard a groan and one or two gasps from where I stood in the doorway, as of someone dying in the room. An instant later Garrett came out, brushing against me as he passed. He stood by me close to the wall at the side of the door and said to me: "That was 'The Kid' that came in there onto me and I think I have got him." I said: "Pat, 'The Kid' would not come to this place—you have shot the wrong man." Upon my saying this, Garrett seemed to be in doubt himself as to whom he had shot, but quickly spoke up and said: "I am sure that was him, for I know his voice too well to be mistaken." This remark of Garrett's relieved me of considerable apprehension, as I had felt almost certain that someone whom we did not want had been killed.

A moment after Garrett came out of the door, Pete Maxwell rushed squarely onto me in a frantic effort to get out of the room, and I certainly would have shot him but for Garrett striking my gun down, saying, "Don't shoot Maxwell!"

As by this time I had begun to realize that we were in a place which was not above suspicion, such as I had thought the residence of Maxwell to be, and as Garrett was so positive that "The Kid" was inside, I came to the conclusion that we were up against a case of "kill or be killed," as we had from the beginning realized such would be the case whenever we came upon "The Kid."

I have ever since felt grateful that I did not shoot Maxwell, for, as I learned afterward, he was at heart a well-meaning, inoffensive man, but very timid. We afterward discovered that "The Kid" had frequently been at this house after his escape from Lincoln, but Maxwell stood in such terror of him that he did not dare inform against him.

By this time all was quiet within the room, and as the darkness was such that we were unable to see what the conditions were on the inside or what the result of the shooting had been, we—after some rather forceful persuasion indeed—induced Maxwell to procure a light, which he finally did by bringing an old-fashioned tallow candle from his mother's room at the far end of the building, passing by the rear to the end where the shooting occurred, and placing the candle on the window sill from the outside. This enabled us to get a view of the inside, where we saw a man lying stretched upon his back dead, in the middle of the room, with a six-shooter lying at his right hand and a butcher knife at his left. Upon examining the body we found it to be that of "Billy the Kid." Garrett's first shot had penetrated his breast just above the heart, thus ending the career of a desperado who, while only about 23 years of age at the time of his death, had killed a greater number of men than any of the many desperadoes and "killers" I have known or heard of during the 45 years I have been in the Southwest.

Within a very short time after the shooting, quite a number of the native people had gathered around; some of them bewailing the death of their friend, while several women pleaded for permission to take charge of the body, which we allowed them to do. They carried it across the yard to a carpenter shop, where it was laid out on a workbench, the women placing candles lighted around it, according to their ideas of properly conducting a "wake" for the dead.

All that occurred after "The Kid" came into view in the yard, up to the time he was killed, happened in much less time than it takes to tell it, not more than thirty seconds intervening between the time I first saw him and the time he was shot. From Garrett's statement of what took place in the room after he entered, it appears that he left his Winchester rifle standing by the side of the door and approached the bed where Maxwell was sleeping, arousing him and sitting down on the edge of the bed near the head. A moment after he had taken this position for a talk with Maxwell he heard voices on the porch and sat quietly listening, when a man appeared in the doorway and a moment later ran up to Maxwell's bed, saying, "Pete, who are those fellows outside?" It being dark in the room he had not, up·to the moment, seen Garrett sitting at the head of the bed. When he spoke to Maxwell, Garrett recognized his voice and made a move to draw his six-shooter. This movement attracted "The Kid's" attention, and seeing that a man was sitting there, he instantly covered him with his gun, backed away and demanded several times in Spanish to know who it was. Garrett made no reply, and without rising from his seat, fired, with the result stated.

This occurred at about midnight on the 14th of July, 1881. We spent the remainder of the night on the Maxwell premises, keeping constantly on our guard, as we were expecting to be attacked by the friends of the dead man. Nothing of the kind occurred, however. The next morning we sent for a justice of the peace, who held an inquest over the body, the verdict of the jury being such as to justify the killing, and later, on the same day, the body was buried in the old military burying ground at Fort Sumner.

There have been many wild and untrue stories of this affair, one of which was that we had in some way learned in advance that "The Kid" would come to Maxwell's residence that night, and had concealed ourselves there with the purpose of waylaying and killing him. Another was that we had cut off his fingers and carried them away as trophies or souvenirs, and of later years it has been said many times that "The Kid" was not dead at all, but had been seen alive and well in various places. The actual facts, however, are exactly as stated herein, and while we no doubt would, under the circumstances, have laid in wait for him at the Maxwell premises if there had been the slightest reason for believing that he would come there, the fact that he did come was a complete surprise to us, absolutely unexpected and unlooked for as far as we three were concerned.

The story that we had cut off and carried away his fingers was even more absurd, as the thought of such a thing never entered our minds, and besides, we were not that kind of people.

The killing of "The Kid" created a great sensation throughout the Southwest, and many of the law-abiding citizens of New Mexico and the Panhandle contributed substantially and liberally toward a reward for the officers whose work had finally rid the country of a man who was nothing less than a scourge.

The taking-off of "The Kid" had a very salutary effect in New Mexico and the Panhandle, most of his followers leaving the country, for the time being, at least, and a great many persons who had sympathized with him or had been terrorized by him, completely changed their attitude toward the enforcement of the law.

The events which transpired at Maxwell's ranch on the night of that 14th of July, to this day seem to me strange and mysterious, as "The Kid" was certainly a "killer," was absolutely desperate and had "the drop" first on me and then on Garrett. Why did he not use it? Possibly because he thought he was in the house of his friends and had no suspicion that the officers of the law would ever come to that place searching for him. From what we learned afterward, there was some reason for believing that we had been seen leaving the peach orchard by one of his friends, who ran to the house where he was stopping for the night, warning him of our presence; upon which he had run out half-dressed to Maxwell's, thinking perhaps that by reason of the standing of the Maxwell family he would not be sought there. However this may be, it is still, in view of his character and the condition he was in, a mystery.

I have been in many close places and through many trying experiences both before and after this occurrence, but never in one where I was so forcibly impressed with the idea that a Higher Power controls and rules the destinies of men. To me it seemed that what occurred in Fort Sumner that night had actually been foreordained.

Billy was placed in a cheap pine box set up on two wooden horses. While the Mexican women prayed during the night, Billy's friends came into the room one by one to pay their respects. First there was only the moonlight, then someone from the Maxwell family brought candles, which were placed at the foot and head of the coffin.

In the morning they buried him in the old military cemetery next to Tom O'Folliard and Charlie Bowdre. There was no priest or minister in the community so each mourner said his own prayers as the sunbaked dirt hit the coffin with a hollow sound.

Billy had lived twenty-one years, seven months, and twenty-two days.

Territorio de Nuevo Méjico } Precinto No. 27.
Condado de San Miguel } Del Primer Distrito Judicial
Al Procurador ~~General~~ del Territorio de Nuevo
Méjico Salud.

Este dia 15 de Julio, A.D. 1881, reciví
mi cama en mi cuarto a cosa de media noche
el dia 14 de Julio entró á mi cuarto Pat. F.
Garrett y se sentó en la orilla de mi cama á
platicar conmigo. A poco rato que Garrett
se sentó entró William Bonney y se arrimó
á mi cama con una pistola en la mano y
me preguntó "Who is it? Who is it?" y entónces
Pat. F. Garrett le tiró dos balazos á dicho
William Bonney y se cayó el dicho Bonney
en un lado de mi fogon y yo salí del cuarto
cuando volví á entrar y á los tres ó cuatro
minutos despues de los balazos estaba muerto
dicho Bonney.

The original coroner's report, in Spanish, on the death of Billy the Kid, First Judicial District, Territory of New Mexico. *Courtesy New Mexico State Records Center and Archives*

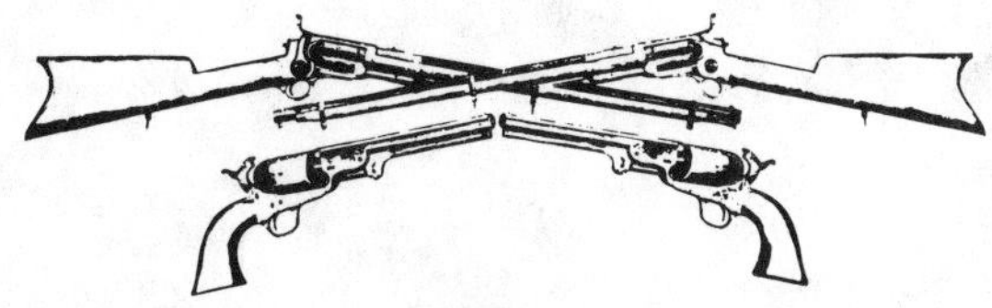

WILD BILL HICKOK

JAMES BUTLER HICKOK, LATE OF TROY GROVE, A SMALL town in La Salle County, northern Illinois, never knew he was a glamorous gunfighter, defender of the helpless, and scourge of evil, until he read an article about himself in the February 1867 issue of *Harper's New Monthly Magazine.*

The author was Colonel George Ward Nichols, who left soldiering in the West under General Sherman to join the magazine as a correspondent.[1]

That year Colonel Nichols had met Hickok in Springfield, Missouri, one of the roughest towns in the Middle Border. It was a time for bloodletting; after Lee's surrender, bands of harassed Union men—"Regulators"—took their revenge against the riders of Quantrill, Bloody Bill Anderson and Bill Todd, who had returned home. It was commonplace to find bodies hanging from trees along lonely roads and turnpikes.

Nichols described Springfield as a busy hamlet, its main street crowded with "men and women dressed in queer costumes; men with coats and trousers made from skins but so thickly covered with dirt and grease as to defy the identity of the animal when walking in the flesh . . . many of these people were mounted on mules or horses, while others urged forward the unwilling cattle, attached to the creaking, heavily laden wagons, their drivers snapping their long whips with a report like that of a pistol shot . . ."

The birthplace of Wild Bill Hickok: Troy Grove, Illinois, seventy miles southwest of Chicago. Wild Bill's father, William Alonzo, established the first general store in the area, then turned to farming. Wild Bill's mother, Polly, died here two years after he was killed by Jack McCall. The building was torn down in the 1920s. *The James D. Horan Civil War and Western Americana Collection*

Then Nichols was introduced to Hickok and was forever lost. He breathlessly recalled:

"I thought John Wilkes Booth was the handsomest man I had ever seen but Wild Bill Hickok was handsomer . . . he had a finer, saner, better balanced more magnetic face and head than Booth . . ."

Nichols spent some time with Hickok who, according to the colonel, gave him a detailed account of his adventures, particularly the gunfight he had been in four years before at a stage stop called Rock Creek Station in southeastern Nebraska.

The station was an important stopover for the wagons moving overland to the Pacific Northwest, passengers of the Overland Stage, and for a change of horses for the Pony Express. The place had been sold to Russell, Majors and Waddell, owners of the lines, by David McCanles, an enterprising farmer and one of the Territory's leading citizens.

After McCanles moved to a new farm in Little Blue Bottom the station was operated by Horace Wellman, his common-law wife, Hickok, the stock tender, and J. W. "Dock" Brink, a stable hand. In the summer of 1861, the line's owners were on the brink of bankruptcy and could no longer meet their payments to McCanles.

On July 12, 1861, probably the most important date in Hickok's life, he was asked by Wellman to join him and Brink in the station. Wellman had just returned from a ten-day visit to the Russell, Majors & Waddell's division offices at Brownsville, on the Missouri River, to learn they could not meet a payment on the money owed to McCanles. Curiously, McCanles's son, twelve-year-old Monroe, had made the trip with him.

David C. McCanles, owner of the Rock Creek, Nebraska, stage depot and Pony Express station. McCanles was killed by Hickok at the station in July 1861. The story in *Harper's* about the so-called Rock Creek Massacre, a fictitious account of how Hickok held off a gang of outlaws, began the legend of Wild Bill. *The James D. Horan Civil War and Western Americana Collection*

A rare daguerreotype of the Rock Creek Stage and Pony Express station. McCanles is on horseback. The plate was discovered many years ago among the effects of Nat C. Stein, general superintendent of Wells, Fargo & Company, by Harry C. Peterson, curator of the Sutter's Fort Historical Museum of Sacramento. Peterson restored the fading image. *Courtesy California State Library*

The Holladay Overland Mail & Express Company with one of their stages "ready to depart for the plains." This photograph was taken before the Civil War. *The James D. Horan Civil War and Western Americana Collection*

McCanles, a brawny, fiery southerner, had accused Wellman of keeping the money so the jittery stage manager wanted as much protection as he could muster for McCanles's next visit. That afternoon McCanles, accompanied by Monroe, his cousin, James Woods, and his farmhand, James Gordon, rode up to the Rock Creek Station. The men were unarmed. Wellman refused to come out and instead sent his wife. There was an argument and Hickok appeared.

McCanles, physically powerful and apparently something of a bully, had contemptuously dubbed Hickok "Duck Bill" because of Hickok's prominent upper lip, hidden for most of his adult life by the familiar moustache. Obviously, they disliked each other.

When McCanles asked for a drink of water Hickok filled a tin cup and gave it to him. The argument continued, then suddenly there was the crash of gunfire. Hickok had shot McCanles from behind a curtain inside the house. Monroe ran to his father's side; the dying man tried to raise himself but fell back dead.

When Woods and Gordon rushed up to the house, Hickok shot Woods. The wounded man staggered a few feet and collapsed. While Mrs. Wellman screamed "Kill them! Kill them!" her cowardly husband armed with a grubbing hoe ran out of the house and clubbed Woods to death. McCanles's son dodged the woman's vicious swings and escaped in the woods. Gordon, also wounded, was tracked to his hiding place and cold-bloodedly killed as he begged for his life.

Four years later in Springfield, Hickok described the events of that day as Nichols eagerly took notes. When the article finally appeared, Hickok had killed the "M'Kandles Gang," ten in all, with his rifle, six-shooter, and bowie knife.

Nichols conceded, it was a "terrible tale" as Wild Bill told it. When the "M'Kandles Gang" raided the station, he began "striking savage blows, following the devils up from one side to the other of the room and into the corners, striking and slashing until everyone was dead . . ."

The Nichols article was the basis of the Hickok legend. Fifteen years later J. W. Buel, a reporter for the *Kansas City Journal,* wrote a sketch of Wild Bill in his *Heroes of the Plains.* He picked up Nichols's improbable details but added more "facts."

Nichols quoted an unnamed army officer as telling him that he had seen the slashed and bullet-torn bodies "an hour after the affair."

Buel in his book identified that officer as Captain E. W. Kingsbury of Kansas City, U.S. chief storekeeper for the Missouri District. The newspaperman claimed Kingsbury arrived at the station an hour after the fight and found Hickok, still on his feet, after having suffered a fractured skull, three "terrible" gashes on his chest, his scalp almost ripped from his head, and various other wounds. Buel also included an interview with Dr. Joshua Thorne, who told how he had treated and bandaged Hickok's wounds.

Buel described the McCanles gang as a band of terrorists who controlled the Territory, killing "more than a score of men and women for the purpose of robbery" but the farmer's power was so great law enforcement officers refused to arrest him or his followers.

From the West—Six Men Killed—Indians—Scouting Parties.

The following we extract from a private letter just received from a reliable and well informed friend residing on the Big Blue:

"Three wagon loads of arms and ammunition passed through the neighborhood below here last week, going westward. On Friday three men were killed at Rock Creek on the Millitary Road about 30 or 35 miles west of this. All we know is that the difficulty originated in the distribution or division of a wagon load of stuff from the Missouri river, and it is supposed it was one of the three wagons above mentioned. During the difficulty some secessionists put a rope around a Union man's neck, and dragged him some distance toward a tree with the avowed purpose of hanging him. He managed to escape. They then gave him notice to leave in a certain time or be hung. At the end of the time five of them went to his house to see if he had gone, when he commenced firing upon them and killed three out of the five; the other two making a hasty retreat.

"A great many of the settlers on the Blue and its tributaries have mooved their families and stock away, and nearly all the rest are preparing to do the same. The excitement is intense. The settlers remaining are going to work to build block houses up and down the river.

The rare *Nebraska Advertiser*, July 25, 1861, notice, containing the first, if garbled, version of the Rock Creek killings. *Courtesy Nebraska State Historical Society*

It was inevitable that Beadle's Dime Library picked up this juicy tale. In 1882 Colonel Prentiss Ingraham wrote *Wild Bill the Pistol Deadshot.* He included the same story with more details from Doctor Thorne, who now claimed he removed eleven bullets from Wild Bill's body as the gallant Lochinvar waved away all offers of an anesthetic.

Contemporary versions of the Rock Creek affair have depended on Emerson Hough's book, *The Story of the Outlaw*; a series written in the *Saturday Evening Post* by Fred Sutton, a former Kansas peace officer; a biography by William Elsey Connelley, secretary of the Kansas State Historical Society; Charles Dawson's *Pioneer Tales of the Oregon Trail and Jefferson County*; and Frank Jenner Wilstach's *Wild Bill, the Prince of Pistoleers.* The last two are the best of the lot. Connelley's overblown biography, glowing with admiration for Hickok, includes some Hickok myths.[2]

Each book offered new "facts." Hough, a popular writer of the World War I period, added motivation for Wild Bill's "heroic defense" of the station; now Hickok was fighting off an attempt by McCanles and his gang to steal the company's horses so vital for the Overland Stage and Pony Express. Connelley brought in Sarah Shull, McCanles's alleged mistress, whom he supposedly brought with him from North Carolina. Connelley, who never saw the woman or gave any source, described her as "voluptuous and beautiful . . . very fair . . . fine blue eyes . . . and a mass of dark hair . . . her relations with McCanles were long standing . . . those who made advances to her at Rock Creek found that she was not to be trifled with . . ."

Connelley has Wild Bill falling in love with Sarah, the result an inevitable triangle. McCanles was pictured—again without any source—as living a life of "progressive degeneracy . . . rascality and crime . . .", was a lover spurned and, of course, hated Hickok. Here is Connelley writing of Wild Bill in love with Sarah:

"Hickok's soul was fused and fashioned into a golden aspiration which was incapable of satisfaction. From her feet he walked through this world a solitary

Sarah Shull (Kate Shell), the legendary "mystery woman" in the Rock Creek tragedy. *The James D. Horan Civil War and Western Americana Collection*

figure, a man in a sort of wandering delirium, silent, suffering torments and reactions of ecstasy which he suppressed as well as he could, capable of great things, plunging into dangers beyond comprehension . . ."

After more of this nonsense Connelley then states that for Wild Bill, Sarah "was the only woman he ever loved . . . to the end of his life there was no room in his heart for any other than Sarah Shull . . ."

Evidently Connelley overlooked the many whores Hickok lived with in the cow towns.

Connelley insists McCanles was carrying a shotgun when he rode up to the station with his two companions, but failed to explain why the frontiersman brought his young son to the station if he expected gunfire.

Connelley had access to material that offered the true story of what happened that July morning. At a July Fourth celebration in 1876 held at Fairbury, Jenkins, one of the Territory's earliest settlers and first member of the state assembly, presented the facts: in 1884 Mrs. McCanles, the widow, told the story in detail before a large audience and on December 29, 1912, at the dedication of the Winslow Monument on the Oregon Trail, Frank Halvey, the stage and Pony Express rider who with his brothers had talked to Hickok shortly after the shooting and had buried the bodies, presented an authentic version of the gunfight.

However, it wasn't until 1927 when George W. Hansen, a pioneering settler and banker of Fairbury, Nebraska, decided to investigate the Rock Creek Station episode that the complete story of one of the West's most celebrated incidents became known.[3] Here is an excerpt from his article, which appeared in the *Nebraska History Magazine* of April-June 1927. Many of the facts came from William Monroe McCanles, at the time a prominent Kansas City lawyer, and records uncovered by Hansen.

The True Story of the Wild Bill-McCanles Affray in Jefferson County, Nebraska, July 12, 1861

On April 22nd, 1861, McCanles sold the West Rock Creek ranch, consisting of 120 acres to Wolfe & Hagenstien, payment for the same to be made in one year from that date. He retained the title as his security, and gave the purchasers a Bond for Deed when its provisions should be fulfilled. This Bond for the sum of $1200.00 was signed by David C. McCanles and wife and witnessed by his cousin, James Woods, and W. N. Glenn, and recorded in the office of the recorder of deeds of Gage County, Nebraska Territory.

In the Territorial archives of the Probate Court of Gage county, I found the original documents. "In the matter of the administration of the Estate of David C. McCanles, "deceased." On April 14th, 1862, James McCanles was appointed Administrator of this estate. On September 2nd, 1862, Wolfe & Hagenstien, having made all their payments as agreed, James McCanles as Administrator made and delivered to them a Warranty Deed for the 120 acre West Rock Creek ranch. It is interesting to notice that the first signature as surety on James McCanles' $4,000.00 bond as Administrator is the well known name of W. W. Hackney, now a resident of Lincoln, who owned and operated the "Hackney Ranch" in 1856 and 1857, merchant of Brownville in the '60s, capitalist and one of the organizers of the Central National Bank of Lincoln, of which his son is President. Mr. Hackney, now in his 92nd year is probably the earliest settler of Nebraska now living.

When the first deferred payment for East Rock Creek Station fell due McCanles called to collect it, and was told by Wellman that the money had not yet arrived. This excuse was made during the month, and on July 1st, when the final payment fell due and was not paid, McCanles demanded full payment or possession of the Station premises. Wellman replied that he would make a trip to the River at once for supplies, and would then collect the money for him. It was arranged that Monroe McCanles, David's 12 year old son, should accompany him, and the next day, July 2nd, they started together for the Missouri River, Monroe with his child's shot gun picking off game along the road, making a perfect holiday of the trip, never dreaming of the terrible tragedy with which it would close.

About ten days were spent in making the trip to the Missouri River and back, and Mr. Wellman and Monroe McCanles arrived at the Station about four o'clock in the afternoon of July 12th, 1861. They were expected several days sooner, but had been delayed by high water, and McCanles had called at the Station on several previous days expecting their return.

When Monroe McCanles reached the Station he saw horses hitched to the ranch of Jack Ney, which was situated a short distance south east of the stage station. He recognized the horses as belonging to his father, and ran over to see if he was there. He found his father, glad to see him again, asking him if he enjoyed the trip and how Wellman had treated him. Monroe says that his father appeared worried by the fact that Wellman had apparently not been successful in obtaining the money due him from the Stage Company. After a little pleasant conversation between father and son, McCanles, accompanied by his boy, immediately went to the Stage Station to talk with Wellman. Gordon and Woods went on down to the barn. These three farmers and the 12 year old boy constitute the entire posse of that notorious "McCanles gang" imposed on a gullible public during the last 60 years by sensation scribblers as a band of cut-throats, murderers and horse thieves which terrified the people of southern Nebraska and northern Kansas for years, and extended their depredations 500 miles west across an unpopulated country into the Rocky Mountains.

The Station building consisted of a one room log cabin 20 feet long by 18 feet wide and a "lean-to" 20 feet long and 12 feet wide. The east ends were curtained off, forming bed rooms. The kitchen, fire place and chimney were at the west end of the building. The barn was situated a short distance to the west and south of the Station proper. Wellman was in charge of the Station, Brink was stock tender and Hickok was his assistant, or stable hand subordinate to Brink. These three men and Mrs. Wellman were positively known to have been at the Stage Station on the afternoon of July 12th, 1861.

On arriving at the Stage Station McCanles and his son, Monroe, went to the kitchen door on the west. There is no reliable evidence that any of these men were armed and subsequent events prove clearly that they had no arms of any description in their possession at that time. McCanles on arriving at the kitchen door, asked for Wellman. Mrs. Wellman appeared and in reply to McCanles' question as to whether Wellman was in, said that he was. McCanles demanded that he come out. Mrs. Wellman promptly informed McCanles that he would not come out. This only added to McCanles' suspicion and anger and he told Mrs. Wellman that if Wellman would not come out he would go in and drag him out. Hickok stepped to the door. McCanles was somewhat disconcerted by Hickok's sudden appearance. He could not understand his motive in taking part in a matter in which he had no personal interest, while Wellman himself remained out of sight.

McCanles' anger at all these maneuvers and evasions increased, and he evidently believed that either the Stage Company was bankrupt and could not pay the money owed to him, or that Wellman had collected it and was planning to trick him out of it. He had mentioned his suspicions to his family frequently during the previous month. He was now determined to collect the money due him or take possession of his property. He had been a sheriff in North Carolina, and during eight years service as such officer had learned considerable law, and now living in a country without courts of justice and peace officers, realized his best and only recourse was quick action, taking the matter in his own hands and obtaining re-possession of his premises by throwing out the occupants by physical force, if necessary. It was his only effective remedy, as there would be no court of competent jurisdiction held in the district for the next two years or more. He was powerful, courageous and unafraid of any living man, and determined on his course.

Not having any quarrel with Hickok, McCanles asked him if they had not always been friends and if they were not still friendly, and being assured that such was the case, asked Hickok for a drink of water. This was a strange request to make in such a tense situation, but McCanles must have sensed the fact that he was in a rather precarious position, and took this method to gain time and survey the situation. While drinking he evidently saw something that aroused his suspicions, because as soon as he had finished drinking he handed the dipper back to Hickok and quickly walked to the other door of the cabin. While he was doing so Hickok had gone behind the flimsy calico curtain which separated the rooms. McCanles realized that, while his business quarrel was with Wellman, he now had

Hickok also to settle with. On the other hand, Hickok knew that by injecting himself into the controversy he had become involved and that he and Wellman together were no match in a physical encounter with a man of McCanles' well known strength and courage. McCanles called to Hickok to come out and if he had anything against him to fight it out square.

On this occasion, in fact at this very moment—Hickok decided on a course which in this case was so successful that he followed it the remainder of his life on the frontier. It was to shoot to kill on his first suspicion of a physical encounter or personal danger.

From his concealed position behind the curtain he shot McCanles, using the rifle McCanles had left at the Stage Station. This shot was not fired in the heat of a conflict or in self defense, but was deliberate and calculated and well aimed and pierced McCanles in the heart.

From all accounts of killings in which Hickok subsequently took part, I have been unable to find one single authentic instance in which he fought a fair fight. To him no human life was sacred. He was a cold blooded killer without heart or conscience. The moment he scented a fight he pulled his gun and shot to kill. So great was his fear of personal harm, and so quick was he to pull the trigger that on one occasion, at Abilene, Kansas, he killed Mike McWilliams, his most intimate friend, before he recognized him.

McCanles fell backward from the doorstep to the ground. His son, Monroe, who was standing by him when he was shot, says: "Father fell to the ground on his back. He raised himself up to an almost sitting position, took one last look at me as tho he wanted to speak, and then fell back dead." The shot was entirely unexpected as McCanles had at no time made an effort to protect himself from rifle fire. He would never have taken his twelve year old son, Monroe, to the door or to the cabin with him had he expected any gun play. He had never in his life on the frontier used a gun nor threatened to use a gun on any man. If, or when, he fought, he fought fair and never with a deadly weapon of any kind, but with his bare fists.

Woods and Gordon, hearing the shots, came running to the cabin, when Hickok came to the door and fired two shots at Woods from a Colt's revolver, wounding him severely. Woods ran around to the north of the cabin, followed by Wellman who had a heavy hoe in his hands.

Meanwhile Gordon turned and ran to get away from the gunfire and Hickok fired two shots at him, wounding him. Wellman had succeeded in dispatching Woods by crushing his skull with the heavy hoe, and, running around the house where young McCanles was kneeling over his father, stupefied at the awful horror of the things taking place around him, struck at young McCanles with the hoe yelling "Let's kill them all." Monroe dodged the blow and ran terrified away, chased by Wellman, but outran his pursuer, and, familiar with every foot of the ground, found a hiding place in the ravine south of the Stage Station.

Mrs. Wellman, who was the common law wife of Wellman, stood in the doorway when the chase began, screaming: "Kill 'em all, kill 'em all." Gordon, altho severely wounded, had succeeded in getting into the brush and about 80 rods down the creek away from the cabin, where he fell exhausted from loss of blood. He was followed by the Hickok crowd and while he begged for his life, was finished with a load of buckshot fired from Brink's shot gun, thus completing the triple murder by the butchery of two of the wounded victims.

During the entire time of the fracas, not a shot was fired by either McCanles, Woods or Gordon, and without any means of defense they were shot down like brutes. Even the twelve year old boy escaped only because of a lucky dodging of a blow, and the speed added to his feet by terror. After succeeding in his escape Monroe ran three miles to his home where he told his mother the horrible story. Breathless and exhausted from the long run, horrified and unnerved by the ghastly and bloody scenes he had witnessed and the same fate he himself had so narrowly escaped, Monroe was unable to return there with his mother. She resolved to go to the Rock Creek Station and face the three murderers, hoping some spark of life might still remain in the bodies of her husband and friends and that they might be nursed back to health. But her errand was only a horror, and all in vain.

After viewing the bodies of the murdered men and realizing the helplessness of herself and five young children in this catastrophe, she sent Tom Finan, a boy employed on the McCanles farm, to the home of James McCanles in Johnson County with the news of the murder. He saddled David's favorite and fastest horse and made the journey of fifty miles during the night and early morning of the next day.

The Hickok-Wellman version of the killing was quickly carried to the neighboring ranches at Big and Little Sandy Creeks and to the settlements along the trail by stage and freight drivers. The following morning the Helvey brothers, Frank, Thomas and Jasper, came to Rock Creek Station, gathered up the bodies of McCanles, Woods and Gordon and buried them, McCanles and Woods in a rude box in one grave and Gordon in a blanket in another. Hickok told Frank Helvey that they killed these men in self defense. Frank Helvey has told me at various times, since my first acquaintance with him in 1870, particularly in 1912 when we were both associated on the committee to mark and dedicate monuments on the Oregon Trail, and again in my office a few weeks before his death, which occurred the Fourth Day of July, 1918, at which time I reduced the main points to writing,—that they found the body of McCanles lying on the ground where he fell backwards from the doorstep; Woods around the corner of the cabin with pistol shots in his body and head crushed with a heavy instrument, and Gordon about 80 rods south of the Station, filled with buckshot, and no guns near any of them, corroborating Monroe's account in its most vital and important features—that there was no fight either in the cabin or outside, and that three unarmed men, (not ten) were killed.

On the day following their murder, the bodies of McCanles, Woods and Gordon were buried. Besides the widow McCanles and her five fatherless children from two to twelve years of age, there were present the following named permanent settlers: Frank Helvey, Thomas Helvey, Jasper Helvey, George Weisel, David C. Jenkins, James Blair, William Babcock, John Hughes. I was well acquainted with all of them up to the time of their deaths, and with Frank Helvey, the last survivor of them, intimately for over forty seven years. They all told the same story—that three men were killed; their bodies laid on the ground where they fell, and no guns near them; that four people were implicated in the affair—Hickok, Brink, Mr. and Mrs. Wellman; that none of these persons showed a scratch or a scar as a result of the controversy.

Monroe McCanles told Hansen, even at the age of seventy-six, "the recollections of those eventful days are burned into my memory and are as vivid and distinct as on the days they occurred."

He gave Hansen a step-by-step account of those July days. When Hansen asked if there had been a court hearing, the old pioneer told him a "trial" had been held in the log cabin of "Pap" Towle at Beatrice, the nearest town before a justice of the peace, but his uncle, James McCanles, had always labeled the trial as a farce.

McCanles also insisted to Hansen that although he was an eyewitness, the judge had refused to let him testify although he accepted the testimony of Hickok and the Wellmans.

In June 1926, Hansen began a search for the court records. Finally, in the office of the clerk of the district court in Beatrice, he discovered an envelope containing a clump of yellowing territorial documents. Among them were the judicial records of the McCanles hearing held before T. M. Coulter, justice of the peace for Gage County.

The records, now in the archives of the Nebraska Historical Society, along with Hansen's interviews with the Helvey brothers, James McCanles, and the others, add up to a prima facie case of murder against Hickok and the Wellmans.

The records confirmed Monroe McCanles's charge that the court had refused to allow him to testify although there is an extant subpoena. They also show that, incredibly, the justice not only refused to let the young eyewitness take the stand but he also banned him from the courtroom so he would not hear the testimony of Hickok and the Wellmans. He then called Mrs. Wellman to testify "in favor of the territory," although she was an actual accomplice in the three murders and the wife of one of the defendants. It would appear Justice Coulter was attempting to weaken the Territory's case against the trio and to strengthen the claim of Hickok and the Wellmans that the killings had been done in self-defense.

It should be pointed out that Hickok and the Wellmans were employees of the Overland Stage Company, the most powerful corporation west of the Missouri, and the cabin in Beatrice was packed with the line's drivers and stable hands.

Coulter also knew at the time of the trial that he intended to run for county treasurer; a few months later he was elected. Evidence reveals he was a thief. After one term he was arrested for embezzlement but escaped from the sheriff's custody and disappeared.

An examination of the Nichols article and the subsequent books on Wild Bill Hickok, which picked up Harper's lurid tale right into the twentieth century, reveal:

Hickok told Nichols he had originally gone to the Rock Creek Station to see "an old friend of mine, Mr. Waltman (Wellman)." Actually he was a stable hand at the time and had been transferred from Leavenworth to the station by the stage company.

Nichols also described how McCanles (he spelled it M'Kanles) was such a "desperado" he once dragged "Parson Shipley along the ground with a rope around his neck, almost dead and horses stamping on him . . ."

County records do not reveal a clergyman by the name of Shipley living in the area at that time but in 1923 Charles Dawson, a member of the family who owned the old Rock Creek Station site, interviewed Robert Y. Shibley, who had settled south of the Rock Creek Station. The eighty-year-old Shibley gave

Territory of Nebraska
County of Gage } Ss

The complainant and informant Leroy McCanles of the County of ~~Jones~~ Johnson Territory afforesaid Made before T. M. Coulter Esquire one of the Justices of the Peace in and for Gage County on the 13th day of July 1861 who being duly sworn on his sworn oath says that the crime of Murder has been committed in the county of Jones and that Dutch Bill. Dock and Wellman (thier other names not known) committed the same

Subscribed and
Sworn to before me J. L. McCanles
This 13th day of July 1861
T M Coulter
Justice of the Peace

The murder complaint against Wild Bill Hickok signed by Leroy McCanles, brother of the murdered owner of the Stage and Pony Express station. Hickok is mistakenly named "Dutch Bill." He was known as "Duck Bill," a name given to him by McCanles because of a protruding lip, later covered by Hickok's celebrated moustache. *Courtesy Nebraska State Historical Society*

Dawson an account of the gunfight at the station naming Hickok as the killer of McCanles; four years later Hansen obtained the same version from Monroe McCanles.[4]

Shibley told Dawson he had worked for McCanles many times and found him to be a good friend and a man of integrity. Obviously, he was the "Parson Shipley" Nichols pictured as being dragged behind McCanles's horse.

Court records reveal that E. B. Hendee, sheriff of Gage County, transported Hickok and the Wellmans to Beatrice for the trial and had also guarded them before the hearing was held. Although the sheriff carefully noted every item of expense for the feeding and housing of his prisoners, nowhere is a doctor's fee listed although Hickok told Nichols: "I had eleven buckshot in me. I was cut in thirteen places. All of them bad enough to let the life out of a man. Dr. Mills pulled me safe through it after a bad siege of many a week."

The name of "Dr. Mills" does not appear in the existing sheriff's accounts.

Hansen's investigation of McCanles disclosed he originally came from Iredell County, North Carolina, where his family had settled before the Revolution. He was educated at an Episcopalian military academy and was appointed Commander of General Musters. At twenty-one he was elected sheriff of Watauga County. He left North Carolina with his cousin, James Woods, and headed for the gold fields of Pike's Peak.

After they had met disgruntled miners McCanles abandoned his search for

83.10

2 Oaths	20
Taking Bond	50
Warrant	50
4 Subpoenas	100
3 Subpoenas	75
1 Subpoena	25
4 Sw Witness	40
new Bond	50
1 Oath	10
2 Subpoenas	50
1 Subpoena	25
1 Oath	10
2 Oaths	20
3 Oaths	30
5 Oaths	50
Stat & Sight	40
3 Oaths	30
	645
Judgment	50
	695

Items of Justices Bills in

Justices fees	695
Hendee Sherriffs fees	83, 10
Meyer Constable fees	40
Witnesses fees	
J & H Ney	10.00
M Ney	5.00
J & S Baker	10.00
Jane Wellman	5.00
Ira Mott	5.00
Fred Hagenstine	5.00
J Holmes	5.30
J H Brown	50
M McCanles	5.00
S. Grason	50
	$141.95

This is the Bill of Costs in the Case of Territory of Nebraska against Wm, B, Hickok J, W, Brink & Horrace G, Wellman, on a Charge of Murder which was not Sustained, and the Costs have to Come off of the County. Said Cause was examined before me on July 15-16 & 18th AD 1861.

T. M. Coulter J. P.

The bill of costs for the murder case against Wild Bill Hickok. *Courtesy Nebraska State Historical Society*

gold to settle on the fertile bottomlands of Little Blue River. As the movement west increased he bridged Rock Creek and established the Rock Creek Station, Nebraska Territory, one of the major stops on the Oregon Trail.

Connelley, on the other hand, viewed McCanles as a thief who stole money entrusted to him as sheriff who was also the tax collector. He based his charges on an obscure regional history of Watauga County published in 1915 and not on court records.

Territory of Nebraska }
Gage County } SS

In the Name ~~of the~~ and by the authority of the Territory of Nebraska,

To all Sheriffs constables and Coroners of Said Territory

It appearing that Dutch Bill. Dock and Wellman has Committed the Crime of Murder in the County of Jones you are therefore commanded forthwith to arrest Dutch Bill Dock and Wellman and bring them before me or Some Other Magistrat of this County to be dealt with according to law

T. M. Coulter Justice of Peace

given under my hand this 13th July AD 1861.

The warrant for the arrest of Wild Bill Hickok on a charge of murdering David N. McCanles. These documents were first uncovered by George Hansen in 1926. Hansen's article in the *Nebraska History Magazine* first exposed the Hickok myth. *Courtesy Nebraska State Historical Society*

There is little doubt that the powerfully built, aggressive McCanles was the local bully ready to challenge anyone. Apparently he had heard rumors, it was no secret at the time, that the line was in financial difficulty and he was eager to get his payments. Wellman, a coward, his wife a harridan, left young Hickok to face this threatening man with the formidable reputation. Rather than face McCanles in a fistfight, Hickok killed him, shot Woods, and allowed Wellman to beat to death the dying man without interfering. He also took part in hunting down and killing the wounded Gordon.

Despite his apologists and romanticists down through the years, there is little doubt Hickok and Wellman were guilty of murder in the first degree in the killing of McCanles, Gordon, and Woods. Wellman's wife should have been indicted as an accomplice. Even a century later the "trial" in the backwoods courtroom appears as an outrageous farce.

Connelley's attempts to set up the "voluptuous" Sarah Shull as the catalyst that touched off the killings is ridiculous. Assuming she was a frontier beauty and both McCanles and Hickok were rivals for her affections, she is hardly the motivation for the bloody events of that day.

McCanles came to the station for money legally due him. He and his companions were killed in that explosive situation when events take over men. If there was a motivation for the slaughter it was fear—fear the cowardly Wellman, his slattern wife, and the young, inexperienced Hickok had for the older, physically tough, bullying McCanles. Yet, it was still guns against unarmed men, and the murderous Wellman with his bloody hoe could have been stopped by Hickok. And certainly nothing can be said in Hickok's defense for shooting the second man and taking part in hunting down and murdering the wounded, unarmed third.

Every happening at a stage station, no matter how trivial, was carried with the speed of the wind across the West. It crossed the land with the pony riders and Overland stagecoach drivers, two hundred miles a day or more, over deserts, mountains, and rivers, through Indian attacks, dust storms, and blizzards to be told to the station keepers, stable men, and drovers. It was pawed over and examined item by item—many times embroidered—and then repeated to the bored, bone-weary travelers who were only too happy to hear something other than the monotonous gossip of fellow passengers, the curses of the drivers, and the moaning, eternal wind of the plains.

A killing was big news and the story of the triple shooting at Rock Creek flew from station to station along the trail from the Missouri River to California. There is no doubt the incident would have been soon forgotten in a few months, wiped out by a sensation such as an Indian attack on a homestead, had it not been that the chief actor became Wild Bill Hickok, one of the most colorful figures in frontier history.

At first Hickok insisted he had killed the three men in self-defense, but gradually he added more touches to his alibi until it was generally accepted. Then Buel, the Kansas City reporter, and the writers who followed him, gave the tale additional flourishes.

With time and repeated telling, the incredible lies became the truth. For example, in San Francisco Nat C. Stein, general superintendent of Wells Fargo, wrote on the back of a daguerreotype identifying the scene as the Rock Creek Station and the lone horseman as:

"McCandless [sic], a desperate character, with two others, was shot dead at the Station last August 1861, by our stock tender. It was done in self defense. Seven of these men attacked our stock tender and he had to cope alone against them but succeeded in killing three and putting the rest to flight. He was brought to trial and honorably acquitted . . ."[5]

When the Civil War broke out, Hickok enlisted as a civilian scout at Fort Leavenworth. He took part in the Battle of Wilson's Creek in August 1861, in which Union General Nathaniel Lyon was killed and his command routed. Hickok escaped and appeared that fall in Sedalia as a wagon master.

A legend without confirmation has Hickok losing a train to rebel guerrillas while transporting supplies for General Samuel H. Curtis, commanding the Union armies in southwestern Missouri. He made his way to Independence where he recruited enough volunteers to go back and recover his train.

Leavenworth, Kansas, as Wild Bill knew it. He first stopped here on his way west in 1856. In the 1860s he brought skins into Leavenworth and bought supplies. *The James D. Horan Civil War and Western Americana Collection*

Again it is legend that insists Hickok won his nickname of "Wild Bill" during his stay in Independence.

The popular version has a bartender friend, who had killed a drunken teamster, appealing to Hickok for protection. When a number of the dead man's friends marched on the saloon, Hickok drew his revolver and pointed it at the crowd.

"Leave or there will be more dead men around here than the town can bury," he warned them.

The teamsters hesitated; they could have rushed him but the cold eyes of the man behind the gun never wavered. And, of course, they had heard the story of Rock Creek. After a few jeers and curses they turned away.

A large crowd had gathered to silently watch the outcome of what had looked to be a lynching party. When Hickok holstered his gun a woman called out:

"Good for you, Wild Bill."

The legends and exploits of Wild Bill Hickok during the Civil War are varied and numerous—narrow escapes from Confederate pistols, swimming rivers under intense rifle fire, and a horse named Black Nell so wonderfully trained the animal once hid in tall grass while enemy troops passed the spot.

Nichols included some of the tales in his *Harper's* article; for years they were picked up by other writers and the myths gradually became accepted as facts. Wild Bill, who was his own best press agent, did not dispute them.

Official documents reveal Hickok enlisted as a scout in 1864 at five dollars a day; his duties probably included spying on enemy movements. In the winter of 1865, Brigadier General John Sanborn, based in Springfield, assigned him to report on Confederates "now on Crowley's Ridge." It was his last wartime mission. On June 9 he was discharged and went on to Springfield, Missouri, and another killing . . .[6]

In Springfield, where he met his first biographer, Colonel Nichols, Hickok killed Davis K. (Dave) Tutt, an Arkansas gambler. Their casual friendship dissolved in a quarrel over "a game of cards." On the morning of July 21, 1865, with most of the town watching, Hickok and Tutt had a shootout in the town's square.

After Tutt missed him Hickok fired so quickly, according to witnesses, that both shots sounded like one. Tutt toppled over, a bullet through his heart. Spectators later measured the distance between the two men. Hickok, it was claimed, had killed his man at seventy-five yards, superb marksmanship considering the poor balance and sights of the period's weapons.

Hickok turned his guns over to the sheriff and was arrested on a charge of murder. He was defended by former Arkansas Governor John S. Phelps and acquitted on the ground of self-defense.[7]

In 1867-1869, Hickok served both as a deputy United States marshal with Fort Riley as his headquarters and an army scout in the Indian Wars. Surviving documents indicate his marshal's duties consisted of recovering stolen government property, mainly horses and mules, arresting the thieves, returning deserters to the army, and escorting prisoners to Topeka. He was assisted by William F. (Buffalo Bill) Cody.

In the fall of 1867, the Cheyenne, Kiowa, and Arapaho under Little Raven, Santana, Kicking Bird, and Ateal began raiding. The Overland Stage Company's stages were burned, horse herds driven off, wagon trains annihilated, and women and children taken captive. Companies of weary troopers from Fort Wallace's tiny frontier garrison rode out again and again to track down and battle the hostiles.

On March 26, 1867, Custer, who commanded Fort Riley, joined General Winfield S. Hancock, commander of the Department of Missouri, in his expedition from Fort Harker against the Indians west of Fort Larned. Hancock reached Harker in April. A few days later he moved out with Custer's Seventh Cavalry, Captain John Rziha's Twenty-seventh Infantry, an artillery company, and an engineer corps.

Included in the civilian scouts was Wild Bill, William Comstock, and Edward Guerrier, Custer's French-Indian interpreter. A council was held with the chiefs on April 14, twenty-one miles from Fort Larned. When the tribes slipped out of their lodges during the night, Custer and his command, Wild Bill, and a party of Delaware Indians took up the chase. After several days they were forced to return on account of lack of forage for the horses.[8]

During this period Henry M. Stanley, who would utter the immortal phrase "Dr. Livingston, I presume?," then correspondent for the *Weekly Missouri Democrat,* interviewed Wild Bill at Fort Zarah. Like Colonel Nichols, Stanley was captivated by the picturesque frontiersman. Stanley left a vivid pen picture of Hickok but it was the Nichols incident all over again; he swallowed Hickok's lies without protest. This time Wild Bill's story was how he had captured a band of fifteen killers who tried to rob him in a Fort Leavenworth hotel. However, Stanley's interview added another dimension to Hickok's growing legend. Other large city newspapers sent correspondents to interview Wild Bill, who made sure they never left without enough implausible adventures to thrill their readers.[9]

Head Qrs. Dist. South West Mo.
Springfield Mo. April 3rd, 1864.

Special Orders
No 89

II ...... Upon recommendation of Major John W. Rabb, 2nd Mo. Light Artillery, Capt. S. H. Julien 2nd Mo. Light Artillery, is hereby detailed on recruiting service for his Regiment at Springfield Mo. This detail to take effect from the 26th day of January, 1864.

III ...... Lieut Timothy Middaugh 6th M. S. M. Cavalry Commanding at Wellsville Mo. will send one Section of his Battery with horses Camp and Garrison Equipage to Springfield Mo.

IIII ...... J. B. Hickok, will be taken up on the Rolls of Capt. Owen, A. Q. M. as Scout, at these Head Quarters, from this date and will be furnished a horse, and equipments while on duty as Scout; His compensation will be five dollars per day.

By Order of Brigadier General Sanborn
W. D. Hubbard
1st Lieut & Acting Asst Adjt General

Wild Bill Hickok's appointment as a Union scout in 1864, as listed in the records of the Department of Missouri, District of Southwest Missouri, the United States Army. *Courtesy National Archives*

George Armstrong Custer, who never forgot his scout Wild Bill Hickok. This is Mathew Brady's photograph of Custer taken in Brady's New York City studio. *The James D. Horan Civil War and Western Americana Collection*

Henry M. Stanley's Interview with Wild Bill Hickok, April 4, 1867

James Butler Hickok, commonly called "Wild Bill" is one of the finest examples of that peculiar class now extant, known as Frontiersman, ranger, hunter and Indian scout. He is now thirty-eight years old and since he was thirteen the prairie has been his home. He stands six feet one inch in his moccasins and is as handsome a specimen of a man as could be found. *Harper's* correspondent recently gave a sketch of the career of this remarkable man which excepting a slight exaggeration, was correct. We were prepared, on hearing of "Wild Bill's" presence in camp, to see a person who would prove to be a coarse, illiterate, quarrelsome, obtrusive, obstinate bully; in fact one of those ruffians to be found South and

The soldiers' barracks at Fort Hays, Kansas, 1873. In the summer of 1868, when the Indians went on the warpath, Hickok was hired at Hays as a guide for the Tenth Cavalry for a sweep of the Republican River. *The James D. Horan Civil War and Western Americana Collection*

West, who delights in shedding blood. We confess to being greatly disappointed when, on being introduced to him, we looked on a person who was the very reverse of all that we had imagined. He was dressed in a black sacque coat, brown pants, fancy shirt, leather leggings and had on his head a beaver cap. Tall, straight, broad compact shoulders, herculean chest, narrow waist, and well formed muscular limbs. A fine handsome face, free from any blemish, a light moustache, a thin pointed nose, bluish-gray eyes, with a calm, quiet almost benignant look, yet seemingly possessing some mysterious latent power, a magnificent forehead, hair parted from the center of his forehead and hanging down behind the ears in long silky curls. He is brave, there can be no doubt; that fact is impressed on you at once before he utters a single syllable. He is neither as coarse or as illiterate as *Harper's Monthly* portrays him.

The following verbatim dialogue took place between us: "I say Bill, or Mr. Hickok, how many white men have you killed to your certain knowledge?"

After a little deliberation, he replied, "I would be willing to take my oath on the Bible tomorrow that I have killed over a hundred a long ways off."

"What made you kill all those men; did you kill them without cause or provocation?"

"No, by Heaven! I never killed one man without a good cause."

"How old were you when you killed your first man, and for what cause?"

"I was twenty-eight years old when I killed the first white man, and if ever a man deserved killing he did. He was a gambler and counterfeiter, and I was in a hotel in Leavenworth City then, as seeing some loose characters around, I ordered a room, and as I had some money about me, I thought I would go to it. I had lain some thirty minutes on the bed when I heard some men at the door. I pulled out my revolver and Bowie knife and held them ready, but half concealed, pretending to be asleep. The door was opened and five men entered the room. They whispered together, "Let us kill the son of a b---h; I bet he has got money."

"Gentlemen," he said further, "that was a time, an awful time. I kept perfectly still until just as the knife touched my breast; I sprang aside and buried mine in his heart and then used my revolvers on the others, right and left. Only one was wounded besides the one killed; and then, gentlemen, I dashed through the room and rushed to the fort, procured a lot of soldiers, came to the hotel and captured the whole gang of them, fifteen in all. We searched the cellar and found eleven bodies buried there—men who had been murdered by those villains."

Henry M. Stanley, the famous African explorer, was a correspondent for the *Weekly Missouri Democrat* in the winter of 1867 when Wild Bill Hickok was a scout for the Seventh Cavalry. Stanley interviewed Hickok at Fort Zarah and, like Colonel George Ward Nichols of *Harper's*, swallowed Wild Bill's lies. *The James D. Horan Civil War and Western Americana Collection*

> Turning to us he asked, "Would you have not done the same? That was the first man I killed and I was never sorry for that yet."

When the Indians became restless and war drums echoed along the Republican, Hickok returned to the army as a scout for the Tenth Cavalry. In the winter of 1869, while delivering dispatches between Fort Lyon and Wallace, he was attacked by a Cheyenne war party. In a running fight he was severely wounded in the thigh by an Indian lance.

Hickok's wound, inflicted by a broad-bladed spearhead, refused to heal. After weeks in the fort's hospital he decided to return home to Troy Hills to recuperate.[10]

Hickok, now thirty-two, was soon restless and bored with the all-female company. Still limping, he traveled to Chicago to visit Herman Baldwin, a boyhood friend. Dressed in buckskin and moccasins, he met Baldwin at the La Salle Station and they quickly found a saloon.

After several drinks they decided to play billiards in a pool hall. Hickok's long hair and buckskins soon became the butt of jeers and comments. Several thugs gathered around Hickok and Baldwin and began fingering Wild Bill's costume, calling him "leather britches."

"Everybody in your part of the country wears rawhide and picks his teeth with a Bowie knife?" one asked, as his companions roared.

"No," Bill replied mildly, "but everyone where I come from knows who his father is."

The gang picked up cues and came at Hickok. The greatest gunfighter in the West soon proved he was as good with a pool cue as he was with a Colt. The affair ended with most of Hickok's tormentors sprawled on the floor, bloody and defeated.[11]

A short time later Hickok left Troy Hills to guide Senator Henry S. Wilson's party of politicians and their wives on a tour of the plains. After five weeks the Wilson party returned to Fort Hays. The senator, chairman of the powerful Military Affairs Committee and the secret lover of Rose O'Neal Greenhow, the glamorous Confederate spy, is said to have paid Hickok five hundred dollars and gave him a gift of a brace of ivory handled, custom-made army Colts, the famous "white-handled guns" he wore for the rest of his days.[12]

Wild Bill never returned to the army as a scout but the men under whom he served, such as Custer, never forgot him. Though there is no official confirmation for the often repeated story that he was chief of Custer's scouts, the general and his wife obviously admired Hickok and left vivid memories of him.[13]

General Custer Recalls Wild Bill Hickok

> Whether on foot or on horseback he [Hickok] was one of the most perfect types of physical manhood I ever saw. Of his courage there could be no question: it has been brought to the test on too many occasions to doubt. His skill in the use of the rifle and pistol was unerring; while his deportment was exactly the opposite of what we expected for a man of his surroundings. It was entirely free of bluster and bravado. He seldom spoke of himself unless requested to do so. His conversation, strange to say, never bordered either on the vulgar or blasphemous. His influence among the frontiersmen was unbounded, his word was law, and many are the personal quarrels and disturbances which he has checked among his comrades by the simple announcement that "This has gone far enough," if need be followed by the ominous warning that when persisted in or renewed the quarreler "must settle it with me."

A street scene in Fort Benton, 1884. *Courtesy Historical Society of Montana*

Wild Bill is anything but a quarrelsome man; yet no one but himself can enumerate the many conflicts in which he has been engaged, and which have almost invariably resulted in the death of his adversary. I have personal knowledge of at least half a dozen men whom he has at various times killed, one of these being a member of my command. [One of a group of cavalrymen who tried to gang up on Hickok in Hays City in the summer of 1870.]

Others have been severely wounded, yet he always escaped unhurt. On the plains every man openly carried his belt with its invariable appendages, knife and revolver, often two of the latter. Wild Bill always carried two handsome ivory-handled revolvers of the large size; he was never seen without them. [Probably the handguns given to Hickok by Senator Wilson.]

Wild Bill as Mrs. Custer Remembered Him

Physically he was a delight to look upon. Tall, lithe and free in every motion, he made and walked as if every muscle was perfection, and the careless swing of his body as he moved seemed perfectly in keeping with the man, the country, the time in which he lived. I do not recall anything finer in the way of physical perfection than Wild Bill when he swung himself lightly from his saddle, and with graceful, swaying steps, squarely set shoulders and well pointed head, approached our tent for orders. He was rather fantastically clad but that seemed perfectly in keeping with the time and place. He did not make an armoury of his waist, but carried two pistols. He wore top-boots, riding breeches, and dark blue flannel shirt, with scarlet set in front. A loose neck handkerchief left his fine firm throat free. I do not at all remember his features but the frankly, manly expression of his fearless eyes and his courteous manner gave one a feeling of confidence in his word and in his undaunted courage.[14]

In August 1869, Hickok was appointed sheriff of Ellis County, which included Hays City, a tough, boisterous army town.

From the very first night he took office, Hickok made it known he intended to keep the peace. Guns dangling from his hip, the butt of an ugly bowie knife showing above his boot, a shotgun in one hand, Wild Bill impressed the rowdiest of citizens.

But there were still some who sought to make a reputation by killing Hickok.

Once a small man named Sullivan jumped out of an alley, his six-shooter pointed at Wild Bill's head.

"I got you, Hickok . . . now I'm going to kill you," he cried gleefully.

While Sullivan was calling out to the gathering crowd to watch while he dispatched the great gunfighter, Hickok's hand inched toward his holster. Suddenly he drew his gun and with one shot killed Sullivan.

"He talked his life away," was Hickok's only comment.[15]

Hickok killed at least two men in Hays City, one the town's bully, until he was finally voted out of office. He left without incident but returned in July to experience one of his narrowest escapes.

According to a Topeka newspaper, he was attacked in a saloon by two troopers of the Seventh Cavalry, killing one and severely wounding the other.

Hickok never backed out of a standup gunfight but he was no fool. The Seventh was a clannish regiment that protected its own; Hickok knew that if he stayed in Hays City he would be facing a mob of wild-eyed troopers who would surely swing him up to the nearest tree or pole. So, as the newspaper reported, Wild Bill "made for the prairie and has not been heard of since."[16]

Wild Bill next showed up in Saint Louis, paying the legislature a visit to "meet many old friends among the members." He was now playing the role of a living legend, the deadliest gunfighter on the frontier. He abandoned the fancy buckskins, beaded moccasins topped with a bright yellow neckerchief for a long-tailed frock coat, fancy embroidered vests, and boots of the finest leather. He still wore his hair, described by magazine writers of the time as "golden brown," shoulder length, and the prominent upper lip that had caused McCanles to nickname him "Duck Bill" was hidden by a long curved moustache.

Then in April 1871, Wild Bill Hickok was appointed marshal of Abilene, toughest of the Kansas cow towns . . .

Abilene was at its peak as a depot for the herds of longhorn coming up the Chisholm Trail when Wild Bill succeeded "Bear River" Tom Smith as its marshal.

Smith, one of the best lawmen in the history of the West, had been killed in the fall of 1870; Wild Bill soon made it clear that unlike Smith who had used his fists he was prepared to use his guns to maintain the peace.[17]

Joseph McCoy, who had built Abilene from a collection of shacks into the most important cattle town on the frontier, recalled Hickok's term as "a rule of iron . . . we had to rule it that way. There was no fooling with the courts of the law. When we decided that such a thing was to be done, we did it. Wild Bill cleaned up the town and kept it clean. But we had to kill a few roughs to do it."

Hickok made the Alamo saloon his headquarters and as he had done in Hays City he patrolled the dusty streets, six-gun strapped to his thigh, the butt of the bowie knife sticking out of his belt, derringers hidden under his frock coat, a shotgun or rifle cradled in one arm.

He had confrontations with Ben Thompson and John Wesley Hardin, the Texas gunfighters, killed Thompson's partner, Phil Coe, in the famous Texas Street battle, and mistakenly killed a local lawman, Mike Williams.[18]

One day a circus came to Abilene. When tents were raised in the vacant spaces near the Drovers Hotel, Hickok appeared to keep order. He was startled when he was introduced to the owner, a striking young woman named Mrs. Agnes Lake Thatcher. She fell in love with the tall handsome marshal and tried to get him to the altar but failed. Wild Bill, as he told one of his friends, didn't intend having a "paper collar" put about his neck. Mrs. Thatcher sadly folded her tents and continued her tour of the rowdy cow towns. She never forgot Wild Bill.

Mrs. Thatcher is an incongruous figure in Hickok's colorful life. Born in Doehme, Alsace, in 1826, she was brought to the United States by her parents who settled in Cincinnati. When she was about seventeen she attended the

Wild Bill Hickok in his fringed buckskins and knife and guns, taken in the 1860s. *Courtesy Kansas State Historical Society*

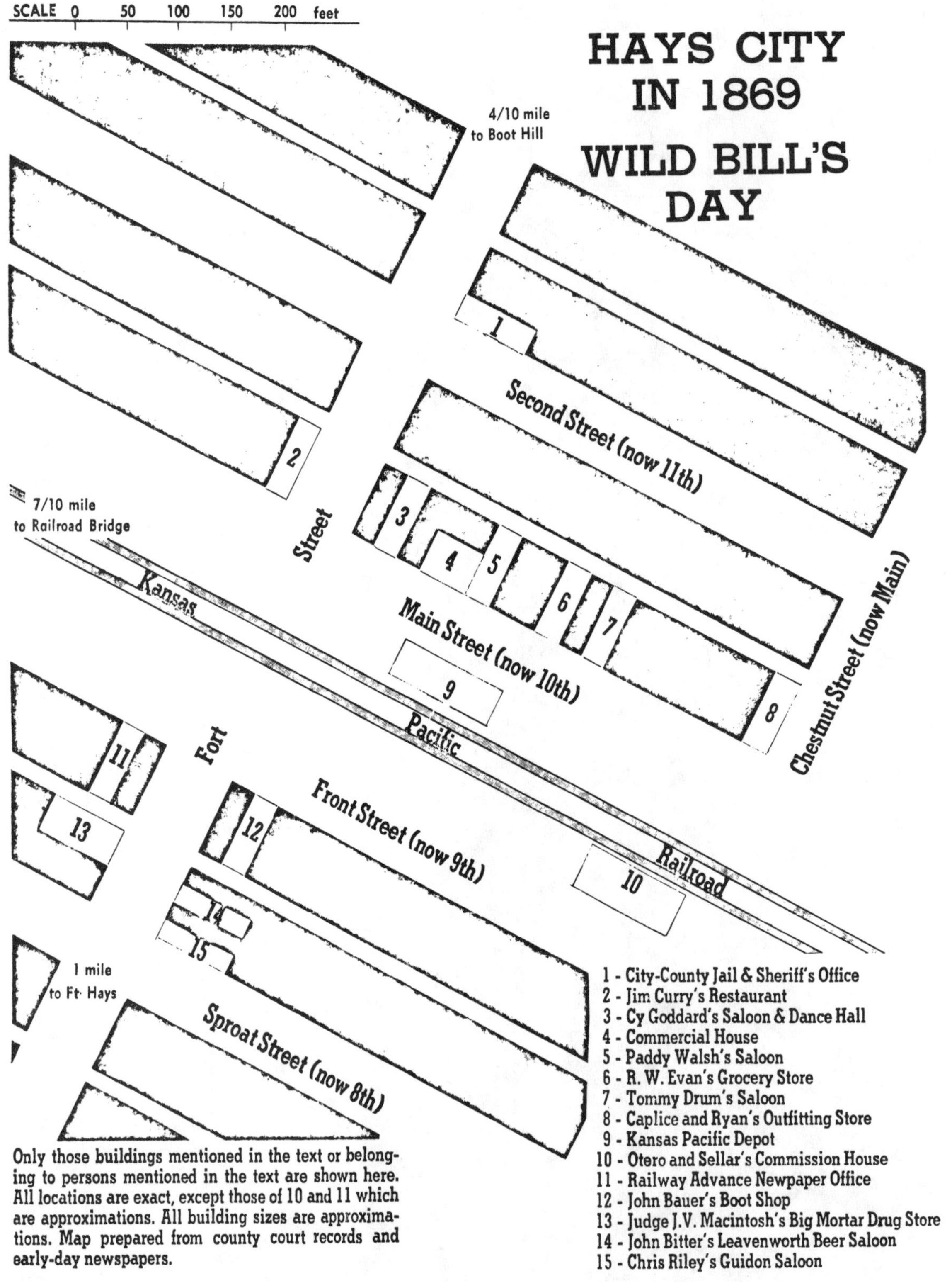

Hays City in 1869, as Wild Bill Hickok knew it. The city, a mile from the fort, was described as "the Sodom of the Plains" by one writer in 1871. Hickok was elected sheriff of Ellis County in 1869 and left Hays in January 1870. In September 1869, after he had killed Sam Strawhun, a local badman, the *Leavenworth Daily Commercial* congratulated him for ridding the town of "such dangerous characters." *Courtesy Father Blaine Burkey, Thomas More Prep: Hays City and the Ellis County Historical Society*

The bodies of troopers Sumner and Welsh, Company "L," Sixth Cavalry, Fort Hays, outside a dance hall in Hays City, September 1873. They had been killed by another trooper, David Roberts, in a drunken gunfight. Roberts was later captured by a posse in Wyandotte, convicted and sentenced to twenty-five years in the state prison. *Courtesy Church Archives, The Church of Jesus Christ of Latter-Day Saints*

4636.

Ellis County
To J B Hickok Dr
To Services as Policeman
1 month + 19 days at
$75.00 per Month $122.50

I certify that the above
account is correct and
remains due and unpaid

J. B. Hickok

Wild Bill's bill for services as a "policeman" for Ellis County. *Courtesy Kansas State Historical Society*

famous Spalding and Rogers Circus and met a young clown named William Lake Thatcher, supposedly the son of a wealthy Bridgeton, New Jersey, family. The young couple fell in love, ran away, and got married.[19]

The Spalding and Rogers show was one of the famous "floating palaces" that were towed up and down the Mississippi by a tug, stopping at small towns and plantations. The show consisted of a large ring in the center of a barge with room for several hundred seats.

When Agnes grew bored she began practicing on the slack wire. She soon became an expert and one of the stars of the show. In the late 1850s her husband went into partnership with John Robinson, and the partners with Agnes as their main attraction then played the river for three years. One of their employees was Fred Bailey who had adopted an orphan named Jim who took his name; he became the famous James A. Bailey of Barnum & Bailey.

During the Civil War period Agnes played her most famous role as Mazeppa in the United States and throughout Europe. Shortly after their return, Lake was shot and killed in Granby, Missouri, by a desperado named Jake Killeon (Kileen, Killyou) after the gunman had been ejected from the show.

Killeen was arrested and served three years. According to one newspaper account, following his release, "he went after a man against whom he had a grudge. The man saw him first and Kileen troubled the world no longer . . ."

The widow continued to manage the circus single-handedly. After Wild Bill declined to accompany her to the altar, she sold her holdings and invested in a Cincinnati lithograph concern. The business failed and she resumed her career with the Great Eastern Circus. Both she and her daughter were expert horsewomen and became stars of the show, each performing in a separate ring. This is said to have been the origin of the two-ring circus.

Not long after the disappointed Mrs. Lake left Abilene, its citizens grew weary of drunken cowboys shooting up their town. In the winter of 1871, the town council published warnings that Abilene would no longer accept "the evils of the cow business" and suggested that drovers seek another shipping point. The Texans took the hint and Abilene soon became just another prairie town. In December the city council thanked Hickok for his service and dismissed him.

After Abilene Hickok began drifting, moving from one cow town to another, living by gambling or occasional jobs as a lawman.

Eyewitness accounts show that in this period he was one of the deadliest gunmen on the frontier. His favorite weapon was a double-action Colt .44 with the catch filed down for hair-trigger action worn in his belt, silk sash, or waistband, butts forward. [Many outlaws used single-action Colt .45s; both Butch Cassidy and the Sundance Kid told Percy Seibert, official of the Concordia tin mines in Bolivia, it was their favorite weapon.]

Robert A. Kane, a big game hunter and editor of *Outdoor Life,* once witnessed an exhibition of Wild Bill's skill with a gun. In the 1870s Hickok was on tour with a theatrical company when Kane and several hunters called at his hotel.[20]

Marshal Thomas J. Smith of Abilene. "Bear River" Smith kept law and order in the cow town with his fists until he was killed by a homesteader. Wild Bill Hickok took his place. *The James D. Horan Civil War and Western Americana Collection*

As his reputation increased, Wild Bill Hickok abandoned his buckskins for a colorful cape, checked pants, and formal coat. This photograph was taken in the late 1860s. *Courtesy Kansas State Historical Society*

Robert A. Kane's Account of Wild Bill Hickok's Marksmanship

When we arrived at his hotel Mr. Hickok treated us with great courtesy, showed us his weapons and offered to do a little shooting for us if it could be arranged for outside the city limits. Accordingly, the early hours of the afternoon found us on the way to the outskirts of the city. Mr. Hickok's weapons were a pair of silver plated S.A.-44 Colt revolvers. Both had pearl handles and were tastefully engraved.

He also had a pair of Remington revolvers of the same calibre.

The more showy pair of Colts were used in the stage performance. On reaching a place suitable for our purpose, Mr. Hickok proceeded to entertain us with the best pistol work which it has been my good fortune to witness.

Standing on the railroad track, in a deep cut, his pistol crackling with the regularity of an old house clock, he struck and dislodged the bleaching pebbles stuck in the face of the bank at a distance of fifteen yards.

Standing about thirty feet from the shooter, one of our party tossed a quart can in the air to the height of about thirty feet. This was perforated three times before it reached the ground, twice with his right hand and once with his left.

Standing between the fences of a country road, which is four rods wide, Mr. Hickok's instinct of location was so accurate that he placed a bullet in each of the fence posts on opposite sides. Both shots were fired simultaneously.

Located between two telegraph poles he placed a bullet in one of them, then wheeled about and with the same weapon planted a bullet in the second. Telegraph poles in that part of the country are about thirty to a mile, or one hundred and seventy feet distant from each other.

Two common bricks were placed on the top board of a fence, about two feet apart and about fifteen yards from the shooter. They were broken with two shots fired from his pistol in either hand, the reports so nearly together that they seemed as one.

His last feat was to me the most remarkable of all. A quart can was thrown by Mr. Hickok himself, which dropped about ten or twenty yards distant. Quickly whipping out his weapons he fired alternately from left to right. Advancing a step with each shot, his bullets striking the earth under the can, kept it in continuous motion until his pistols were empty.

No matter how elusive the target, even when shooting at objects tossed in the air, he never seemed hurried. This trait was of course natural and in part due to his superb physique, which combined and supplemented by his methods and practice and free wild life in the open, developed in him that perfect coordination of hand and eye which was essential to the perfect mastery of the one-hand gun.

In the spring or early summer of 1872, Wild Bill met Colonel Sidney Barnett, son of a Niagara Falls, New York, museum owner. Barnett had hired John B. Omohundro, known as "Texas Jack" to the frontier, to ship several buffalo to Niagara Falls for what was to be advertised as a "buffalo hunt." Texas Jack and a band of Major Frank North's Pawnee were to stage the hunt near Barnett's museum.

Barnett encountered many difficulties and obstacles. Grown buffalo weighing tons were not easy to lasso and load on wagons and in captivity they died. The Pawnee Indian agent refused North's request to allow the Indians to join the show and Barnett ended up with no braves and a few sickly animals.[21] Still determined to put on his show, he sent an agent to Wichita where the town's *Weekly Eagle* reported he was "hiring Mexican greasers" and buying horses, buffalo, and longhorn for the "great sell."

Barnett met Wild Bill in Kansas City and signed him up to manage "the Niagara Falls Buffalo hunt." It is not known how much Hickok was paid.

The show took place on August 28 and 30, 1872, in a large open area near the falls. From newspaper accounts Hickok put on an exciting show with a band of Sac and Fox braves staging a buffalo hunt using blunt arrows, then finally lassoing the big beasts. There were also war dances, a championship lacrosse game between two tribes (undoubtedly Iroquois), a regimental band, and a Canadian tightrope walker. The crowd was disappointingly small and Barnett suffered a staggering financial loss that eventually forced him to sell the museum.

Wild Bill returned to the gambling halls and saloons of Kansas City, Wichita, and Topeka. The following year he was recruited by Buffalo Bill to join him and Texas Jack in Cody's most successful play, *Scouts of the Plains.*[22]

Hickok was a popular attraction but playacting irritated him. Once when he was passed a jug during a tense scene in the play, he spat the liquid on the stage and said:

"Any damn fool would know that was cold tea."

Before he would continue, Buffalo Bill had to replace the tea with whiskey. Hickok also refused to say such lines as "Fear not, fair maiden, by heavens you are safe at last with Wild Bill, who is ever ready to risk life if needed in the defense of weak and helpless womanhood."

He often improvised to the delight of the audience.

A season on the boards was all Wild Bill could stand. He returned again to the West, teaming up at various times with Cody and Texas Jack to guide parties of Englishmen on hunting trips to the North Platte country. Hickok next showed up in Cheyenne. According to Bat Masterson's friend, Alfred Henry Lewis—certainly the most unreliable of sources—Hickok sent messages to the editors of newspapers between Cheyenne and Abilene warning them he would pass through their "prairie dog villages" with his hair worn long as usual. Most frontier editors were proud, fiercely aggressive, intelligent men, and if the story were true they would have answered Hickok on their front pages. A search of the newspapers of the period failed to find any mention of Lewis's obvious fiction.

In March 1873, when Hickok learned from a Missouri newspaper that he was "really dead," killed in a gunfight with a Texan, he quickly sent a note to the editor.[23]

Horatio N. Griffith, A. Augustus Porter.

Office of Griffith & Porter,

Attorneys & Counselors at Law.

Niagara Falls, N. Y., July 3d 1872

Hon. F. A. Walker
Indian Commissioner
Washington D.C.

Dr Sir. At the direction of Mr Sidney Barnett of Clifton, Ontario, I write you to enquire whether there is any way in which, consistently with your duties and in accordance with existing laws and treaty regulations, the services of the indians for the proposed buffalo hunt can be obtained.

Mr Barnett has expended a large amount of money in preparation under the mistaken idea that there would be no difficulty in procuring the men. Mr. Barnett is a reliable man and ready and willing, if possible, to furnish any reasonable amount of security for the safe transfer and return of the indians to their reservations, and is prepared to give ample evidence of his reliable character. It is not the business now office of Govt. I am aware to help men out of bad speculations, but Mr. B. as a young man does not like to begin life with any suspicion of humbug.

Please inform me whether your action can in any way be modified & oblige— Yours &c

A. Aug Porter

The letter of the attorney for Sidney Barnett, son of the owner of a Niagara Falls museum, to the Indian Bureau, asking for the "services" of some Pawnee Indians so the grand buffalo hunt starring Wild Bill Hickok could be staged. *Courtesy National Archives*

A rare photograph of Hickok, second from left. Next to him with a six-shooter in his belt are Buffalo Bill and Texas Jack Omohundro. There is no positive identification for the figures at either end. The man next to Hickok may be Colorado Charley Utter who was with Hickok when he was killed in Deadwood. *Courtesy Denver Public Library, Western History Department*

Wild Bill Denies He Has Been "Corraled"

THE ORIGINAL REPORT:

It begins to look as if "Wild Bill" was really dead. The latest report is that the Texan who corraled the untamed William did so because he lost his brother by Bill's quickness on the trigger. When the Texan shot Wild Bill he asked the crowd in the bar-room if any gentleman had any desire to "mix in"; if so he would wait until he was "heeled" and then take pleasure in killing him. No gentleman expressed a desire to be killed, the Texan got on his horse, and remarking that he had business in Texas, slowly started for the Lone Star State.

WILD BILL'S REPLY:

Springfield, Mo., March 13, '73

To The Editor of the Democrat:

Wishing to correct an error in your paper of the 12th, I will state that no Texan, has, *nor ever will* [newspaper's italics], "corral William." I wish to correct your statement on account of my people. Yours as Ever,

J. B. Hickok

P.S. I have bought your paper in preference to all others since 1857.

J. B. Hickok
or
"Wild Bill."

OPERA HOUSE!
KEOKUK.
Fri. & Sat. April 17 & 18

LINKS BETWEEN CIVILIZATION AND SAVAGERY
ON THE TRAIL!

THE Originals!
LIVING HEROES!

BUFFALO BILL
Hon. WM. F. CODY.

BORDER PERILS!
INDIAN FIGHTS!

TEXAS JACK!
J. B. OMOHUNDRO.

DARING DEEDS!
Representative Men!

WILD BILL!
J. B. HICKOK.

DANGER!
PEACE CONFERENCES!
INDIAN POLICY
TREACHERY!

THE PEERLESS
MORLACCHI!
IN A NEW AND THRILLING DRAMA OF WESTERN BORDER LIFE
Scouts of the Plains!
FULL DRAMATIC COMPANY!
Elaborate Dresses.
HARRY MINER, Business Manager

A rare poster of *Scouts of the Plains*, starring Buffalo Bill, Texas Jack, and Wild Bill Hickok. *The James D. Horan Civil War and Western Americana Collection*

Wild Bill Hickok in New York City in the 1870s. This photograph was taken by George Rockwood. *The James D. Horan Civil War and Western Americana Collection*

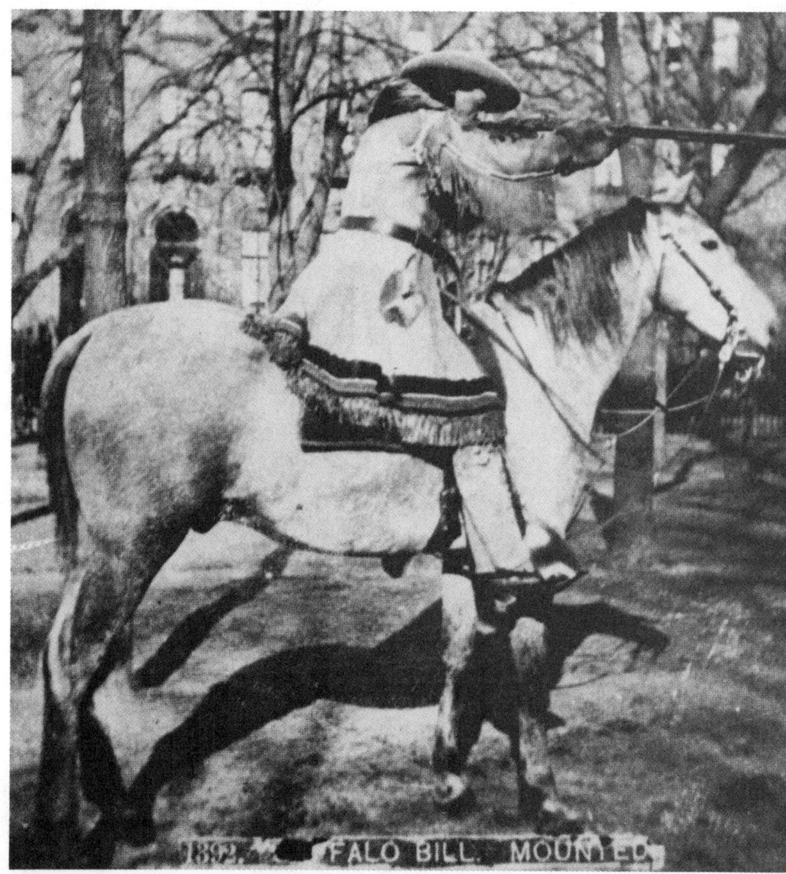

> We take much pleasure in laying Mr. Hickok's statement before the readers of the *Democrat,* most of whom will be glad to learn from his pen that he is "still on deck." But in case you *should* go off suddenly, William, by writing us the particulars we will give you just as fine an obituary notice as we can get up, though we trust that sad pleasure may be deferred for years.
>
> "Wild Bill" or any man killed by mistake in these columns, will be promptly resuscitated upon application or mail. It is not necessary for the deceased to call in person. He will receive just as much by writing.

While Hickok was in Cheyenne it became evident to his friends and admirers that he was suffering from eye trouble that has been variously described as glaucoma, ophthalmia, or an injury resulting from an explosion of a light near his eyes during the tour of the Cody show.[24]

If there were any gunmen eager to gain a reputation by testing Wild Bill's fading eyesight, they never showed up in Cheyenne to make a play against this still formidable giant with the reputation of a man who never misses.

Then on a winter's day in 1876, Agnes Lake Thatcher arrived in Cheyenne from a successful European tour. She had never forgotten Wild Bill and after what appears to have been a month's courtship, they were married in the home of Agnes's friend, A. L. Moyer.

As the *Omaha Daily Bee* commented:[25]

Wild Bill's Wedding to Agnes Lake Thatcher

> Lake's circus has now a new manager. Mrs. Lake ostensibly came to Cheyenne for recreation but really to take advantage of the privileges which leap year gives the ladies. Hickok has always been considered wild and wooly and hard to curry but the proprietress of the best circus on the continent wanted a husband of renown so she laid siege to the not over susceptible heart of the man who has killed his dozens of both whites and Indians.
>
> The contest was short, sharp and decisive and "Wild Bill" went down in the struggle clasping his opponent in both his brawny arms, and now sweet little cupids hover over their pathway and sugar, cream and honey form a delicious paste through which their [they] honeymoon.
>
> Success and happiness attend them, and while on the road of life, may they have every joy vouchsafed to mortals, and we feel confident that Mr. Hickok will see to it that they are never lacking "small hills."

Following a brief honeymoon in Cincinnati, Wild Bill left his bride to go to Deadwood, the new booming gold camp where he would be dealt the dead man's hand . . .

Wild Bill Hickok arrived in Deadwood in the summer of 1876 when the camp was at its peak. The ebb and flow of gold seekers, carts, wagons, and horsemen crowded the one narrow muddy street. The air was filled with jeers, curses, and the pistol shot sounds of drivers' whips. The old buildings were weather-beaten shacks, the new, hastily built structures of raw unpainted pine. Saloons,

A rare photograph of Buffalo Bill in New York City's Central Park. *The James D. Horan Civil War and Western Americana Collection*

An early photograph of Leadville taken by the famous western photographer William Jackson. *The James D. Horan Civil War and Western Americana Collection*

gambling houses, and brothels were open twenty-four hours a day. The common menu was beans and whiskey.

When Hickok stepped down from the wagon, 25,000 men and women lived in the dead end canyon town carved out of the Dakota wilderness. Gamblers, fugitives, gunmen, madams, and whores arrived every hour; among them was Calamity Jane, the pathetic drunk whose ominous name has won her a niche in frontier history.

Hickok soon made his headquarters at Nuttall & Mann's No. 10 saloon on Main Street; the bartender was Harry Young, whom he had known in Hays City. Hickok and Colorado Charlie Utter pitched a tent nearby and settled down to days and nights of continuous gambling.

On the afternoon of August 2, 1876, Hickok was playing poker with three old friends: Carl Mann, owner of the saloon, Captain William R. Massie, a former Missouri River pilot, and Charles Rich, gambler, gunman, and friend of Wild Bill. For the first time Hickok sat with his back to an open door and not against a wall.

Luck was against Hickok and he was forced to borrow fifty dollars in chips from Young, the bartender. He had just picked up his next hand when Jack McCall, a twenty-five-year-old drifter whose ambition was to be known as a famous gunfighter, walked in and shot Hickok in the back of the head, killing

Denver, which Wild Bill left in 1874 guiding a party of "English millionaire hunters." *Photograph by William Jackson, The James D. Horan Civil War and Western Americana Collection*

him instantly. As Hickok's body fell back, his cards fell to the floor—the ace of spades, ace of clubs, two black eights, and the jack of diamonds, from then on known as "the deadman's hand."[26]

The next day McCall was tried by a miners' court and acquitted despite the testimony of Massie, Rich, and Young. The quick verdict may have been returned because interest in the killing vanished after a new sensation had sent shock waves through the gold camp that same day; Indians were moving in for an attack. Word had been brought to the camp by Francisco Moros, a Mexican bullwhacker, who exhibited the head of a warrior he claimed to have killed.

Annie Tallent, a Dakota pioneer, recalled the events of that exciting day in Deadwood.[27]

Annie Tallent Recalls the Murder of Wild Bill Hickok

Late in the afternoon of August 2nd, 1876, the denizens of Deadwood, in the vicinity of lower Main street, were startled by a loud pistol report, immediately followed by the hurried tramping of a multitude of human feet, when the excited cry of "Wild Bill is shot! Wild Bill is shot!" rang out above the wild tumult of the

Holy Bible

MARRIAGE CERTIFICATE

This is to Certify

That Mr James Butler Hickok of Cheyenne in the State of Wyoming and Mrs Agnes L. Thatcher of Cincinnati in the State of Ohio were by me joined together in

HOLY MATRIMONY

on the 5th day of March 1876 in Cheyenne W.T.

Witness

S L Moyer

W. F. Warren
Pastor M. E. Church

The marriage certificate of Wild Bill Hickok and Agnes Lake Thatcher, well-known equestrian and high-wire artist of the 1870s. She is credited with inventing the two-ring circus. *Courtesy Connecticut State Library, Photograph by Gus Johnson, Windsor, Connecticut*

gathering crowd. At almost the same time a man might have been seen backing away up Main street, holding a loaded revolver in each hand to keep at bay a large posse of excited citizens, who were following in close pursuit. After a short chase the desperate man was captured and brought back to No. 10, the scene of the shooting, where he was held in custody to await his fate.

A strong guard was placed around the building to keep the prisoner from the clutches of an excited mob, determined to give him short shrift for his crime. Just at a critical time a force of about fifty well-armed men—the body-guard of Carty, who had just been acquitted of the murder of Hinch—arrived from Gayville with their charge. After setting Carty free at the lower end of town they consented to aid in protecting the prisoner from the threatening mob.

While Wild Bill was playing cards in Nuttall & Maw's [sic] saloon, known as No. 10, wholly unconscious of threatened danger, McCall walked in behind his victim, raised his revolver and fired, the ball entering the back of his head and coming out at the center of his right cheek, killing him instantly.

A meeting of the citizens was called at the theater building, at which Judge W. L. Kuykendall was chosen to preside at the trial of the case. Isaac Brown was elected sheriff, a deputy and twelve guards being appointed by the court. Col. May acted as prosecuting attorney, and Judge Miller defended the prisoner. The only evidence given was by the prisoner himself, who testified that Wild Bill had killed his brother, somewhere in Kansas, and confessed to committing the crime in retaliation. The jury chosen to try the case, after a brief deliberation of about thirty minutes, returned a verdict of "not guilty," much to the surprise and dissatisfaction of hundreds of the people of Deadwood, who declared that trial by jury in the Black Hills was pretty much of a farce, and that in future murder cases Judge Lynch would preside.

Wild Bill's remains were taken charge of and buried by his friends in the old burying-grounds overlooking the Whitewood. His remains were afterwards removed to "Moriah Cemetery," where his ashes now repose. His grave, inclosed by an iron fence, is marked by a rough sandstone obelisk, about six feet in height, surmounted by a bust of the famous scout. This bust has been sadly defaced by relic hunters, by reason of which it to-day bears but a little resemblance to the long-haired, dashing frontiersman of a quarter of a century ago. On the front of the stone beneath crossed revolvers is a carved scroll, bearing, in addition to the ordinary inscription, "Custer was lonely without him."

After McCall was acquitted by a miners' court in Deadwood, he left the camp for Cheyenne and Laramie. As the days passed he grew boastful, describing in detail how he had murdered Wild Bill. One night in August 1876, United

Gayville in Deadwood Gulch, Black Hills, 1876, as Wild Bill knew it. *The James D. Horan Civil War and Western Americana Collection*

States Deputy Marshal Balcombe quietly joined the crowd listening to McCall; the next day the killer was arrested.

It was not a case of legal double jeopardy; the miners' court had taken place on Indian land and as a vigilante action was not recognized by the government.

In October 1876, McCall was indicted for murder and his trial held in Yankton in December.

Carl Mann, the saloon owner, one of the witnesses for the prosecution, gave an excellent eyewitness account of how McCall killed Wild Bill.[28]

Carl Mann Tells How Jack McCall Killed Wild Bill Hickok

I reside at Deadwood and was there August 2nd of this year. The place was then a town of two hundred houses. It is on White Wood Creek. Gayville is about a mile and a half west of Deadwood gulch. Crook City is very nearly east of Deadwood—a little north of east. Bear Butte is a little north of east from Crook City. Deadwood may be about eight miles further west than Bear Butte.

On the second of last August I had a house in Deadwood. There was a saloon there that some of them said I was keeping it. I do not know as I ought to answer questions about my keeping a saloon because it might get me in trouble. There was a building there in which I had an interest in and I knew a man named Wild Bill.

Saw both him and defendant that day in the building. Know of a shooting affair there that day. It was after dinner, about three o'clock probably. Three of us were playing cards with Wild Bill. I heard somebody walking on the floor and when I looked up I saw defendant raise a pistol and fire it at Wild Bill's head. It kind of knocked Bill's head forward and then he fell gradually back.

I saw where a bullet came out on his face before he fell. The pistol was from one foot to eighteen inches from Bill's head. It was a navy sized revolver. The same ball hit Capt. Massie in the arm. I slipped off to get something to defend myself. All went out of my house. McCall pointed his pistol at me and head [had] it on me all the time. He went out before I did. Do not know of any inducements to defendant to confess.

Heard men say that if McCall got up and said Wild Bill killed his brother the jury would clear him. Did not hear any body say so to McCall.

McCall said Wild Bill had killed his brother and he had killed Wild Bill. Did not hear him saying anything more about him doing it again. Saw McCall only twice before this happened and in this house. Bill was there and McCall weighed out some gold dust to get some chips to play poker with Wild Bill and others.

Bill won $23 or $24. Am not certain of the amount. He then went out and came back and played again. After playing a short time he took out a purse and bet five or six dollars and Bill bet twenty or twenty-five more. McCall shoved his purse further onto the board and says, "I call you." Bill won and they came to the bar and asked me to weigh out $20 or $25.

The purse was $16.50 short. Bill said, "You owe me $16.25." McCall said, "yes" and went out. He came back shortly and Bill said, "did I break you?" McCall said, "yes." Bill gave him all the change he had, 75 cents, to buy his supper and told him that if he quit winner in the game he was playing he would give him more. McCall would not take the money and went out in fifteen or twenty minutes.

The cross-examination revealed nothing new.

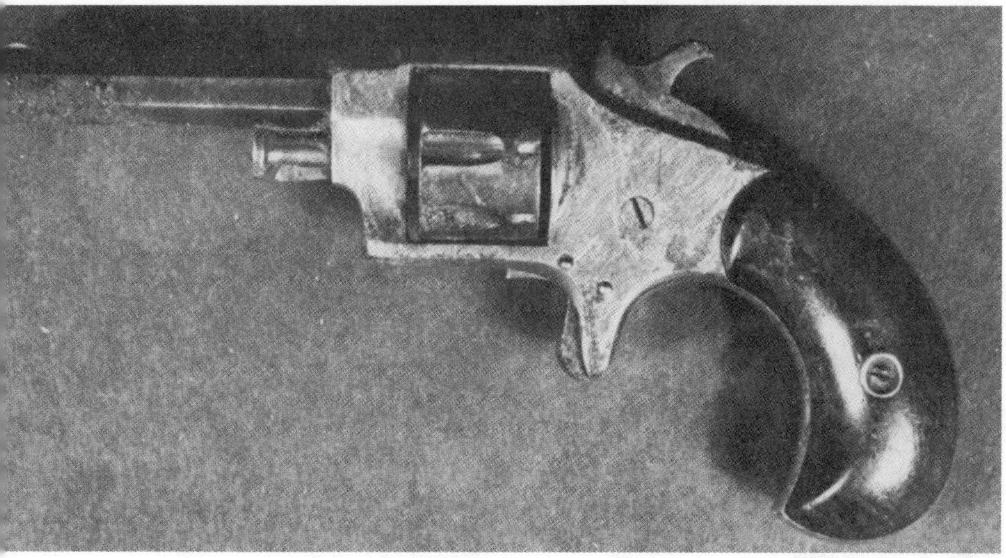

A .22-caliber pistol taken from Jack McCall, who shot and killed Wild Bill Hickok in Deadwood, South Dakota. The weapon was found on McCall after he had been arrested the second time. A miners' jury had acquitted him in Deadwood. The government did not recognize the verdict because the trial had taken place on Indian land. The weapon was owned by Sergeant Theodore Benson, Company C, Fifth Regiment, at Fort Fetterman, who may have been a member of the patrol which arrested McCall. Benson was discharged three days before Custer left for Little Big Horn. *Courtesy Wyoming State Archives and Historical Department*

A Cool Customer.

The following is a copy of a letter recently written to a friend in Denver by Jack McCall, Wild Bill's convicted murderer:

YANKTON, D. T. Jan. 13th, '77.

DEAR FRIEND:

I received your letter and will drop you a few lines to let you know how I am getting along. I am in good health and spirits, hoping when this reaches you that you will be in the same. I have not heard or seen Jack Kelly since I seen you last. McCarty is here yet and will get his trial in April. I have got my trial and will be hung Thursday, the 1st day of March, 1877. I have not heard from any of the boys in the hills. We have had very cold weather here. But comfortable place here. I hope you will get out. You asked me if I thought it would pay to go to the hills in the spring. I think it would if you save your money and above all things let whisky alone. So farewell forever on this earth. Yours,

JACK MCCALL

A letter from Jack McCall, "A Cool Customer," in the *Cheyenne Leader*, February 6, 1877. *Courtesy Wyoming State Historical Society, Research and Publications Division*

Calamity Jane, who legend has chasing Jack McCall, Hickok's killer, and capturing him with a meat cleaver. Jane might have been in Deadwood at the time but took no part in capturing McCall. *The James D. Horan Civil War and Western Americana Collection*

Wild Bill Hickok's grave in Deadwood. He was first buried in Ingleside, then in June 1879, his body was exhumed and removed to Mount Moriah, Deadwood's permanent cemetery. Hickok's Sharps rifle was buried with him. Off to the right is the grave of Calamity Jane who asked, as she lay dying, to be "buried near Bill." In 1891 a statue of Hickok was erected but was mutilated by "relic hunters." In 1902 another statue was placed over the grave. The heavy screen was cut open and the second statue was also defaced. It was finally removed many years ago. *The James D. Horan Civil War and Western Americana Collection*

After a brief trial the case went to the jury, which returned a guilty verdict. Following some minor legal skirmishing that fall, McCall was sentenced to death on January 3, 1877. After the Dakota Territory Supreme Court upheld the verdict, McCall's attorneys appealed to Attorney General Alphonso Taft. On February 19, 1877, the chief clerk, Department of Justice, wired United States Marshal J. H. Burdick at Yankton that the attorney general refused to interfere with the ruling of the territorial high courts. McCall was executed on March 1, 1877, two miles from Yankton.[29]

Yankton, Dakota Territory, where the Jack McCall trial and execution was held. *The James D. Horan Civil War and Western Americana Collection*

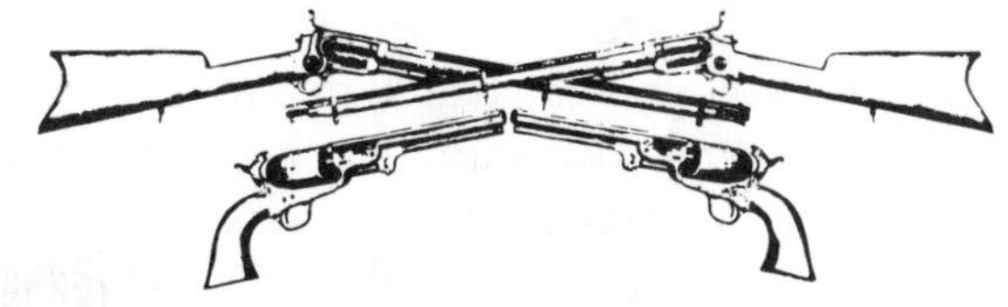

BEN THOMPSON

THERE WERE FEW MEN ON THE WESTERN FRONTIER WHO took part in more historical events or crowded more drama into a forty-three-year life-span than did Ben Thompson—Confederate cavalry officer, secret agent behind federal lines, major in Maximilian's army, Indian fighter, gambler in every cow town of the West, and a precise and ruthless killer.

"It is doubtful, whether in his time there was another man living who could equal him with a pistol in a life and death struggle," wrote Bat Masterson who had worn a tin star in Dodge City during its wildest years.

Only his fellow Texan, John Wesley Hardin, equaled Thompson in the skill of handling a gun, and Kid Curry, Tiger of the Wild Bunch, was his only match for the casualness with which he viewed his own life and those of the men he faced in solitary combat.

Ben was born of English parents in Nova Scotia in 1843. When he was nine his family moved to Austin, Texas. His father, a former British sailor, spent most of his time in saloons. Before he was twelve, Ben and his younger brother Billy, were fighting daily battles with bullies who tormented "drunken Thompson" as he reeled home.

Men who knew Ben as a boy recalled him as "bright, handsome, full of promise and owning an explosive temper." He was thirteen when he shot another youngster in a dispute over his marksmanship. As a frontier newspaper account reported, the extent of the boy's wounds was picking bird shot out of his body while Ben "through some means got clear of punishment." Ben also fought a duel with shotguns in a dispute over some geese.[1]

By this time Ben's father had gone to sea, never to return. He left Ben and Billy to support their mother, "a handsome English woman," and two sisters, by selling fish.

Ben had earlier caught the eye of Colonel John A. Green, a prominent Austin attorney who sent him to Professor Swancoat's private school. Young Thompson proved to be a bright pupil and for two years took honors in every class until he was forced to return home and support his mother.

Colonel Green got him a job in the composing room of Austin's *Southern Intelligencer* where he soon became an apprentice printer. After a year he moved to the *New Orleans Picayune.* One day while riding a horsecar Ben noticed a young Frenchman "forcing his unwelcome attentions on a young woman." Ben interfered, there was a fight—and he threw the Frenchman off the car.

The Frenchman, Emile de Tours, traced Ben to the newspaper office and challenged him to a duel with pistols or swords. But Ben, as the challenged party, had the right under the code duello to choose his weapons, so the young Texan shocked de Tours and his seconds by insisting they enter a darkened room with knives and fight blindfolded to the death.

After some argument de Tours agreed. One morning at dawn they were both blindfolded, each given a bowie knife, and guided into an abandoned icehouse on the outskirts of the city. Then the door was locked on the outside.

The seconds waited in a tense silence. After a few minutes there was a knock and they rushed to open the door. Ben, still blindfolded, stepped out; behind him on the floor was de Tours's slashed lifeless body.

That night de Tours's friends searched the city for Thompson but his friends had insisted he leave at once for Austin.[2]

For a while he worked again in the *Intelligencer*'s composing room, spending his spare time gambling. When he discovered he had a singular skill with cards and guns he discarded his printer's stick for the gambling tables.

He became as good with a six-shooter as he was with cards. Once a notorious gambler with a reputation as a killer called Ben a cheat and challenged him to a gunfight. When the smoked cleared the gambler was dead.

Austin at the time was a rough frontier settlement. Beyond its borders lay the open wilderness, endless herds of buffalo, and the Comanche and Kiowa. It was not unusual for the townspeople to fight off raiding hostiles who swept into the dusty streets. Once when a party of warriors thundered into Austin to take five young girls as hostages, Ben joined the posse that finally caught up with the band. His marksmanship emptied the Indians' saddles until only one escaped and the children were rescued.

Records show Ben joined the Second Cavalry in San Antonio when the Civil War broke out. At Fort Clark he got into a brawl with a lieutenant and a sergeant and killed both. He was jailed but escaped to sign up with another cavalry outfit and took part in several engagements, including the disastrous Battle of LaFourche Crossing in 1863 when his regiment was decimated during a frontal attack under heavy fire. While on leave Ben returned to Austin and married

Catherine Moore, daughter of a local farmer. He returned to duty as a lieutenant assigned to Colonel John (Old Rip) Ford's regiment patroling the Rio Grande.

Trouble and Ben Thompson were never far apart. In Laredo he killed two Mexicans in a gambling hall dispute and outrode a posse to return to Austin. A short time later he was imprisoned for killing a man named John Coombs, again over cards. He escaped and rejoined the army until the surrender at Appomattox.[3]

Back in Austin, Thompson found the war was not over. Federal troops occupied Texas and carpetbaggers controlled the law and the courts. Only a short time after he was reunited with his wife and brother Billy, both Thompsons were arrested and charged with the Coombs shooting.

Like many other prisoners in postwar Texas, Ben and Billy languished for months without a hearing. Their appeal for bail was denied; they were refused particulars of the charge and an opportunity to hire a lawyer.

In Mexico Emperor Maximilian, struggling to retain his throne, had sent out agents to recruit former Confederate officers to help his failing army. Ben accepted a lieutenant's commission. His guards were bribed and one night he slipped out of prison to cross the Rio Grande into Matamoros, Mexico, where he joined the regiment of General Tomas Mejia.

Thompson's adventures as a mercenary were extraordinary. In June 1866, he commanded a company of fifty-eight infantrymen attached to a regiment escorting a "treasure train" headed for Camargo. On the way they were attacked by two Republican army brigades. Thompson, as he recalled, "fought as I have never fought before or since."[4]

He was also present at Queretaro when the city was surrounded by Republican forces under Benito Juarez. Before his escape he witnessed the surrender of the generals, including Mejia, who were later executed.

The role Thompson played in Mexico is not well known. For some reason he never mentioned that period in his life to newspaper or magazine interviewers. However, a short time before he was killed, he agreed to assist his biographer, William M. Walton, an Austin judge, "who has known him as a child." Thompson gave Walton a number of long and detailed interviews in which he told of his experiences in Mexico and on the frontier. Walton had the good sense to use the interviews as he had recorded them. Here are two sections of that now extremely rare book, *Life and Adventures of Ben Thompson*, published in 1884, the year the gunfighter was killed, in which he tells of his service as an officer in Maximilian's army.[5]

The Battle of the Treasure Train

We went out in fine style, all dressed in the gayest and finest Mexican clothes, high spirits, laughing, singing, anticipating a pleasant journey. Quite a number of the ladies, accomplished and beautiful, accompanied their friends for a few miles, and were escorted on return by a squadron of cavalry. My company was the advance guard on the march. No danger was looked for. Escobedo was thought to be many miles in the interior, and no other enemy in force had been reported; nevertheless I kept as vigilant a watch as if I had known an attack would be made. We marched and camped, and marched the next day until nearly four o'clock, when I was ordered to join the main body, as an attack was threatened from the rear. I hastened to obey the command, but by the time I reached the command the attack had been made, and the fight became general. I obeyed orders, and fought as I never fought before, nor since. Every man, not only of my company, but of the entire force, bore himself as if the success of the fight depended on his single arm. The attack was made by two brigades, and they stood to their work like demons gathering Christian souls. Our men fought for the train, over it, under it, around it, it was no use, the attack was too strong to resist, the fight continued until sundown; out of the fourteen hundred splendid soldiers, we had lost over eleven hundred. Out of my fifty-eight, with which number I went into the fight, I now had but seventeen, and eight of them seriously wounded, the forty-one were not wounded, they were dead, and yet I had not been touched in the flesh; my clothes had many holes in them. Our commander (not Mejia, but a subordinate general, whose name I think was Ignacio Morales, but am not certain), had been struck twice, left arm broken, and a flesh wound in the side. Mules in every team had been killed. We were terribly whipped; the treasure lost. Nothing could be saved but the lives of the few who remained. It was suicidal to fight longer. The general gave the order to retreat, and in darkness and silence we left our dead comrades to the mercy of the jackals and crows.

Ben Thompson at the Fall of Queretaro and His Escape

Maximillian had met with the most serious reverses, his armies defeated, the fickle people rising, and some of his own generals pronouncing against him. He was on the retreat from the City of Mexico. The convocation of his council had failed. General Bazaine had orders from Napoleon to withdraw the French troops, and he was on the march to Vera Cruz.

Mejia was ordered to join Maximillian at Queretaro by rapid marches. Mejia, though a full-blood Indian of low birth, had, by native talent and fortunes of war, risen to high command, and he was faithful to the Emperor, one of the few Mexicans who did not turn traitor to him when the crisis came. He was prompt to conclude and instant in action. Volunteers were called for; he well knew that only such as would volunteer would remain faithful even to him in this hour of adversity; besides, a slow march could serve no purpose, and would only expose him in the open field to attack and destruction by the enemy. Seven hundred and sixty-one men volunteered, I among the number. Preparations for the march were made instantly, and four o'clock in the morning named as the hour to leave the city. The news of the situation had gone abroad in the streets and confusion reigned everywhere. The Mexican is fickle, ungrateful and treacherous. They saw the certain downfall of Maximillian; no power on earth within reach could save him. Ever ready to espouse the stronger side, the soldiers who did not volunteer, joined by the citizens, were ready to declare for Juarez and massacre those who adhered to the Emperor. They were particularly malignant towards the alien mercenaries, and I fell within that class; but the general animosity did not deter me from going, not only on the street, but where I pleased. It is true, I had some personal friends among the natives, and was in less danger than most other aliens. I determined that before the hour of departure I would take one more round to the gambling houses and other places of amusement (they were in full blast, notwithstanding the excitement). The truth is, my finances had again run low, and I was bound to undergo whatever danger there might be in order to fill my purse. The gambling failed me. I came out poorer than when I went in. I drifted around with my friends, and at last entered a fandango hall and was soon engaged in dancing with the handsomest and most graceful senorita I ever saw, and in my life I have seen many. I danced as if there was no hereafter. Oh, how she enjoyed it! As we passed a couple who attracted considerable attention by the energy they displayed in their movements, my eyes encountered those of the man. The recognition was mutual and instantaneous. He was the man who had punched me with the pistol. That, however, was not the place or time for me to have an explanation with him. I went on with the dance, but I did not lose sight of my quick motioned friend, although I did not wish him to see that I had my eye on him.

After a time the dance ended. My partner was seated, and, as is customary, I asked her what wine, confection or ices I should bring her. Before she answered, this man touched me on the shoulder and asked me to step outside the door with him. I excused myself on the plea of the lady. The devil was already jumping out of him through his eyes. He insisted, but had stepped back a pace or two, as if he expected me to comply with his request. I again said "No, you will excuse me." He then had his hand on his knife. He seemed to hesitate a moment, but only a moment, drew quickly and dashed at me. I was just in time; a step sideways and backward avoided the blow. I struck him on the head with my pistol, and then, as rapidly as thought, shot him four times. I don't think he even moved after he fell—and he commenced falling on the first shot—nor did I shoot after he touched the floor. The sound of the report had not ceased before I was out at the door and in the dark. Pursuit was made, but I was some distance ahead, and safely reached the quarters of General Mejia. His kindness will never be forgotten, nor even grow dim on the records of my memory. I explained to him. He said: "Never mind, we will soon be far from here." He handed me two rolls of gold—two thousand dollars—and remarked: "Every man must be his own commissary." It was verging on to three o'clock. The general had not slept, nor did he propose to do so. I wrote to my wife, and also dispatched a note to Nestor Moxan at Brownsville, then law partner of Judge Stephen Powers, asking him to send over and get my mule Dan and keep him for me. I was then ready for the ride, let it end where or how it might. Nestor Moxan was as brave a man and true a friend as ever stood in the breach where danger was hurled from within or without. He was afterwards killed in a duel with de Pana y Pana, on the West bank of the Rio Grande River, in sight of where I was born.

Four o'clock came, and every man was ready—gun, pistol, knife, lasso, jerked beef, prepared corn, water gourd, active horse, brave heart and love for General Mejia, who rode at the head brave, as faithful to the Emperor, as we to him. "To Vueretaro to succor the Emperor," cried he; "my comrades follow, endure and fight with me." The distance was three hundred and sixty miles as the crow flies—somewhat further as the roads ran. I have been on a great many rides, but this was the most energetic, determined, constant and compact I have ever participated in. The distance whatever it was, submitted to us in less than ninety-six hours, and but twenty-three of the men fell by the way—they from exhaustion, and not from want of will to do or attachment to our glorious leader. We entered Queretaro on the fourth night a little after twelve o'clock. I am no admirer of emperor or kings, as such, but when the dignity is embodied in a grand personage, no man can fail to accord some degree of homage. Mejia was entitled to see and speak to his chief, whom he idolized. I could go where Mejia went. I was his close follower and humble friend; he recognized and treated me as such. I heard the greeting between these men. It was full of fidelity on one side and gratitude on the other. I am not able to forget the impression Emperor Maximillian made on me. His presence was the magnificence of human appearance. I will not try to describe him. He knew that a few hours would decide his fate. Escobedo, the late antagonist of Mejia, the revengeful enemy of the Emperor, with a large force was in hot pursuit of the now fleeing head of the nation, Queretaro was the final point of retreat—this, all who reasoned, knew.

Escobedo, flushed with victory on many treacherously fought fields, followed, like the waves of the sea, relentless, and if animate insatiate. The interview and consultation between the Emperor, Miramon and Mejia hardly ended before the dread flag of Escobedo, the champion of Juarez, appeared with demand for unconditional surrender. Surrender was death; defence impossible. Maximillian tried to retrieve a fatal step. His capitol was his strength; he had unadvisedly left it, and now sought to regain it. Escobedo—impatient, fiery, impetuous—had not waited for a reply under his flag. Preparing to assault the wall, he was met with open-handed treachery; the defences were yielded, and before the Emperor was even aware that other than truce was meant he and his generals were surrounded by Escobedo's best and most trusted men.

The Emperor, Miramon and Mejia were prisoners, with no hope of rescue.

Not so the men, though weary to death by the long and desperate ride. Jean Lefebre and I determined to escape if we could. The capture of the Emperor and his two trusted, most trusted generals, Miramon and Mejia, gave a confused rejoicing to the enemy that permitted escapes that would otherwise have been impossible. We did escape from the town, changed our horses by force, or fraud, if you choose to call it so, and fled in the direction of Vera Cruz, whither we knew General Bazaine had withdrawn the French troops, the desire of our lives was to reach and get inside the French lines. The ride towards Queretaro, under Mejia, was to succour the imperiled Emperor; now it was to save our own lives—no longer useful to the chief, but dear to us. Our lives! What will we not do to keep them—unless, worthless, depraved as they may be—Vera Cruz, Bazaine, the French.

Two hundred and eighty miles; no American, no Frenchman, who was not friend to Maximillian; the country aroused; every Mexican an enemy, and none but Mexicans on the line of flight. How we reached the protection of the tricolored flag and rested under the folds of Fleur-de-lis, I never knew and will not try to tell.

History has recorded the fate of the captured, and of him who hesitated. Better had it been to then die than in after years, by solemn trial, be declared traitor to his country and his race, and, by the ruthless hand of executioner, despoiled of the insignia of rank and honor.

Slowly dragged along the toiling column; the wounds of the wretched soldiers re-opened; the strong and robust became pale and emaciated; the tropical sun reached and scorched them to the marrow; they fell, and died where they fell; thousands were reduced to hundreds, and hundreds to tens, and yet the march continued.

I had, by great effort, fought blighting disease, and beat it back from me, while thousands died on the march, but at sight of the city, energy gave way and I was seized with the most malignant type of the yellow fever.

After we joined the French it was a matter of serious and earnest thought with me as to what course I should pursue. To Vera Cruz I must go; this I knew; but after reaching there, what then? My mind recurred to my early dream of seeing the Pacific slope, and trying my fortune there; the desire, reawakened by the memory of the dream, was not impossible of gratification. I had the money, and all I had to do was, when comparative quiet should be restored, to pass back to Queretaro to the great City of Mexico; from thence to Mazatlan, and onward to San Francisco. It was feasible. By day and night the thought, the hope, the dream danced through my mind I had resolved; I would do it. But when the fever struck me I saw my hopes fade as the shadows lengthen in the rays of the descending sun. The conviction fastened itself upon me that this sickness would end in death. I had seen thousands die; so few recover in sickness so deadly as mine. But I did not die; the sickness was long, and I rose a skeleton. Months had elapsed. The French were gone, and I, indebted for my life to the noble Sisters of Charity, Sister Josefa having had special charge of me, who there, as the world over, are the most devoted and unselfish women who live. When I was sufficiently recovered to think and to look about me, I found my money greatly decreased, though I know as I live that all the missing coins had been expended on me in my sickness and invalidism; besides, a stray newspaper, the New York Herald, found its way to me, and from it I learned that civil government had been established in Texas, J. W. Throckmorton elected governor. My heart longed for home. There was no barrier to my return; no reason why I should longer expatriate myself. I had done nothing for which I was afraid to meet the gaze of twelve jurors and hear the charge of any honest judge. I returned, and was again clasped in the arms of my wife and to the heart of my mother.

Thompson arrived in Austin to discover Congress had dismissed the newly elected governors and legislatures of southern states and ordered the military to retain order. Ben insisted to his biographer that, although he carefully avoided any trouble on his return, the Yankees had a long memory and he and his brother Billy were arrested as fugitives from justice, ironed and placed in the bullpen.

A military court was convened a mile from the pen; Ben and Billy were forced to walk the distance carrying their chain and ball, which weighed a hundred pounds.

At the conclusion of a five-week trial, they could barely hobble because of the deep wounds caused by the leg shackles. The court returned a guilty verdict and both were sentenced to ten years at hard labor in Huntsville Prison. After serving two years they were released when a civil government replaced military rule.

Herds of Texas longhorn were now moving up the Chisholm Trail to the railheads of Kansas; by 1871 more than 600,000 steer were in the pens of Abilene. Returning drovers reported to Ben the town was wide open and a gambler's mecca. In June Thompson arrived in Abilene with only enough money to buy a night's lodging and breakfast.

Gambling houses, saloons, and brothels were open day and night, poker and monte games went on continuously with fortunes sliding across the tables. Ben pawned his six-shooter and sat in the first poker game he could find; when it ended several hours later he had won $2,583.

Another Austin gambler who arrived in Abilene about the same time was Phil Coe, a tall, slender, mild-mannered man who had served on the Rio Grande with Ben. Coe had several thousand dollars so they formed a partnership and

Dodge City in 1879, "the Beautiful Bibulous Babylon of the Frontier," as one editor called the raw trail's end town. *Courtesy Kansas State Historical Society*

A rare photograph of building one of the first hotels in Dodge City. *The James D. Horan Civil War and Western Americana Collection*

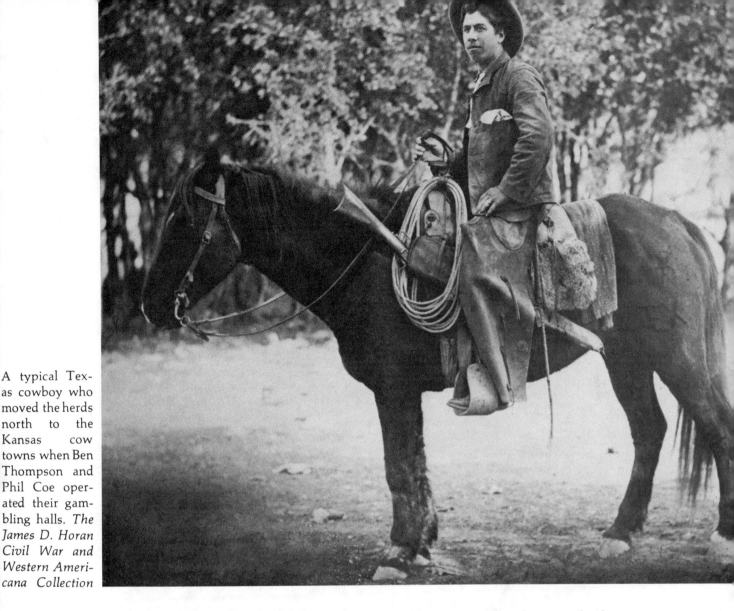

A typical Texas cowboy who moved the herds north to the Kansas cow towns when Ben Thompson and Phil Coe operated their gambling halls. *The James D. Horan Civil War and Western Americana Collection*

opened the Bull's Head Saloon, the most notorious gambling house and saloon in Abilene's rowdy history.[6]

Wild Bill Hickok wore the town's tin star; the flamboyant lawman, fresh from Hays City, controlled the wildest of Kansas cow towns with only two deputies and his reputation as the deadliest of gunfighters. He had the difficult task of keeping the wild Texas cowhands under control and still make sure they spent their money in the town.

The Texans found Wild Bill a formidable figure. A cowhand who had watched Hickok patrol Abilene's streets recalled:

"He wore a low-crowned, wide black hat and frock coat. When I came along the street he was standing there with his back to the wall and his thumbs hooked into his red sash. He stood there and rolled his head from side to side looking at everything and everybody from under his eyebrows—just like a mad old bull. I decided then and there I didn't want any part of him."[7]

The Bull's Head was a booming success, patronized by the thousands of Texans who came to Abilene with the herds. The other saloon owners resented its popularity and the legendary tale is that they conspired with Wild Bill to kill Thompson.

THE

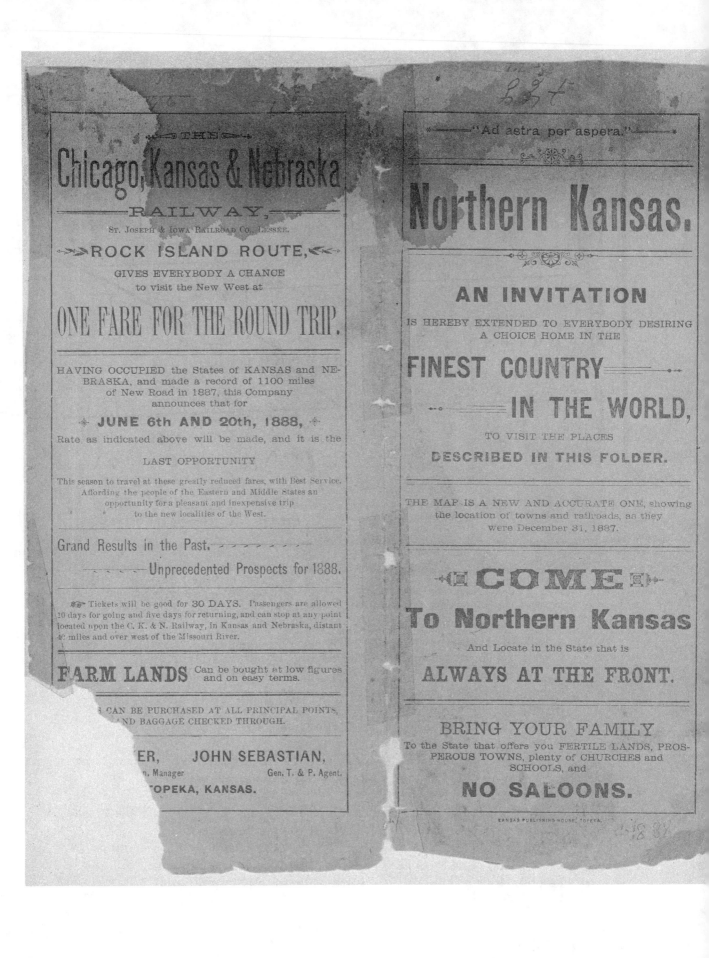

Chicago, Kansas & Nebraska

RAILWAY,

St. Joseph & Iowa Railroad Co., Lessee.

ROCK ISLAND ROUTE,

GIVES EVERYBODY A CHANCE
to visit the New West at

ONE FARE FOR THE ROUND TRIP.

HAVING OCCUPIED the States of KANSAS and NEBRASKA, and made a record of 1100 miles of New Road in 1887, this Company announces that for

JUNE 6th AND 20th, 1888,

Rate as indicated above will be made, and it is the

LAST OPPORTUNITY

This season to travel at these greatly reduced fares, with Best Service. Affording the people of the Eastern and Middle States an opportunity for a pleasant and inexpensive trip to the new localities of the West.

Grand Results in the Past.

Unprecedented Prospects for 1888.

Tickets will be good for 30 DAYS. Passengers are allowed 10 days for going and five days for returning, and can stop at any point located upon the C. K. & N. Railway, in Kansas and Nebraska, distant 40 miles and over west of the Missouri River.

FARM LANDS Can be bought at low figures and on easy terms.

…S CAN BE PURCHASED AT ALL PRINCIPAL POINTS, …ND BAGGAGE CHECKED THROUGH.

…ER, JOHN SEBASTIAN,
…n. Manager Gen. T. & P. Agent.
…TOPEKA, KANSAS.

"Ad astra per aspera."

Northern Kansas.

AN INVITATION

IS HEREBY EXTENDED TO EVERYBODY DESIRING A CHOICE HOME IN THE

FINEST COUNTRY IN THE WORLD,

TO VISIT THE PLACES

DESCRIBED IN THIS FOLDER.

THE MAP IS A NEW AND ACCURATE ONE, showing the location of towns and railroads, as they were December 31, 1887.

COME

To Northern Kansas

And Locate in the State that is

ALWAYS AT THE FRONT.

BRING YOUR FAMILY

To the State that offers you FERTILE LANDS, PROSPEROUS TOWNS, plenty of CHURCHES and SCHOOLS, and

NO SALOONS.

KANSAS PUBLISHING HOUSE, TOPEKA.

WASHINGTON,

The county seat of the "banner corn, stock, and tame-grass county of Kansas," extends a cordial invitation to people desiring a home in a substantial and enterprising city of 3,000 population, largely American. We have six churches, fine graded schools, a $40,000 court house all paid for, electric lights, beautiful homes, solid business houses, two railroads, and not a dollar of debt. This year we will build a city hall, go 2,000 feet, if necessary, into the earth for good coal or gas, and build a large number of business houses and residences. We want good farmers, fruit-raisers, dairymen and stock-raisers to come here and get rich. If you are coming west you will find friends in Washington city and county. We never had a boom and never want one, but we guarantee safe and satisfactory investments for all. We raised as good corn, oats, fruit, tame grasses, etc., in 1887, as were ever raised in any place, and the prospects for 1888 are grand. We never had a failure of crops, and we have the cheapest land in Kansas, considering that the county is 25 years old and in the best and safest part of the best State in the world. A grand reunion of old soldiers will be held at Washington during the fourth week in August. All invited. Address S. PICKARD, President Board of Trade.

WATERVILLE,

Marshall county, is situated in the valley of the Blue river, on the Missouri Pacific Railroad, 100 miles west of Atchison. Our location is in one of the finest agricultural sections in the State. Marshall county is one of two in the State that has averaged 50 bushels of corn to the acre. Hard-wood timber in abundance sells for $3 to $4 per cord. Fine gypsum beds within two miles of the city. Magnesian stone in abundance. Our streams are rapid, with rock bottoms. Two fine water-powers of 500 horse-power within 1½ miles of the city. Wheat worth 75 cents per bushel at our mills, being fully Chicago prices. Have two fine steam elevators, fine stone school building—cost $12,000. Have room for two more flouring mills. Practically no debts, and taxes reasonable. What more can you ask? We invite the agriculturist to one of the finest portions of the great State of Kansas, and to those seeking investments in factories, etc., to the finest water-powers in the State. Address W. J. COWGILL, City Clerk, Waterville, Kansas.

TAXES! TAXES!!

Eastern people read of the high taxes in the West, but it is true that taxes are no higher in Kansas than in the East. The difference is in the assessed value, and most men see no more hardship in paying *five dollars* tax on a property worth $500 but assessed at $100, than in paying the $5 if the property is assessed at $500, though in the first case the rate is five per cent. and the second but 1 per cent.

☞ *In all cases where no address is given, write to any of the names mentioned in this folder, and request further information. It will be sent you.*

Look out for the excursions of 1888. ONLY HALF FARE. Be sure that you come to Kansas this year.

10

"Come to Northern Kansas," a rare original pamphlet, issued by the Chicago, Kansas & Nebraska Railway to encourage settlers. *The James D. Horan Civil War and Western Americana Collection*

Ben Thompson in the role of a successful frontier gambler. *The James D. Horan Civil War and Western Americana Collection*

From their first meeting Thompson and Hickok viewed each other with suspicion and hostility. Even without the Bull's Head as a source of disagreement, they would have been enemies on an open prairie. Ben hated Yankees and Wild Bill was contemptuous of Texans, particularly Texas gamblers.

City officials demanded that Thompson and Coe change the Bull's Head sign, an exaggerated painting of a longhorn's sexual organ. When the gamblers ignored their complaint, Hickok marched to the saloon and stood outside with a shotgun while painters made the necessary alterations.

Hickok continued to harass the Bull's Head; a few weeks later he forced the owners to move their faro equipment out of the back room to the front of the saloon.

Ben and Wild Bill never had a confrontation, but tension mounted every night when the long-haired Hickok walked down Texas Street to enter the Bull's Head's crowded bar. Thompson thought his troubles were over when John Wesley Hardin came into town with a herd. The young Texan's reputation as a killer had reached the cow towns but instead of facing the young gunman with a six-shooter, Hickok wisely sat down with Hardin and, over a bottle of champagne, made him promise not to "embarrass the marshal" during his stay in Abilene. A few nights later Hardin killed a man in a fight and left for Texas.[8]

By the midsummer of 1871, Abilene quieted down as the cattle business started to fall off preparatory to the panic of 1873; unemployment was increasing in the eastern cities and the demand for meat was declining.

Ben, lonely for his family, telegraphed his wife to join him. Kate and their six-year-old son arrived at Kansas City, Missouri, but with tragic results—their carriage overturned on the city's outskirts, severely injuring all three. Kate's crushed arm had to be amputated, their son's foot was broken, and Ben's leg fractured.

Doctors treated them for the rest of the summer at the Lincoln Hotel in Kansas City until Ben decided he had enough of Abilene. He and Coe sold the saloon and in late September the Thompsons started for Texas, moving short distances by rail and stagecoach. Coe remained behind to work as a professional gambler. Somewhere on the trail Ben met Bud Cotton, a Texas drover returning after selling his herd in Abilene. He stunned Ben by informing him he was bringing Coe's body back to Austin for burial.

As Cotton told the story, shortly after Ben had left, Coe and Wild Bill had a bitter argument over Jessie Hazel, a pretty young tart. There was no gunplay because Coe was unarmed.

On October 5 the Dickinson County Fair opened; cattlemen and cowhands announced it would be their farewell to Abilene. Hickok, who evidently didn't want the wild Texans killing any visiting farmers or homesteaders, announced that anyone firing a gun within the town's limits would be arrested.

Coe, accompanied by a singing, whooping crowd, walked down Texas Street toward the Alamo. For some reason Coe, who seldom carried a gun, had strapped on a gun belt and six-shooter. On the way to the saloon the exuberant Coe fired a shot in the air.

Hickok stormed out of the Alamo, his favorite saloon, and demanded to know who had fired the shot. Coe, gun in hand, admitted he was the lawbreaker.

When Hickok started cursing him, Coe fired, the bullet going through Wild Bill's coat. Hickok's six-shooter roared and Coe crumpled on the wooden sidewalk. Hearing the shots, Deputy Marshal Mike Williams came running around the corner. Hickok, who was holding off the angry, threatening crowd, spun around and fired at the approaching shadow, killing Williams by mistake.

After he discovered he had killed his friend and deputy, Hickok went on a wild rampage, smashing up the Texas Street bars, shooting out their lights, and challenging the cowhands to get back to their camps or fight. No one stood up to the wild-eyed man in the frock coat and shoulder-length hair.

As Cotton told Thompson: "There was only one man who would have faced him—and you weren't there, Ben."

When Cotton took Thompson back to his camp, the cattleman later recalled Thompson put his head on Coe's casket and wept.[9]

The death of Coe and the injuries of Ben's wife and son shattered him. For months he was moody and irritable, seldom visiting his gambling house in Austin and refusing to sit in the big monte or poker games. It was a year before he was back at the tables—this time listening to the drovers and cowhands describe Ellsworth, the Kansas cow town that was twice as big and open as Abilene . . .

Ben and Billy Thompson arrived in Ellsworth in June 1873, and opened a gambling house in the rear of a saloon. Ben was popular with the cowhands and his "gambler's roost," as the town's newspaper called it, was a success.

For all its boasting Ellsworth was not as wild as Abilene. Cowhands fresh from the trail would ride in shooting at signs and shattering windows and streetlamps but there were few gunfights. A force of deputies under Sheriff Chauncey B. Whitney, veteran of the Indian Wars, allowed the hands to blow off steam, then made them pay the damages and usually bought them a drink. More than once Ben helped Whitney disarm a drunken, would-be gunfighter and he and the sheriff became close friends.

On the afternoon of August 15, 1873, the famous Battle of Ellsworth took place. It began in a saloon when Ben asked Jack Sterling, another gambler, to pay off a debt. Sterling, who knew Ben was unarmed, struck him in the face. Ben went for Sterling but Deputy Sheriffs Happy Jack Morco and Edward Hogue held him off with six-shooters.

Later Ben and Billy went looking for Sterling and Morco. By Billy Thompson's own admission, he had been drinking heavily all afternoon and was drunk when he joined his brother. They met near the railroad depot with Ben offering Sterling and Morco a chance to fight. Sheriff Whitney, who had been summoned, tried to act as peacemaker.

Unarmed, he walked toward the Thompsons, calling out:

"Boys, let's not have any fuss or difficulty."

"We don't want any trouble, sheriff," Ben replied, "but we intend to defend ourselves if they want to fight."

"Put up your guns and I will see that you will be protected," Whitney promised.

"I'm satisfied that you will," Ben told him. "Let's have a drink and get Billy to put his gun away."

The railway station, Ellsworth, Kansas, 1872, where Ben Thompson and his brother, Billy, had their confrontation with Deputy John "Happy Jack" Morco and gambler Jack Sterling. *Courtesy Kansas State Historical Society*

Main Street, Ellsworth, Kansas, 1879. At the peak of the cattle drives, the local newspaper boasted that Ellsworth would be "the liveliest town in Kansas." County Sheriff Chauncey B. Whitney was killed by Billy Thompson on Main Street during the famous Battle of Ellsworth on August 15, 1873. *Courtesy Kansas State Historical Society*

The trio walked back up Main Street to Brennan's saloon, a popular meeting place for cowhands and drovers. Billy and Whitney walked in but as Ben was about to follow someone shouted:

"Look out, Ben, here they come with guns!"

Ben whirled about to see Sterling and Morco, guns drawn, advancing toward him. As he pulled his six-shooter, Sterling and Morco jumped into a store entrance and Ben's shot splintered the wood where they had been standing.

How Sheriff Whitney was killed was described by Thompson to Judge Walton.[10]

Left: Billy Thompson, Ben's wild, younger brother, whom Bat Masterson once rescued from an Ogallala, Nebraska, jail where he was waiting execution for a killing.

Right: Ellsworth County's sheriff, Chauncey B. Whitney, was accidentally killed by the drunken Billy Thompson during the Battle of Ellsworth, August 1873. *The James D. Horan Civil War and Western Americana Collection*

The Killing of Sheriff Whitney in the Battle of Ellsworth

The hostility towards me on the part of the police at Ellsworth arose from my repeated interference to prevent them from robbing Texans. I have seen those men arrest a stranger (who incautiously exposed money) on grounds as false as a moonless night is dark, and searching him, pretendedly for arms, seize his money, and, when complained of, be sworn out by their friends committing the boldest perjury. When this game was sought to be played on some of the cowboys I vetoed it, and they did not press on or over it; but it gained for me a burning and malignant hatred from them that nothing could appease but my life which would have been taken at almost any time could they have caught me off my guard. I did not want Billy to go out to the engine with me. I felt assured, from the magnitude of the demonstration, that I would be killed, and I did not want him involved with me. Besides, he was drinking too much, and I did not see that he could materially aid me. I felt certain that I could kill enough of the assailants to make a bloody compensation for my life long before they could murder me. The man Hogue, a sort of Deputy Sheriff, and Happy Jack, policeman, were my most inveterate enemies; I had interfered with them more than any others. Their activity in arousing public feeling against me was constant. This I had known for some time, and I deliberately concluded to be certain to kill them if any rush was made on me. I got a shot at each of them, and why I missed them I have never known; there must have been something the matter with the gun. If I had not acted as promptly as I did in firing at them, they would have a lodgment from which they could have shot me to death, in time, if I had not turned my back and sneaked away—a thing I have never done, and never expect to do. I may be killed; but, if so, whether by knife, gun, or pistol, the mortal wound shall enter me in front.

After firing at these men, as has been stated, the eagerness that had been manifested by many to take part in the recontre greatly abated. When Hogue and Happy Jack fled, the mob had no head or leaders, and a coolness and hesitancy showed themselves. It was at this time that Sheriff Whitney came out to where I was. He was my friend and I esteemed him highly. He was an excellent officer, impartial, energetic, merciful and brave. He asked what was the cause of the disturbance. I told him how the matter occurred, and stated to him my belief that it was the intention of Hogue and Happy Jack to murder me. He asked me to surrender my arms to him, and that he would disarm them. This I declined to do until they were first disarmed, saying, "I know they are treacherous and malignant." To this he agreed, and I gave my promise not to be aggressor on them.

We started to the Grand Central Hotel, he and Billy walking in advance, I in the rear. I kept a vigilant watch in every direction, believing, as I did, that either of the two men I have named would not hesitate to assassinate me, although in the hands, or rather in charge of the Sheriff. Glancing behind me when near the hotel, I saw Happy Jack, about sixty yards away, come around the corner of a store, gun in hand, and in the attitude of presenting it at me, though for him to have would have as likely hit the Sheriff and Billy as me. I right-about faced instantly, and drew my gun down on him and fired; but he dodged behind the corner from which he had come, too quick for me. This conduct on his part enraged me, and I concluded to have it out with him then and there, and for that reason started in a rapid walk toward him. This shooting drew the attention of the Sheriff and Billy, the latter of whom stopped, while the other started toward me. Just then Happy Jack stepped from behind the corner again in an excited manner, holding his gun in both hands. I heard the report of a gun behind me, and, turning, found that Sheriff Whitney had been shot. I ran to him, all thought of Happy Jack leaping out of my mind. I also saw Billy lowering his gun; I exclaimed, "My God, Billy, what have you done; you have shot our best friend." He came running up, and said, "Christ, what a misfortune! I tried to shoot Happy Jack, I stumbled and shot Whitney."

It flashed through me instantly that this incident would intensify the excitement to such an extent that there would be but little chance to control it; accident it was, and as undesigned a killing as ever took place. Mr. Whitney died with no malice in his heart toward Billy, firmly believing that neither Billy nor myself, would intentionally have harmed a hair on his head, for any consideration in the world. The storm was at hand now; accident, this it was; but a hated Texan was the author. Sheriff Whitney was greatly beloved by the better class of people, and the rabble had already been worked up to fever heat; he was evidently mortally wounded. He called his wife. The spectacle was pitiable indeed; but the living claimed attention. I knew the mob would be present in a moment. I urged Billy to fly. The misfortune seemed to have confused him worse, instead of shocking him into a sober state of mind; Captain Millett, then of Seguin, furnished a fleet horse, and some money; I gave him one of my pistols and more money, mounted him, and ordered him to ride for his life. He was not sensible of the imminent danger, foolishly rode about shooting his pistol off in the air. I was well nigh crazed myself, but about him. My appeals at last prevailed, and he left. I had made up my mind that if the mob should get hold of him to shoot him down—him, my own brother—and then to empty my gun and pistol in the mob ranks as completely as I could, up to the moment they killed me, for of my death there was no doubt, under such circumstances.

But he left, and thus saved me from that complication. I stood my ground. I had done nothing to put me in flight. Several Texans were around; I was standing by a post, at which horses were usually hitched. Here came Ed Hogue and two others, supported by some citizens at a distance, all armed with muskets, pistols and guns ready for action. They came right up, but strange as it may seem, yet it is faithfully true, they did not see me. Their attention was directed to the squad of Texans, who had been standing a little way from me, who ran to arm themselves when they saw Hogue was coming. They came up and Hogue in a loud voice asked:

"Where are those murderers, the Thompsons?" Their guns were ready for instant use. I saw my chance and improved it. I was in less than ten feet of the policemen. I presented my gun at them and said: "The man who moves I shall kill." They stopped as if petrified. I now said: "Lay your arms down, don't hesitate." They laid them down. I said: "Step away from there, and I will talk to you." They obeyed. I then said: "What is it you want, Billy is gone. He it was who accidentally shot Sheriff Whitney. Why do you apply the term murderer to me?" Hogue replied that he was ordered to arrest me as being concerned in the killing. 'That you cannot do." I said: "I will talk about surrendering to another officer, but you cannot arrest me, nor be concerned in doing so, and you should have known better than to make the effort." "Well," said he, "I will go up and send some one else down." "No," I replied, "you stand right where you are, there will be officers enough here, directly. Where is that scoundrel, Happy Jack, I suppose he is sneaking around some corner to get a sly shot at me?" "I don't know where he is, a moment ago I saw him going toward the mayor's office," replied he. "Very well, let him keep out of my sight, for he is the sole cause of all this trouble, except the contemptible part you have played in it. And were I to do you, as you and Jack have sought to do me, I would shoot you where you stand." The poor fellow was white as a sheet, trembled like a coward, as he was, and would have stood there as long as I might have desired. His two companions were frightened about as badly as he was.

While standing with my gun on these men, a rather laughable incident occurred. A few days before I had borrowed two dollars from a young man by the name of McKinney to make change, and afterwards put the money to repay the loan in my vest pocket, but did not happen to meet him. While standing there as stated, he, in the excitement, came out of the hotel, and in doing so my eye fell on him, and I immediately thought of the money I owed to him. I then held the gun in one hand, took the money out with the other, and called to him to come and get it. He hesitated, did not like to come, but I called positively. He came in a trot, got his money, and away he went; and I have never seen him since. I thought of this matter afterwards, and laughed heartily over the cool impudence of the act.

While thus standing, life hanging on a thread, because no one could tell when the disarmed policeman would be reinforced. The mayor, Mr. Miller, appeared. He is a man of great decision of character, and brave, too. He had been given an exaggerated account of the circumstances, and was disposed to go right over me, but the Henry rifle soon brought him to his senses, and he stood along by the side of Hogue and others. I said to him: "Mr. Mayor, I respect you, and am inclined to surrender to you, but before doing so, must have your word of honor that no mob shall in any way interfere with me and besides Happy Jack and Hogue must be disarmed, or rather the first must be disarmed, and the other not permitted to resume his," and I said further: "I had nothing to do with the unfortunate killing of Sheriff Whitney; his death came through an accident—a lamentable one. He was one of my best friends; but I know people do not reason under excitement, and particularly so when malignity moves them to action. Here is Mr. Larkin, the proprietor of the hotel. He will vouch for me. If you will go and disarm Happy Jack, and declare to me that Hogue shall not again be armed, until the law has dealt with me, I will surrender." He at once agreed to this proposition, and Larkin satisfying the mayor that I would stand, and at an agreed moment surrender, they went off together to disarm Happy Jack. Hogue and his two cubs in the meantime being in a sort of "pound" which I surrounded with my Henry rifle. In a short time, shorter than it would take to tell the facts and circumstances, the mayor and Mr. Larkin returned with Happy Jack unarmed. The mayor was an honorable man, at least I believed it. When he gave the assurances I required I willingly surrendered, knowing that the law could not and would not touch me, so far as the death of Sheriff Whitney was concerned.

After surrendering, I went with the mayor to his office, and it being too late to have an examining trial, I proposed to give bond for my appearance when wanted. The mayor hesitated, but at last concluded to take bond, if resident citizens would go on it—this was an impracticable condition without considerable figuring around; my Texas friends came promptly to the front, and offered to deposit, in money, the amount of the bond—ten thousand dollars; but no, that would not do, there must be bondsmen; but we were equal to the occasion. Seth Mabry and Captain Millett deposited the amount to the credit of responsible citizens, procured their signatures, and I was released; but not before an altercation occurred. When I was taken to the court, a lawyer, who appeared as county attorney for the State, said: "Why there is nothing against this man, he should be turned loose—it is false imprisonment to hold him under restraint." At this point my friend Hogue appeared and said: "You red headed son of a sea cow, what have you to do with this case, you are the misdemeanor attorney," and with that he kicked my friend down stairs, and he did so vigorously. Oh, how I did long to be loose, to throttle Hogue. My friend took his kicking meekly, and went his way—a sorry and humiliated way, I imagine.

This circumstance reminded me of an anecdote of Colonel J. K. McClung, the celebrated duelist of Mississippi. On one occasion he deemed himself insulted by a man in a bar-room and straightway kicked him out of the room; the man uttered no word, but went off. Several days elapsed when the colonel was passing another saloon, and saw a man come sprawling out on the pavement. He stopped and looked in and saw that the man whom he had kicked, was the kicker in this instance. He said to him, "Look here, how is this. I kicked you out of a saloon the other day, and you did not and have not resented it, and now I find you kicking another man out into the street; how is this." "Oh colonel," replied the man, "You and I know who to kick." The bonds were arranged and I was discharged. From there, I went to the theatre, and while sitting there absorbed in the play, which was "She Stoops to Conquer," a friend tapped me on the shoulder, and said: "Billy is in the city." If a streak of lightning on a clear day had struck me I should not have been more surprised. I sat still for a few moments to not attract attention by a sudden leaving, and then departed. I have forgotten to state, that as soon as Billy left and even before I was arrested, a great many officers, regular and special, had left in squads, in pursuit of him, and they were scouring the country in every direction. I knew where Billy would very likely go to when he returned to the city, and I took a round-about way, and went there. He was in a small up-stairs room, and quite sober. His jaunt had shaken off the effects of the whiskey. "What in the name of God, Billy, are you doing here, you ought to be at least thirty or forty miles away." "No, I ought not," he replied, "because you see the country for a long distance is full of officers, the authorities have certainly telegraphed in all directions, and for me to try to pass from this locality now, would end in my arrest. I studied out what they would do, and come to the conclusion to come back to the city, and here I am." "But, what are you going to do," I asked

> him. "I am going to disguise myself as well as I can, and go out to the herds, before daylight, and drive stock in, as I have done for a few days, and then leave with the first bunch that is driven away." "I don't like your plans, but suppose it is the best that can now be done, if we can make your disguise complete." I then studied out a plan of disguise. His hair was very long, hanging down on his shoulders. I first cut that as best I could by shingling it, then made him strip, and colored him to the hue of a Mexican, from head to foot, even between the toes, and then, with yellow paint stained his milk white teeth to the color that is given by tobacco juice; changed his shoes for boots, not new ones, then replaced his Mexican hat with a cap, and his black clothes with second-hand army blue blouse and brownish pants, and he was ready for the road. His most intimate friend would not have known him—should not have known him myself, had I met him accidentally. I instructed him to speak nothing but Spanish, which he could do fluently. I did not want any of the boys to know him, indeed, no one, except Maj. Mabry or Captain Millett. Thus disguised, he drove cattle in and out of Ellsworth for several weeks, without being recognized, and in due time went off in perfect safety.
>
> The next morning I appeared in accordance with the conditions of my bond, but for some reason no witnesses appeared against me, and the prosecution was dismissed.

A short time later Ben left for Kansas City. Whitney's death was followed by another gunfight between Cad Pierce, a popular Texas drover and a deputy. When Pierce died of his wounds a mob of Texans threatened to burn Ellsworth to the ground.

This led to vigilante action. Bands of armed citizens patroled the streets, raiding hotels, saloons, and gambling houses, and giving "undesirables" only a few minutes to leave town "or be the guest of honor at a necktie party."

As the *Topeka Commonwealth* commented: "The trains East are freighted with more infamy than is usually transported in one day . . . the day of August 12 will be remembered in Ellsworth for the exodus of the roughs and the gamblers . . ."

When he heard the gamblers had been forced to leave Ellsworth, Ben returned to Texas. He continued to open gambling houses in cow towns and boom mining camps. Dodge City knew him and so did Leadville, Colorado, when a major gold strike was made there in 1879. He also took part in the Colorado railroad "war" between the Atchison, Topeka and Santa Fe and the Denver and Rio Grande, joining forces with Bat Masterson to lead an army of professional gunfighters who were hired to protect the Sante Fe property.

Ben commanded a company of Texans assigned to guard a large roundhouse south of Pueblo. When the courts finally ordered the Sante Fe to surrender its property to the Denver and Rio Grande, a Pueblo sheriff and one hundred deputies surrounded the roundhouse and ordered Ben to surrender.

Ben answered he had been hired by the railroad and would only give up the property upon written instructions. The sheriff then shouted he and his men had come "to disperse a mob" but Ben only replied there was no mob, "only construction workers."

The following day Ben was taken prisoner after he was lured outside on the pretext of holding a parley with the sheriff. With their leader in jail, Ben's "troops" surrendered. Masterson returned to Dodge City, and Ben, accompanied by a jovial sheriff who drove him to the depot, went back to Austin—richer by $2,300 and several diamonds, which ironically would someday lead to his death.[11]

By the 1870s Ben had the reputation as one of the most dangerous gunfighters on the frontier. Mythmakers credited him with killing twenty-one men, but coroners' inquests, yellowing newspaper clippings, and his many court appearances total his victims at about eight.

Bat Masterson, who probably was a witness to more gunfights and killings during his lawman's career in Dodge City than any man in the West, recalled Thompson's skill with a six-shooter.[12]

Bat Masterson on Ben Thompson

> It is doubtful if in his time there was another man living who equalled him with a pistol in a life-and-death struggle. Thompson in the first place, possessed a much higher order of intelligence than the average man killer of his time. He was absolutely without fear and his nerves were those of the finest metal. He shot at an adversary with the same precision and deliberation that he shot at a target. A past master in the use of a pistol, his aim was as true as his nerves were strong and steady.
>
> Wild Bill Hickok, Wyatt Earp, Billy Tilghman, Charlie Bassett, Luke Short, Clay Allison and Jim Curry were all men who played their part on the lurid edge of our western frontier at the same time Ben was playing his and it is safe to assume that not one of them would have declined the challenge of battle had he flung it down. However, I am constrained to say that little doubt exists in my mind that Thompson would have been the winner . . .

By 1875 Thompson's reputation as a gunfighter had become so widespread that the editor of the *New York Sun* sent a reporter to Texas to ask Thompson to describe his gunfighter's technique.[13]

Ben Thompson on Ben Thompson

> I always make it a rule to let the other fellow fire first. If a man wants to fight, I argue the question with him and try to show him how foolish it would be. If he can't be dissuaded, why, then the fun begins but I always let him have first crack. Then when I fire, you see, I have the verdict of self-defense on my side. I know that he is pretty certain in his hurry, to miss.
>
> I never do.

In the fall of 1879, Ben Thompson, gunfighter, killer, and gambler, ran for city marshal of Austin. His campaign circular was simple and direct. He challenged any man to prove he had ever been dishonest or had ignored the pleas "of the defenseless, timid and weak to protect them from the aggressions and wrongs of the over bearing and strong."

The Robin Hood image failed to enchant the majority of Austin's citizens and

GOVERNOR'S PROCLAMATION.

WHEREAS, C. B. Whitney, Sheriff of Ellsworth County, Kansas, was murdered in the said county of Ellsworth, on the 15th day of August, 1873, by one William Thompson, said Thompson being described as about six feet in height, 26 years of age, dark complexion, brown hair, gray eyes and erect form; and Whereas, the said William Thompson is now at large and a fugitive from justice;

NOW THEREFORE, know ye, that I, Thomas A. Osborn, Governor of the State of Kansas, in pursuance of law, do hereby offer a reward of **FIVE HUNDRED DOLLARS** for the arrest and conviction of the said William Thompson, for the crime above named.

IN TESTIMONY WHEREOF, I have hereunto subscribed my name, and caused to be affixed the Great Seal of the State. Done at Topeka, this 22d day of August, 1873.

THOMAS A. OSBORN.

By the Governor:

W. H. SMALLWOOD, Secretary of State.

Kansas Governor Thomas A. Osborn's proclamation for the arrest of Billy Thompson. *Courtesy Kansas State Historical Society*

Ben Thompson's Austin, Texas, saloon and gambling hall. *The James D. Horan Civil War and Western Americana Collection*

Ben Thompson as city marshal of Austin, Texas. After he had served for a year, the city was described as one of the safest in Texas. *Courtesy Kansas State Historical Society*

he was defeated. However, at the next election he was elected by slightly more than two hundred votes.

Curiously, Ben was an excellent police officer. White, black, or Mexican complainants or prisoners were treated alike. The crime rate fell and records reveal there wasn't a murder or burglary within the town's limits during his term.[14]

In the summer of 1882 Ben resigned after killing an old enemy, Jack Harris, a well-known Texas gambler and owner of San Antonio's Vaudville Theatre, probably the best-known nightclub on the frontier. Its patrons were mostly wealthy cattlemen who not only played for high stakes but also came to see the Irish and German comedy teams, magicians, gymnasts, and the theatre's celebrated high-kicking chorus line.

Ben and Harris had their confrontation at the latter's theatre on July 11, 1882, after an argument over the value of the diamonds Thompson had received as part of his payment in the Colorado railroad "war." Harris, hearing Thompson was gunning for him, prepared himself with a double-barrel shotgun. It was twilight when Ben approached the gambling hall. A screen stood between the entrance and the interior of the place. The theatre's band was blaring on the outside balcony as Ben peered through the blinds and saw Harris cradling his shotgun. There was an exchange of profanity and Harris swung around to fire but Ben, always fast on the draw, got off the first shot, then fired two more into Harris's body as the dying man vainly tried to pull the trigger of his shotgun.

Thompson's murder trial attracted wide attention, not only in the Southwest but in the eastern press. Large crowds flocked to the city to catch a glimpse of the famous gunfighter.

The prosecutor tried to prove that Thompson had actually provoked the fight but eyewitnesses testified Ben was only obeying the frontier's code of self-defense. The jury deliberated for a few hours, then acquitted him.[15]

Ben's return to Austin was unforgettable. His train arrived at sundown but the depot had been packed for hours. A brass band crashed into a lively tune as he stepped down from the coach and several of Austin's city officials and leading merchants hurried forward to greet him as the plaza echoed with cries of "Welcome home, Ben . . ."

When Ben joined his family in a carriage, some of his admirers detached the horses and, followed by the band and crowd, they pulled the carriage to the state capitol while men and women from housetops and windows waved the Confederate stars and bars, hats and handkerchiefs . . .

"Hurray for Ben Thompson . . . Welcome home, Ben . . ."

Then what followed were a number of incidents in Ben's life, some dramatic, some comic, and not a few pathetic.

He returned to his gambling house but curiously the returned hero found business bad. Days when he was forced to close early for lack of customers, he sat alone in the darkened bar drinking and brooding. He suffered from insomnia and prowled the deserted streets of Austin—the police always found it convenient to be in other places—shooting at signs and streetlights, cursing the furies that haunted him. Once he found an Italian organ grinder returning home and shattered the organ with gunfire. The next day, chagrined and apologetic, he hunted up the frightened man and paid him twice the value of his instrument.

Newspaper composing rooms seemed to fascinate him. When he couldn't sleep and there were no more streetlights to shatter, he would visit the composing rooms of the *Daily Austin Statesman* and reminisce about his early days as a printer on the *Austin Intelligencer*. But there were nights when he would come in roaring drunk to kick over the boxes of type and send the printers fleeing from his gunfire.

One night he took a box at the Austin Theatre where a traveling repertory company was presenting *East Lynn.* At the peak of the melodrama he stood up, denounced the villain, took out his six-shooter, and began firing at the actors who dove behind props, leaped into the audience, or fled into the wings. The theatre emptied within minutes leaving Ben shaking with laughter. He had loaded his gun with blanks.

On another occasion he decided to attend the annual dinner of the Cattleman's Convention. He entered the hall flourishing his gun and using the water pitchers for targets. As one account reported, Shanghai Pierce, the famous cattleman, "carried the window sash with him."[16]

Another time, while the judge was on the bench, Ben beat up a complainant who he claimed had "insulted" him. When a warrant was served on him he appeared in court on horseback.

Gradually the Austin newspapers turned against him.

The block of buildings in Austin that was occupied by the *Austin Statesman* and Ben Thompson's gambling hall. The gunfighter, a former printer, visited the *Statesman*'s composing room many times to see old friends. When drunk, however, he would shoot up the composing room, sending type and printers flying. *The James D. Horan Civil War and Western Americana Collection*

El Paso's Sheldon Block, with the Plaza and Hotel Vendome in the distance, as Ben Thompson knew it. *The James D. Horan Civil War and Western Americana Collection*

The First National Bank and the Wells Fargo office in El Paso, as Ben Thompson knew it. *The James D. Horan Civil War and Western Americana Collection*

A rare early photograph of the El Paso National Bank in Ben Thompson's time. *The James D. Horan Civil War and Western Americana Collection*

J. King Fisher, the Texas gunfighter, who was killed with Ben Thompson in the Vaudville Theatre in San Antonio, March 1884. *The James D. Horan Civil War and Western Americana Collection*

"He is a curse to Texas . . . what kind of meat is he eating?" one asked editorially.[17]

Sober, Ben Thompson was soft spoken, courteous, impulsively generous, and fiercely loyal to his friends. Liquor completely changed his personality. Intoxicated, he became arrogant, belligerent, and ready to fight. Danger turned him into a calculating, nerveless killer.

There was an inevitability about his death. He died as he lived by the gun in company of King Fisher, who has blustered his way into the folklore of the West as a handsome, dashing gunfighter, idolized by every young cowhand who made the trip north with the herds.

In reality Fisher was a six-gun bully, a swaggering killer who terrorized Maverick and Uvalde counties with a large band of rustlers, killers, and fugitives from every territory in the West. Napoleon A. Jennings, a Texas Ranger, recalled Fisher in his memoirs as a boasting menace who dressed in flamboyant Mexican clothes and carried two silver plated six-shooters.

Ben Thompson deserved better company in death . . .

The shootings took place on March 11, 1884, in San Antonio. Although he had vowed never again to enter the Vaudville Theatre where he had killed Jack Harris—"it would be my graveyard," he was quoted as saying—Ben allowed Fisher to persuade him to go to the combined theatre, gambling hall, and saloon.

He knew he had many enemies in the city and was aware that Joe Foster, Harris's partner, had warned the police there would be trouble if Thompson entered his place.

To this day controversy surrounds the death of Ben Thompson and King Fisher; every few years an article appears in a scholarly journal of Southwest history debating the details.

There are two versions: testimony taken before the coroner's jury on the

San Antonio's famous Vaudville and Variety Theatre where Ben Thompson and J. King Fisher were killed in 1884. *The James D. Horan Civil War and Western Americana Collection*

morning of the double killing and eyewitness statements obtained by reporters for the *Austin Statesman,* which indicated both gunfighters had been ambushed and killed. Many years later the newspaper's "eye-witness accounts" were confirmed by the memoirs of a well-known Texas newspaper editor.[18]

Fisher, then a deputy sheriff of Uvalde County, was in Austin on business when he met Ben and joined him on a tour of the local bars. After making these rounds Fisher talked Ben into stopping off at San Antonio on the way to Fisher's home in Uvalde. Finally Ben agreed to go. Both men had been drinking for hours and Ben was in an ugly mood.

They reached San Antonio about 8 P.M., saw a play at Turner's Hall, then set out for the Vaudville Theatre, operated by Joe Foster and Billy Simms, Ben's boyhood playmate and former classmate at Professor Swancoat's private school. Years before, Ben had staked Simms in his first attempt as a professional gambler but there had been a dispute over a game and Thompson had forced Simms to leave Austin. But the coolness between the two men had gradually dissipated; they had become casual friends and occasional opponents across a monte table.

There is little doubt that news of their coming to the Vaudville Theatre preceded them. The *San Antonio Light* revealed a warning telegram was sent to Foster by his friends in Austin. Foster had alerted the city police that Thompson and Fisher were on their way to San Antonio and there could be violence.

The gunfighters were greeted by Simms. When they were joined by a policeman, Jacob S. Coy, the quartet sat at a table and began drinking. Then Ben demanded to see Foster who appeared. He refused to shake Ben's hand or accept his offer of a drink.

At this point guns crashed, tables were overturned, glass shattered, and the crowded smoky hall was thrown into wild confusion. When the gunsmoke drifted away, Ben and Fisher were dead, Foster critically wounded, and Coy had been shot in the foot.

An examination of the testimony taken before a coroner's jury on March 13 discloses all witnesses agreed Thompson started the fight after Foster refused to shake his hand. Coy, the policeman, claimed the gunfighter drew his gun but that he had prevented Thompson from firing at the theatre owner because he "grabbed it by the cylinder . . . there were thirteen shots fired all together . . ."

Witnesses swore they did not see anyone shoot Thompson and Fisher. Other policemen, including a captain, testified they arrived after the shooting was over to discover the two men dead on the floor.

While a crowd of three thousand milled outside the courthouse the jury retired and quickly returned a verdict: the two gunfighters had been killed by officers in self-defense.

Rumors swept the frontier that Thompson and Fisher had been ambushed and assassinated by hired guns. Then the *Austin Statesman,* which editorially voiced suspicion the double killings had been planned, shook the Southwest on March 16 with a page one story containing the statements of two eyewitnesses who agreed in independent versions that Thompson and Fisher had been gunned down by hidden killers without a chance to defend themselves.

Under the headling "The Facts," the newspaper described the witnesses as two salesmen "from the North," one for a liquor company, the other for a tobacco house:

"They appear very candid, truthful men, and the story they give corresponds so closely with the post-mortem examination there can be no doubt but it is a correct statement of the tragedy."[19]

Eyewitness Accounts of Alex T. Raymond and John R. Sublett to the Killing of Ben Thompson and King Fisher, March 11, 1884

We happened to be in San Antonio the night of the tragedy. We stayed with an old acquaintance and he insisted that we see the sights of the city. We went to see Ada Gray and then our friend proposed we see some of the variety shows and in that way we were at the Vaudville Theatre when Thompson and Fisher came in.

It was between eleven and twelve when Thompson and Fisher entered the bar. Our friend informed us they were the notorious Ben Thompson and King Fisher. It was the first time we had even seen him [Thompson] and our curiosity was aroused. Our friend informed us Thompson had killed a man in this very bar, Jack Harris, and that the present manager had been the partner of the man killed by Ben Thompson and he thought it strange that Thompson should come to this place.

Neither Thompson nor Fisher were drunk. They talked in an ordinary conversational tone and both appeared to be in the best of humor. Soon a man came into the bar who our friend said was Simms and he came up to Thompson and said:

"Hello, Ben, I'm glad to see you."

Thompson then introduced him to Fisher and Fisher and Simms shook hands. Then Officer Coy came into the room and he shook hands with both the men.

Simms then said to Ben Thompson: "Ben, I'm awful glad to see you here. Let's forget the past and be friends in the future."

Thompson replied: "I desire to be friends and I have come here with my friend Fisher to talk the matter over and have a perfect understanding. I have a perfect right to do that, have I not?"

Simms said: "Yes Ben, that is right and I know we can be friends."

Ben said, "I have nothing against you or Foster. I am not afraid of you. I am here surrounded by my friends but I want to be friends with you and I have come to talk it over."

Simms said, "That is all right. Come upstairs and see Foster."

After taking a drink, Thompson and Fisher went upstairs to the theatre. Neither the policeman nor Simms went upstairs with them. With our friend we followed them and took a seat a short distance from them.

In a short time they were joined by Simms and Coy who sat by the sides of Thompson and Fisher and some pleasant conversation passed.

Soon a girl came along and Thompson ordered drinks. After they had drunk he teased the girl about paying for them, but finally pulled out a very large roll of bills, saying, "I have lots of money. I have $20,000 in this roll."

He paid the girl for the drinks. Then he turned to Simms, saying;

"I thought you brought me up here to see Foster. Billy don't play any games on me. I didn't come up here for any fuss and I don't want any but you must treat me fair."

Simms said, "It's just as I told you, Ben. I will go and tell Foster you want to have a friendly talk with him."

"Yes, go and get him," Fisher said. "I want to make you fellows good friends before I leave. I have invited Thompson here, he did not want to come but you all are friends of mine and I want you to be friends. I told him to come over and talk the matter over like gentlemen together and bury the past. Thompson is willing to do so and I want Foster to come over and meet him halfway."

Simms said: "All right, I will go and get him."

Then he went into a box and came out with Foster and they came down to where Thompson and Fisher were. As they came up and without rising, Thompson extended his hand to Foster and as he did so, Fisher said:

"I want you and Thompson to be friends. You are both friends to me and I want you to shake hands like gentlemen."

Foster said: "I cannot shake hands with Ben Thompson nor can he and I be friends and I want him to keep out of my way."

As he said that both Simms and Coy stepped to one side, at least two feet from where Thompson and Fisher were seated and Foster was about the same distance on the other side of them.

Thompson and Fisher sprang up, neither of them had a revolver in his hand, and before they got to their feet a volley that sounded as though there were a dozen carbines, was fired from a box that was a little to the left and considerably above the doomed men and both went down instantly.

Neither Thompson nor Fisher drew their revolvers nor did they have time to do so. Any statement to the contrary is without the slightest foundation. Thompson fell on his right side and as he did so, Simms or Coy rushed by and drew his revolver and bent over, putting the muzzle close to his ear and fired. He then fired other shots into his head and body and the other man shot Fisher in a similar manner.

Foster tried to draw his revolver but it caught and he gave it an angry jerk, bringing it out but the jerk discharged it and the ball went into his leg and he fell and the crowd then gathered around the dead men.

972 Estate of Ben Thompson, dec'd

And now on this May-9-1884, comes on for examination the Inventory and appraisement filed herein by R. B. Underhill, Admr, which is found to be in all things sufficient,

It is therefore ordered by the Court that said Inventory and appraisement be and is hereby approved

972 Estate of Ben Thompson, deceased.

And now on this May 9-1884, It is ordered by the Court that said Inventory and appraisement herein and above approved be here recorded towit

972 Inventory and appraisement of property belonging to estate of Ben Thompson, deceased, the same being community property of Ben and — Thompson, his wife:

Real Estate:

Lot 1. Block 28, City of Austin, with small frame house, valued at 1500.00

Lots 14 & 15, Block E. Pattons addition to town of

A. Mobeetie, valued at 50.00

Real Estate in Bastrop County Texas. one lot valued at 600.00

B. 1/3 interest in North half of lot 2, Block 69. City of Austin, on which there are vendors liens to amount of $4000. & accumulated interest. This being the property of Holman, Marshall and Thompson. See note for further explanation of condition of this property, property valued without reference to debt 4000.00

Personal Property:

1/3 interest in furniture in business rooms of Holman, Marshall and Thompson. The entire value of said furniture being $672. Thompsons interest therein being 1/3	224.00
1 Horse (at Millers) valued at	200.00
1 English Dog Cart "	200.00
1 Set Harness, Dog Cart	20.00
1 " "	15.00
1 Basket Phaeton at Paggis	60.00
Property of estate of Ben Thompson, which in pledge for debt	
1 Diamond ring & diamond scarf pin, valued at	400.00
In pledge with Sam de Cordova, for debt of 300.00	
99 shares of stock in Savings and Loan association cert 39. Series 1. against which Driscol, Purner and Brush hold debt to amount of $669.40 & have a transfer of the stock for debt &c &c, transfer however is merely as collateral	1133.00
Saddle at Reudy and Parkers, on which there is a lien for $20.00 of value	100.00
1/3 int in & to 50 shares stock in Savings and Loan association, sd shares being in name of and are partnership property of Holman, Marshall & Co. & sd 1/3 int of Thompson is valued at	190.83 1/2

Note with reference to real estate mentioned above:

A. The lot situated in Bastrop is subject to mortgage for 300.00

B. This property is subject to vendors liens to amount of $4000. & interest. Is partnership property of firm of Holman, Marshall and Thompson — Thompson is due the firm of H M & T. about $2500. which is a charge on his interest in the property, in advance of claims of general creditors of Thompson.

C. This is the family homestead on which there are vendors liens to amount of $2500.00

> [Mr. Raymond added to his statement:]
>
> It is monstrous the evidence those fellows gave at San Antonio and the whole town seems to be in mortal fear of the crowd who have their headquarters at that den of infamy, The Vaudville.
>
> Thompson, no doubt, was a bad man but that crowd who murdered him ought to be hanged for it was coldest bloody murder ever committed.

Thompson's death attracted as much national attention as the killing of Jesse James in Saint Joseph, Missouri, two years before. After the *Austin Statesman* published the statements of the two eyewitnesses, Thompson's family demanded the investigation be reopened. A postmortem performed by two eminent Texas physicians revealed both men had been shot by persons hidden above them and using Winchester rifles.

The results of the postmortem led the *Austin Statesman* to call for a grand jury investigation and the killers be indicted. But despite the uproar there was no grand jury action nor did the San Antonio police or prosecutor appear interested. Gradually Thompson and Fisher faded into the myth and folklore of the American West.

Half a century later *Glamorous Days,* the memoirs of Frank H. Bushick, once city editor of the *San Antonio Express,* was published and confirmed the *Austin Statesman*'s charge that Fisher and Thompson had been ambushed and murdered in the Vaudville Theatre.[20]

He disclosed that both gunfighters had been killed by three "hangers-on" at the theatre—a bartender, gambler, and variety performer, who had been armed with rifles and hidden in a nearby box. After they had killed Thompson and Fisher, the trio slipped out of town.

Bushick explained that for "political reasons" city officials were "friendly" to the gambling syndicate and the coroner's jury inquest was perfunctory. However, neither Bushick's memoirs, the testimony before the coroner's jury, nor the *Austin Statesman*'s investigation explained the role played by King Fisher that bloody night. Ninety years later the mystery is still unsolved. Was Fisher, who his friends claimed after the shooting had always been contemptuous of Ben Thompson despite his show of friendship, acting as a decoy? And had Fisher, the double crosser, been double-crossed himself by the gamblers who may have viewed him as a bully and a potential threat?

The gunfire in the balcony of the Vaudville Theatre produced strange twists of fate. Foster's leg bone had been so badly shattered by the ball from his own six-shooter that it was amputated. He died a short time later. Coy, who told the coroner's jury he had only suffered a slight wound, discovered it was more serious than he first thought; he became a cripple for life.

In Austin, Thompson's friends and admirers, who had given him a triumphal welcome following his acquittal from the Harris shooting, gave him a monumental farewell. Crowds overflowed the church and the line of mourners stretched for blocks. One of the many carriages was filled with weeping orphans; it wasn't known until the funeral that Ben Thompson, the man killer, was providing for their clothes and food . . .

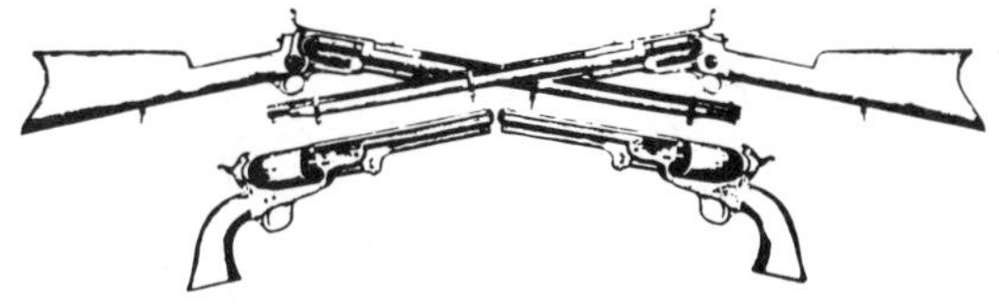

JOHN WESLEY HARDIN

JOHN WESLEY HARDIN, WHO ONCE DESCRIBED HIMSELF AS "a warrior born of battle, a man who belongs to no man or set of men," is credited with forty killings in stand-up gunfights, ambushes, and running battles on horseback. The number may be accurate; whenever Hardin rode out of a frontier town, dead men were always left behind.[1]

The reason may be in his own philosophy: "There always seemed to be a man with a challenge and I never refused one . . ."

Wes, as he was called, was born May 25, 1853, in Bonham, Fannin County, Texas, son of James C. Hardin, a circuit riding preacher who named his newborn after the fiery British founder of Methodism, and Elizabeth Dixon Hardin, "a cultured woman from an educated and comfortable family."[2]

Hardin lived most of his formative years in Sumpter, a small town in southeastern Texas, where he received formal schooling in an academy established by his father. He was a tall, slender, handsome boy, a natural born leader who organized footraces, wrestling matches, and contests shooting at marks. "We all carried guns in those days," he once explained.

One day after school Hardin accepted a challenge for a wrestling match with a fellow student, Charles Sloter, older and bigger. After Wes pinned him down, Sloter attacked him with a knife. Someone tossed Hardin a blade and the pair slashed at each other. Sloter broke away first, running home with blood stream-

A rare daguerreotype of twenty-year-old John Wesley Hardin. By this time, as one of the deadliest gunfighters in the Wild West, he had killed a number of men, had a confrontation with Wild Bill Hickok in Abilene, and was wanted by the Texas State Police and Texas Rangers. *Courtesy Southwest Texas State University Library, San Marcos, Texas*

ing from his wounds. Wes, also cut, washed up in a nearby stream. Sloter's parents protested to the school board and sheriff, but Wes was cleared after his schoolmates told how he had to defend himself from Sloter's knife attack.

When war broke out Reverend Hardin, although he had voted against Secession, organized a company and was elected captain. At the urging of his men, however, he resigned to remain behind.

"You can be of more good use at home than off fighting Yankees," he was told.

Wes and Manning Clements, his cousin and closest friend, ran off to join the company but were brought back by Hardin's father who gave him "a sound thrashing."

In the violently pro-Confederate county, Hardin recalled he saw Lincoln "burned and shot to pieces in effigy so many times. I looked upon him as a demon incarnate who was waging a relentless and cruel war on the South to rob her of her sacred rights . . . the way you bend a tree, that is the way it grows. I grew up a Rebel . . ."[3]

In 1862 the Hardins moved to Polk County where his father opened a law office. Three years later the family returned to Sumpter. Reverend Hardin continued his practice and also taught at the local school. Wes and his older brother, Joe, "being regular scholars."

By the time he was twelve Wes was an accomplished hunter of deer, raccoon, possum, and wildcats. Many years later he remembered those days when "I was a child of nature" as being the best of times.[4] Before he was fifteen, in a frontier world where most adults used firearms as casually as they rode horses, Wes was recognized as one of the best marksmen in the county.

Manning Clements, John Wesley Hardin's cousin and closest friend. Clements joined Hardin in driving a herd of 1,200 steers to Abilene. It was through Clements that Hardin met sixteen-year-old Jane Bowen, whom he later married. *The James D. Horan Civil War and Western Americana Collection*

The following year his father bought a plantation on Long Knife Creek near Livingston, Texas, but soon grew weary of "country living." He brought his family back to Sumpter and turned the place over to his brother, Barnett Hardin, and his wife, Anne. The plantation was the scene of John Wesley Hardin's first killing.

In 1865 when he was twelve, Hardin, "carrying my pistol," joined his uncle, kinfolk, and several farmhands in the annual cane sugar harvest. After the cane had been cut and gathered, a cousin, Barnett Jones, matched himself and Hardin in a wrestling match with a burly Negro hand named Mage. The two boys threw him twice but in the second fall Hardin's ring scratched Mage's face and the wrestling match turned into a fistfight that was stopped by the spectators. Mage, shouting threats, was forced to leave by Hardin's uncle.

The next morning while he was on his way home, Hardin met Mage on the road. When the hand tried to knock him from his horse with a club, Hardin shot him.

Hardin returned to the plantation and brought back his uncle and several friends. It was obvious Mage was dying so Barnett Hardin ordered his nephew to ride to Sumpter, tell his father about the shooting, and "to look out for the Yankee soldiers who were all over the country at the time." Mage died soon after.[5]

Reverend Hardin and his wife, "distracted" by the news of the killing, realized that if they surrendered their son to the Yankee dominated courts, he would certainly be sentenced to death.

Wes was sent to a friend who had an isolated ranch, until, as his father told him, "Yankee bayonets should cease to govern."

Wes spent his time rounding up wild cattle and hunting until the morning a rider appeared to warn him a Union patrol was approaching the ranch to arrest him for killing Mage.

Wes decided to ambush the troopers at a creek crossing. He killed three in what he termed "a war to the knife . . . I had no mercy on men who wanted my body to torture and kill."[6]

As in Missouri and Kansas there was no Appomattox on the Texas frontier . . .

In January Hardin rejoined his father who had been appointed head of the Old Word School in Pisga, Navarro County. There was a teacher's vacancy so the school board hired Wes as a temporary replacement. It makes a fascinating picture of the teen-age killer teaching reading, writing, and arithmetic to the class of twenty-five boys and girls, some older than himself.

Apparently he was satisfactory; after three months the board offered him another term but by now Hardin had enough of books and classrooms. He turned down the board's offer and told his father he was joining his cousins, Manning Clements and Tom Dixon, rounding up and selling the wild longhorn that belonged to anyone who had the courage and skill to rope them.

It was a free, unrestricted life of gathering the steers and driving them to the nearest shipping point. Hardin, Clements, and Dixon, all teen-agers, spent their nights in the frontier gambling halls, saloons, and on racetracks. In addition to becoming skilled in the use of a Colt .44, Wes became an expert at poker, euchre, and seven-up, his favorite game, and a good judge of race horses. As he wrote:

"I liked fast horses and would soon bet on any kind of a horse race, a chicken fight or dog fight and on anything down to spitting at a mark . . ."[7]

He was still on the lookout for Union patrols. When his friend, Frank Polk, killed a man in Coriscana, Wes was accused of being an accomplice although he could prove he was not in the same county when the shooting had taken place. Polk was captured but, as always, Wes was warned by friends and escaped.

While he was on the dodge he met Simp Dixon, a cousin who was waging a one-man war against Union troops. Dixon's mother, brother, and sister had been murdered by a marauding federal patrol and he had sworn to "kill Yankees as long as he lived."

Union cavalrymen trapped them in the Richland Bottoms and after a fierce gun battle Hardin killed two troopers.[8]

Although he sympathized with his cousin, Hardin refused to join him in this senseless vendetta; he said good-bye and drifted around Navarro County until he was persuaded by his father to hide out at the Barnett Hardin plantation. For the rest of the year he speculated in hides and cotton, rounded up and sold wild cattle, raced horses, and dodged Union patrols.

By the fall of 1869 when he was sixteen, John Wesley Hardin had the reputation of being one of the deadliest gunfighters in southwestern Texas. After his election, Texas Governor Edmund J. Davis publicly vowed to have the young man killed, jailed, or hanged.

With legislative approval, Davis formed what he called the "Texas State Police." This law enforcement body of ruthless man hunters would become incredibly corrupt and a terror to most Texans.[9]

Hardin was one of their principal targets; patrols began to search the county for him but friends and kinsmen in cow camps and frontier towns never failed to warn him when police were in the vicinity.

In the winter of 1869 he rode into Towash, a wild cow town where brothels, saloons, and gambling halls were open twenty-four hours a day. The community was ruled by Jim Bradley, a desperado and killer who owned a crude racetrack on the edge of town and enforced his own law with a band of fugitives and gunfighters.

Even in this outlaw haven trouble was never far from Hardin. In a daylong poker game he cleaned out Bradley, who refused to let him pick up the winnings but took Hardin's boots and drove him out of the shed where the game was being played. The outraged, bootless Hardin borrowed a rifle, killed Bradley, and drove off his gang.

After playing hounds and hare with a Towash posse, Hardin finally reached Brenham on January 20, 1871. In a short time he killed two men, one a circus performer who drew first after Hardin had accidentally bumped into him, and a confidence man who used a young girl to lure him into a house to be robbed. Hardin took out fifty dollars in gold pieces and said it was all he had but promised to get the rest from his saddlebags. When the confidence man reached for the money, Wes let some of the pieces fall to the floor.

As he told the story:

"He stooped down to pick them up and as he was straightening up I pulled my pistol and fired. The ball struck him between the eyes and he fell over, a dead robber . . ."[10]

The Brenham gambling halls saw a great deal of young Hardin. Here he met Ben Thompson and J. King Fisher, who would die together in San Antonio, and Phil Coe, who would be killed by Wild Bill Hickok in Abilene. It was Coe who gave him the nickname "Little Seven-Up" from Hardin's favorite poker game.

Hardin remained in Brenham only a few months. In March he left when he heard a patrol of state police were coming after him with a murder warrant. After months of drifting he ended up in Evergreen, Texas, where he won $300 from the notorious Bill Longley.

When he rejoined his father who was teaching school in Mount Calm, the Reverend Hardin urged Wes to continue his studies in Professor Landrum's Academy in Round Rock where his brother, Joe, was studying law. Wes, weary of running and drifting, agreed and rode to Round Rock where he enrolled in the academy.

He attended classes only one day when his father sent word the state police were on their way to arrest him. Hardin, as he recalled, left his classes but studied with his brother by the campfires of his hideouts. Professor Landrum agreed to give him an examination, which he passed; he picked up his diploma virtually on horseback with the state police only a few miles away.

In the winter of 1871, the Hardin clan moved into the north central Texas town of Comanche. Joe, who brought his wife and their baby daughter, Dora Jean Joe Belle Hardin, was followed by his parents, "Preacher" Hardin as he was to be known and his wife; their daughter Matt, a young son, Jeff, and several other children. Mrs. Hardin's relatives also joined them, including Tom and Buddy Dixon who were close to John Wesley Hardin and Manning Clements. As soon as he arrived, Joe became active in the tiny community. He joined the Masons and the Friends of Temperance, hung up his lawyer's shingle, and practiced real estate. A few years later he was appointed postmaster.

Assured by his father that "when the Democrats regained power I could get a fair trial but not under the Carpet-bagger rule," Wes said good-bye to his parents and rode for Shreveport, Louisiana, where he intended to hide out with relatives until the Yankees left Texas.

Before he could reach the border he was mistakenly arrested in Lake View for another man. There the state police caught up with him and made plans to remove him to the stronger Waco jail.

Hardin bought a .45 Colt "with four barrels loaded" from a prisoner for fifty dollars and his overcoat. He tied the weapon under his arm, killed his state police guard on the banks of the Trinity River, and rode back to Comanche. After a brief reunion with his mother and father, Wes took off for Mexico.

On the road between Belton and Waco he was taken into custody by a trio of state police. When the officers got drunk that night, Hardin killed them with their own weapons.

"I took an oath right there never to surrender at the muzzle of a gun," he wrote.

Traveling at night he finally reached Gonzales where Manning Clements persuaded him to join a cattle drive to Abilene.

While the ranchers rounded up their steers, Wes attended a relative's wedding party where Clements introduced him to Jane Bowen, the pretty, dark-haired sixteen-year-old daughter of a local rancher. Hardin later recalled he fell in love with Jane the moment he saw her; she would always be "my life and my everlasting love . . ."[11]

Jane was attracted to the handsome, reckless young man with the awesome reputation. Before the drive started in late February they were engaged, with Hardin promising to return as soon as possible. Finally the herd was ready, the ranchers held a meeting and, although Wes was the youngest hand, he was elected foreman. Then one morning, the order was given, "Point 'em North," and the steers began heading for Abilene, the cow town with the magical name that made young Texans dream of beautiful "calico girls," endless barrels of whiskey, poker games without a limit—and a towering marshal named Wild Bill Hickok who didn't particularly like Texans . . .

To John Wesley Hardin of 1871, badmen and legendary marshals "had as much influence on me as a snaffle bit has on a wild horse." The young puncher in worn boots, patched jeans, and battered hat looked amazed when he was confronted on Texas Street in Abilene by the stylishly dressed Hickok, by this time a living legend on the frontier as a man of consummate skill with firearms.

Hickok demanded that Hardin turn over his guns; the young Texan surrendered them—butts first. When Hickok reached out to take them, Hardin whirled the guns about in a "road agent's spin" and Wild Bill found himself looking

A rare daguerreotype of eighteen-year-old Jane Bowen Hardin in her wedding dress. She had met Hardin two years earlier when he was "on the dodge" from Texas state police patrols. *Courtesy Southwest Texas State University Library, San Marcos, Texas*

Joseph Clements, John Wesley Hardin's cousin, who accompanied him on the drive to Abilene where Hardin confronted Wild Bill Hickok. Hardin and Clements won $3,000 on horse races in Comanche, May 26, 1874, when Hardin killed Deputy Sheriff Charles Webb. *The James D. Horan Civil War and Western Americana Collection*

into the muzzles of two six-shooters. Hickok quickly suggested they have a drink and talk things over.[12]

In his autobiography Hardin recalled that incident:

John Wesley Hardin Faces Wild Bill Hickok in Abilene

I have seen many fast towns, but I think Abilene beat them all. The town was filled with sporting men and women, gamblers, desperadoes and the like. It was well supplied with bar rooms, hotels, barber shops and gambling houses, and everything was open.

Before I got to Abilene I had heard much talk of Wild Bill, who was then marshal of Abilene. He had a reputation as a killer. I knew Ben Thompson and Phil Coe were there, and had met both these men in Texas. Besides these I learned that there were many other Texans there and so, although there was a reward offered for me, I concluded to stay some time there as I knew that Carol and Johnson, the owners of my herd "squared" me with the officials. When we went to town and settled up, Jim Clements insisted on going home, although they offered him $140 per month to stay. I continued in their employ to look after their stray cattle at $140 per month. Thus we settled our business and proceeded to take in the town.

Columbus Carol got in a fuss with a policeman that night at a notorious resort. Carson was the policeman's name and he drew a pistol on Carol. I was present and drew mine on Carson, making him leave the place. I told him not to turn his head until he got to the corner of the next street and to go and get "Wild Bill," his chief, and come back and we would treat him likewise. But "they never came back."

Next morning Carol and myself met Carson and Wild Bill on the streets, but nothing happened.

Jim Clements took the trail and went back to Texas. Phil Coe and Ben Thompson at that time were running the Bull's Head saloon and gambling hall. They had a big bull painted outside the saloon as a sign and the city council objected to this for some special reason. Wild Bill, the marshal, notified Ben Thompson and Phil Coe to take the sign down or change it somewhat. Phil Coe thought the ordinance all right, but it made Thompson mad. Wild Bill, however, sent up some painters and materially altered the offending bovine.

For a long time everybody expected trouble between Thompson and Wild Bill and I soon found out that they were deadly enemies. Thompson tried to prejudice me every way he could against Bill and told me how Bill, being a Yankee, always picked Southern men to kill, and especially Texans. I told him "I am not doing anybody's fighting just now except my own, but I know how to stick to a friend. If Wild Bill needs killing, why don't you kill him yourself?"

He said: "I would rather get someone else to do it."

I told him then that he had struck the wrong man. I had not yet met Bill Heycox [Hickok], but really wished for a chance to have a set-to with him just to try his pluck.

One night in a wine room he was drinking with some friends of mine when he remarked that he would like to have an introduction to me. George Johnson introduced us and we had several glasses of wine together. He showed me a proclamation from Texas offering a reward for my arrest. He said:

"Young man, I am favorably impressed with you, but don't let Ben Thompson influence you; you are in enough trouble now and if I can do you a favor I will do it."

I was charmed with his liberal views, and told him so. We parted friends.

I spent most of my time in Abilene in the saloons and gambling houses, playing poker, faro and seven-up. One day I was playing ten pins and my best horse was hitched outside in front of the saloon. I had two six-shooters on and of course I knew the saloon people would raise a row if I did not pull them off. Several Texans were there rolling ten pins and drinking. I suppose we were pretty noisy. Wild Bill came in and said we were making too much noise and told me to take off my pistols until I got ready to go out of town. I told him I was ready to go now, but did not propose to put up my pistols, go or no go. He went out and I followed him. I started up the street when some one behind me shouted:

"Set up. All down but nine."

Wild Bill whirled around and met me. He said:

"What are you howling about and what are you doing with those pistols on."

I said: "I am just taking in the town."

He pulled his pistol and said: "Take those pistols off. I arrest you."

I said all right and pulled them out of the scabbard, but while he was reaching for them I reversed them and whirled them over on him with the muzzles in his face, springing back at the same time. I told him to put his pistol up, which he did. I cursed him for a long-haired scoundrel that would shoot a boy with his back to him (as I had been told he intended to do me). He said, "Little Arkansaw, you have been wrongly informed."

By this time a big crowd had gathered with pistols and arms. They kept urging me to kill him. Down the street a squad of policemen were coming, but Wild Bill motioned them to go back and at the same time asked me not to let the mob shoot him.

I shouted: "This is my fight and I will kill the first man that fires a gun."

Bill said: "You are the gamest and quickest boy I ever saw. Let us compromise this matter and I will be your friend. Let us go in here and take a drink, as I want to talk to you and give you some advice."

At first I thought he might be trying to get the drop on me, but he finally convinced me of his good intentions and we went in and took a drink. We went in a private room and I had a long talk with him and we came out friends.

I had been drinking pretty freely that day and towards night went into a restaurant to get something to eat. A man named Pain was with me, a Texan who had just come up the trail. While we were in the restaurant several drunken men came in the restaurant and began to curse Texans. I said to the nearest one:

"I'm a Texan."

He began to curse me and threatened to slap me over. To his surprise I pulled my pistol and he promptly pulled his. At the first fire he jumped behind my friend Pain, who received a ball in his only arm. He fired one shot and ran, but I shot him as he started, the ball hitting him in the mouth, knocking out several teeth and coming out behind his left ear. I rushed outside, pistol in hand and jumped over my late antagonist, who was lying in the doorway. I met a policeman on the sidewalk, but I threw my pistol in his face and told him to "hands up." He did it.

I made my way to my horse and went north to Cottonwood about thirty-five miles, to await results. While I was there a Mexican named Bideno shot and killed Billy Coran, a cow man who had come up the trail with me. He was bossing a herd then, holding it near by Abilene for a market. His murder by this Mexican was a most foul and treacherous one, and although squad after squad tried to arrest this Mexican, they never succeeded in either killing or arresting him.

Many prominent cow men came to me and urged me to follow the murderer. I consented if they would go to Abilene and get a warrant for him. They did so and I was appointed a deputy sheriff and was given letters of introduction to cattle men whom I should meet. About sunrise on the 27th of June, 1871, I left the North Cottonwood with Jim Rodgers to follow Bideno. Of course, we proposed to change horses whenever we wanted to. This was easy to do, as there were many horses around the herds and we knew they would let us have them when we explained our purpose. We hoped to catch up with him before he got to the Nation, and especially before he got to Texas. Off we went in a lope and got to Newton, about 50 miles away, by 4 p.m. I had learned of a herd there bossed by a brother of the dead Billy Coran and I sent a messenger to him telling him (the messenger) not to spare horseflesh. Coran came and one Anderson with him. I told him of his brother's death and we were soon on the trail with fresh horses and four instead of two in our party.

We had not yet heard one word from Bideno. We expected to reach Wichita that night. About twelve miles from Newton, just about dusk, we came upon a herd bossed by Ben McCulloch, who was afterwards Assistant Superintendent of the Huntsville Penitentiary, while I was there. We changed horses again and took the trail, having as yet heard nothing of Bideno. We reached Wichita about 11 o'clock that night, having traveled 100 miles since starting. We concluded to rest until morning and then go on the south side of the river and make inquiry. I knew there were several Mexican herds near the river which Bideno might have gone to for a change of horses. We went next morning to these herds, going from one to the other hunting for information. Finally we struck a Mexican who said that a man had stayed at his camp about 10 o'clock last night and had traded horses with one of his men early in the morning. He said the horse he had traded for was the best in camp. We were convinced that this must have been Bideno, so changing horses and flushed with hope we hit the trail again about 7 a.m. in a long lope.

We saw a herder about 8 o'clock who told us that two hours before he had seen a Mexican wearing a broad brimmed hat and going south in a lope, keeping about 200 yards from the trail. We were now satisifed we were on the right track and pulled out again, expecting to change horses at Cow House creek, about fifteen miles further on.

We met a man near Cow House who told us that he had seen a Mexican wearing a broad brimmed hat and going south in a lope. When we got to Cow House we changed our horses at once and found that Bideno had done likewise an hour before. It was now about 10 o'clock, and hoping to overtake him before we got to Bluff Creek, twenty miles off, on the line of Arkansas and the Indian Territory, we pushed our fresh horses to a fast lope. We heard from him several times, but he was always in a lope and always off the road.

After going about twenty miles we again changed horses so that if we ran up on him our horses would be fresh. When we got within two miles of Bluff Creek the road forked. Anderson and I went through the city, while Rodgers and Coran took the other fork; all agreeing to meet in the Indian Nation on the other side of the creek.

Anderson and I, before going far got direct information that Bideno had just unsaddled his horse and had gone up town inquiring for a restaurant. We fired our pistols and by this means got Coran and Rodgers to hear us and come back.

We soon got to Bluff, which was a town of about fifty houses. There were some bar rooms and restaurants in a line and we agreed to ride up like cowboys, hitch our horses and divide into two parties each going into different places. Anderson and I went into a restaurant, but before we reached it we had to go into a saloon. I called for drinks and took in the situation. I asked if we could get dinner and if a Mexican herder was eating dinner back there. They said there was; so I told my partner to get out his gun and follow me. We stepped into the entrance and I recognized Bideno. With my pistol by my side I said.

"Bideno, I am after you; surrender; I do not wish to hurt you and you shall not be hurt while you are in my hands."

He was sitting at the table eating and shook his head and frowned. He then dropped his knife and fork and grabbed his pistol. As he did it I told him to throw up his hands.

When he got his pistol out I fired at him across the table and he fell over a dead man, the ball hitting him squarely in the forehead.

Hearing the firing Coran and Rodgers rushed in also. Coran said: "I just want to shoot my brother's murderer one time. Is he dead?"

I told him he was, but he wanted to shoot him anyway. I would not let him but he took his hat as a trophy anyway.

In the meantime the waiter was jumping up and down, begging us not to kill him; that he was a friend of cowboys, etc. I quieted him by telling him if he did not get out he might, perhaps, get shot accidentally, and he promptly acted on my suggestion.

We all went into the saloon and the bartender said: "Take what you want." We took some good whisky and he would not let us pay for it.

Quite a crowd had gathered by now and they all wanted to know what the shooting was about. I got outside the saloon and told the crowd how this Mexican had murdered a prominent cow man on the 26th at North Cottonwood; how we had followed him and demanded his surrender; how he had refused to give up and had drawn his pistol, when I was forced to shoot him. I then introduced John Coran, the dead man's brother. They all commended our actions and we gave these people $20 to bury him.

We all started back to Abilene, rejoicing over our good luck. We reached Wichita that night, which was about fifty miles away. As we had ridden about 150 miles in 36 hours we all rested that night in Wichita.

There I told my companions my trouble in Abilene. We all agreed to go to Newton and thence to Abilene, where they were to stick to me against anything.

I had heard that Wild Bill had said that if I ever came back to Abilene he would kill me, so I determined to go back there and if Bill tried to arrest me to kill him.

We stopped next at Newton and took in the town in good style. The policemen tried to hold us down, but they all resigned I reckon. We certainly shut up that town.

We went on to Abilene fearing nothing but God. While we were opening wine there, Wild Bill came in and asked me if I remembered our talk in the "Apple Jack."

"Well," he said, "you can not 'hurrah' me, and I am not going to have it."

I told him, "I don't wish to hurrah you; but I have come to stay regardless of you."

"Well," he said, "you can stay and wear your guns, but those other fellows must pull them off. You are in no danger here. I congratulate you in getting your Mexican. Come in and invite your friends. We will open a bottle of wine."

The boys had been watching us pretty closely and we all went into a room, they having their guns on. The marshal said nothing about their pistols then and after drinking a couple of bottles of wine left.

I then told my companions that Bill was my friend and had asked me to see that they took their pistols off. They asked me why I did not pull mine off. I told them that the marshal had not demanded that of me, but I knew he was our friend and would protect us all, and if he did not, I would. Well, they said that if Wild Bill was all right with me they would go home, which they did.

Everybody at Abilene wanted to see the man that killed the murderer of Billy Coran and I received substantial compliments in the shape of $20, $50 and $100 bills. I did not want to take the money at first but I finally concluded there was nothing wrong about it, so took it as proof of their friendship and gratitude for what I had done. I think I got about $400 in that way. Besides this, some wealthy cow men made up a purse and gave me $600, so I got about $1000 for my work. I wish to say, however, that at the time I killed him I never expected to receive a cent, and only expected to have my expenses paid.

It was about the 2nd of July that John Coran, Jim Rodgers, Hugh Anderson and myself parted at Abilene. In a day or two Manning and Gip Clements came into Abilene and hunted me up. They found me with Jake Johnson and Frank Bell. To celebrate the meeting we opened several bottles of wine and then Manning said:

"Wes, I want to see you privately."

He, Gip and myself went up to my private room. Manning said:

"Wes, I killed Joe and Dolph Shadden last night, but I was justified."

"Well," said I, "I am glad you are satisfied, but I would stick to you all the same, even if you were not satisfied with your action."

Manning said that he was bossing a herd for Doc Burnett in Gonzales county and was driving them here. He had selected his own hands and had hired these Shadden boys. Everything had gone on smoothly until they crossed Red River. Then the Shaddens commenced playing off and refused to go on night duty. When they were ordered to do so they became insulting and demanded their time and money. When told they could quit they wanted pay for all the time had they gone through to Abilene. This Manning refused to do, but offered to pay them for the time they had actually worked. He told them it was either this or leave camp or to do night duty and stay. They stayed and did night duty. All the time going through the Nation they were trying to make the other hands dissatisfied and told them that they intended to kill Manning before they got to Abilene, where they knew that Jim Clements and Wes Hardin were and they would take Manning's part of course.

When they crossed the Canadian they gave up work entirely. Manning then offered them their full pay if they would leave. This they would not do, so he told Gip and the rest of the hands to watch them in word and actions. Manning would actually stay away from camp at night to avoid trouble, as he knew they were fixing to kill him there. They began to talk about his cowardice in sleeping away from camp at nights. When the herd crossed the Arkansas, Manning told a friend of his that had their confidence too, that he was not going to sleep out of camp any longer.

The Shadden boys then said: "Well, if he comes back to sleeping in camp at night we will kill him."

Manning was told of their intention and told his brother Gip in their presence to make down his bed in a certain place, which he did.

When they had gone, Manning told Gip what was up. Manning went on duty first that night and a hand came out to the herd and begged him not to go back to camp that night as these Shadden boys were sitting up waiting to kill him. Manning, however, took a friend and went to camp. He got there later than they expected and called out in a loud voice: "Gip, get up and go on herd." Gip said, "all right." Joe Shadden jumped up with his pistol, but Manning had on a slicker and also had his pistol in his hand. Manning fired first and put a bullet through Joe's head. Dolph, meanwhile, had fired at Manning, the ball going through his slicker and vest. Manning and Dolph Shadden then rushed together and scuffled, but Manning managed to fire, shooting him through the breast.

He fell back on his bed, telling Manning that he had killed him. Manning then turned the herd over to one of his hands, got his young brother Gip and came on here. When Manning told me this I said: "I have a heap of trouble, but I stand square in Abilene. Wild Bill is my particular friend, and he is one to help you here if papers come from Texas for you. Now, Manning, pull off your pistols until I see Bill and fix him." I made Gip do the same thing. I then saw Columbus Carol and Jake Johnson and it was agreed that Columbus see Wild Bill and square Manning Clements. But, unfortunately, Columbus got drunk and squared nothing. That evening we all dropped into a gambling hall and began to buck at monte. Wild Bill came in and said: "Hello, Little Arkansaw." Bill bought $20 worth of checks and lost them. Then he bought $50 and then $100. Manning and I walked out and went over to the American House to get supper. I had finished eating, but

Manning and Gip had not, when in walked Wild Bill and McDonald. I knew in an instant that they had come in to arrest Manning. Bill gave me a wink. In a few minutes he said, "How did you come out?" I told him about $25 ahead and I asked him what he did. "I lost $250," said he. I told him I knew all the time he was playing the house's money when we had left. He laughed and said yes, that those fellows knew better than to refuse him. By this time Manning had finished eating and Wild Bill said:

"Are you through eating?"

Manning told him "yes," and he said: "I suppose your name is Clements. I have a telegram here to arrest Manning Clements; so consider yourself under arrest." Manning said "All right." I told Bill to let McDonald guard his prisoner a moment and told Bill I wanted to speak to him privately. I asked him if Columbus Carol had posted him.

"No," said he, "he is drunk. Why did you not post me yourself?"

I then told him that he had once promised to do anything I asked of him; that Manning was a cousin of mine and relied on me for safety. I then asked Wild Bill what I could expect from him. He told me he would turn Manning loose. I told him that was the only way of avoiding trouble. It was agreed that he should protect himself and his reputation as an officer by taking Manning to the Bull's Head saloon (Phil Coe's) and from there to the lock-up. I asked him to tell me exactly what time he would turn him out and he said 12 o'clock. I then called Manning in and told him that Columbus had gotten drunk and had not posted Wild Bill and he must go to jail, but would be turned out at 12 o'clock.

Wild Bill and McDonald then took Manning to jail, while I went to Jess McCoy and bought a horse and saddle for Manning to ride. By this time they had landed him in jail and Bill had sent for me to come up town. Jake Johnson was cutting up about the arrest and had a band of twenty-five Texans ready to liberate him. The police were also gathering at the jail. I took Jake off and told him that Columbus had gotten drunk and had not posted Bill. I explained it all to him and told him to bring his men up to Phil Coe's saloon and stay there. I went up to Phil Coe's and privately agreed to break open the jail at 12 o'clock if Wild Bill did not turn him loose at the appointed time. We went to work then and got fifty men, stationed them in the back of the Bull's Head saloon, just across the street from the jail. I told Phil Coe that Wild Bill and I had set our watches together and so he and I set ours together. I agreed with Phil Coe that he should get the key by 10 minutes to 12 and if at that time he had not gotten it to send me word. I told him where Wild Bill and I would be exactly at that time. I told him if I did not get word from him by 5 minutes to twelve I would kill Wild Bill, but whether he heard shooting or not to break open the jail if he did not get the key. At 10 minutes to 8 by my watch I went to meet Wild Bill and we commenced to take in the gambling houses, etc. We began on monte and the banks we did not break closed. Then we tried faro, and after a while they closed, too. Bill played the bluff racket and I bet with him, so where they paid him they paid me as well. I think we won about $1000 that night. On going over town we learned that a policeman named Tom Carson had arrested some female friends of ours and we determined to see them turned loose and to whip Tom Carson, although he was chief deputy of Wild Bill. We went to the calaboose and met Carson, but Bill did not say anything to him then, and called to the turnkey to bring the key. The prisoners got a hack and went home rejoicing. Tom Carson asked Wild Bill what he did it for and Bill answered his question by knocking him down and then jumping on him with both feet. It was a bad beating up, for Wild Bill was a man six feet high and weighed 200 pounds. He was light complexioned, blue eyed and his hair hung down his shoulders in yellow curls. He was a brave, handsome fellow, but somewhat overbearing. He had fine sense and was a splendid judge of human nature. After this we again went up town and directly I asked Bill what time it was. He said, "15 minutes to 12," and handed me the key wrapped up in a piece of paper. I sent it at once to Phil Coe's at the Bull Head saloon and sent word where Manning could find me. Manning soon joined me; we had some wine and then went to our horses.

We rode to Smokey river, where we got down and talked matters overs. I had provided him with money and everything else necessary for the trip. It was agreed that we should meet again at Barnett Hardin's in Hill county, Texas, and that I should take care of his younger brother, Gip, whom he left with me. We parted with this understanding and he went to Texas, while I went back to Abilene, reaching the town about 3 a.m.

In those days life was constantly in danger from secret or hired assassins, and I was always on the lookout.

On the 7th of July Gip and I had gone to our rooms in the American Hotel to retire for the night. We soon got to bed, when presently I heard a man cautiously unlock my door and slip in with a big dirk in his hand. I halted him with a shot and he ran; I fired at him again and again and he fell dead with four bullets in his body. He had carried my pants with him so I jumped back, slammed the door and cried out that I would shoot the first man that came in. I had given one of my pistols to Manning the night before, so the one I had now was empty.

Now I believed that if Wild Bill found me in a defenseless condition he would take no explanation, but would kill me to add to his reputation. So in my shirt and drawers I told Gip to follow me and went out on the portico.

Just as I got there a hack drove up with Wild Bill and four policemen. I slipped back and waited until they had gotten well inside the hotel and then jumped off over the hack. Gip came after me. I sent Gip to a friend of mine to hide him. I hardly knew what to do. I was so sleepy in the first place, and without arms or clothes. I knew all the bridges were guarded and the country was out after me, believing that I had killed a man in cold blood, instead of a dirty, low down, would-be assassin. I concluded to slip around and sleep in a hay stack which I knew of. I heard them come and look for me, one remarking that he believed that I was in that hay stack and started to set it on fire. I crawled away into the hay stack, knowing they would not set it on fire, because it was too close to a store. If they had done so you would have seen a lad 19 years old in his night clothes crawling away from the officers and the fire in a hurry. I crawled to the edge of the stack after awhile and saw two squads of police not far off. I crawled to a cornfield in roasting ears, keeping the hay stack between me and the police. Presently I saw a lone cowboy riding up within a few yards of me. I asked him if he knew me. He said he did. I put my hand to my side and told him to get down on the other side. He did it and I got up. The police saw this move and I turned my nag loose. The police were right after me and we had a hot race to the river, three miles off. I got there a quarter of a mile ahead and plunged my horse in. He swam like a duck and I got across in safety. They fired several shots at me from the other side and their bullets whistled unpleasantly close to me, so I soon put space between myself and pursuers. I went about a mile, when I looked back and saw three men coming at full speed, but I rode on and at that time few men could outride me. I weighed 155 pounds and was confident of myself, even though I was undressed and unarmed. I let that dun mare go a gait that I thought she could stand and that would put me in camp at least half an hour ahead of my pursuers. I looked back again and saw them coming about four miles off. It was about five miles to camp and up hill most of the way so I let her go and made it in about twenty minutes.

I was a sorry spectacle when I got to that camp. I was bareheaded, unarmed, redfaced, and in my night clothes. I went to work at once to meet my pursuers and got two sixshooters and a Winchester. The cook had prepared dinner and as I had eaten nothing since the evening before, I certainly relished it. The camp was on the north bank of North Cottonwood and I dropped down under the bank while my pursuers rode up. Tom Carson and two others inquired of the cook where I was. He told them I had gone to the herd and asked them to get down and have dinner.

When they were eating I stepped up near them, but not near enough for any of them to grab me. I covered Tom Carson with my Winchester and told them, "all hands up or I'll shoot." All their hands went up, and I told the cook to relieve those gentlemen of their arms and told them any resistance on their part would mean certain and untimely death. The cook did his work well, and I told them to finish their dinner, while I sat on a dry goods box with my Winchester in my hands.

When they were through I made Tom Carson and his two men pull off their clothes, pants and boots, and sent them all back in this condition to face a July sun for thirty-five miles on a bald prairie.

I waited out on Cottonwood several days until Gip Clements came out.

On the 11th of July, 1871, Gip and I left Cottonwood for Texas, well armed and equipped in every way.

Hardin returned to Texas to prepare for his wedding. On a horse-buying trip to Smiley he killed a Negro policeman who tried to arrest him and later single-handedly held off a fifteen-man posse, killing three and driving off the rest. The shooting at Smiley enraged Governor Davis who ordered his police to bring in Hardin dead or alive. Wes ignored the threats and returned to Gonzales and Jane, confident the governor's man hunters could not penetrate the tightly knit circle of kinsmen and friends in the county.

During the winter of 1872 Jane's father gave his consent and they were married in March. Hardin later insisted that as a married man he studiously tried to avoid strangers, who might be seeking to make a reputation as a gunfighter by killing him, saloon brawls, poker games, and Governor Davis's "carpetbaggers and scalawags," as he described the state police.

In July 1872 he was putting together a racing stable with Manning Clements and rode to Trinity City to inspect a mare making a reputation at the local racetracks. While waiting for a relative in John Gates's saloon and tenpin alley, he got into a game with a man named Phil Sublette (Sublet). There was an argument over a wager and Sublette threatened to kill Hardin. Wes lost his temper, slapped Sublette, then pacified him with a drink, and the game continued. After he had won Sublette's money he invited the customers to have a drink.

At the bar he suddenly noticed that Sublette had slipped out. Wes retrieved his guns from behind the bar as Sublette, armed with a shotgun, rushed in. Hardin, "hoping to avoid any new kind of trouble," fired over his head. A drunk grabbed Hardin and held him as Sublette fired, the gun's load hitting him in the stomach. Bleeding badly, Hardin staggered after Sublette who dropped his shotgun and ran. Hardin got off one shot, hitting Sublette in the shoulder. He continued down Trinity City's one street, firing at Sublette as he dodged from house to house. Finally Hardin collapsed, telling his friends:

"If all the gold in the world belonged to me I would freely give it to kill him. I have one consolation, however, I made the coward run."[13]

The unconscious Hardin was removed to a hotel where surgeons operated on his wounds. Manning Clements arrived with Jane and they remained at the bed-side; Jane was told her husband would probably die. A few days later Clements rushed into the room with news that several armed state troopers had heard of the shooting and were riding toward the hotel.[14]

While the horrified surgeons protested that he wouldn't last the hour, Clements and Jane helped Wes to dress and get on a horse. As Clements and Hardin slowly rode out of town, the troopers discovered Wes had escaped and set off in pursuit. In a wild gunfight on the outskirts of town, Hardin killed two troopers and received another wound in the thigh. But he and Clements drove off the patrol. As darkness closed in, they escaped into the hills.

By the following day Hardin was bleeding badly from both his operation and the new thigh wound. Leaving Wes at a hideout, Clements arranged his cousin's surrender with Cherokee County Sheriff Richard Regan, who promised not to turn him over to the dreaded state police.

Hardin, supported by Clements, rode to a rendezvous with Regan. He was put in a wagon and with Regan and his deputies riding on both sides, they drove to Rusk, then later to the Austin jail where, as the *Austin Statesman* reported, "Hardin is evidently tired of his troubles and seems to have no thought except to get through with it." In the fall of 1872 Hardin was transferred to the Smiley jail to await trial for killing the policeman.

A jubilant Governor Davis disclosed Hardin's capture and predicted the young gunfighter would soon be hanged. When he announced plans for his state police to take over the Smiley jail, Manning Clements arranged for his cousin's escape, probably by bribing the guards.

Battered, weak, and subdued, Wes rode back to Gonzales, promising Jane he would hang up his guns forever and return with Clements to their racing stable. Two daughters, Molly (Mollie) and Nan, were born, then a son, John Wesley Hardin, Jr.

While Wes Hardin was slowly recovering in the Austin and Smiley jails, the smoldering feud between the Sutton and Taylor families of Gonzales and DeWitt counties had erupted into one of the most savage of feuds in the Wild West.[15] Towns and counties were armed camps, dead men were found on their doorsteps, on lonely roads, and cut down before the horrified eyes of wives and children. The feud's inception is obscure, probably beginning in the Carolinas, the birthplace of both families.

The Sutton band was the stronger, and had the political blessing of Governor Davis and his state police.

The Taylors, friends of the Clements and Dixons, urged Hardin to join their ranks but Jane begged him not to get involved so he refused, although it was difficult to walk a narrow path in the violent counties. Only Hardin's reputation as a deadly man with a gun saved him from numerous confrontations.

One day in Cuero, Texas, Wes was openly challenged by J. W. Morgan, the town's sheriff and a Sutton supporter. Hardin tried to ignore him but when Morgan tried to take him into custody at gunpoint, Hardin drew and killed him.[16]

He rode back to Gonzales only to discover that Bill Sutton, leader of the Sutton faction, had threatened Jane and their infant daughters. Hardin then joined the Taylors; at a clan meeting he was elected leader.

The raging war continued with blood spilled on both sides. Under Hardin's planning, Jim Cox was killed and Wes and Jim Taylor trailed Jack Helm, a notorious gunfighter for the Suttons, to a cow town in Wilson where Wes killed him in a standup gunfight.

Hardin later wrote that he had received "many letters of thanks from the widows of the men Helm had killed, while many of the best citizens of Gonzales and DeWitt counties, patted me on the back and told me it was the best act of my life."

The part Governor Davis's state police played in the feud and evidence of their corruption and brutality forced the Texas legislature to disband the group. Then in April of 1874 the frontier was shocked when Billy and Jim Taylor trailed Bill Sutton, the leader of the clan, to the old port city of Indianola and killed him and Gabriel (Gabe) Slaughter as they boarded the steamboat *Clinton.*[17]

Slaughter, a rancher, was an innocent bystander, and aroused citizens demanded that newly elected Governor Richard Coke end the feud and bring peace to DeWitt and Gonzales counties. Coke ordered Texas Rangers dispatched to the two counties with orders to arrest John Wesley Hardin, credited with planning Sutton's murder.

Hardin sent Jane, his daughters, and son to Comanche, Comanche County, and organized a drive north with the faithful Manning Clements, Jim and Joe Taylor, and Tom and Billy Dixon. Hardin and Taylor rode to nearby Brown County, rounded up some steers, and drove them back to Gonzales.

When Brown County Deputy Sheriff Charles Webb heard Hardin and Taylor had been in his county, he was infuriated, denouncing Comanche Sheriff John Carnes as a coward for not arresting Hardin and Taylor and publicly promising, "I'm going to arrest or kill John Wesley Hardin before sundown or die in the attempt."[19]

On May 26, 1874, Webb rode into Comanche with a large following of Brown County residents who had come to attend the horse races held on the edge of town. Hardin's story, supported by eyewitnesses, which he later recounted in many petitions to governors and judges, was that he had been warned Webb was coming to town to kill him.

They first met at the racetrack. Hardin, wearing his six-shooters, carefully watched the deputy, whom he had been told would attempt to get the drop on him during one of the races. Manning Clements and the Dixon brothers, all armed, trailed Webb through the crowds until the deputy realized it would be suicide to kill Hardin among his friends.

It was Hardin's twenty-first birthday and a glorious day for the young gunfighter. His horses were the best on the track and by that afternoon he and his brother, Joe, than a practicing lawyer in Comanche, had won $3,000 in cash, horses, wagons, and produce. He gave Jane the cash and the Dixons drove the mounts and wagons to his ranch, while he, his brother, Joe, and Clements rode into town to celebrate Wes's birthday at Jack Wright's saloon.

It was evident that the large crowd of Brown County residents, many of them bitter at losing to Hardin, were crowding the town saloons and gambling halls. There were several near clashes but Hardin ignored the insults and curses.

Suddenly Webb, followed by several friends, walked into the saloon and approached Wes who was determined to "avoid any difficulty."

As he recalled: "Webb had a big pistol and stopped near me, eyeing me closely. He had been announced to me as the man who had promised to kill me before sundown or die in the attempt."[18]

Webb, apparently confident with his backing of followers, kept one hand behind his back.

"Your name is Webb, isn't it?" Hardin asked.

"That's right," the deputy replied.

"Do you have papers for my arrest?" Hardin demanded. "My name is John Wesley Hardin."

"I know who you are," Webb replied. "I have no papers for your arrest."

"What do you have in your hand behind your back?" Hardin inquired.

Webb slowly brought his hand around to his waist and held up the stub of a cigar. His followers roared.

"I heard the sheriff of Brown County said Sheriff John Carnes is no man and no sheriff because he was harboring the notorious John Wesley Hardin," Wes said. "I further understand that the sheriff of Brown County had said he was coming over here to attend to the Carnes business and that he intended to kill me before sundown or die in the attempt."

Webb stared at Hardin. "I'm not the sheriff of Brown County, I'm a deputy and I'm not responsible for what the sheriff does or says. Besides I think John Carnes is a brave officer and a gentleman."

Hardin said promptly, "Well, then sir, that settles it, there are no differences between us. Will you join me in a drink and a cigar?"

"I will sir," Webb replied.

As Hardin turned to give his order to the bartender, Webb started to draw his gun.

Hardin later wrote:

"There came a voice to me, like the voice of God, 'Look out, Jack,' and his [Webb's] game was up and he himself died."

Hardin's superb reflexes had acted automatically. Webb's revolver had not cleared his holster when Hardin spun around, drew, and killed him with one shot.[19]

As Webb's body crashed to the floor, the sun was slowly setting . . .

For a moment there was a taut silence, then the saloon exploded with shouts, curses, and gunshots. Hardin and Manning Clements fought their way free of the gathering mob but the Dixon brothers and Joe Hardin were taken into custody by Sheriff Carnes and put into the jail at Comanche.

A mob of Brown County residents quickly gathered, fought off the Comanche supporters of Hardin, stormed the jail, and lynched the innocent Joe Hardin and the two Dixons.

Hardin always insisted a company of Texas Rangers had moved into town but refused to stop the lynchings. A short time later two more of Hardin's cousins were killed as they tried to escape a Brown County mob.

Hardin realized Texas was no longer safe; he sent Jane and his children to her parents in Comanche, then fled to Alabama where he became a horse trader, stockman, and saloon owner under the name of James W. Swain. Ironically, the real Swain was a Texas marshal and Hardin's friend.

In August 1876, Jane, Molly, and John met him in Polland, Alabama, where Hardin had become a partner in a prosperous logging business on the Stick River.

In the meantime Brown Bowen, Jane's brother, who was under a murder indictment, joined them in Polland. After a few weeks he foolishly wrote to his father, Neal, Hardin's father-in-law in Gonzales County, revealing where the Hardins were living.

Some time before a young stranger who said he was interested in buying the Bowen general store had moved in with the Bowens as a boarder to familiarize himself with the business. He gave his name as John Duncan. Jane's father was impressed with Duncan's energy and courtesy and sold him several shares in the business. He was soon accepted as a member of the family, dining with the Bowens, joining them on the porch in the evenings, and playing cards with Neal Bowen.

Duncan was actually a Texas Ranger assigned to find John Wesley Hardin by Captain John Armstrong who had vowed to capture the famous gunfighter with the impressive list of dead men to his credit—and possibly collect the $4,000 reward the state of Texas had now posted for the capture of Hardin.

Captain John Armstrong of the Texas Rangers, who trailed Hardin to Decatur, Alabama. Hardin was living in Alabama under the name of John D. Swain and Armstrong arrested him in August 1877, after a gun battle in which Hardin's friend Jim Mann was killed. Hardin in letters to his wife, Jane, insisted Mann was shot in the back and he was taken without a warrant. *The James D. Horan Civil War and Western Americana Collection*

One day Duncan saw the letter from Brown Bowen. Late that night he read its contents. A coded dispatch was shortly on the way to Armstrong, advising him to investigate the mysterious James W. Swain in Polland, Alabama.

Undercover rangers were sent to Florida and Alabama; Swain was quickly identified as John Wesley Hardin. The gunfighter was shadowed and reports detailing his movements were delivered to Armstrong, recovering from a bullet wound in the leg. The Ranger captain, using a cane, obtained special permission to work on the case with Duncan.

On a hot August day in 1877, Hardin, accompanied by an old friend, Jim Mann, boarded a train at Pensacola, Florida, for Alabama. Without waiting for a court warrant Armstrong surrounded the train with his Rangers and local law enforcement officers. Four, dressed as passengers, casually boarded the smoking car directly behind Hardin. As the gunfighter sat down they leaped on him, handcuffing and disarming him. Mann, who was not wanted, ran down the station and was quickly riddled by rifle and six-shooter fire from the Rangers.

As Hardin bitterly wrote to Jane:

"They had me foul, very foul, four men grabbing me by the arm and legs . . . poor Jimmy was shot dead by the crowd [of Rangers] who were on the outside . . ."[20]

Hardin was indicted and convicted of Webb's murder, despite the testimony of witnesses that Webb had attempted to shoot him in the back. There is little doubt the Rangers viewed Hardin as a menace and were determined to get rid of him at any cost. Hardin later claimed some of his witnesses had been warned not to testify in his behalf. Comanche Judge Fleming sentenced the gunfighter to twenty-five years at hard labor in the dread Huntsville prison. The Texas court of appeals affirmed the conviction and sentence, not because Hardin killed Webb, but because of his reputation and "the enormity of his crimes and his associates. . . ."

John Wesley Hardin served nineteen years in Huntsville. During that time he wrote many letters to his wife, Jane, his mother, members of his family, and to friends. Each one was carefully hidden away by Jane. Numbering more than three hundred, they are preserved in the Southwest Texas State University's library at San Marcos.[21]

They contain not only a rare insight into the character of one of the most famous gunfighters of the Wild West but can be viewed as the personal history of a man who matured in dank cells and dungeons from a wild, reckless killer to a soft-spoken, graying attorney who finally said good-bye to his jailers.

And too, there is a full panoply of emotions exposed: Hardin rebellious, belligerent, dangerous as he plots a mass escape; furious, frustrated at the cold, impersonal law, and in the next moment depressed, anguished, as he yearns for Jane. Curiously there are none from Jane; obviously she wrote as did their two daughters and son but the letters are lost. However, writing to a cousin, Wes quoted a portion of Jane's last letter to him written shortly before she died, lonely, sad, and expressing her deep sorrow at their long parting.

We can feel his torment when he wrote that he could "feel your strong hugs . . . our love is beyond all language."

J. S. CLARK & DAVID P. LEWIS,

Attorneys at Law,

Give full names of all parties to suits.
Non-residents must give security for costs.

Decatur, Ala. .... Aug the 25 1877

The rare first letter written by John Wesley Hardin to his wife Jane after he had been captured by Captain John Armstrong and his Texas Rangers. Hardin, writing on his lawyer's stationery from Decatur, Alabama, told Jane how he was taken "foul, yes very foul." He signed the letter "J. H. Swain," the alias he used as a fugitive. *Courtesy Southwest Texas State University Library, San Marcos, Texas*

John Wesley Hardin committed many sins but the most grievous were those against the ones he loved . . .

When he entered Huntsville, Hardin was told he could only write once a month but he soon found a way to "get pass the eyes of the Supt."; a guard with the wonderful name of James C. Outlaw agreed for a price to smuggle out his letters to Jane and other members of his family.

Hardin, a born leader, led groups of prisoners several times in escape attempts, once almost capturing the prison's armory. Although he was repeatedly flogged with thick straps and confined for long periods in solitary dungeons on bread and water, the guards could not break his spirit. In all his letters he never complained to Jane. He dismissed the beatings and solitary as a mild form of punishment, assuring her that convict friends, even the guards, supplied him with extra blankets, food, and candles.

Hardin's letters also reveal his progress as a scholar. While he had attended school and had a better education than the average frontier young adult, his early letters had little punctuation, misspelled words, and grammatical errors. The letters improved as he began to study law and theology, encouraged by Ben McCulloch, the Texas frontiersman and Huntsville's assistant warden. McCulloch, who knew Hardin from their trail driving days, is credited with persuading Hardin to accept his long sentence and work for a pardon. In the end Hardin's petition to Governor James S. Hogg was a polished document, filled with impressive legal arguments and citations. Here are excerpts of Hardin's letters to Jane, his children, and relatives.

In his first letter to Jane after he had been captured by the Texas Rangers, Hardin charged he was taken "without a legal warrant." He denied that "I have ever murdered anybody, nor robbed anyone but what I have done in Texas was to save my life." He told Jane to write to him at the Austin jail under his alias James H. Swain and informed her it was her brother's letter that led to his capture. He described the Ranger Duncan as a "State Detective of Texas."[22]

A few months later he reviewed his case for Jane, pointing out that "the first insulting word had come from Webb who shouted, 'Damn you,' pulling his pistol and firing at the same time. I defended myself but not until he fired the *1st* time . . . Jane, my darling, you do not know how often I think of you. Jane, dearest, do not grieve for me for it will do no good but look for a bright future which yet may come. I am able to bear my troubles and will do it like a man."[23]

That same year Brown Bowen was arrested and indicted for murder. His father, Neal, visited Hardin and begged him to confess to the killing so his son, Brown, Jane's brother, would be freed.

On March 26, 1877, Hardin wrote all this to Jane, declaring her father and brother "are now against me, they have done all they can against me. He [her father] tried to lay his foul and Disgraceful deed against me but they don't go worth a cent."

In May Hardin asked Jane to be "cheerful and live in hope of better days. Do not grieve or trouble your mind, my dear wife, your troubles have been

Dec the 5th 1877

Austin Travis county
Texas

Mrs Jane Hardin

My Darling and affectionate wif I received your kind and most welcome letter to day. which give me much satisfaction to know that you had been able to get one letter from me and also to know that you & the family were all well. Jane this leaves me well and in joy better health than I have since I came here. about 2 weeks ago I had a severe attact of my side but received good attention and did not last long. Jane I am wel cared for and kindley treated have all the medical aid that may be necissary for me to have. Jane I am in good spirits as one could be under the same circumstances. one of my Lawyers have been to see me since I wrote to you he says that for me to be in good spirits that my case is shore to be reversed & remanded. Jane if so I am shore to come clear yet. he says that I should of come clear at the communche trial. according to Evidence and say that the courts of appeals wil say so. for the testimony was that there was no insulting language or threats made by me and that the first insulting word was from web which as follows. No god damn you puling his pistol and firing at the same time then I defended my self but not untill he fired the 1st shot. J.W.H.

A rare letter from John Wesley Hardin to his "darling and affectionate wife" some months after his capture and when he was in the Austin jail. The famous gunfighter gave his version of how he killed Deputy Sheriff Charles Webb, insisting that Webb drew first and he did not fire, "not until he fired the 1st." *Courtesy Southwest Texas State University Library, San Marcos, Texas*

great and I do wish I could bear them for you. Let my fate be what it may, but dear, my case will be decided soon, reversed or affirmed."

A short time later after the Texas court of appeals had affirmed his conviction and sentence, Hardin wrote a bitter letter to Jane denouncing the "false newspaper reports and the lies of cowardly murderers to prejudice the minds of the people and the courts of the state of Texas against me . . . but Dear One, I can bear it all."[24]

He also revealed that her father had again visited him asking for the statement to clear Brown Bowen of the murder charge.

"I told him no, it was not honorable and I hoped he wished me not to make a false one. In fact, I said true statements will do him no good and a False one I cannot make . . . I cannot be made a scapegoat . . . May God forgive him . . ."

Brown Bowen was hanged on May 17, 1878, in Gonzales, and Neal Bowen never forgave his son-in-law . . .

In June, after another appeal had been turned down, Wes swore to Jane he would never give up: "I know that your love is beyond any language . . . it seems that the strong hand of Man is against us . . . the current is against me and besides I have cost the State of Texas to much monie to be allowed my liberty whether right or wrong. So can you see what publick opinion can do for man and men . . ."[25]

A short time later Hardin cautiously indicated to Jane he was thinking of escape: "My friends say they will help me at the right time . . . Kiss the children and do not let them forget me . . ."

Hardin did not attempt to break out that summer. In October he was again full of plans for another appeal and possibly a pardon.

"My intention is to live as a quiet & peaceful citizen should I ever be allowed that . . . I dream and pray for you, my beloved one of all . . . tell Mollie [his daughter] to mind her ma and Grama . . . tell JWH [his son] to be a good boy."

In December 1878, after his final appeal had been turned down, a desperate John Wesley Hardin organized a gang of fifty prisoners in a mass jailbreak. Led by Hardin, they fought their way to the armory, which they were near capturing, when reinforcements arrived and drove back the convicts armed with crude, homemade weapons. After a daylong siege they surrendered. Hardin was flogged into unconsciousness, then throw into the solitary dungeon.

Later he casually wrote Jane that he had been "punished for the break, spending five days in a dark cell. But you bet the guards & convicts treated me well and I had all the candles, extra grub and blankets I needed. None of which is allowed a man in a dark cell." There was only one bitter note: "If this place must be beat, [there is] no telling what I might do in the time to come . . ."

In the same letter Wes ordered Jane to "write to M. C." (Manning Clements) and advise him "to come down this Spring, that horses will bring a good price," which may have been a signal for the faithful Clements that Wes was already preparing another escape attempt.[26]

Hardin was in solitary for a long time. When he finally emerged in February 1879, he cheerfully assured Jane: "I'm doing as well as circumstances will admit . . ."

In July Wes told Jane the prison grapevine informed him that Johnny Ringo,

Mollie (Molly) Hardin Billings, John Wesley Hardin's eldest daughter. In the summer of 1892, Mollie notified her father that her mother Jane was seriously ill.

A rare photograph of John Wesley Hardin, Jr. In a letter written in 1886 from his cell in Huntsville prison, John Wesley Hardin urged his son to "make arithmetic, grammer, spelling, reading and writing a speciality, have honor and you will succeed." *Courtesy Southwest Texas State University Library, San Marcos, Texas*

the Arizona gunman, had been killed in Arizona. Ringo, leader of a gang of outlaws near Tombstone, had become friendly with Hardin when they had been together in the Austin jail.

During the next few years Hardin wrote faithfully to Jane but by 1883 his letters gradually ceased. In the winter of 1884 he explained to Jane he had been seriously ill for some time with an infection from an old gunshot wound suffered in Trinity City. He had been months in bed, he wrote, "all the time not able to get up."[27] Hardin's health deteriorated. By August of the following year when Ben McCulloch was appointed assistant warden, Wes wrote to him begging for medical assistance:

"I don't know whether I have Bright's Disease, Cancer or heart Disease or whatever else it is, but it gives me much pain beyond description . . . I am wasting away from this disease and have suffered for two years . . ."[28]

McCulloch apparently had prison physicians examine and give him treatment. After he recovered, McCulloch obtained permission for Hardin to study law and theology and put him on the prison's debating team, which Hardin later headed. The former gunfighter and one of the most dangerous men on the frontier wrote Jane that his team won a debate. The subject: "Women's Rights."

When Hardin left his children they were infants, now Molly, Nan, and John Wesley Hardin, Jr., were teen-agers. In 1886 Hardin wrote to his son:

"You compose and write well for a boy of your age. When you write a letter, think over carefully what you want to write. That is, what happened or transpired, what would be worthy to speak of, if brought face to face with the person addressed, since the last time you saw him . . . I have made these suggestions to improve your manner of writing, hoping that you will profit by my advice. As I said before, you do well but I wish to see you do better. Large streams from little creeks grow; full trees from small acorns grow; then great men from little boys. Make arithmetic, Grammer, Spelling, Reading and Writing a speciality; have honor and you will succeed . . ."[29]

On February 1, 1889, Hardin wrote an appeal "to the Lawmakers of Texas Assembled at Austin," suggesting reforms in the laws governing homicide cases, the length of imprisonment after conviction, and procedures used after a convict's release from prison. The appeal was signed by ninety-seven convicts and delivered to Austin.

In the fall of 1890, Wes urged Jane "not to lose all your good looks—save them for me." He dismissed his recurring illness which again had confined him to bed for some time, adding: "But Jane, considering all things I am doing life is splendid. I am not hacked or discouraged and hope to re-enter the arena of life ready to battle for my rights as I understand them." He asked her to "watch the children carefully, encourage them in healthfull sports, make their home as pleasant as possible, don't scold them or grumble at them in order to govern them but rather rule them with kind words backed by reason and love . . . keep your children in the path of virtue and rectitude and you will do well." He ordered John not to be "quarrelsome but to be kind and obliging to every one, not to drink whiskey or go with roudies [sic], not gamble but to make an honest living for your Ma and your sisters . . ."[30]

In 1892 Hardin wrote his old classmate, William Teagarden, a well-known lawyer and a power in the Democratic party, that his health was precarious and he had been confined to his bed for as long as eight months from his old gunshot wounds.

Now it was another time, the frontier was gone, and men like Teagarden urged that Hardin be pardoned. Newspaper articles recalled the early wild days of the Texas frontier with a touch of pride and how John Wesley Hardin was one of the last links to the days when the state was struggling against the Carpetbaggers and the Yankees and the drives to the Kansas cow towns were making history.

With well-known leaders in the Democratic party working for his pardon, Hardin grew more hopeful: In one letter to Jane, "My beloved with a soft sweet good morning," he pictured their new life together.

Then in the summer of 1892, Hardin's daughter, Molly, wrote that Jane was seriously ill. He replied to Molly: "My anxiety cannot be expressed . . . I only wish it was possible for me to suffer in her stead . . ." He hoped that his "angelic wife" would soon recover, "that true and loyal wife of mine whose love is like the driven snow . . ."[31]

Hardin, distraught over Jane's illness, begged his daughters and son "not to let your sweet mama do any work . . . tell her she must take care of herself for her children's and my sake." In September 1892 he was writing to his cousin, Buck Cobb, urging him to call on Jane "and cheer her up." He expected his pardon would be issued the following month. He added proudly:

"My freedom will be based on legal endeavor and not that liberty that will have me play hide and seek with the officers of the law . . . tell her [Jane] that when I am free, my highest ambition is to do one act, say some word, that will cheer her and make her happy . . ."

Jane, at the home of relatives in Kingsbury, Texas, continued to sink. In her last letter to Wes, she wrote:

Huntsville Feb the 1st 1889

To the law makers of Texas assembled at Austin Texas. It is with veneration that we the unfortunate inmates of the Huntsville prison whose names are attached to day address you and forward to that august assembly this our petition for the amendment of the Statute that portion that section and that article which defines and describes the crimes which the Statute shall run against or be outlawed after a certain limited time has expired and respectfully pray that the crime of Homicide be added thereunto under certain circumstances and conditions, Namely, When a person charged with the crime of murder for which he has not been tried is confined in the penitentiary for any crime and remains in the said penitentiary for seven years who bears his true name at the time of entrance to the penitentiary or makes known his real name within three months after entrance to the penitentiary that all such persons shall receive the benefit of this amendment and that said person or persons shall stand acquited of murder because the State has not used due dilligence to bring the said person or persons to justice and when any person or persons charged with murder establish this fact that he has served in a penitentiary in the State of Texas [illegible] his own true name and that the [illegible] committed [illegible] Sentence which the State so generously [illegible] do not believe this law has any potent influence for good upon such [illegible] when he knows that the agent of the State stands ready at the expiration of his term to lead him back in irons to the scenes of former days at a time when his health is broken without friends money or witnes[ses] with the odium of having been a convict which allmost warrants conviction according to the convict view. This idea seems to obtain namely that the agent of the State says obey the rules and gain good time and at the expiration of your sentence we will take you out try you for murder and hang you or give you a life sentence and we believe that it is a prison organizer for it is noted fact that one individual evilly inclined often does a great deal of harm and causes trouble untold by inducing men leading to mutiny to insubordination to conspiracy his fellow convicts 5, 10, 20, and even more, to accomplish their designs they often take Therefore we beseech you with great deference to amend this law. [Th]en trusting in the justness of our cause, and confiding in your superior wisdom your patriotism and your love for reform for justice for mankind and your God we transmit this our petition hopefully to that august assembly for their deliberation with the fervent wish that this law [be] amended. Names.

John W. Hardin
Bill Templeton
[illegible]
A. L. George
[illegible] Pierson

Mit Day
Sam Feagan
J. B. Gough
A. C. Barber
H. M. Harp

J. G. Spurs
W. H. Kiser
Forbs Miller
A. J. Rinford
H. L. Reafer

A rare 1899 petition written by John Wesley Hardin for his fellow inmates in the Huntsville prison to the "lawmakers of Texas assembled at Austin," in which he suggested changes in the state's penal code. He was the first of ninety-seven convicts to sign it. Hardin by this time was studying law. *Courtesy Southwest Texas State University Library, San Marcos, Texas*

"John, it seems so hard that we must be apart but that cannot be helped now. But to be away from my children is harder still under the circumstances and I am going to try and avoid this in the future. Your loving wife until death, Jane . . ."[32]

A short time later on November 6, 1892, Jane died.

Wes was stunned by his wife's death; Jane had been always there, waiting. Now she was gone. As he wrote Buck Cobb, "only Time alone can wash away the tears of [my] grief . . ."

In the fall of 1893 new difficulties threatened to postpone his pardon. Neal Bowen, who had never forgiven Hardin for refusing to confess to a killing and save his son, Brown, from the gallows, had testified that Hardin had killed Deputy Sheriff J. B. Morton, the Sutton supporter, some years before in Cuero. Wes pleaded guilty and was sentenced to two years but persuaded the courts to agree the sentence would run concurrently with his long term.

On January 1, 1894, Hardin petitioned Governor Hogg for a pardon. The document is professional, carefully reviewing the Webb killing, citing opinions of the Texas court of appeals, including legal citations, and analyzing the testimony of eyewitnesses who swore Hardin fired only in self-defense after Webb had pointed a pistol at his back.

Hardin pointed out that the state's vital testimony from Deputy Sheriff William Cunningham of Comanche County quoted Hardin as saying to his friend Jim Taylor when he saw Webb on the street:

"Did you ever see anything coming up finer in your life?"

Hardin stressed to Governor Hogg that the state's attorney had failed to supply proof he was even on the street at the time. He also charged Cunningham and other state witnesses to have been ringleaders of the mob that lynched his brother, Joe, and his cousins, Tom and William Dixon. Hardin pointed out that a company of Rangers stationed nearby failed to stop the mob. They were lynched, Hardin swore, because Tom Dixon was an eyewitness to the Webb shooting and Joe had promised to make sure his brother received a fair trial. Hardin wrote:

"While the state, through Webb's friends, offered a reward of $4,000 for my capture, no money was ever offered, nor was there an investigation into the leaders of the mob who lynched Joe Hardin and the Dixons."

John Wesley Hardin was pardoned in the spring of 1894. He emerged from Huntsville a graying, pale, gaunt man, to enter a strange, alien society that viewed him as a curiosity, an anachronism from the "old days."

Hardin found former cow camps were now towns. Austin, where he recalled citizens fought off raiding parties of Comanche and Kiowa, was a bustling city. El Paso and San Antonio had trolley cars, brick houses, impressive stores, and public buildings.

Rutherford B. Hayes had been president when he entered Huntsville; now five presidents later, Benjamin Harrison was sitting in the White House. Old friends and enemies were long dead: Wild Bill Hickok—he now described Hickok in a letter as, "no braver man ever drew breath"—and Phil Coe, who had given him the name of "Little Seven Up"; Ben Thompson, who tried to talk him into killing Hickok during the wild days in Abilene. The Sutton and Taylor

Parties corresponding with prisoners must observe carefully the following directions, viz: Write plainly. Confine yourself strictly to family and business matters. In directing letters put prisoner's name plainly on envelope, and address care of box 32, Huntsville, Texas. Daily papers are not admitted. All letters and papers are examined. Prisoners can write but once a month at the expense of the State; they may be permitted to write a second letter at their own expense, and to see friends once a month, so long as their conduct is good. Prisoners are permitted to receive underclothing.

DO NOT INTERLINE.—WRITE ONLY ON RULED LINES.

PUT YOUR NAME HERE.	PUT FULL ADDRESS OF YOUR LETTER HERE. Give Post Office, County and State.
Name. John W. Hardin	Miss Molly. E. Hardin
Molly Dear daughter	Sedan Gonzales County
y precious child and	Texas

Huntsville, Texas, Aug the 21st 1892

my faithful daughter Your loving father received your
ief letter last night with fatherly gratitude and joy. Yet I
nnot describe or explain on paper my deep and my sincere solic-
ude for the health of your most estimable mother, my anxiety in regard to her bad
ndition cannot be expressed. I only wish that it was possible for me
 suffer in her stead. I do hope ere now, ere this reaches you that my
riceless wife that my angelic wife will have regained her accustomed
 normal health, and being hopeful brave and loving. I shall
ope to the God of love of hope of mercy to cause to restore to health
at adorable woman that loving and beloved mother that true
yal wife of mine whose heart and mind is free from guile
d whose love is as pure as the driven snow. tell your
ving mother and your sweet sister and your noble brother
hat papa sends them his love with a kiss. Buck I received
your welcome letter about three weeks ago, your cousin was
lad to hear from you and I wish to say that my sensibility would
 dense indeed if I did not appreciate your aid and friendship
 me and mine and I do hope and believe that the ties that bind you
nd I in brotherly love are stronger than steel more durable
an brass more permanent than adamant more lasting than iron
 and will last as long as our lives last. Buck I am not only
roud and grateful to you for your friendship, but I am eq-
ually proud and grateful to others of your section who have stood
p for me and have done all they could for me and mine. I have
atched the Houston convention with an interesting and with a critical eye I unqualifiedly approve all the hog (or regular democratic
convention) done, I believe and hope they will win easy, The Clark faction
bolterots lost but would not give the stakes up but the people will see
t they do in november, yet I expect to be pardoned by the middle of
ov for I see with pleasure and hope that the indomitable the wi

A rare letter from John Wesley Hardin to his daughter Molly, after he had been notified that his wife Jane was seriously ill. Here the gunfighter told his daughter he wished that it could be "possible for me to Suffer in her Stead." Jane died before Hardin was released from Huntsville prison after serving nineteen years of his twenty-five-year sentence. *Courtesy Southwest Texas State University Library, San Marcos, Texas*

feud was long forgotten; the buffalo were gone along with the Indians, whom Hardin once told Jane he feared meeting on the Plains; only a few longhorn were kept by sentimental ranchers; and the great drives to the northern cow towns were fading memories cherished by white-haired men. Even Manning Clements, who had faithfully visited Wes every month in prison, was dead.

Hardin found his children adults, married, and with their own families. He was alone, a weary, sick middle-aged man, suffering constant pain from old bullet wounds and still grieving for the woman who had waited so long to join him.

Hardin had come out of prison a recognized lawyer. In October 1894, he opened his first office in Gonzales. From his letters he appeared to have had a respectable practice among the Mexican-Americans in that town and neighboring counties.[33]

One shadow hung over his life, the fear that a gun-happy youngster might attempt to kill him to gain the reputation as the man who killed "the notorious John Wesley Hardin," as the newspapers called him. During the first years of freedom Wes carefully avoided saloons, gambling halls, and argumentative strangers.

Hardin started his autobiography shortly after he was released from prison; there were many volunteers to help him. One admirer wrote that he was the only one who could do the task: "Don't let anyone else do it, I want to write it myself."[34]

Publishers were also interested, one calling him "a thoroughly reformed gentleman interested in publishing a book."

Hardin, who had read a great deal in prison, continued his love of books, purchasing some from the Gilbert Publishing Company which advised him of their "book credit plan."

In the winter of 1894, Hardin met Callie Lewis, a flirtatious, pretty young woman, many years his junior. Callie, intrigued by Hardin's colorful past, encouraged his attentions. In one letter, Captain Len L. Lewis, who may have been her father, warned him that "Callie is full of Hell . . . perhaps your matter [marriage] should sleep awhile . . ."

But Callie had completely charmed Wes and he courted her intensely. They were finally married, but after a month Callie returned to her family.[35]

The breakup with Callie was a shattering blow to Hardin. Depressed and embittered he returned to the gambling halls and saloons. He became irritable, morose, and overbearing. He entered politics, opposing a nominee for sheriff of Gonzales. He vowed in a letter to a local newspaper that "if he is elected I will not continue to live in this county." When the other man was elected, Hardin kept his promise and moved to El Paso where he opened a law office.

He was welcomed by the *El Paso Times*, which reminded its readers that Wes had been a part of Texas history, a man "who in his younger days was as wild as the broad western plains on which he was raised . . . forty-one years had steadied the impetuous cowboy down to a peaceable, dignified quiet man of business . . ."

Hardin was making a reputation as a criminal lawyer in El Paso when he met the attractive wife of Martin McRose, a cattle rustler. McRose, "on his way to talk about terms of surrendering," was killed by Ranger Jeff Milton and Depu-

TUESDAY AUGUST 20, 1895.

J. W. Hardin
John Selman

WES HARDIN IS KILLED.

This Noted Character Dies by John Selman's Pistol.

THE FATE OF ALL BAD KILLERS.

The First Bullet Hit Him in the Eye and Passed Through his Brain—A Sketch of Hardin's Life in Brief by one who has Known Him Since Boyhood.

Last night between 11 and 12 o'clock San Antonio street was thrown into an intense state of excitement by the sound of four pistol shots that occured at the Acme saloon. Soon the crowd surged against the door and there, right inside lay the body of John Wesley Hardin, his blood flowing over the floor and his brains oozing out a pistol shot wound that had passed though his head.

Soon the fact became generally known that John Selman, constable of Precint No. 1, had fired the fatal shots that had ended the career of so noted a character as Wes Hardin, by which name he is better known to all old Texans.

For several weeks past trouble has been brewing and it has been often heard on the streets that John Wesley Hardin would be the cause of some killing before he left the town. Only a short time ago, Policeman Selman arrested Mrs. M'Rose, the mistress of Hardin, and she was tried and convicted of carrying a pistol. This arrest angered Hardin and when he was drinking he often made remarks that showed that he was bitter in his feelings against young John Selman. Selman paid no attention to these remarks, but attended to his duties and said nothing. Lately Hardin had become louder in his abuse and had continually been under the influence of liquor and at such times he was very quarrelsome, even getting along badly with some of his friends. This quarrelsome disposition on his part resulted in his death last night and is a sad warning to all such parties that the rights of others must be respected and that the day is past when a person having the name of being a bad man can run rough-shod over the law and the rights of other citizens.

This morning early a HERALD reporter started after the facts in the case and found John Selman, the man who fired the fatal shots and his statement were as follows:

"I met Wes Hardin about 7 o'clock last evening close to the Acme saloon. When we met Hardin said: 'You've got a son that's a bastardly, cowardly s— -of-a-b——!' I said, 'Which one?' Hardin said: 'John, the one that's on the police force. He pulled my woman when I was absent and robbed her of $50, which they wouldn't have done if I had been here.' I said: 'Hardin, there is no man on earth that can talk about my children like that without fighting, you cowardly s— -of-a-b——!' Hardin said: 'I am unarmed.' I said: 'Go and get your gun; I am armed.' Then he said: 'I'll go and get a gun and when I meet you I'll meet you smoking, and make you —— like a wolf around the block!' Hardin then went into the Acme saloon and began shaking dice with Henry Brown. I met my son, John, and Captain Carr and I told

What Metal Is Worth.	
Silver	66¾
Lead	3.37½
Copper	11
Mexican pesos. El Paso	52
" " Juarez	52

Some shots were fired after he was down. F. F. PATTERSON.

Mr. E. L. Shackelford testified as follows:

My name is E. L. Shackelford—am in the general brokerage business. When I came down the street this evening I had understood from some parties that Mr. Hardin had made some threats against Mr. Selman who had formerly been in my employ and was a friend of mine and I came over to the Acme saloon where I met Mr. Selman. At the time I met Mr. Selman he was in the saloon with several other parties and was drinking with them. I told him I understood there was occasion for him to have trouble and having heard the character of the man with whom he would have trouble I advised him as a friend not to get under the influence of liquor. We walked out on the sidewalk and came back into the saloon, I being some distance ahead of Mr. Selman, walking toward the back of the saloon. Then I heard shots fired. I can't say who fired the shots as I did not see it. I did not turn around but left immediately. The room was full of powder smoke and I could not have seen anything anyhow.

E. L. SHACKELFORD.

Mr. R. B. Stevens the proprietor of the Acme saloon was seen by a HERALD reporter this morning and gave the following account of the affair:

"I was on the street and some one told me that there was likely to be trouble at my saloon between Wes. Hardin and John Selman, Sr. I came on down to the saloon and walked in Selman was sitting outside the door. Hardin was standing just inside the door at the bar, shaking dice with Henry Brown. I walked on back into the reading room and sat down where I could see the bar. Soon Selman and Shackelford came in and took a drink. I then understood Shackelford to say to Selman: 'Come out now, you are drinking and I don't want you to have any trouble.' They went out together. I then supposed Selman had gone away and there would be no trouble. I leaned back against a post and was talking to Shorty Anderson and could not see the front door. While I was in that position the shooting began. I could not see the front door and do not know who came in. When Selman and Shackelford came in they took a drink at the inside end of the bar. Hardin and Brown were standing at the end of the bar next to the door. I did not see Selman when the shooting took place. When I went into the bar room Hardin was lying on the floor with his head near the door and was dead. I walked to the door and looked out. Selman was standing in front with several others, Captain Carr among them. When Captain Carr came into the saloon I asked him to take charge of Hardin's body and keep the crowd out. He said he could not move the body until the crowd viewed it. I saw Carr take two pistols off Hardin's body—one was a white handle and the other a black handle. They were both 41 calibre Colts. At the time of the shooting Shorty Anderson and myself were in the reading room, Frank Patterson was attending bar and Hardin and Brown were standing at the bar.

The bullet that passed through Hardin's head struck a mirror frame and glanced off and fell in front of the bar and the lower end. In the floor where Hardin fell there are three bullet holes in triangle shape and about a span apart. They range straight through the floor.

I agreed and shook first, he shook back and said he'd bet me a quarter on the side he could beat me. We both had our quarters up and he and I were shaking dice. I heard a shot fired, saw a flash and Mr. Hardin fell at my feet at my left side. I heard three or four shots fired I then left, went out the back door and don't know what occurred afterwards when the first shot was fired Mr. Hardin was against the bar facing it, as near as I can say, and as near as I can say his back was towards the direction the shot came from. I did not see him make any effort to get his sixshooter. The last words he spoke before the first shot was fired were "Four sixes to beat." and they were addressed to me. For a moment or two before this he had not spoken to anyone but me, to the best of my recollection.

I had not the slightest idea that anyone was quarrelling there from anything I heard.

H. S. BROWN.

The following evidence was given Justice Howe this afternoon by the three physicians whose names are signed thereto.

We the undersigned practicing physicians hereby certify that we have examined the gun shot wounds on the person of the deceased John Wesley Hardin and its our opinion that the wound causing death was caused by a bullet wound. That the bullet entered near the base of the skull posteriorly and came out at the upper corner of the left eye.

S. G. SHERARD.
W. N. VILAS.
ALWARD WHITE.

Justice Howe issued a warrant for John Selman's arrest this afternoon and ordered him held under arrest until bail was fixed.

The wounds on Hardin's body were in the back of the head coming out just over the left eye; another shot in the right breast just missing the nipple and another through the right arm. The body was embalmed by Undertaker Powell and will be interred at Concordia at 4 p. m.

A rare copy of the *San Antonio Herald-Post* with a number of eyewitness accounts of how John Selman killed John Wesley Hardin in the Acme Saloon in August 1895. Hardin had just completed his autobiography when he was killed. *Courtesy El Paso Public Library*

ty U.S. Marshals George Scarborough and Frank McMahon. The trio of lawmen were later indicted for the killing.

One night Hardin, drinking heavily, boasted in a saloon that he had hired Milton and Scarborough to kill McRose so he could marry the rustler's wife.

The lawmen were outraged. Milton went looking for Hardin and found him in a saloon. He offered to let John Wesley go for his gun but Hardin refused to face the younger man. Instead, for the first time he backed down and told the crowded bar:

"When I said that about Captain Milton I lied."

Later he wrote a note of apology to Scarborough.

John Wesley next encountered the Selmans, father and son. The younger Selman, an El Paso policeman, arrested the now widowed Mrs. McRose on a charge of carrying a gun. Hardin bailed out his sweetheart and went into a public tirade about officer Selman.

Like Hardin, the senior John Selman had a violent past. Charlie Siringo, the cowboy-detective, knew him as a dangerous man who had hunted Billy the Kid and more than once was on both sides of the law in the early days of territorial New Mexico.

Now he was chief constable of El Paso, a pillar of the community, and a very proud man.

When troublemakers reported what Hardin had said about his son, chief Selman went looking for him.

On August 19, 1895, he found Hardin shaking dice for drinks at the bar of the Acme Saloon. Now the once superb reflexes, the deep hidden instinct of the hunted, failed to flash their alarm. Hardin never turned as Selman drew his gun, carefully aimed, and shot him in the back of the head as he raised his dice cup for a toss.[36]

Selman was charged with murder and was defended by Albert Fall, who many years later would become one of the central figures in the Teapot Dome scandal. A jury acquitted him and he went back to wearing a tin star.

Ironically, several months later Selman was killed in a gunfight with United States Deputy Marshal George Scarborough, the lawman who had forced Hardin to apologize.[37]

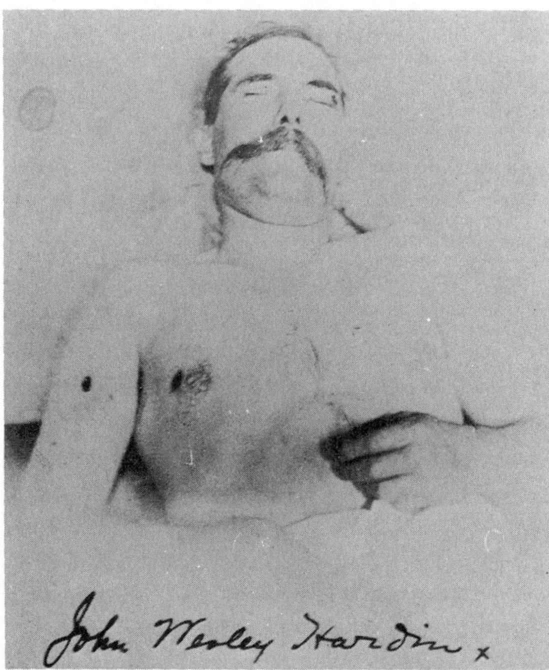

A rare photograph of John Wesley Hardin on a slab of the El Paso morgue shortly after he was killed by Sheriff John Selman on the afternoon of August 19, 1895, at the bar of the Acme Saloon. According to testimony of the bartender, Selman shot Hardin in the back of the head; the photograph reveals two gunshot wounds in the chest and upper arm. *Courtesy Southwest Texas State University Library, San Marcos, Texas*

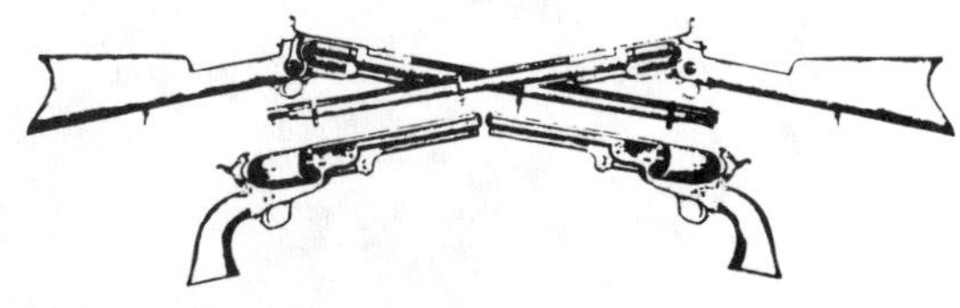

KID CURRY AND THE LOGANS OF MONTANA

HARVEY LOGAN, ALIAS KID CURRY, ONE OF THE MOST DANgerous men in the Wild West, was no tall ruggedly handsome Gary Cooper; photographs taken in the 1880s make him appear to be a mild-mannered man of medium height with melancholy dark eyes and dressed rather formally in a blue suit and wing collar. Lawmen who trailed him across the West—and beyond the grave—credited him with killing fifteen men "on the record"; he once rode hundreds of miles to wait patiently all night to gun down a rancher he held responsible for his younger brother's death.[1]

There was a sense of suppressed violence about him that men never forgot; he was so fast on the draw that witnesses in Knoxville, Tennessee, where he was finally captured, testified his shots came so fast it was hard to believe he had drawn his six-shooter and not fired through a coat pocket. He was slight in build but had enormous physical endurance. When he disappeared into the Tennessee wilderness known as "Jeffrey's Hell," mountaineers predicted they would find his bones in the spring but Kid Curry, as Logan was known in the West, appeared a month later in Denver carrying a suitcase of money, probably from a train robbery, generously tipping bellboys like a prosperous drummer and advising old friends he was glad to be back and promising, "I'll cut my way through hell before they'll take me again . . ."

He was proud of his reputation as a badman and killer. While the nation

The famous group photograph of the Wild Bunch. Kid Curry is standing to the right with his hand on Butch Cassidy's shoulder. *Courtesy Pinkertons, Inc.*

eagerly read newspaper accounts of the Northwest manhunt for Harry Tracy, a fellow Wild Bunch rider, Logan wrote a friend in Montana: "If I don't give them a better run for their money than that cub, Harry Tracy, then my name isn't Harvey Logan . . ."

Women were attracted to him. They flocked to his Knoxville cell bringing flowers, "fine foods," and bribing guards to deliver their love notes.

So many "fine presents from Knoxville women" filled Logan's cell the sheriff cut off all packages to the outlaw.

Logan was always accompanied by attractive women when he was "on the dodge" following a train or bank robbery. They were not all girls from Fanny Porter's Sporting House, the Texas frontier brothel where Logan hid out when he wasn't touring the country on stolen bank notes; Catherine Cross, a member of what the Knoxville newspapers called "a good family," may have helped him to escape from prison. She was later murdered by an infuriated drunk or madman because she insisted on singing a ballad about the Kid and his exploits.

Maud Davis described him as a "gentleman, clean through"; to Annie Rogers, who had her picture taken with one arm around Logan, "he was a fine man who never said a bad or cross word to me . . ."

Logan not only impressed Fanny Porter's whores and dazzled the matrons of Knoxville, but he also left lasting memories with the cowboys and ranchers who

A rare photograph of Landusky, Montana Territory, in Kid Curry's time. *Courtesy Alvin J. Lucke Collection*

knew him in Montana's beautiful country of the Little Rockies. A former cowboy and broncobuster, white-haired but still vigorous in the early 1950s, described Kid Curry to me as a loyal and generous friend.[2]

> I had worked with Harve in Montana. When I met him in Landusky I was sick and busted up inside from a bad ride and flat broke. I was real low down. Harve stood me to a drink and listened to what I had to say. Then he took a roll from his pockets, pushed some bills into my pocket and said it was a grubstake to help me get back on my feet. When things got better I could pay him back. I had a little outfit and the money helped me to keep the place and survive. When I got going again I tried to find him and pay back the loan but the Kid was on the dodge with the rest of the [Wild] Bunch after those train robberies. I left word at the Curry boys' saloon [The Club Saloon run by Lonny Curry in Harlem, Montana] but Lonny Curry [the Kid's brother killed in Dodson, Missouri, in 1900] was gone and the Kid never came back to the territory. Then I heard he got winged after a train robbery and killed himself. Maybe he did a lot of things that were outside the law but up here [Little Rockies country] there are still some alive who remember him as a man of his word and a man you could trust. That was a lot in those wild, early days . . .

But thirty years ago Lowell Spence, the Pinkerton detective who trailed Kid Curry for many years, gave me another view.[3]

Lowell Spence Recalls Kid Curry

It was almost suicide to go after him. He wasn't the kind to run and hide, he would plot and plan to ambush you.

He was an expert with a handgun and a rifle and could endure the most difficult weather conditions. He wasn't a big man physically nor was he a braggart but he was a cold, calculating killer. I recall when he was finally captured in Knoxville and I was asked by the United States Attorney to come down to the Knoxville Jail to formally identify him because the Kid calmly insisted his name was, I believe, Wilson. Of course this was in the days before fingerprints.

Logan came out to the bars and stared at me. We exchanged a bit of small talk then before I turned away to tell the United States Attorney this was really Harvey Logan, the Kid said quietly:

"I've been looking for you a long time, Spence. When I get out of here I'll be sure and look you up."

Logan knew I had been trailing him for years and we sort of knew each other. It gives me a chill even now, many years later, to recall him staring out at me through the bars. I am sure I was number one on his list. When he named a man he was going to kill, like that rancher Jim Winters, the Kid never failed to make good his threat.

After he escaped from Knoxville I trailed him for months. It was a very tense time. I never knew when he would suddenly appear, gun in hand . . .

As the *New York Times* said of Harvey Logan's life in the Wild West, "It reads like a dime novel, of the sensational type." His beginnings, however, were quiet and ordinary.

The four Logan brothers, Hank, Harvey, John, and Lonny, were born in Rowan County, Kentucky. While very young they came to live with their aunt, Mrs. Hiram Lee, her son, Robert E., and a daughter, Lizzie, in Dodson, Missouri. Mrs. Lee, their father's sister, operated a farm situated on a hill between Dodson Road and Troost Avenue, sixteen miles from Kansas City. Why the boys left Kentucky is not known. In 1900 Justice Douglas, who knew the Lee family, was quoted in the *Harlem* (Montana) *Enterprise:*

"Not much was known of their background. Even Mrs. Lee did not know a great deal about their parents. They came to live with her at the farm, the main house was a two-story frame house which Mrs. Lee and her husband, Hiram, occupied since the end of the Civil War."[4]

The elder Lee was an invalid, possibly a Confederate war veteran, who could be seen every day sitting in a rocking chair on the front porch while the Logan brothers and their cousin, Bob Lee, worked the farm. Neighbors recalled Harvey as quiet and reserved, Lonny outgoing and mischievous, and Johnny impulsive and owning a quick temper. Hank, the oldest, "kept the boys in hand."

Cherokee blood showed in their thick black hair, black eyes, and dark skin.

In their teens the four brothers, accompanied by Bob Lee, "left Dodson for the west to become cowboys."

Hank and Harvey joined the Circle outfit in Montana's Little Rockies country in the summer of 1884. As extra riders they were paid off in the fall and spent the winter chopping forty cords of wood, which they sold in the spring before rejoining the Circle.

They were all illiterate. "Dad" Marsh, a Missouri River trader, taught the young cowboys to read and write. Marsh recalled: "Every moment they had was put to studying and one day Hank brought in an order for some goods at my store, written in his own hand. I was astonished. The boy was very proud of his accomplishment."[5]

Harvey and Hank pooled their savings and with Jim Thornhill, another Circle rider, bought a ranch six miles south from the cow and mining town of Landusky. The town was named after Powell (Pike) Landusky, one of Montana's earliest pioneers. Landusky, who first came to the mining camp of Last Chance in 1872, was a tough Missourian with extraordinary long arms who liked to boast of his physical strength.

"If he liked you he would go to the gates of Hell for you," a friend recalled many years later. "If he disliked you, watch out. I don't know if he ever killed any white man, he just beat them until they couldn't fight any more. His hatred for Indians was a mania. No man knows how many he killed."

In 1880, while on a drunken spree, Landusky killed the wife of White Calf, a Blackfoot. The warrior hunted him down and shot him with a Buffalo gun. The blast tore away part of his lower left jawbone. Landusky lived for seventeen days on whiskey while friends took him overland in a wagon to the nearest surgeon.[6]

"After that it was hard to tell how good looking he might have been," a pioneer remembered.

In June 1894, the miners and stockmen of Chouteau County officially named Pike's trading post Landusky. It soon became a stopping-off place for gunmen, rustlers, army deserters, fugitives with a price on their heads, along with respectable ranchers and miners.

Landusky's partner was Jake Harris, known in the history of Montana's Little Rockies country as "Jew Jake." A saloon occupied the front part of the log building with a counter in the rear where gloves, overalls, and overshoes were sold.

In the early 1880s Harris had lost a leg from wounds he received in a gunfight with the sheriff of Great Falls. He walked with crutches but a Landusky pioneer resident described him:

"When Jake had the shift at the bar he used only the left hand crutch, leaving the right hand free to use a No. 8 sawed off shotgun he always kept within reach. If it was an exceptionally lively night in the bar he used the shotgun as a crutch . . ."[7]

After a year of ranching Hank left Montana, legend has him going to California, "the only honest Logan." Harvey was then joined by John and Lonny, the youngest. About this time, for some reason, the Logans changed their name to Curry; in Montana's frontier history they are known as "the Curry boys."

Their nearest neighbor was Landusky. The Missourian evidently respected Harvey, known as a quiet, almost aloof man, skilled with a six-shooter, "who made few friends and none of the, what you would call intimate friends . . . he and his brothers stuck pretty much together. Johnny was the wild one, always carrying a gun and trying to be a desperado . . . But it was Harvey the tough boys avoided. There was something about Harvey that made the so-called badmen walk around him . . ."

The Currys and Landusky remained friends and neighbors until one day there was a row; legend has it over a plow that Landusky borrowed and refused to return but a more logical reason is Landusky's buxom daughters. Two had been married but Lonny was courting Elfie, single and attractive. Landusky protested to Harvey, then threatened to shoot Lonny. In Jew Jake's saloon Harvey softly replied that if anyone hurt his brothers they would have to answer to him. And that included Pike Landusky.

The feud simmered for a year until Pike had Harvey and Johnny arrested on a rustling charge. The sheriff of Chouteau County put the pair in Pike's custody until a hearing was held in Landusky. Once when Harvey wasn't carrying a gun, the Missourian tied him to a log with a chain and "threatened him with a nameless indignity." He constantly warned the Kid he would shoot him on sight if he ever appeared in Landusky.[8]

Kid Curry calmly accepted the beatings and threats. The younger Johnny insisted they confront Landusky in a stand-up fight but Harvey quietly told him he would settle with Pike in his own way and in his own time. The rustling charge was eventually dismissed.

A rare photograph of a street scene in Landusky, Montana Territory, at about the time Kid Curry and his brothers would ride in and shoot up the town. *Courtesy Alvin J. Lucke Collection*

In the fall of 1894 someone in the town suggested a community Christmas dinner and dance. "From that time until the day, Landusky was all feverish activity." Riders spread invitations across the lonely frontier; Landusky was entertaining, all were welcome.

The guests drifted in from the badlands sixty miles away, from grassy valleys in the foothills, alkali flats, posts far down the river breaks, and in gullies deep in the Little Rockies. They came on horseback, in boats, on mules, wagons, some even walked into town. On Christmas Eve there were more than a hundred guests, the largest gathering recorded in that section of the Territory.

A rare photograph of Susie Landusky with her schoolmates and teacher of the one-room schoolhouse that served Landusky. Susie is the girl on the left with the flat hat. The feud between the Curry brothers and Pike Landusky is said to have begun over Lonny Curry's attentions to his daughters. *Courtesy Alvin J. Lucke Collection*

The highlight of the Christmas dinner was four quarts of oysters carefully brought up the river and prepared by "Tie Up George, the best cow cook in the Little Rockies." The Curry brothers loaned their large new barn for the dance, while Lonny, an excellent fiddler, provided the music along with a tiny Mason and Hamlin organ, which had been tied on a wagon and brought to Landusky from a ranch many miles in the interior.

A rare photograph of Kid Curry's barn on the Jim Thornhill and Curry ranch outside Landusky, Montana Territory. This may be the barn that the Curry brothers turned over to the people of Landusky and their guests for the rousing Christmas dance in 1894. Lonny Curry, described as an "excellent fiddler," provided the music. *Courtesy Alvin J. Lucke Collection*

For two days and nights the guests danced, ate, and drank. Known gunmen, rustlers, and outlaws with a price on their heads checked their guns before joining in the dance at the Curry barn. As a frontier newspaper reported:

"If they wanted to awake the echoes for a moment, they would borrow a gun from the bartender and have a go at it . . ."

Finally the dance ended and guns were strapped back on. Many of the guests seemed reluctant to return to the deadly winter monotony of their ranches, cabins, and mines; the town remained crowded, the drinking confined to Jew Jake's saloon.

On December 27, 1894, a light snow fell. About 10:30 A.M. Pike Landusky and a friend stood at the rough bar. Suddenly the door opened and Kid Curry followed by Lonny and Jim Thornhill, walked to where Landusky was standing and slapped him on the shoulder. As the Missourian turned, Curry hit him on the jaw, sending him sprawling on the floor. Lonny and Thornhill drew their guns and waved the crowd back as Curry leaped on Landusky's back. Pike, then about fifty years old and wearing a thick bearskin coat, fought desperately to get to his feet but Kid Curry kept beating him unmercifully. Finally Pike was forced to do what he had never done before: cry out for help.

Tommy Carter, an old prospector, appealed to Lonny and Thornhill to stop the beating but they refused. Curry continued smashing Pike's head against the floor until the older man weakly waved his hand to surrender. As he got to his feet a gun appeared in his hand. However, "it was a new type he found difficult to work." In the second that Pike fumbled with his weapon, Kid Curry drew his single-action Colt .45 and killed him with two shots.

Customers ran out into the street along with Jake Harris who left on one crutch; he knew Thornhill or Lonny would have killed him if he had touched his shotgun. Johnny Curry, who may have been waiting, drove up in a wagon. Kid Curry, Lonny, and Thornhill jumped aboard and were gone within minutes.[9]

Kid Curry's life as an outlaw and gunfighter began with Landusky's death. The Curry brothers had a number of friends who urged the Kid to stand trial but he rode off after a murder warrant was issued for his arrest. Thornhill and Lonny, tried for conspiracy to commit murder, were quickly acquitted by a jury whose members made it plain they considered the fight between Pike and the Kid to have been one of survival; Kid Curry had killed in self-defense.

While Kid Curry rode to Wyoming, Johnny and Lonny continued to operate the ranch. In the summer of 1895 James M. Winters and A. Gill bought the Dan Tessler outfit adjacent to the Curry spread.

Shortly after the new owners had moved in, Johnny Curry rode over to tell them he not only owned the ranch but also all irrigation rights. Winters showed him their bill of sale but Curry, in a rage and slapping the gun on his hip, shouted they had only ten days to get off the land or suffer the consequences.

Winters, "who was good with a gun," as the *Harlem Enterprise* put it, drove him off the ranch.

A few weeks later a visitor at the ranch borrowed a horse. As he rode down

rare photograph of Abram Gill, partner of n Winters, killed by Kid Curry. Gill and inters refused to be driven off their ranch Johnny Curry. Gill was present when Win-s killed Johnny and later took the dying inters in a wagon to Fort Benton after he had en ambushed by Kid Curry in revenge for e death of his younger brother. Gill disap-ared along with his horse and saddle and s never seen or heard of again. *Courtesy vin J. Lucke Collection*

A rare photograph of the ranch near Landusky, Montana Territory, owned by Jim Winters and Abram Gill. Johnny Curry claimed the ranch and ordered Winters and Gill to "get out of the country," but both ranchers drove him off their land. Winters killed Curry. Later Harvey Logan, Kid Curry of the Wild West, ambushed Winters outside the main house in the photograph. *Courtesy Alvin J. Lucke Collection*

a road a hidden gunman fired, the bullet going through the crown of his hat.

"They're out to get me," Winters was quoted as saying. "If they want me, they know where I am."

On the morning of February 1, 1896, Johnny Curry rode up to the front door of the Winters-Gill ranch. As Winters, armed with a shotgun, stepped out, Curry fired, the bullet narrowly missing the rancher. The blast from Winters's shotgun knocked Johnny out of his saddle; he died a short time later in the Fort Benton hospital.

Winters surrendered at the fort where a coroner's jury ruled he had killed Curry in self-defense.[10]

In Wyoming, where he had joined Flat Nose George Currie's gang of rustlers and horse thieves, Harvey sent back word he would never forget it was Jim Winters who had killed his younger brother.

After he had buried his brother John, Lonny Curry sold the ranch and with his cousin, Bob Lee, moved to Harlem where he opened a saloon. Harvey was feared, Johnny despised, but Lonny, handsome and friendly, was well liked in the county. His bar, The Curry Bros. Club Saloon, prospered.

Little is known of Lee who had dropped his illustrious name of Robert E. Lee for Bob Curry. After they had arrived in the Little Rockies from Dodson, Missouri, Bob had become a miner in Last Chance and Cripple Creek, Colorado. He

Bob (Curry) Lee, the Logans' cousin, who left Dodson with them when they went west to become cowboys. Lee was arrested in Cripple Creek for taking part in the Wilcox, Wyoming, train robbery and was sentenced to a long term in the state prison. In trying to escape, his leg was so badly injured it was amputated. *Courtesy Pinkertons, Inc.*

FORM 55-2, '95-1 M. H. AB. 1671

P.N.D.A. **Agency.**

X431

Name Bob. Lee

Alias Bob. Curry

Residence Dodson Mo.

Nativity American

Occupation Gambler + Hold ups

Criminal Occupation Train Robber

Age 34 *Height* 5 ft. 9 in.

Weight 175 *Build* Heavy

Complexion Dark *Eyes* Brown

Color of Hair Black

Color of Mustache Black

Color of Beard Black

Style of Beard

Date of Arrest Feb. 28, 1900.

Where Arrested Cripple Creek

Crime Charged Train Robbery

Peculiarities of Build, Features, Scars, Marks, etc.

Small scar on left cheek about one inch from base of nose

A rare photograph of Lonny Logan (left), Kid Curry's brother, taken in a Harlem, Montana Territory, saloon, before he joined his brother in holding up the Union Pacific. Lonny, well liked in the Little Rockies country, was killed by a posse in Dodson, Missouri. His companions at the bar are cowboys and ranchers. *Courtesy Alvin J. Lucke Collection*

was also a monte dealer and when times were bad, had turned to rustling. He was a stolid, stocky man, dark-skinned like the Logans.

Those who recalled them said Bob did most of the bartending while Lonny courted the widows and young girls of Chouteau County.

"Lonny's reputation with women was not enviable," one frontier man recalled.[11]

Lonny was also Harlem's favorite fiddler and supplied the music for the town's dances. After he took over the Club Saloon he decided he looked too youthful and grew a moustache and wore dark business suits instead of puncher's clothes. In the summer of 1894 he had saved enough to contemplate buying the Shufelt works, the largest quartz mill in Lewistown, and made frequent trips into the mining country, "seeking to make investments."

"Both Lonny and Bob Curry have conducted themselves in a peaceable law abiding manner, in fact almost exemplary," the *Harlem Enterprise* commented in 1900.[12] Meanwhile in the Hole in the Wall country, Kid Curry and the other Flat Nose George Currie riders were driving stolen horse herds along the outlaw trail, as far south as Alma, New Mexico.[13]

From stealing horses and steers, the Kid turned to bank and train robbery. On the morning of June 2, 1895, he and Flat Nose George Currie led the gang that held up the Union Pacific's Overland Flyer, east of a bridge and siding known as Wilcox, Wyoming, 113 miles west of Cheyenne. The riders included Lonny and Bob Curry who had left their saloon to join the Kid. The technique was typical Wild West: the engineer eased his train to a stop when he saw the waving red lantern. As he stepped down from his cab, six armed men, faces blackened with burnt cork and wearing bandannas as masks, ran out of the darkness. Robert J. Harvey, the train's conductor, described Kid Curry's role:[14]

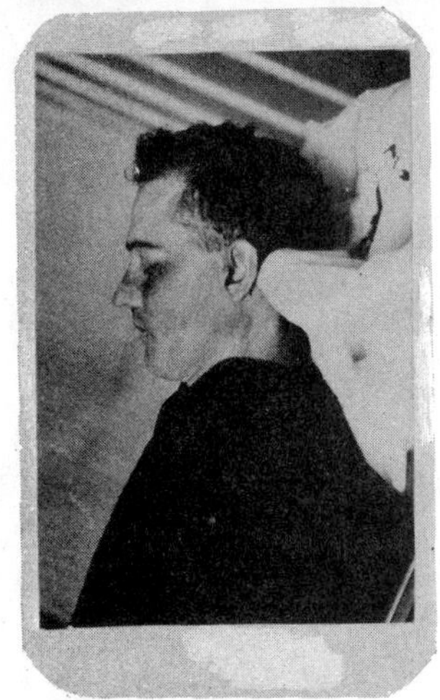

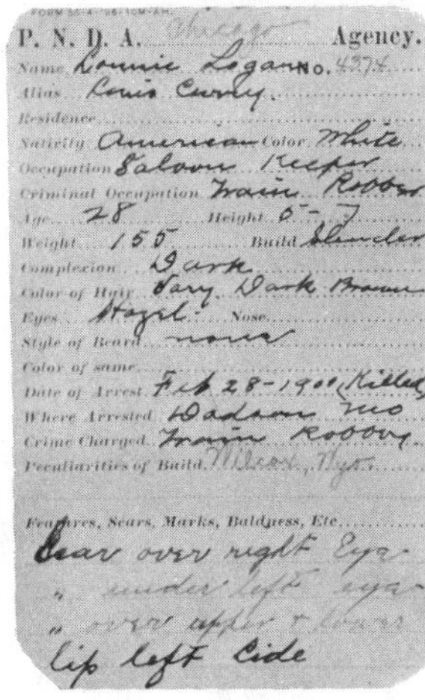

P. N. D. A. Chicago Agency.
Name Lonnie Logan No. 4374
Alias Louis Curry.
Residence
Nativity American Color White
Occupation Saloon Keeper
Criminal Occupation Train Robber
Age 28 Height 5-7
Weight 155 Build Slender
Complexion Dark
Color of Hair Very Dark Brown
Eyes Hazel. Nose
Style of Beard none
Color of same
Date of Arrest Feb 28-1900 (Killed)
Where Arrested Dodson Mo
Crime Charged Train Robbery.
Peculiarities of Build Wilcox, Wyo.
Features, Scars, Marks, Baldness, Etc.
Scar over right Eye
" under left eye
" over upper & lower
lip left side

Lonny (Curry) Logan, in the Kansas City morgue, shortly after he was killed by a posse outside his aunt's house in Dodson, Missouri. *Courtesy Pinkertons, Inc.*

On the morning of February 28, 1900, a posse of Pinkertons and local police surrounded the farmhouse.

Lonny, who may have wanted to draw fire away from the house, ran out. He was wearing a heavy overcoat and the snow was deep. He tried to reach a strip of timbers but when warning shots whistled about him he dropped behind a mound and returned the fire of the lawmen. After a brief, savage exchange he abruptly rose and stumbled toward the posse, his six-shooter blazing. In moments he was riddled and fell dead in the snow.[22]

A shadow continued to hover over the outlaw brotherhood. A few weeks later Bob Curry, working as a monte dealer in the Antelope Club, Cripple Creek, was arrested. A white-handled, single-action .45, along with a clipping of the Wildox robbery, was found in his valise. "Not a cent of money was found on his person," the *Harlem Enterprise* reported.

The Wild Bunch, the largest and most colorful band of outlaws in the Wild West, was broken up by the turn of the century, its riders scattered, resting in Boot Hills or serving long terms in prison like Bob Curry who had been convicted of the Wilcox robbery and sentenced to twenty years in Wyoming's state penitentiary.

Butch Cassidy had begged Kid Curry to come to South America with him, Harry Longbaugh, the Sundance Kid, and Etta Place. Curry declined, refusing to believe the Wild West was finished, that it was nothing but a romantic memory, especially to the large eastern newspapers that periodically published full-page feature stories about the gang.[23]

The Kid told Butch he intended to travel, leisurely spending his share of the train and bank robberies, then would organize another gang.

In the fall of 1901 he began a tour of the South. Apparently he was never without an attractive woman. There was Annie Rogers, a slender redhead, who stayed with him in Nashville and found him always a gentleman; Maudie Davis, who remembered how he bought her a fox skin. The Kid was also attracted to cameras; although he was one of the most wanted men in the country, he posed with Annie for a loving portrait in a Nashville, Tennessee, studio. She draped his arm over her shoulder while the Kid gazed at the lens with a slightly amused expression. His hair and moustache were neatly combed and trimmed. His dark double-breasted suit, polished boots, and wing collar made him appear a mild-mannered prosperous drummer.

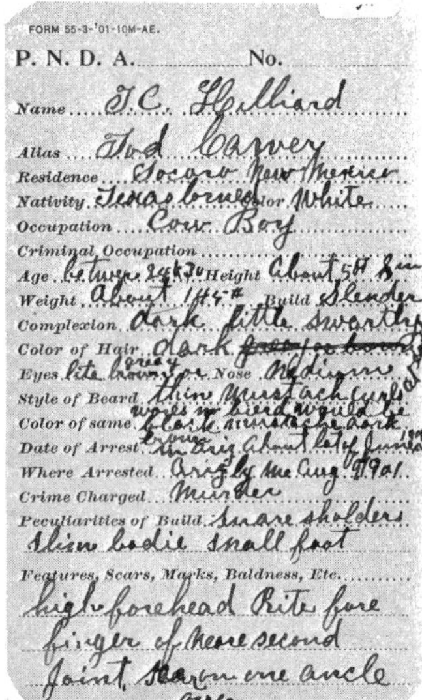

FORM 55-3-'01-10M-AE.

P. N. D. A. No.

Name T.C. Hilliard

Alias Tod Carver

Residence Socorro New Mexico

Nativity Texas born Color White

Occupation Cow Boy

Criminal Occupation

Age between 24 & 30 Height About 5 ft 8 in

Weight About 144 # Build Slender

Complexion dark little swarthy

Color of Hair dark

Eyes lite brown Nose Medium

Style of Beard thin Mustach

Color of same

Date of Arrest

Where Arrested

Crime Charged Murder

Peculiarities of Build Square sholders thin bodie small foot

Features, Scars, Marks, Baldness, Etc. high forehead Rite fore finger of [illegible] second joint scar on one ancle

The handsome Tod Carver, member of the Wild Bunch and one of Kid Curry's favorite riders. *Courtesy Pinkertons, Inc.*

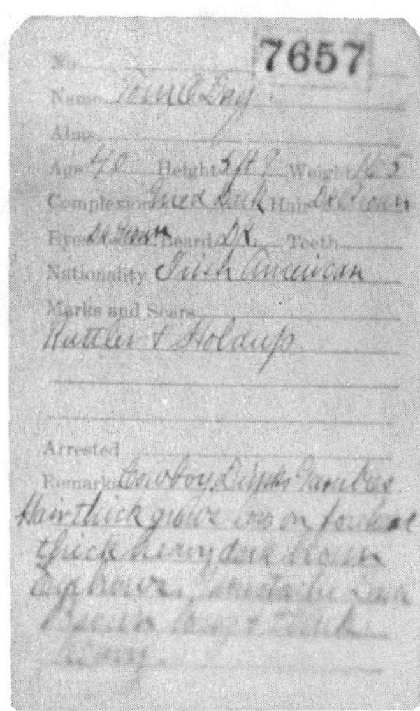

No. 7657

Name Tom O'Day

Alias

Age 40 Height 5 ft 8 Weight 165

Complexion [illegible] Hair [illegible]

Eyes [illegible] Beard [illegible] Teeth

Nationality Irish American

Marks and Scars

Rustler & Holdups

Arrested

Remarks Cowboy [illegible] Gambler [illegible]

Tom O'Day, one of Kid Curry's riders. Gambler, rustler, and train robber, O'Day was nicknamed "Peep," because of the many times Curry and Butch Cassidy used him as a lookout for their bank robberies. *Courtesy Pinkertons, Inc.*

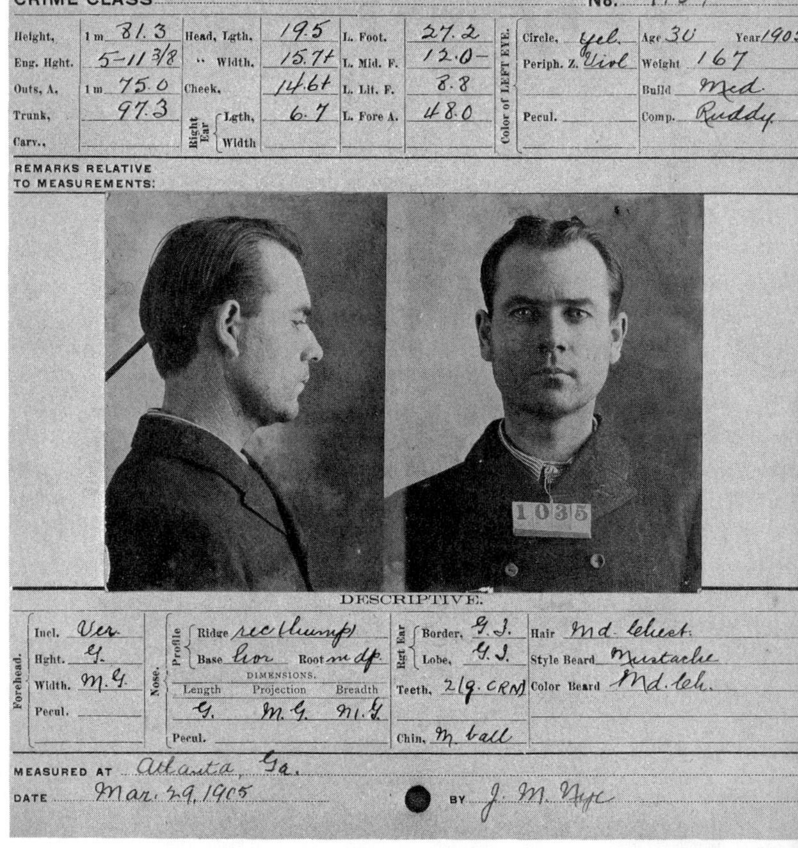

CRIME CLASS No. 7109

Height,	1 m 81.3	Head, Lgth.	19.5	L. Foot.	27.2	Circle,	yel.	Age 30	Year 190[illegible]
Eng. Hght.	5-11 3/8	" Width.	15.7+	L. Mid. F.	12.0-	Periph. Z.	Viol	Weight	167
Outs. A.	1 m 75.0	Cheek.	14.6+	L. Lit. F.	8.8			Build	Med.
Trunk,	97.3	Right Ear Lgth.	6.7	L. Fore A.	48.0	Pecul.		Comp.	Ruddy
Carv.,		Right Ear Width				Color of LEFT EYE			

REMARKS RELATIVE TO MEASUREMENTS:

1035

DESCRIPTIVE.

Forehead.		Nose.		Rgt Ear			
Incl.	Ver.	Profile Ridge	rec (hump)	Border,	G. I.	Hair	Md. Chest.
Hght.	G.	Profile Base	hor Root m dp.	Lobe,	G. I.	Style Beard	Mustache
Width.	M. G.	DIMENSIONS. Length / Projection / Breadth	G. / M. G. / M. G.	Teeth,	2 (g. CRN)	Color Beard	Md. Ch.
Pecul.		Pecul.		Chin,	M. ball		

MEASURED AT Atlanta, Ga.

DATE Mar. 29, 1905 BY J. M. Nye

Ben Kilpatrick, the "Tall Texan" of the Wild Bunch, a close friend of Kid Curry. The illiterate Kilpatrick would always order beans and ham in the frontier saloons because he could not read the menus whitewashed on the bar mirrors. *Courtesy Pinkertons, Inc.*

Flat Nose George and the others were captured but Kid Curry held out; he surrendered only after he was convinced the situation was hopeless. The fugitives were lodged in the Deadwood jail for the Belle Fourche robbery but not for long. Some weeks later Curry overpowered the sheriff, unlocked the cells, and the gang escaped.

Fleeing, they held up post offices, stole horses and supplies, and fought off posses. On April 17, 1900, Flat Nose George Currie was killed while rustling steers at Thompson, Utah. A posse led by Sheriffs William Preece of Uintah County and Jesse M. Tyler of Grand County trapped Currie after they had driven off his horses. He refused to surrender and was killed in a gunfight.

In Brown's Hole, Kid Curry assumed leadership of the gang, later merging with Butch Cassidy's Wild Bunch. On July 3, 1901, near Wagner, Montana, almost 200 miles east of Great Falls, the Kid, Cassidy, Harry Longbaugh, the Sundance Kid, Ben Kilpatrick, the Tall Texan, and Camilla Hanks, known as "Deaf Charley," held up the Great Northern, shattering the express car with dynamite and charges of black powder.[16]

They rode off with $65,000 in unsigned bank notes consigned to the Helena, Montana, bank. The gang scattered but the Kid had a mission to finish in Montana: the murder of Jim Winters who had killed his brother Johnny five years before.

He arrived at the Winters-Gill ranch late Wednesday, July 25, 1901. All night he patiently waited for Winters to appear. At sunup, the rancher came out on the back porch with a pan of water and started to brush his teeth. As he bent over, Kid Curry, resting his rifle on the bars of the corral, shot him twice. Gill, who ran out, saw a man in a crouching run leap on his horse. He swore it was Kid Curry.

$2500 REWARD.

will be paid by us for the capture of the four men hereinafter described. $625 reward will be paid for each man. These men are wanted for attempting to rob this bank on Monday June 28, 1897.

Description.

GEO. CURRIE—About 5 ft 10 in., weight 175, age 27, light complexion, high cheek bones, flat forehead, flat pug nose, big hands and bones, stoops a little, long light mustache, probably clean shaven.

HARVE RAY—About 5 ft 8 1-2 in., weight 185, age 42, dark complexion, round full faced, bald headed, heavy long dirty brown mustache, might have heavy beard, dark gray eyes, hair quite gray above ears and inclined to curl, bow legged.

— ROBERTS—About 5 ft 7 1-2 in., age 32, rather small, weight about 140, very dark complexion, possibly quarter breed Indian. Formerly from Indian territory.

— ROBERTS—Rather small man. About 5 ft 6 in. weight 130. age 28, very dark, probably quarter breed Indian, large upper front teeth protruding from mouth.

$100 reward for information leading to their arrest. Please destroy former circulars.

BUTTE COUNTY BANK,
Belle Fourche, S. D.

July 28th 1897.

A rare wanted poster naming Kid Curry as the leader of the gang that robbed the Butte County bank in Belle Fourche, South Dakota, June 28, 1897. Kid Curry, Flat-Nose George Currie, and "Peep" O'Day were captured, but Curry staged a jailbreak and the gang rode back to Hole-in-the-Wall. *The James D. Horan Civil War and Western Americana Collection*

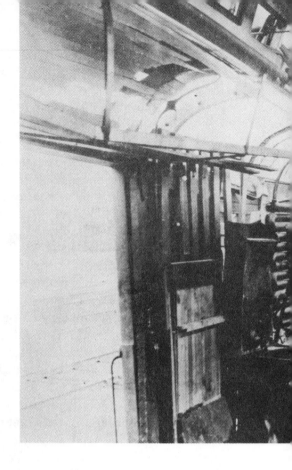

A rare photograph of a device used by outlaws in the Wild West to outwit posses. Horseshoes were nailed to shoes in an attempt to confuse trackers. *Courtesy Wyoming State Archives and Historical Department*

A typical wooden jail in the West. Once an indignant Kid Curry and his gang raided a similar building, released their rider, and burned down the jail. This one was used in the Wyoming Territory in 1893. *Courtesy Wyoming State Archives and Historical Department*

Camilla (Deaf Charley Hanks, a member of th Wild Bunch, Kid Curry' friend, and a fellow trai robber. "He's a good ma in a tight spot," Kid Curr told a Knoxville reporte "He came well recom mended." *Courtesy Pink ertons, Inc.*

The interior of the Union Pacific's express car blown apart by dynamite or black powder by Kid Curry and his riders at Tipton, Wyoming, August 29, 1900. *Courtesy The Union Pacific*

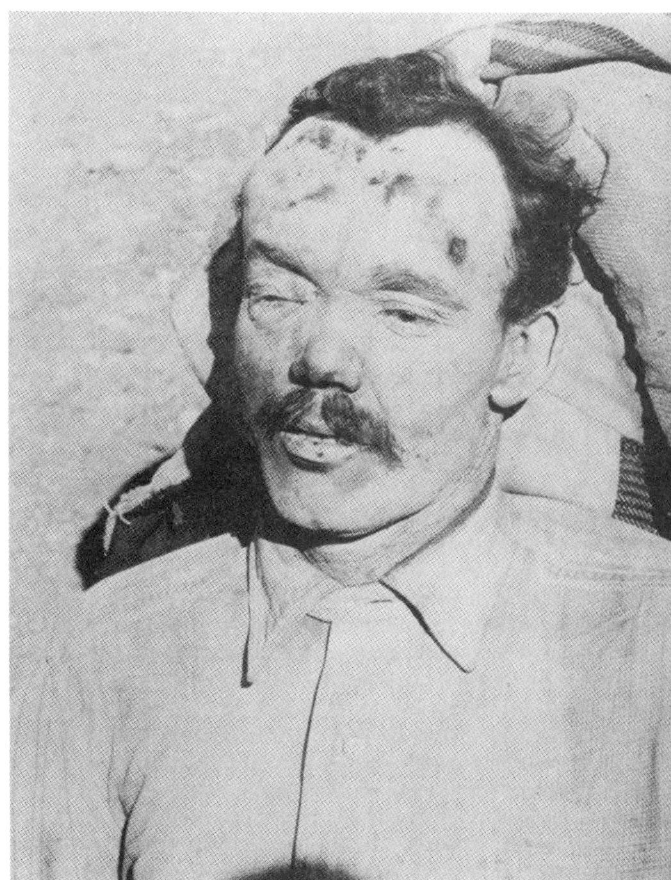

A rare original photograph of "Flat Nose" George Currie, taken shortly after he was killed by lawmen. He was caught using a rustler's running iron and was shot during a gun battle. *The James D. Horan Civil War and Western Americana Collection*

55-3.1900-2M A-sy.
A. Chicago Agency.
C Hanks No.
as Jones Deaf Charley
Los Vegas New Mexico
American Color White
Cowboy
ccupation Train Robber
38 Height 5 ft 10 in
156# Build Good
Sandy
ir Auburn
Sunken Nose Regular
ard Mustache if any
me Sandy
est Summer 1894
ested Teton Co Montana
ged Robbery N.P. Express
of Build Leans head
tly to left Somewhat Deaf
Scars, Marks, Baldness, Etc.
m burn size of 25¢ piece
ight forearm
scar right leg above
le middle near
ht nipple

Charlie Siringo, the famous "Cowboy Detective." This picture was taken during the time he was trailing Kid Curry after a train robbery. *The James D. Horan Civil War and Western Americana Collection*

The nearest physician was in Harlem, sixty miles away. Gill and his hands put Winters in a wagon and drove to the town. It was an agonizing journey over the rutted roads in the blazing heat. Winters died shortly after he arrived. The Kid's marksmanship was impressive; two soft-nose .30-caliber bullets were found within an inch of each other near the dead man's navel.[17]

While his brother Harvey was carefully getting Jim Winters in his rifle sights, Lonny was courting Hattie Nichols, daughter of a Lewistown rancher. The *Harlem Enterprise* noted they had been seen riding together to the ranch of Jim Thornhill, Harvey's old partner.[18]

In Harlem Bob Curry was still behind the bar of the Club Saloon. On November 3, 1899, he made a drastic mistake when he sent five bank notes taken in the earlier Wilcox robbery to the Stockmen's National Bank at Fort Benton for redemption. The notes, torn by the dynamite blast that shattered the express car, still retained their numbers. They were routinely passed on to the bank's Chicago representative, who forwarded them to the First National Bank of Portland, which had been assigned the bank notes by the United States Treasury.[19]

The methodical banking process continued. Letters, telegrams, and memoranda passed between Fort Benton, Chicago, Portland, and the United States Treasury, tracing the journey of the bills from Washington to the express car; finally they were pinpointed as part of the Wilcox loot.[20]

The Pinkertons, representing the American Bankers' Association, took over the case. Operatives sent into Montana finally ended in Harlem. Friends warned Lonny Curry that detectives were in town. On January 6 he hastily sold the Club Saloon to a local businessman, George J. Ringwald, and with Bob Curry left on horseback for the Little Rockies country. At Zurich, "a water tank accommodation stop," they boarded the train for Havre. From there they went to Shelby Junction, then on to Cripple Creek, Colorado.

Detectives relentlessly followed their trail, finding out where they had stayed in hotels or ranch houses, taken trains or hired horses at livery stables. Lonny shaved off his moustache and substituted "cowboy clothes" for his neat dark suit.[21]

In Cripple Creek he visited the post office every morning, asking for a registered package. Finally it came, money from the loyal Jim Thornhill. A few hours after the arrival of the package, Lonny said good-bye to Bob; the only refuge left in his violent world appeared to be Aunt Lee's place in Dodson, Missouri. His cousin decided to stay behind in the mining camps.

Mrs. Lee, that "estimable little old lady who had no knowledge of the sort of life her nephew led," as the *Kansas City Post* later reported, gave Lonny a prodigal's return. For weeks the outlaw hid out in the frame farmhouse on the hill. In early February, either through carelessness or overconfidence, he spent one of the torn Wilcox robbery bills in Dodson. Routine banking procedures in Kansas City spotted the bill; a message was sent to the Pinkertons in Chicago. Orders were flashed to the Kansas City, Missouri, office. Operatives quickly discovered Lonny Logan, who lived with the Lees, had passed the bill.

The Union Pacific's express car blown up by Kid Curry's riders at Wilcox, Wyoming, June 2, 1899. *Courtesy The Union Pacific*

The posse chasing Kid Curry and his riders. *Courtesy The Union Pacific*

A posse with saddles and guns in the Union Pacific baggage car. The horses were in the adjacent car. *Courtesy The Union Pacific Archives and Western History Department, University of Wyoming Library*

A rare photograph showing the posse that chased Kid Curry and other train robbers who held up the Union Pacific at Tipton, Wyoming, in August 1900. The posse was about to ride overland in an attempt to cut off the gang. The lawmen and their horses had just left the train carrying them. *Courtesy Wyoming State Archives and Historical Department*

Harvey Logan and the Wilcox Train Robbery

> My train was running along smoothly one night when we struck a small patch of woods. All at once the train slowed down and I ran out to see what was happening.
>
> I found the front of the train surrounded by a gang of men, all armed with six shooters and rifles and they made the engineer and fireman get down and raise their hands. Then they ran the train a distance while some of the gang, led by Kid Curry, went back to the express car and started to bore into the safe.
>
> The Kid told us that if we made any resistance he would kill us. He wasn't excited but the way he spoke we all knew he meant every word he was saying.
>
> Finally they blew the safe and cleaned it out of all the money it contained. Then the Kid led the robbers up to the engine and it stopped where they had some horses waiting. They were gone within minutes.
>
> We got up a posse and used bloodhounds. We found their trail and kept after them. In fact we got so close Logan killed the hounds, all four of them. It cost the Union Pacific one thousand dollars for each of the dogs that were sent in from Kansas City.
>
> The gang got away in the mountains. Logan or Kid Curry as we knew him, planned that robbery. He was the most feared man in the West, deadly with a gun and if he said he was going to kill you there wouldn't be a place you could hide. He'd follow you to hell if necessary.

Within the next two years the Currie gang had become one of the largest in the West. Using the K-C ranch on Powder River as an operational base, they plundered sheep and cattle ranches, robbed post offices, trains, and banks in Utah, Montana, South Dakota, and Wyoming. Currie, as the oldest and most experienced, was nominally in command but it was Kid Curry whom the riders obeyed and followed.

In April 1897, Deputy Sheriff William Deane foolishly tried to capture the gang single-handedly. As he rode up to the front gate of the K-C ranch, he shouted "Hands up" to Curry and two others. Before the echo of his command had died away, the Kid had spun around and shot him out of his saddle. The body was dragged through the brush at the end of a rope and left by a road to be discovered the next day by a passing rancher.

On June 28, that same year, the Kid took part in his first bank robbery. Shortly after the Butte County Bank in Belle Fourche, South Dakota, opened, six masked men walked in and, as one newspaper reported, "cleaned out the money in sight."[15]

A posse finally cornered the gang near Levins, Fergus County, Montana.

Ben Kilpatrick, the "Tall Texan," and his sweetheart, Laura Bullion, were captured, and Deaf Charley Hanks was almost taken by a posse, but Kid Curry casually continued his tour. Sometime in the early winter he may have visited old friends in Rowland County, Kentucky; in December he appeared in Knoxville, Tennessee, as the city was preparing for Christmas. As he later said, he wandered about "window shopping," decided he liked Knoxville, and found lodgings in a rooming house.

The Kid was never long without a "woman companion," as the papers of the day discreetly described a mistress. Somehow he met and wooed Catherine Cross of whom little is known.

It was evident that Curry, killer, outlaw, rustler, and fugitive, completely charmed the young woman.[24]

However, there were times when Catherine may have bored him. On nights when he didn't see her he sought out the company of two young hookers. They remembered him as a rather bashful customer who wore elegant underwear and boasted his clothes came "from Denver's best men's shop."

In between courting Catherine and visiting the whores, the Kid found time for his favorite pastime, playing pool. He selected Ike Jones's combination pool hall and saloon at Central and Commerce streets as his headquarters.

There was nothing of the western desperado about Logan; Ike Jones, the pool hall owner, described him as "a drummer type, just passing through, a quiet man, standing treat many times and playing many games of pool."

As a mark of his affluence, Logan drank nothing but apricot brandy and smoked the most expensive brand of cigars. Those who played pool with him

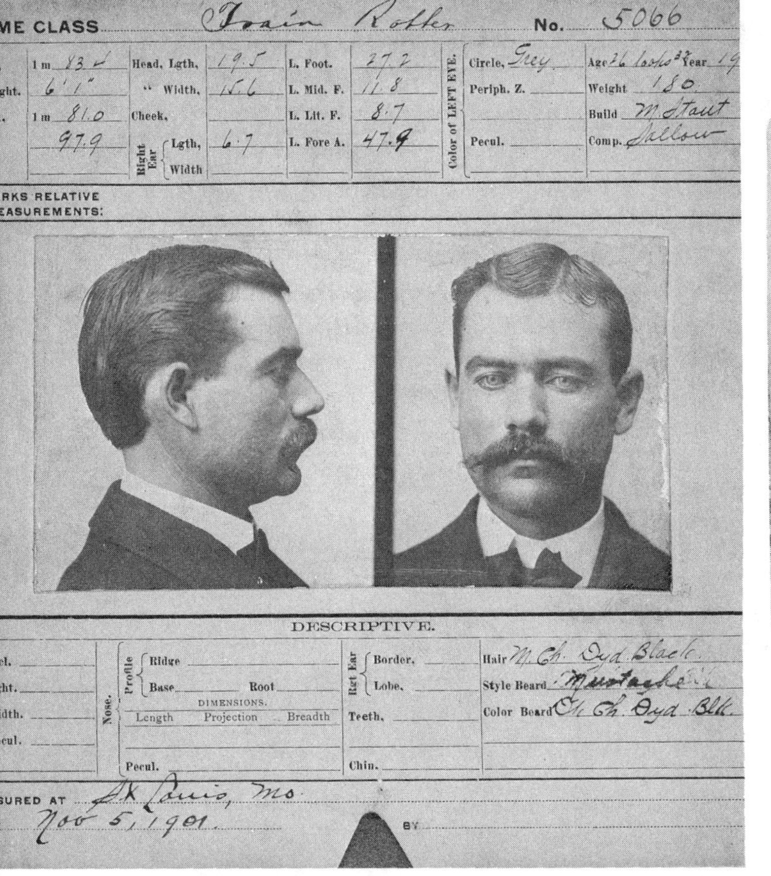

ME CLASS Train Robber No. 5066

1 m 83	Head, Lgth. 19.5	L. Foot. 27.2	Circle, Grey	Age 26			
6' 1"	" Width. 15.6	L. Mid. F. 11.8	Periph. Z.	Weight 180			
1 m 81.0	Cheek.	L. Lit. F. 8.7		Build M Stout			
97.9	Right Ear Lgth. 6.7 / Width	L. Fore A. 47.4	Pecul.	Comp. Sallow			

ARKS RELATIVE
EASUREMENTS:

DESCRIPTIVE.

Nose. Profile Ridge / Base Root — DIMENSIONS. Length Projection Breadth — Pecul.
Rgt Ear Border. / Lobe. — Teeth. — Chin.
Hair M. Ch. Dyd Black
Style Beard Moustache
Color Beard Ch. Ch. Dyd Blk.

SURED AT St Louis, Mo
Nov 5, 1901 BY

Ben Kilpatrick after he was arrested in Saint Louis with his sweetheart, Laura Bullion. *Courtesy Pinkertons, Inc.*

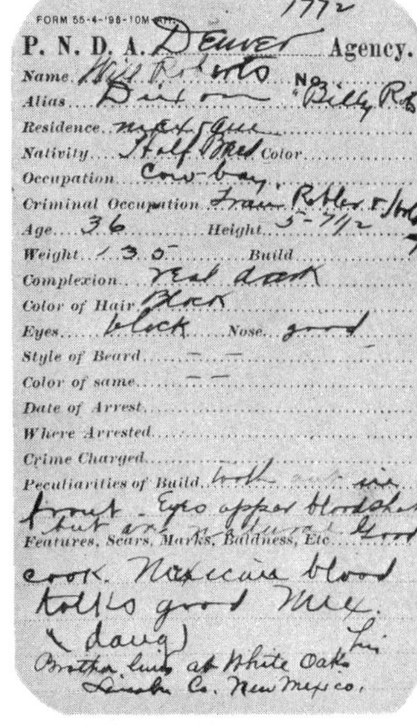

FORM 55-4-'98-10M 1772

P. N. D. A. Denver Agency.

Name Will Roberts No.
Alias "Billy R"
Residence
Nativity Half Breed Color
Occupation Cow-boy
Criminal Occupation Train Robber
Age 36 Height 5-7½
Weight 130 Build
Complexion Real dark
Color of Hair Black
Eyes black Nose good
Style of Beard — —
Color of same — —
Date of Arrest
Where Arrested
Crime Charged
Peculiarities of Build
Features, Scars, Marks, Baldness, Etc.
cook. Mexican blood
talks good Mex.
Brother lives at White Oaks
Lincoln Co. New Mexico.

Willie Roberts, who rode with Kid Curry and the Wild Bunch. His brother lived in White Oaks, New Mexico, where Billy the Kid fought off a posse. *Courtesy Pinkertons, Inc.*

Harry Longbaugh (the "Sundance Kid"), and Etta Place, his common-law wife, who had worked as a prostitute in Fanny Porter's Sporting House. Longbaugh, a friend of Kid Curry's, was arrested with him for the robbery of the Butte County bank, but they both escaped. This photograph was taken in 1901 in New York City by Joseph De Young, a society photographer whose studio on 10th Street was once occupied by Mathew B. Brady, the famous Civil War photographer. Both Longbaugh and Butch Cassidy begged Kid Curry to accompany them to South America, but Curry refused. *Courtesy Pinkertons, Inc.*

recalled he was friendly "but not the talking kind." When someone asked what he did for a living he solemnly replied he was "a railroad man."

Bartenders on the western frontier were a trusted breed; it wasn't unusual for cowhands to leave their bedrolls, six-shooters, and money with them for safekeeping. The Kid liked J. D. Finley, Ike Jones's bartender, and entrusted him with $3,500 in bank notes—part of the Wagner, Montana, train robbery loot.

Curry, who went by the name of William Wilson, settled down to a routine of playing pool, drinking the sweet, syrupy brandy, courting Catherine, and occasionally visiting the hookers.

A dark streak of violence ran deep and strong in the Kid, however; it took only an implied insult to turn him homicidal. On the afternoon of December 13, 1901, he was quietly playing pool with two small-time local criminals, Luther Brady and Jim Boley, when an argument started. The Kid put down his cue and walked to the bar. He tossed off a drink, then returned to the table, knocked Brady over a barrel, and started to strangle him. When Boley tried to stop him,

Pinkerton's National Detective Agency

FOUNDED BY ALLAN PINKERTON, 1850

WM. A. PINKERTON, Chicago, }
ROBT. A. PINKERTON, New York, } Principals.

GEO. D. BANGS, Gen'l Sup't, New York.

D. ROBERTSON, Ass't Gen'l Sup't Middle Division, CHICAGO.
JAS. MCPARLAND, Ass't Gen'l Sup't Western Division, DENVER

Attorneys:
SEWARD, GUTHRIE & STEELE,
New York.

CONNECTED BY TELEPHONE.

OFFICES.

DENVER,	OPERA HOUSE BLOCK.
J. C. FRASER, Sup't.	
NEW YORK,	57 BROADWAY.
BOSTON,	30 COURT STREET.
PHILADELPHIA,	441 CHESTNUT STREET.
CHICAGO,	201 FIFTH AVENUE.
ST. PAUL,	GERMANIA BANK BUILDING.
KANSAS CITY,	622 MAIN STREET.
PORTLAND, ORE.,	MARQUAM BLOCK.
SAN FRANCISCO,	CROCKER BUILDING.
MONTREAL,	STREET RAILWAY CHAMBERS.

REPRESENTING THE AMERICAN BANKERS ASSOCIATION.

$18.000 REWARD.

It has been definitely ascertained who were THREE of the men concerned in the hold-up of the Union Pacific Train at Wilcox, Wyoming, and the robbery of the Pacific Express Co's safe, by the use of dynamite, early on the morning of Friday, June 2nd, 1899. The parties committing this robbery were also guilty of the MURDER of Sheriff Josiah Hazen, of Converse County, Wyoming (near Casper) on the afternoon of Sunday June 4th. Sheriff Hazen at the time of his death was leading a pursuing posse.

The following are the names and discription of

THREE OF THE ROBBERS.

LOUIS CURRY, alias LONNY CURRY. Age 28 years, height five feet seven inches, weight 155 pounds (about), build, slender; hair, dark brown, thin and curly; eyes, hazel and slightly sunken; nose thin, long and slightly turned up at end; mustache, dark brown, small and curly at ends; scar over the right eye, is not noticeable except on close inspection; wears a No. 8 shoe.

HARVEY CURRY alias KID CURRY. Age 34 years; height five feet nine inches; weight 170 to 180 pounds; build, heavy; hair, dark brown, and straight, usually wears it cut short; nose, prominent, long and straight; mustache, dark brown, and medium size; talks slow; is very quiet; is a good horseman

R. E. Curry, alias Bob Curry, alias Bob Lee. Age 36 years; height five feet nine inches; weight 175 to 180 pounds; build strong well proportioned and heavy; shoulders round; eyes, hazel; hair, black thick and straight; mustache, black, heavy and hides mouth even when smiling; hands, indicate work; fingers short and thick; nose small, broad and flat at norstrils, looks like negroes- face full, round and somewhat "dished" (i. e. if rule was laid on face it would about touch the forehead, nose and chin). Has a bull dog expression of countenance, but not unpleasant; front view, rather good looking. Has small bunch of hair, like a mole, at base of nose on left cheek. Wore flannel shirt, and soft hat pulled down over right eye. Wore gold cuff buttons with initials: "T. M." on them. Louis and Harvey Curry are brothers.

R. E. Curry has passed as a brother of Louis Curry. He is supposed to be related, but is not a brother. His right name is not positively known, it may be Robt. Lee.

Louis Curry was proprietor of "The Club" saloon at Harlem, Choteau County, Montana, until January 6th, 1900, when he and his supposed relative, Bob. Curry, finding they were suspected of this robbery, left Harlem well mounted and heavily armed. It is surmized they will eventually join Harvey Curry. When leaving they had in their possession a part of the $3,400.00 UNSIGNED CURRENCY of the First National Bank of Portland, Oregon, which was stolen at the time of the robbery and is described fully below.

A part of this currency consisting of TWENTY $100.00 BILLS and TWO $20.00 BILLS ARE MUTILATED, THE LOWER RIGHT HAND CORNER HAVING BEEN BLOWN OFF IN THE EXPLOSION.

The following is the full description of the money

	Bank numbers in lower left hand corner	Treasury numbers in upper right hand corner.
22 $ 50 notes,	A3705 to A3726 inclusive.	A744372 to A744393 inclusive.
22 $100 "	A3705 to A3726 "	A744372 to A744393 "
2 $ 20 "	A5641 to A5642 "	T130922 to T130923 "
2 $ 10 "	A5641 to A5642 "	T130922 to T130923 "
2 $ 10 "	B5641 to B5642 "	T130922 to T130923 "
2 $ 10 "	C5641 to C5642 "	T130922 to T130923 "

Banks receiving this circular are earnestly requested to be on the lookout for the above described money.

There may have been five or six men in this robbery.

The Union Pacific Railroad Company and the Pacific Express Company have jointly offered $2.000.00 reward for the arrest of either of the robbers. This means for their detention and surrender to an officer duly authorized to receive them on behalf of the State of Wyoming, or in case either of the robbers should be killed in attempting their capture, the reward would hold good.

The United States Government has also offered an additional reward of $1,000.00 for each of the robbers.

The photograph on this circular of Louis Curry, is a fairly good picture of him.

Parties furnishing information leading to the arrest of either of the robbers will share in the reward.

Information sent to the undersigned, or to either of the above listed offices by telegraph or mail, will receive prompt attention.

PINKERTON'S NATIONAL DETECTIVE AGENCY,
ROOM 219 OPERA HOUSE BLOCK, DENVER, COLO.

Or
J. C. FRASER, Resident Supt.
February 23, 1900.

A rare wanted poster for Kid Curry, his brother Lonny, and their cousin Bob Lee, for the Union Pacific robbery at Wilcox and the killing of Sheriff Josiah Hazen of Wyoming's Converse County. *Courtesy Pinkertons, Inc.*

Pinkerton's National Detective Agency.

FOUNDED BY ALLAN PINKERTON, 1850.

ROBT. A. PINKERTON, New York, } Principals.
WM. A. PINKERTON, Chicago. }

GEO. D. BANGS, General Manager, New York.
ALLAN PINKERTON, Asst. General Manager, New York.

JOHN CORNISH, Gen'l Sup't., Eastern Division, New York.
EDWARD S. GAYLOR, Gen'l Sup't., Middle Division, Chicago.
JAMES McPARLAND, Gen'l Sup't., Western Division, Denver.

Attorneys.—GUTHRIE, CRAVATH & HENDERSON, New York.

TELEPHONE CONNECTION.

OFFICES.

CHICAGO, 201 FIFTH AVENUE.
J. H. SCHUMACHER, Sup't.
NEW YORK. 57 BROADWAY.
BOSTON, 30 COURT STREET.
PHILADELPHIA, 441 CHESTNUT STREET.
MONTREAL, MERCHANTS BANK BUILDING.
ST. PAUL, GERMANIA BANK BUILDING.
ST. LOUIS, WAINWRIGHT BUILDING.
KANSAS CITY, 622 MAIN STREET.
DENVER, OPERA HOUSE BLOCK.
PORTLAND, ORE. MARQUAM BLOCK.
SEATTLE, WASH. BAILEY BLOCK.
SAN FRANCISCO, CROCKER BUILDING.

REPRESENTATIVES OF THE AMERICAN BANKERS ASSOCIATION.

INFORMATION CIRCULAR No. 3.

$5,000 REWARD.

PHOTOGRAPH OF HARVEY LOGAN.

The above is the aggregate amount of reward offered by the GREAT NORTHERN EXPRESS CO. for the arrest and identification of the four men implicated in the robbery of the Great Northern Railway Express train No. 3 near Wagner, Mont., July 3, 1901. A proportionate amount will be paid for one, two or more, and **$500 Additional for each Conviction.**

Under date of Aug. 5th, 1901, we issued a circular bearing a picture of **HARVEY LOGAN** showing him with a full beard, making it difficult to identify. We herewith present a later and better picture of him which has been identified in Nashville, Tenn., as a good likeness of the companion of a woman arrested there for attempting to exchange some of the stolen currency.

DESCRIPTION.

Name, **HARVEY LOGAN.**

Alias Harvey Curry, "Kid" Curry, Bob Jones, Tom Jones, Bob Nevilles, Robert Nelson and **R. T. Whalen.**

Residence, last known, Landusky and Harlem, Montana.

Nativity, Dodson, Mo.

Color, white.

Occupation, cowboy, rustler.

Criminal Occupation, Bank robber, train robber, horse and cattle thief, rustler, "hold up" and murderer.

Age, 36 years (1901).

Eyes, dark.

Height, 5 feet, 7½ inches,

Weight, 145 to 160 lbs.

Build, medium.

Complexion, dark, swarthy.

Nose, prominent, large, long and straight.

Color of Hair, dark brown, darker than mustache.

Style of Beard, can raise heavy beard and mustache, color somewhat lighter than hair.

Marks, has gun-shot wound on wrist, talks slowly, is of quiet reserved manner.

On Oct. 27th, 1901, a man believed to be GEORGE PARKER, alias Butch Cassidy, whose photograph and description appeared in our circular of Aug. 5th, 1901, attempted to pass one of the $20 bills of the stolen currency at a Nashville store. He escaped from officers after a severe struggle.

On the night of Nov. 5th, 1901, the St. Louis Police arrested Harry Longbaugh, alias Harry Alonzo, one of the train robbers, after he had passed four of the stolen bills at a PAWNSHOP. A female companion was also arrested. They had in their possession about $7,000 of the stolen notes.

Officers attempting to arrest these men are warned that they are desperadoes, always carry firearms and do not hesitate to use them when their liberty is endangered.

Wanted poster for Kid Curry, using part of the photograph he had taken with Annie Rogers, naming him as the leader of the gang that held up the Great Northern Railway train at Wagner, Montana, July 3, 1901. *Courtesy Pinkertons, Inc.*

$18,000.00 REWARD

THE UNION PACIFIC TRAIN ROBBERS.

On Friday morning, June 2d, 1899, a party of masked robbers held up the first section of train number one of Union Pacific Railroad Company, about ten miles west of Rock Creek Station, Albany County, Wyoming, and after dynamiting bridges, mail and express cars, and robbing the latter, disappeared. The second section of this train, being the Overland Limited Passenger, following ten minutes behind, was fortunately stopped by the brakeman of the first section who escaped from the robbers.

Three of the robbers went north mounted and were followed eight hours later by a posse. The robbers crossed the Platte River at Casper about three o'clock Sunday morning, and were followed from Casper by another posse from that point, who overtook them about four o'clock in the afternoon about twenty-eight miles northwest of Casper, where a running fight occurred, the robbers shooting three of the horses of the pursuing party, and escaping to a point about fifteen miles further on, where they were again overtaken the following Monday morning by both posses, at which time Sheriff Hazen, of Converse County, was shot and killed from ambush. In the confusion which followed, the robbers eluded the posses, and are supposed now to be somewhere in Johnson or Big Horn Counties, and are being closely followed by the pursuing parties.

A description of these three robbers is as follows: One man about 31 or 32 years of age: height, five feet eight or nine inches; weight, 185 pounds; complexion and hair light; if moustache, likely to be long but not heavy; blue eyes; peculiar nose, flattened at bridge and heavy at point; round, full, red face; walks slightly stooping; may be slightly bow-legged; bald forehead; when last seen wore number eight cow-boy high-heel boots. Two men look like brothers; smaller, five feet seven inches; age about 28; weight 135 pounds. Largest, five feet, five inches; age about 30; weight 145 or 150; may have slight growth of whiskers; complexion of both very dark; one-quarter Cherokee Indian; smaller man sometimes wears moustache; both have dark hair, indicating the Indian; eyes dark.

When overtaken about forty miles north-west of Casper where Sheriff Hazen was murdered, their horses were captured, described as follows:

An Arabian horse, weighing 1100 or 1200 pounds; strawberry roan in front, shading lighter to the rear; rump and back, white, with small black spots; has collar mark on right shoulder; short mane and tail; indistinct brand on right shoulder.

Second horse; dun color, or clay bank, with white mane and tail; weighs about 1100 pounds; is branded "spade or heart J" on left shoulder; has worked in harness.

Third horse; small sorrel, well shaped head; weighs about 950 pounds; white face and white hind legs; white ring around right fore-leg at knee joint; several indistinct brands on left shoulder, one resembling the letter "H", another resembling a "flying diamond"; also three perpendicular bars—long bar in center. These horses are now in safe keeping at Cheyenne.

It is probable that these three robbers, when driven from their present hiding, will make for the north into adjoining states, or possibly British Columbia. Have not up to this time succeeded in locating the other three men, but it is probable will be able to do so soon.

In order to prevent the escape of these three robbers who are being pursued, it is important that posses be organized without delay in your state, and that they be dispatched at once in the direction of the present supposed hiding in northern Wyoming, to capture them if they attempt to cross the line.

Union Pacific Railroad Company and Pacific Express Company have jointly offered two thousand dollars per head, dead or alive, for each of these men, and the United States Government has also offered a reward of one thousand dollars each, making three thousand per head for each of these men.

Any information concerning these bandits should be promptly forwarded to Union Pacific Railroad Company and the United States Marshal of Wyoming, at Cheyenne.

UNION PACIFIC RAILROAD COMPANY.
PACIFIC EXPRESS COMPANY.

OMAHA, NEBRASKA, June 10th, 1899

A rare wanted poster for the Wilcox train robbers before they were identified as the Kid Curry gang. The killing of Sheriff Hazen is described. *The James D. Horan Civil War and Western Americana Collection*

the Kid continued to choke Brady with one hand and with the other shot Boley. Bystanders told the police "he fired the shot with such speed he just had to fire the pistol from inside his pocket." Later, when Curry was captured, police could not find a bullet hole in his coat pocket . . .

After he shot Boley, the Kid left the gasping Brady on the floor and started to clean out the bar. When Officers Robert Saylor and William Dinwiddle arrived, Curry had reduced the furniture to splinters and had taken on the customers who were fast losing their enthusiasm for battle.

When the Kid refused to stop fighting, Saylor broke his billy over the outlaw's head. Curry, with his fast draw, shot Saylor four times and Dinwiddle once before he decided he had enough of Knoxville.

As the *Knoxville Journal and Tribune* reported, "his face knitted in a demon-

Kid Curry and his girl friend, Annie Rogers, an attractive redhead who insisted the deadly Kid was "always a gentleman." She was arrested in Nashville, October 14, 1901, as an accomplice of Curry, but was acquitted June 19, 1902. *Courtesy Pinkertons, Inc.*

ical fury," he leaped through a back door only to fall twenty feet into an open railroad cut.[25]

Battered, bleeding, coatless, and limping from a badly sprained ankle, the Kid dodged the posses and their bloodhounds for three days in subzero temperatures.

On the afternoon of the fifteenth near Jefferson City about twenty miles from Knoxville, this fugitive from the Wild West encountered an enemy he had never faced before—the telephone. A. B. Carey, a Jefferson City merchant, called the Knoxville police to report he had seen a man walking down the road who he believed was the much wanted fugitive. While waiting for the Knoxville posse to appear, Carey and three Jefferson City merchants decided to hunt down the outlaw.

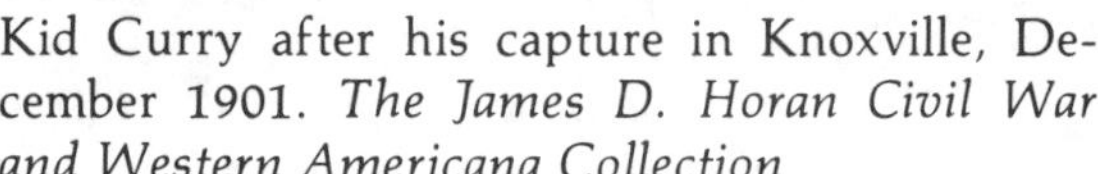

Kid Curry after his capture in Knoxville, December 1901. *The James D. Horan Civil War and Western Americana Collection*

A rare photograph of Fanny Porter, owner of "Fanny Porter's Sporting House" in San Antonio's "Hell's Half Acre," a frontier brothel, where Kid Curry, Butch Cassidy, and the rest of the Wild Bunch would hide out after a train or bank robbery. When he was arrested, the Kid refused to explain a terse message from Fanny found in his pocket. *Courtesy Pinkertons, Inc.*

They finally discovered Logan huddled over a small fire.

"He was slow in putting up his hands," Carey explained, "but he finally surrendered."

When the man hunters returned to Knoxville a crowd variously estimated as between 2,000 and 5,000 jammed the depot hoping to catch a glimpse of the desperado. It was typical of the Kid to give his silver watch to a posseman who had shown him some kindness and in passing to insist his name was Wilson.

On the seventeenth, Lowell Spence, then assistant superintendent of the Chicago office of the Pinkertons, arrived in Knoxville. A few hours later United States Attorney Wright announced Spence had identified the prisoner as Harvey Logan, alias Kid Curry, the western outlaw. Spence's original notes show that Logan had "jet black hair and a beard three days old . . . 5 ft. 7 in. . . . peculiar dark eyes, reserved manner . . . speaks quietly but positively and is slightly bowlegged. He acts cool and collected . . . there is a gunshot wound scar on his right wrist . . ."

When Logan was searched, a baggage check was found for the checkroom of the Southern Pacific Depot. There "a telescope bag" yielded $3,130 of the stolen Helena bank notes, three suits "from a fine Denver men's shop," and a note from Fanny Porter, operator of the famous Texas bordello in Hell's Half Acre. It read: "Will wait until parties arrive."

When he was asked about the meaning of Fanny's cryptic note, the Kid only shrugged. Later, Ike Jones's bartender reluctantly gave up the bank notes entrusted to his care by Logan.

Kid Curry became a celebrity in jail. Large crowds stood outside in the bitter cold hoping to catch a glimpse of the badman. It is hard to believe, but Knoxville's Sheriff James W. Fox declared an "open house" that Christmas week; anyone interested in shaking hands with the notorious killer and western outlaw was welcome.

Thousands stood in line from dawn to late afternoon: men and women with small children, mountaineers cradling rifles, farmers and residents of other states paraded down the jail corridor to peer in at the outlaw or shake his hand.

A Knoxville reporter remained outside Logan's cell for a day and wrote a detailed account of what took place.[26]

Many Callers: An Afternoon with Harvey Logan

Logan stood at the bars of his cell most of the time receiving and indulging in fun with his visitors. He answered the questions politely unless there were some things asked that he didn't care to make public.

Most of his visitors simply asked how he felt, just to hear the sound of his voice but some just looked at him as one would a corpse, then pass on. He was the recipient of many cigars. The public had read in *The Sentinel* he did not smoke cigarettes and none of these nor the material used in making them were offered to him.

A visitor who amused Logan perhaps more than any other was a Cooke County constable. He did not say how long he had been an official but his experience with criminals had not been extensive. He told the sheriff his friends up in Cooke County said he was "A Plumb Good Detective" so he was anxious to see the badman who had been able to avoid the western officers for so long.

"He didn't run long here," said the constable. "As soon as we seed *The Sentinel* that he was here we were ready for him. I was on the lookout for him myself, and if he had come up our way I'd a knowed him from his description in the paper."

Jailer Bell took the constable to the cell and Watchman Clark introduced him to Logan who said he was delighted to meet him.

"I'm sure glad I didn't meet you on the outside," smiled Logan who saw at a glance what he was up against.

The constable was somewhat embarrassed but his mountain nature soon overcame him.

"I 'spect it better ye didn't," he replied in much the same tone and showed in a moment that he could "give and take" as they say in the mountains.

"You weigh about 158 pounds, I should judge," the constable said, giving the outlaw a good sizing up.

"No, I weigh 180 pounds," Logan said with a smile. "If I stay here and get this good beef I'll reach a ton by spring."

"I 'loud you will," said the constable.

"Have you made many arrests?" asked Logan.

"Yes, a few but I have studied the business a heap."

"You'll find that's the safest part of your business," Logan said solemnly.

"How's that?"

"I say the studying part is the safest."

The constable laughed and Logan fairly roared.

When they shook hands Logan told him:

H. D. Kampmann, Proprietor.
McLean & Mudge, Managers.

C.1.

The Menger,
San Antonio, Texas.

Logans Log

June 2, 99, Wilcox Wyo
June 5, 99, Killed Josiah Hazen Sheriff leading Posse nr Casper
Aug 19, 1900 Rawlins. Wyo.
Aug 29, 1900 . Tipton Wyo
Sept 2 to 23rd/1900 Jim Ferguson Ranche in Black Mtns.
~~Oct to Nov. Unknown~~
Oct 1900 . San Antonio - at Fanny Porters with Will Casey.
Oct 1900. Ft Worth, Denver, Shoshone, &c.
Nov 21st/1900 Had Photo taken group of 5. Ft Worth
Dec 10 to 20/1900 Came back to Ft Worth with Casey & 2 women
Dec 22 to 30th/1900, Laclede Hotel San Antonio with Ben K & Will C,
Feb 3/1901. San Angelo. wrote to Miss L. D. Watson [illegible]
Feb 10 to 25th/1901, Knickerbocker with Will Casey, Ben K.
March 1st to 26/1901 Christoval with Will Casey & [illegible]
March 27/1901. Camped nr [illegible] Rock with Ben, Will & another
March 27/1901 J. W. Thornton Killed, gang fled wounded.
Ap 2/1901, Bill Carver Killed Sonora by E. S. Briant & Geo Kilpatrick
Ap 1901. Geo & Ed Kil[patrick] Indicted for Thornton murder, Logan in it too,

"Logans Log" kept by Lowell Spence, who hunted Kid Curry for years. It was Spence who finally identified the Kid after he had been captured in Knoxville. Later Spence determined the exhumed corpse of a train robber was Kid Curry. *Courtesy Pinkertons, Inc.*

C2

Tipton Witnesses

E. J. Kerrigan, Cond,
C. E. Woodcock Mess, Exp train men,
H. O. Granburg Road Master, Rawlins, Wyo.
Wm Running Tipton
Mrs Wm Running "
Chas Calkins "
W. S. Cooper "
Lizzie Warren "
(Running & wife kept Eating house – Saw [illegible] go towards Engine. Saw a 2nd man. Gang may have eat there or some of them. Calkins & Cooper boarded at Runnings. Lizzie Warren [illegible] one of robbers a [illegible] to be [illegible] whom Mrs Running [illegible])
Harry Wesner . Trainman
Henry Wallenstein "
A. Iverson. Red Desert Wyo. (Saw 2 men leading 2 horses Couple days before robbery)
Joe J. Maloney, Bitter Creek. of Lewis Bruces Stone gang now residing at 1242 So Tremont St Denver. Can identify one of 3 men. Saw 2 men with horses, grey horse. [illegible] 2 or 3 dys before R. one wore Blue Shirt, Corduroys
Courtney A. Joyce. Cook, Bitter Creek Wyo address [illegible] J. E. Markell Omaha. outfit #28. Sold 2 men [illegible] would know one [illegible] the dark complected man
Lewis Bruce % Joe J Maloney 1242 So Tremont
Scotch Bob Rawlins Wyo. (Saw Bob & Curry [illegible] Sunday before the robbery [illegible] So of [illegible])

A list of witnesses Lowell Spence gathered for the United States attorney in Knoxville. They were used in the government's case against Kid Curry. *Courtesy Pinkertons, Inc.*

"You just keep on studying. Don't be in a hurry to graduate and be careful when you go and put your detective education into practice—"

"Why?" asked the constable.

"Some farmer might beat you to death with a cornstalk," Logan told him.

Later the outlaw was given some diversion when the W.C.T.U. ladies held services on his floor. He was a respectful and interested listener. After the services Mrs. Skillman called him to the bar[s an]d talked to him for some time privately. Logan gave her a respectful audienc[e]

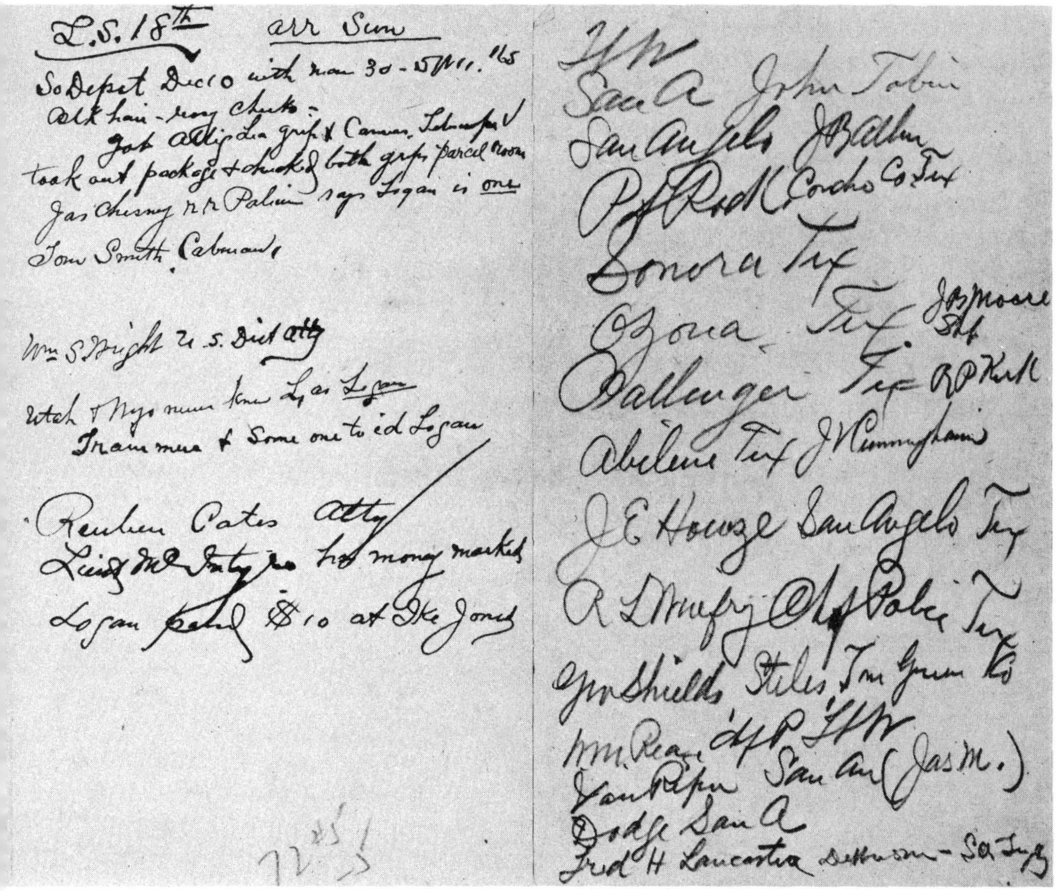
Wm S Wright U. S. Dist Atty

Reuben Cates Atty

Sonora Tex

Ozona Tex

Abilene Tex

J E Howze San Angelo Tex

Spence's witnesses were also interviewed in Texas. One of his notes indicated Kid Curry's valise, containing some of the stolen bank notes, was found in the Knoxville railroad baggage room. *Courtesy Pinkertons, Inc.*

> There was an unusual stir late in the afternoon when Sheriff Fox reported his brindle bulldog, "Dock Croker," was lost. He is only nine months old and full of play. The back gate was left open and he followed someone out. Sheriff Fox will be obliged if anyone who sees the dog will notify him.
>
> Jailer Bell reported that almost 2,000 were turned away. He said some were mountain people who had come down with their rifles. They said they wanted to see if a western badman was a better shot than they were . . .

Rather than return Logan to Montana for trial where he had many friends, the Great Northern Railroad officials and the United States Attorney decided their case against the outlaw would consist of his forging and passing the Helena bank notes. In Knoxville he was indicted on nineteen counts, each an incident in which he used a bank note for currency.

The staff of the United States Attorney in Knoxville carefully built a case that traced the journey of the stolen bank notes from the time they left the United States Treasury for the Helena bank until they were removed from the express car's safe at Wagner, Montana. Each mile of the railroad line from Washington to Montana was described by witnesses and confirmed by vouchers and bills of lading as the bank notes were passed from messenger to messenger. One of the highlights of the trial was the testimony of M. F. O'Neil, the engineer of the Great Northern, who nervously described in detail how the Wild Bunch riders robbed the train and how Logan blew up the safe. C. H.

Smith, the young messenger, produced the only laughter when he told how Logan had put a Colt to his head and said:

"All I want from you is Jim Hill's money." (Hill was president of the Great Northern Pacific.)

After he put the bank notes in a sack, Smith testified Logan looked about the car, shattered by dynamite, and spotted a bolt of silk.

"Open up the sack," he told one of the bandits, "I'm going to take this back for the old lady."

Smith said, as the outlaws were jumping from the car, he asked Logan for his .44 Colt.

The Kid stared at him. "What for, young fellow?"

"Something to remember this event by," Smith replied.

The witness told how Kid Curry laughed, fired the last shot in the six-shooter, and tossed it to him.

The trial ended, the Kid was found guilty, and remanded for sentencing.

Kid Curry, like all other gunfighters of the West, had an enormous ego and tremendous self-confidence. They showed in his bold visits to photography studios when he was nationally hunted with large rewards offered for his arrest, his almost studied indifference to lawmen, and his casual visits to big cities and towns where his wanted posters were prominently displayed.

Although he was never known to brag of his skill with a six-shooter or of his physical toughness, the Kid was quietly proud of his reputation. To his many women visitors he never failed to point out that Knoxville newspapers were calling him "the Napoleon of Crime" and "the noted western desperado."

Confinement in a cell was torture for this man of the open plains. By Christmas 1902, a year after his capture, Curry's "health is fast giving away and his confinement is telling on him very much," the *Fort Benton River Press* reported. In the beginning the Kid had systematically exercised but as the months passed he did less and less. He constantly paced up and down, the frustrations and tensions slowly building. One day he went into a rage and tried to strangle a fellow prisoner who had taunted him as a "cowboy." It took all the guards on the cellblock to pry him loose from the man's throat.

He also became weary of the crowds that still paraded outside his cell on weekends and once put a blanket over his head "as a protest to being put on display like an animal."

By Christmas 1902, the Kid was planning his escape. That month he wrote a revealing letter to his old friend Edward Hanlon, a fellow rancher in the Little Rockies.

As Curry explained, to get the letter past the guards he "shot" it out his cell window with a rubber band; on the envelope he had written, "please mail this letter." The outlaw had shrewdly predicted that someone would pass the jail, pick up the letter, and mail it without questioning how it got there or where it was from.

Kid Curry was obviously planning an escape from the Knoxville jail. After the sheriff discovered that women who were attracted to the outlaw were smuggling in boxes of "fine foods," he ordered an embargo on all packages sent to the Kid. *The James D. Horan Civil War and Western Americana Collection*

SHERIFF MAKES TIMELY DISCOVERY.

KNOXVILLE, Tenn., Sept. 20.—A box intended for Harvey Logan, the alleged Montana train robber in jail here, was intercepted by the sheriff today. The box contained several packages of tobacco and six cob pipes with long stems. Over the mouths of the pipes were seals. These were broken by the sheriff who found a steel saw twenty-two inches long in each pipe.

The letter was published in the *Lewistown Democrat News,* December 5, 1902.

A Letter from Kid Curry

I will get out of this scrape yet. I will show these people that they are not dealing with a soft thing. They call me "the Napoleon of Crime" and you should see how they flock to see me when the trial is on.

And when I get out of this, Ed, look out for me. They talk about Harry Tracy,* but if I don't give them a better run for their money, my right name is not Harvey Logan. I'll cut my way through h--l before they'll take me again.

I am now waiting for my sentence. It will be a light one for the people out here are with me and I've got all sorts of friends. Well, goodby old friend, it won't be long before I'll be back in Montana and when I am there'll be h--l to pay!

On November 30, 1902, Logan was sentenced to twenty years at hard labor in a federal penitentiary and fined $5,000.[27]

Law enforcement agencies warned Sheriff Fox and the president of the Union Pacific—a favorite of the Wild Bunch—that Logan was undoubtedly planning an escape from the Knoxville jail and guards should be doubled. They also insisted Logan should not be imprisoned in the Columbus penitentiary because "his pal, Ben Kilpatrick (the Tall Texan), is imprisoned there after having been convicted of train robbery in the United States court at St. Louis, Missouri . . . we think it would be very bad policy to have both these men confined in the same penitentiary . . ."

Logan's impressive team of attorneys, which included a former congressman, appealed his conviction. After a lengthy hearing in the spring of 1903, his conviction was upheld by the United States Circuit Court of Appeals, Sixth District. In June preparations were made for federal marshals to deliver Logan in irons to a federal penitentiary.[28]

But as the lawmen had predicted, Logan broke out of the Knoxville County jail in one of the most bizarre escapes in the nation's history.

Logan lassoed jailer Frank Irwin with a wire he had taken from a broom and tied him with strips of a canvas hammock he had hidden in his cell—which the jailers and sheriff had insisted earlier to the U.S. Attorney's office had been empty of anything, including the outlaw's personal effects.

After tying up Irwin and another guard, Tom Bell, Logan took their guns, selected the sheriff's fine bay, and casually rode out of town to disappear in the mountain wilderness.

Statements taken by the United States Attorney W. D. Wright reconstructed the escape.[29]

Statement of Knoxville Jail Guard Frank Irwin

I frequently talked to Logan and Saturday afternoon about 4:15 P.M. he got up from his bunk and walked to the end of the corridor when I approached.

"I think the river is rising slowly from so much rain," he said.

It had been raining almost steadily but this afternoon was clear, with the sun striking the water it made a nice sight. I continued to look at the river and he said, "It's a nice sight, isn't it?"

*See the chapter on Harry Tracy.

I agreed with him and was about to turn around when suddenly he tossed this loop of wire from between the bars like it was a lariat, and twisted it hard.

"I got the advantage of you, Frank," he said, "and I'm going to get out of here. If you move I will kill you. Just do as I tell you, don't yell and you'll be all right."

Then he made me poke my hands through the bars of his cell and while he held the lasso tight around my neck with one hand, he tied my hands securely with strips of canvas, using his right hand and his teeth to make knots.

"I'm going to get out of here, Frank," he said again when he had finished, "and you can be a dead man. I like you, Frank, and it may be that I will be stretched out here on the floor in a few minutes. I don't want to hurt Tom [Bell, the other jailer] but he has got to turn me out."

I told him not to hurt Tom as he had nothing against him. Then he left me and went to work on the box.

He had some pieces of window molding and he bound those together with canvas strips. Then he took a hook he had hidden under his mattress and attached it to the sticks. He stretched out on the floor of the corridor and using the sticks and hook reached a cardboard box that was on the floor. In the box were two guns, a .45 calibre Colt and a .38 Smith & Wesson. He stuck both guns in his belt. Then he took out my pocket watch, looked at it and replaced it.

"I don't want your watch," he said, "I just want to see what time it is. Now call Tom."

I knew that he had me and would kill me if I made any trouble. I could do nothing but call Tom.

Statement of Jailer Tom Bell

I was so surprised when he shoved a gun in my face that I hardly realized what had happened.

"Open up, Tom," he said. "I'm going to get out of here. I don't want to hurt you but I will kill you if you do not open this door. I have nothing against you but Fox [Sheriff] better stay out of my way. Now open up—I'm going to get out of here."

There was nothing I could do, I knew the man and I knew he meant every word. I opened the door, then he told me to work the combination of the door leading from the second ward to the main office. I was so nervous I couldn't work the combination and Logan poked the gun in my face and warned me not to fool him. Finally it opened and he marched me down to the main office, down the basement steps and out into the yard.

The sheriff's bay was out there and so was R. P. Swanee, the Italian helper. He commanded me to saddle the horse and told Swanee to assist me. When we got the bay saddled he swung up, a pistol still in his hand.

Then the sheriff appeared on the porch above us and asked what was the matter. I told him that he would soon find out what was the matter if he did not get back into the house. I said this because I knew Logan was ready to kill him [Fox] and the sheriff didn't have a gun.

The sheriff ran back into his house to get a gun but Logan galloped out into Prince Street. I ran back into the jail and met Jim, our colored cook, and together we freed Irwin who had been tied by the neck to the bars with the wire lasso.

When we got back to the courtyard the sheriff had his gun but Logan by this time was gone.

There were many bizarre circumstances surrounding Logan's escape. An hour after the outlaw had fled, United States Attorney W. D. Wright and United States Marshal R. W. Austin passed the jailhouse. What happened is described in Austin's statement:

Statement of United States Marshal R. W. Austin

About half past five o'clock, Saturday afternoon, W. D. Wright, the United States Attorney, and myself left my office. We had been in consultation on some matters. We had not at that time heard of Logan's escape. As we left the building I saw Sheriff Fox passing in a leisurely manner.

I said, "Fox, how is Logan?"

He replied, "He's gone."

I replied, "You must be joking."

"No," he replied, "It is a fact."

Mr. Wright and Mr. Fox went to my office where we obtained the story from Mr. Fox. Mr. Fox also stated to us that he found out two weeks before that Logan had a map of the country south of the river.

We also learned that Logan had the use of the inner corridor. Mr. Wright stated that he had given orders to the sheriff not to allow Logan out of his cell, and I had given the same orders.

I asked Mr. Fox if he had done anything about hunting Logan and he replied that he would have a posse to go after him. That was about an hour after Logan had escaped.

I then began to phone all over the country, calling to my aid all the deputy United States marshals and sheriffs. Both the sheriffs of Blout and Sevier counties stated they would start with posses and they did. I was in frequent communication with all parts of the country and had the telephone companies notify all their patrons of Logan's escape, giving a description of him.

This information was sent in every direction. Telegraph was used to handle many other points.

We left Sheriff Fox about six o'clock under a promise to meet Mr. Wright and myself at my office at 8:30 o'clock that same night.

At nine o'clock he had not returned and so we went out into the streets looking for him.

Then we were notified that he was in the office of Charles T. Cates, where he wanted to see us. We went there and found there these gentlemen, William Epps, E. E. McMillan and John C. Houk. Mr. Houk is Logan's attorney.

Sheriff Fox acted as their spokesman. He told the story of Logan's escape and made the statement that Irwin's neck showed where the wire had caught him.

I then asked him, "Did you not tell me that when you examined Irwin's neck there were no marks on his neck?"

He admitted that was true. Mr. Wright and I left the office rather than discuss the matter in the presence of Logan's attorneys. I also notified Judge D. C. Clark who ordered me to make the most careful investigation of Logan's escape.

Also notified was the Department of Justice at Washington, the Pinkerton's National Detective Agency and the Great Northern Express Company.

Later with Mr. Austin we examined the cell and the corridor. I also looked carefully at the neck of Irwin the guard. There were no marks of violence on his neck or anything to show he had been roughly treated.

What of Catherine Cross, so "infatuated" with Logan, that police said she "planned to leave the city with him"? Kid Curry's arrest and identification as a notorious western outlaw and killer only increased her devotion. She visited him as often as possible, "showing him much attention." A ballad had been written about the Kid and his exploits and became quite popular that winter in Nashville and Knoxville.

Catherine loved to sing it and entertained the Kid, the guards, and other prisoners with her version. One night Catherine sang the ballad—where in Knoxville is not clear. A man demanded that she stop. When she refused, he stabbed her to death. Whether her assailant was a disgruntled suitor, drunk, or a madman is not known. She died in the hospital, whispering to police that she and the Kid had made plans to leave Knoxville together for the West.

Had Catherine acted as the Kid's courier, passing bribe money and smuggling guns into the cell? Was she to have met the Kid after his escape or had Curry simply used her? There are no answers . . .

Although posses searched the mountains with local guides, Logan was never captured. Mountain people in the remote section of the wilderness known as Jeffrey's Hell reported they had seen the outlaw, carrying a small bag of provisions, making his way through the dense undergrowth. They insisted he would lose his way and exhaust his food.

"Come spring, we'll look for his skeleton," one mountain man said. "We'll find it like we found the skeletons of those two others who went in that hell last year and never came out . . ."

But somehow, Harvey Logan, on foot, in poor physical condition because of his long confinement, and with a small amount of food, made his way across Jeffrey's Hell and eventually reached the West. In the winter of 1904, the *Great Falls Tribune* reported the Kid had been in Denver's Oxford Hotel carrying two suitcases filled with money that the outlaw insisted on carrying himself.

When a bellboy entered the room with a pitcher of water he saw Logan bending over the opened suitcases. In each were bundles of "new currency and a large revolver beside them." The startled boy notified the desk clerk who contacted the police. When they arrived, the Kid "had made his escape by a side entrance."

There were reports he fled to the Little Rockies country "where he had many friends." One said he had seen him and was told by the Kid, "I'll cut my way through here before they'll take me again." Then on June 7, 1904, three masked men held up the Denver & Rio Grande Railroad at Parachute, Colorado. They dynamited the express car but found the safe empty. A posse trailed them for two days, finally cornering the trio in a gully near Rifle.

In the gunbattle one man was hit. The posse heard his companions call out to ask if he was wounded.

"I'm hard hit and going to cash in quick . . . you go on," was the reply.

At dawn the posse rushed the gully. They found a dead man, six-shooter in hand, and a bullet in his temple. His companions had made their escape during the night. He was identified as Tap Duncan, a cowboy who had worked on local ranches.[30]

During the early days of the West, the Pinkertons had established a system in which local lawmen would send them photographs of dead outlaws. When the photographs arrived at the agency, experts would match them with Bertillon charts—exact physical description—of wanted men. If the photographs and charts matched, the agency arranged for the local sheriff or marshal to collect any existing reward—and the fugitive's records were placed in the "Dead and Inactive File."

Before the Colorado train robber was buried, the sheriff had the local photographer snap pictures of the corpse identified as Tap Duncan, stretched out on a plank. He sent the photographs along with a superficial description to the Pinkertons.

Apparently, it took some time for the sheriff to finally mail the material because the photographs and sheriff's letter did not reach William A. Pinkerton's desk in his Chicago office for some weeks. On a hunch, Pinkerton ordered Lowell Spence to try and determine if the dead outlaw was Logan.

This is Lowell Spence's story as he gave it to me more than twenty-five years ago.

How Lowell Spence Trailed Kid Curry Beyond the Grave

After I had been ordered by Mr. Pinkerton to determine if the train robber who had committed suicide near Rifle was or was not Harvey Logan, I went to Colorado and interviewed everyone who had known the dead man when he was working as a cowhand under the name of Tap Duncan.[31]

I was particularly interested in scars, manner of speaking, walking, drinking habits and skill with firearms. A great deal of the information I collected began to piece together a picture of the Harvey Logan I knew so well.

I next went to the sheriff and requested that the body buried in Glenwood Springs be exhumed. This was done on July 16, 1904. With me was W. S. Canada, Special Agent of the Union Pacific and R. Brunazzi of the Globe Express Company. The corpse had not been embalmed and was badly decomposed. I took what measurements I could and tried to find as many scars, such as bullet wounds, as was possible.

I also had copies made of the original shots the sheriff's photographer had made of the man immediately after death.

I then returned to Knoxville. I showed the photographs and the two Bertillon charts to the sheriff, jailers, United States Attorney, United States marshal, defense attorneys and as many members of the jury which had convicted Logan as I could locate.

They all agreed with my conclusion; the dead man was Harvey Logan, alias Kid Curry.

I returned to Chicago and made my report to Mr. Pinkerton. After more comparisons of the charts and photographs by our experts the Agency came to the conclusion Harvey Logan was dead and buried in that tiny western graveyard.

Our findings were released to the press which published stories across the country from New York to the West Coast.

Some disagreed with my findings, such as Special Agent Canada and Mr. Brunazzi. They both insisted the dead man was not Kid Curry.

SAINT PAUL PIONEER PRESS
TUESDAY, JULY 12, 1904.

KID CURRY IN HIS GRAVE

Photographs Reveal That Notorious "Bad Man" Killed Himself While Chased After Committing Train Robbery.

BANDIT "KID CURRY."
Notorious Western train and bank robber who, wounded by pursuers, kills himself.

The exhumed body of Harvey Logan (Kid Curry), who had been buried as "Tap Duncan," a cowboy and train robber, who killed himself when trapped by a posse. *The James D. Horan Civil War and Western Americana Collection*

Mr. Canada and Mr. Brunazzi said certain scars were not found on the body. That is true, there was a lack of scars. However the corpse was decomposed and this could have made any scars invisible.

I had known Kid Curry better, I think, than any other officer in the West. I had hunted him day and night for years, as Assistant Superintendent of the Chicago office of the Agency, I had helped direct others in hunting him.

In Knoxville I was at his side from the moment he was put into his cell until the day he was found guilty by the jury and then sentenced to prison.

I knew the man intimately. I knew his face, how he talked, his features—and I am certain now as I was so many years ago, that the dead man buried as Tap Duncan was Harvey Logan.

I think it is significant that we never heard from Harvey Logan again.

Logan or Kid Curry, who I believe was the most dangerous man in the West, had taken his life in that gully because he could not face the possibility of being sent to prison.

As he had told his jailers and his defense attorney in Knoxville, he would rather die than spend a long time in prison.

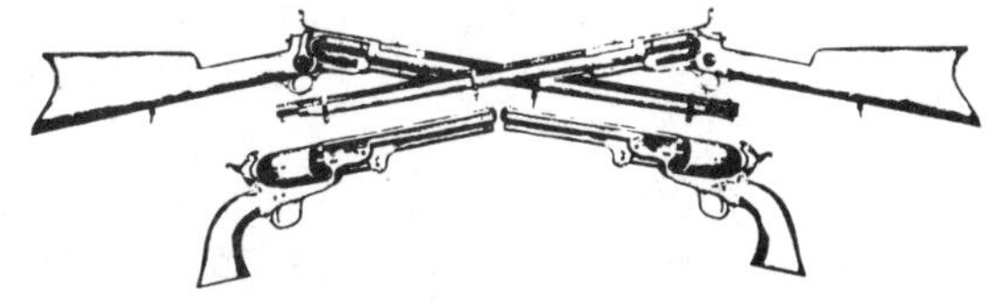

TOM HORN

ON THE WESTERN FRONTIER WHERE TOM HORN'S GUN WAS for hire, he gave his cattle baron employers full measure of what they paid for and took their deadly secrets with him into eternity.

As his adoring young schoolteacher, Glendolene Myrtle Kimmel, described him, "He was a man who embodied the characteristics, the experiences and code of the old frontiersmen."

The extent of Horn's experiences in the Wild West were extraordinary: stagecoach rider, cowboy, Indian scout, and interpreter, the man who captured the Apache chief Nana and persuaded Geronimo to surrender; rodeo champion, skilled marksman—and hired killer, "my stock in trade," as he would boast.

When he died on the gallows in Cheyenne on a November morning in 1903, the city was under martial law after rumors had been printed that Horn's "cowboy friends" would storm the jail and release him. Such a thing was not a Wild West fantasy; not many years before Butch Cassidy and his Wild Bunch riders had been prepared to free his fellow outlaw Matt Warner from a Utah jail until Warner's wife begged him not to do it.

The West held its breath until the trap was sprung to let Horn's big body dangle at the end of the hangman's rope. Horn had been hired by prominent men in the cattle industry and the prosecutor had indicated his death sentence might be commuted to life imprisonment if he talked. Horn scorned the offer.

He was a cool calculating killer but, as his adoring Miss Kimmel had said, he never broke the code; to betray an employer or a friend was unthinkable.

Horn was born near Memphis, Scotland County, Missouri, November 21, 1860. His father was a prosperous farmer, his mother, as he recalled her, "was a powerful woman . . . a good old fashioned Campbellite." He was fourteen when he left home after a "disagreement" with his father.

He first worked on the railroad in Kansas, then joined a team of freighters to get to Santa Fe. His next job was driving a stage for the Overland Mail from Santa Fe to Prescott, Arizona.[1]

His first contact with the Apache was near Camp Verde where he worked as a night herder. When he left a year later he could speak fluent Spanish and Apache. At sixteen he was employed by the quartermaster's department to herd horses for the army posts.

At Fort Whipple he met Al Sieber, the famous Indian scout, and joined him as Mexican interpreter at San Carlos for $75 a month. Horn always said his years on the large Apache reservation were the happiest of his life.

It was a nomadic life: hunting with the bucks, living in the village of Pedro, the old war captain of Victorio, the famous Apache chief, and letting the squaws "throw a stick." (Apache women threw a stick at a man to show she was ready for courtship.)

He also met Mickey Free, the celebrated one-eyed Apache-Mexican scout, who became his close friend. In 1876 at Pedro's request, Sieber appointed Horn as a liaison scout between the Apache and the army at San Carlos and Fort Apache. When the Indian Bureau scandal shook Washington, all civilians were banned from the Indian agencies, and the army scouts lost their jobs. According to Horn's autobiography, he and Sieber joined Ed Scheflin and watched the birth of Tombstone. While Sieber worked a claim they had staked out, Horn supplied the camps with venison at $2.80 a deer.[2]

In October they were recalled to Fort Whipple to join the Sixth Cavalry as scouts. After he and Sieber helped to bring in Geronimo for the first time, they were again fired in the spring of 1877 when federal appropriations ran out.

For a year Horn worked for Tuly, Oches & Co. in Tucson, supplying beef for the Apache at San Carlos. Once again civilians were issuing the rations and corruption was rampant. As Horn recalled, one agent when arrested could not account for $54,000 in food and clothing he had received between six and eight months at San Carlos.

In May 1880, the Chiricahua Apache broke out, killing the agent, his native policeman, and cutting down the telegraph poles. To alert the army, Horn made the thirty-two-mile ride to Fort Thomas, swimming his horse across the swollen Gila.

The Apache war had begun. Horn first served under Colonel Forsyth, hero of Beecher's Island battle, then as a scout when Captain Adam R. Chaffee's troopers of the Third and Sixth Cavalry met the Apache at Chevelon's Fork on the Little Colorado River. Chaffee was well known on the frontier for the order he had given during the peak of the Kiowa-Comanche war in the 1870s:

"Forward! If any man is killed, I'll make him a corporal!"

Tom Horn's mother, "a good, old-fashioned Campbellite," as he described her in his autobiography. *The James D. Horan Civil War and Western Americana Collection*

After conferring with Sieber, Chaffee sent two detachments east and west into Devil's Canyon to outflank the hostiles. It was a deep gorge, with steep walls that Horn and the troopers finally scaled, as he later said, "by our fingernails."

A heavy fire fight finally ended in a fierce rain and hailstorm that Horn called the worst he had ever seen in the West. The Apache had lost a number of warriors and withdrew to be pursued by Chaffee until they agreed to return to the agency.

In the summer of 1886 after a tiswin (corn beer) spree, Geronimo led a large number of warriors into Mexico. General George Crook ordered Captain Emmett Crawford, one of the finest young officers in the Indian Fighting Army, to track down the wily chief; Horn, as chief scout, accompanied the expedition.

Under a new treaty allowing American troops to move into Mexico to seek out runaway Apache bands, the tiny army crossed the border and continued on into the Sierra Madre.

On the Aros River, Horn and his scouts found the Apache chief's camp. While they engaged the hostiles, they were attacked by Mexican irregulars and Crawford was killed.

For many years, especially after Horn had been executed, the army refused to credit him for the part he had played during the Apache campaign. Apparently the generals had no desire to share credit with civilians.

Even after Horn's autobiography—finished a short time before he died on the gallows—was published, young officers contemptuously dismissed him as a braggart. However, veterans of the campaign remembered the tall, courageous young scout who spoke Spanish and Apache and had an uncanny ability to persuade Geronimo, Natches, and the other chiefs to listen to the army's proposals.

In the section of his autobiography that describes the Apache wars, Horn does not brag; his accounts are simple and vividly written. His bravery, courage, and dedication to the army are a bewildering contrast to his later role as a killer for hire.

Here Horn tells how Crawford was killed and of his capture of Nana, Victorio's ancient war captain.[3]

Mickey Free, who served as a scout with Tom Horn under Generals Crook and Miles during the Apache campaign. Al Sieber, chief of scouts, once described Free as "Half Irish, Half Mex, and whole son of a bitch." *The James D. Horan Civil War and Western Americana Collection*

An original photograph by C. S. Fly, the famous Tombstone photographer, of Geronimo and Natches, ready for the peace conference with General Crook, March 27, 1886. Natches with hat on, Geronimo's son by his side. Geronimo asked Fly to take this photograph. *The James D. Horan Civil War and Western Americana Collection*

A rare original photograph taken by C. S. Fly during the Apache campaign. Fly, an eyewitness to the gun battle of the O.K. Corral, was present at the peace councils held by General Crook and Geronimo. *The James D. Horan Civil War and Western Americana Collection*

The cavalry camp at Zuni, New Mexico, as Tom Horn knew it as a scout. These are troopers of the Sixth Cavalry preparing to move out for Fort Apache during the Apache campaign. *The James D. Horan Civil War and Western Americana Collection*

Captain Emmet Crawford. Horn was with Crawford when he was killed in the Apache campaign. *Courtesy Arizona Historical Society*

A rare original photograph of Nana, famous Apache chief, captured by Tom Horn during the Apache campaign. *Portrait by A. F. Randall, May 1884. The James D. Horan Civil War and Western Americana Collection*

The Death of Captain Crawford and the Capture of Nana

All of us began to stir at daylight, and very shortly after we saw Mexican soldiers coming toward us. I saw they were getting ready to make a fight, and I could hear their orders as plainly as I could hear Captain Crawford's, who stood beside me. I told the scouts to get ready for a scrap, and to listen to me and do as I said, and not fire one shot if they could keep from it.

I heard the Mexican commander say to his men to throw out flankers on each side of us, and for some of them to get ready to charge. I got Shipp out on one side to stop their flankers, and Maus on the other side to do the same, and told each of them to start the game when they were compelled to for their own protection. I yelled to the Mexicans many times, that we were American troops from the line, but that did not stop them. They must have heard me, for Captain Crawford and I could hear them plainly. They had formed for a fight about three hundred yards from us. We had ample time to get into position, and we were in a strong natural fortification. I knew a thousand Mexicans could not move us.

Finally, I heard the commander ask if the men were all in position for the flank move, and the answer came back that they were all waiting.

"Follow me, valientes!" cried the Mexican Captain, and at us they came on a run across a little basin, directly toward us.

Crawford said, "My God, Chief, can't you stop them? These scouts will kill them all!"

I ran out towards them, and Crawford jumped up higher still, on a big prominent rock, and had a white handkerchief in his hands. He could not speak Spanish, but he could swear in a moderately clever way, not like Sieber or Chaffee, but still he was doing very well. I kept on talking to the Mexicans all the time, and was also talking to the scouts and telling them not to fire.

When they reached the middle of the basin the Mexicans began to shoot. Some would stop and shoot, and then come on towards us on a trot, and others would do the same, so that some were coming on a trot and some were firing all the time.

One of my scouts yelled to me to come back, that Crawford was killed. I was half-way down meeting the Mexicans, and was out in the opening. I was wondering why it was that they did not hit me, and then all at once I wondered no more, for I was struck in the arm. My scouts saw I was hit, and they yelled, "Come back!"

I did not start right away, although the Mexicans were within fifty feet of me, but I yelled to my scouts to give it to them! All my scouts seemed to shoot at once, and how it did paralyze those Greasers! They went down in groups and bunches! Their advance was stopped as though they had come to the end. Some of my scouts wanted to be down where I was; and, Chi-kis-in and about a dozen came down and kept on shooting at some of the wounded Mexicans who were trying to crawl away.

I believe the Mexicans afterwards said there were thirty-six killed and thirteen badly wounded. There were one hundred and fifty-four Mexicans, so they said later. After all the Mexicans had gotten out of sight, one of them yelled over to us:

"O, you white man that talks Mexican, I want to talk to you."

I said, "What do you want? I spoke to you many times and you would not answer."

They replied, "Now we want to talk."

I had gone over to where I had left Captain Crawford standing on a rock. Some of the Indians had said that he had been killed, and I wanted to see if it were true.

The scouts told me he was lying out in front of a big pile of boulders. I ran around there, and sure enough, there he lay. Shot in the center of the forehead, a glancing shot, but it had torn out a whole lot of his brains—I should say as much as a handful.

When I stepped around to where he lay I guess I was in plain view of the Mexicans, as they commenced to shoot at me again, and I tried to get Crawford back, but I had only one arm that I could use, and I could not lift him. I could not get the scouts to help me, as they do not like to do anything with a wounded man. So I had to drag him with one hand. It was about fifty feet from there to the sheltering rocks, but I finally got him around there. He was unconscious. I poured a little water down his throat, but he did not revive any.

The fight was going on again quite briskly, and it was not worth my while to try to stop it! Chi-kis-in came to me and wanted to scatter out our men and go after the Mexicans and kill all of them, but I talked to them and told them not to do so until I ordered them.

Old Nana came crippling up to me and said:

"Captain, though I am a prisoner and an old man, I would like to take the rifle and ammunition of the dead Captain and help to entertain the Mexicans."

I gave him the gun and belt and told him to do as I told him, or rather as I told the rest of the scouts. He said, "I will do so. If this is a fight to the death, here I will die, for I will never be shamed by running, as I did yesterday."

I went around among my scouts and told them not to waste their ammunition too freely, as we were in the Mexicans' country, and two weeks' travel from the line, and may be the Mexicans had taken in all our command, I did not know, and could not guess, why we had been attacked. I thought Mexico and the United States were at war, and that we were in it. I was sure the Mexicans did not want to do anything but fight, and I knew, also, that my men were wanting to advance awfully bad, and I knew, also, that if I did let my scouts go they would kill all of the Mexicans, or nearly all, as an Apache has no fear of Mexicans.

I went and saw Lieutenant Maus, and had a talk with him, and told him how things were.

We could not make out why we were attacked by the Mexicans, unless Mexico had declared war against our country, and, as we had left Bowie on December 1, 1885, and it was now January 11, 1886, we had not had any word for a long time from the line.

Maus was now in command, as Crawford was dying, and I asked him if I should turn the Indians loose and make a ramp on the Mexicans. Maus said to speak to them again, and if they did not answer, to do as I wanted to, which, I tell you, meant go to 'em!

Just then I caught sight of Lieutenant Shipp and his bunch of scouts, right around over where the Mexicans were, and in a splendid commanding position. I could see that the Mexicans were getting excited, also, and so I spoke to them and asked them how they liked the entertainment. One of the Mexicans asked me who we were, and I told him we were a bunch of sports down from the United States, looking for some game, and thanked him for the nice little time we were having, and invited him to get his "valientes" together again, and try another charge.

He asked me what those Apache were doing, getting up over them, and I told him that if they did not charge or run soon, my men were going to try it, and see how charging went; but as we were now on three sides of them, and a steep ledge in front of them, that they had better act as though they had some sense.

"What do you want?" asked the Mexicans.

"Everything you have," replied I.

They talked a while among themselves, and then they asked what the soldier they saw (meaning Crawford) and I were doing with the Apaches. I told them that our business originally had been to hunt down renegade Chiricahuas, but that we were attacked by their outfit and that we had to defend ourselves, which we were perfectly able and willing to do.

Just here a loud yell broke out on the side of the Mexicans that we did not have guarded, and old Geronimo bobbed up and began to call to me. He shouted to me to give the word, and we would all strike the Mexicans at once and kill them all and get their pinole. Mexicans, when they go upon a campaign or trip, take only pinole, a kind of parched meal, and the Indians all like it—would do anything to get it. Some of Geronimo's men began to talk to the Mexicans in Spanish. I could easily distinguish old Jose Maria among them.

The Mexicans were getting pretty badly worked up by this time and they asked me to come over there to their camp. I went and saw Maus and told him I was going over, and then I told the scouts that I was going and to be sure to kill all the Mexicans if they killed me. I told Geronimo, also, that I was going into the Mexican camp, and I heard Jose Maria tell the Mexicans that if they harmed me that the scouts and renegades would combine and kill every mother's son of them!

Then I walked over. I went in among them and asked where their commander was, and they said that he lay dead on the field of battle. I told them we had not had a battle yet, only a skirmish; that if their commander had been killed they had better go back home and get a new one; that we were the same as Mexican troops, as we were; and were allowed all the rights and privileges of Mexican troops within certain limits and that we were within those limits, and that on this occasion, by our treaty, our rights and privileges were equal to their own. I told them that they had come and attacked us, and that we had merely defended ourselves.

One of them then asked me who I was, and I told him. "Well," he said, "we don't know anything of this treaty you are talking about, but we think it is all right, and we will let it go, though we have had many men killed and among them is Don Maurice Corredor, the bravest man that ever lived. We will have to take you with us to the city of Chihuahua to settle this thing."

I told them that I would have to decline the order or invitation, whichever it was, and they said they would take me anyhow, and that I was their prisoner!

Geronimo was closer to me than my own men and I spoke to him and told him what these Mexicans were talking of doing, and he yelled to my scouts what I had told him, and in a minute every scout and renegade commenced to yell and get ready for an advance. The Mexicans asked me what the Indians were doing, and I told them that I was chief of the Indians, and they did not propose to see me taken away.

"What did you say to the Indians?" asked the Mexicans. I informed them that I had told the Indians I was a prisoner. The Mexicans could see that they were surrounded and that they would be exterminated in a few minutes more.

"We will kill you," said one of them, "if the Apaches fire upon us."

"I know you will," replied I, "and I know, also, that you will never smile again after you do kill me, for no one but myself can handle or control those Indians, and when they know I am killed you will all be killed. Not one of you will escape."

All the Indians were closing in now, and one Mexican said to me: "Go quick and stop them, and then come back and see if we can not fix this thing up."

I called to Geronimo not to fire till I told them, or till they saw me fall. I was in plain sight of the Chiricahuas and of most of the scouts, and I stepped up where I could be more plainly seen by all of them. I then asked the Mexicans if they did not think it unnecessary to take me to the city of Chihuahua, as my presence was very necessary there with my scouts.

"Have you not got a commissioned officer with your outfit?" asked one, and I told him that there were two of them with the scouts.

"You go over and take care of the scouts, and send one of the officers over and let us talk to him."

"Neither of them can talk Mexican," said I.

"Well, if you can control the Indians, go on back to them," said one of the Mexicans.

I went back and told Maus all about the whole business; also that the Mexicans, such as were there, were a very uncertain lot and would not do to trust. Maus asked me to go and get one of the prominent Mexicans to come over and talk to him. I went back to the Mexican camp and asked them to send over a man or two, or a dozen if they liked, to talk to our officer.

Two of them concluded to go. Jose Maria, of the Chiricahuas, asked me what we were going to do, and I told him. "May I come over, too, and hear what they have to say?" And I told him yes, to come on. Jose Maria came down and the four of us went over to our camp. I introduced them to Maus and told them who Maus was. The Mexicans then told Maus that they had made a mistake and did not know we were from the United States, that they were sorry for what they had done, and that they had suffered a much more serious loss than we had, as Maurice Corredor was a great man and would be a great loss to Mexico. I did not tell them of Crawford being shot. They wanted to know if we had any men killed and I called a scout that had gotten a shot in the wrist, and told him there were our wounded.

The Mexicans did not know what to do and I could not see that we were doing any good, so I told them to go on back to their camp. We had not had any breakfast and it was 10 o'clock by this time, so we went to work to get something for all hands.

Along about noon a Mexican came over and asked if I could let our doctor go over and attend to their wounded. I told Dr. Davis he could do as he liked, and he went over and dressed a whole lot of wounds for them. Dr. Davis said one of them was shot eight times. While Dr. Davis was over there, one of them came over and asked for Maus to go over, as they wanted to talk to him. I told Maus not to go, as he could not do any talking to amount to anything, but he said he would go, and go he did.

About the time Maus went over, Dr. Davis came back and said he did not like the looks of things. That the Mexicans did not treat him right. Presently Maus sent over a note, saying he was held prisoner; that the Mexicans wanted us to divide our rations with them; they wanted our mules to carry their wounded and they wanted everything we had.

They talked of taking him to Chihuahua. I told the Mexican who came over with the note, to go over and get men to take the mules and grub back; told him to bring four or five men. This he did, and the man who came back to receive the mules and rations said he was the man now in charge of the Mexicans.

He had four men with him, making five altogether. I told them that I was surprised that they should hold Lieutenant Maus as they were doing, and he told me that they were bound to have their own way, and we had better not make any trouble. I told him if that was their game, they should see how it was going to work. I told them to get upon a rock that was close by.

"What are you going to do?" asked their spokesman.

"You are playing a Mexican trick of bluff on us," said I, "and I am going to show you what joy means."

I made them get up on the rock, and then I called old Nana and Jose Maria, and about a dozen of my scouts, and told them to get ready to do as I told them.

I told them that as soon as I gave the word, I wanted them all to shoot into the Mexicans. By this time the Mexicans could see that they were going to be executed. I told them to call over to their comrades and tell them just the kind of a fix they were in, and after they told them that Lieutenant Maus must be sent back in one minute, or I would allow the Apaches to shoot them.

The man then commenced to tell his companions how things were, and that they would surely be killed in a minute if Maus did not appear.

For many a day we laughed at the way that Mexican did talk! Nana and Jose Maria were also telling them that they were all the same as dead men already, and how much pleasure they were going to have. I did not wait long till I told them that it was no use; that their friends had quit them, and they would have to die. Their friends wanted to talk, but I told them "No savvy," and it was getting time for my lieutenant to be coming.

The talk of this man sounded so sincere that the lieutenant came over and said that the Mexicans were doing a lot of bluffing on him, but they would not do any more. Maus said the Mexicans demanded everything when he got over there, and he could not talk much Spanish, and the Mexicans could not understand a word of American, and I guess there had been big doin's.

Well, that ended the row. I told the Mexicans to come over and get a lot of extra horses I had, and I took about forty head of the best and turned the rest of the captured horses (and there must have been three hundred of them) over to the Mexicans.

The Mexicans came from the Chihuahua side of the Sierra Madre, and the horses belonged to the Sonora side, but I was not going to take any more horses to the line or to Bowie, as I already had enough of that.

Late that evening the Mexicans pulled out, and I sent half a dozen scouts to follow and watch them. They were in very bad shape, as they had a good many wounded. I let old Jose Maria go back to the renegades, and told him to tell Chihuahua, and any others who wanted to talk to me, to come on the next day to where we would camp.

Crawford was unconscious, and remained so till he finally died, three days later. He had a great hole in his head, and it looked as though a handful of brains had been shot out; but with all that, he lived until the third day, and died while on the way out of the mountains. We were carrying him in a travois, carried by pack mules. We were rather a sorrowful lot ourselves, as we pulled towards home. We did not want to bury Crawford there in the mountains, so we were taking him out to the nearest settlement, which was Nacori.

I had sent five scouts on ahead with dispatches from Maus to our camp at Nacori, and two others we sent to General Crook. From Nacori we could send in helio dispatches, and by the time we arrived at Nacori with the body of Captain

Crawford, all the world knew of his death, and how it came about.

We buried Crawford at Nacori. The packers and soldiers had the grave prepared when we arrived there with the body. His body was taken up the next summer and sent to either Lincoln or Beatrice, Nebraska, where his mother and sister lived, and I have always understood that it was buried at Lincoln.

To go back to the Chiricahuas. As we went into camp, the first day after we left the battle ground, a woman came and told me Chihuahua was close there, and for me to come out, as he wanted to see me. I told Maus I was going out to see him, and he told me to do as I liked, and to come back and see him, and tell him what Chihuahua wanted.

I went with the squaw, and joined the chief, and he said he would follow Geronimo no more, as Geronimo was "all on the run and drink muscal." He said Geronimo was the war chief, and it was the custom of all other chiefs to obey the order of the war chief. He said Geronimo was too much on the talk; and gave me to understand that he was going to follow him no more.

He wanted me to make arrangements for him to meet General Crook and talk to him, and said he would be a renegade no more. Chihuahua was one of the most determined, and of the best hereditary standing of any chief in the Chiricahua tribe, but he never aspired to rank high as chief. Natchez and Chihuahua were half brothers, and both of them grandsons of old Cochise, the most noted of all old-time Chiricahua chiefs.

Natchez was the greatest warrior, and the best man physically, in the bunch of renegades; he was also a man of great personal pride and courage. So, knowing his pride, I asked Chihuahua to try to see if he could not get Natchez to come with him. He said he would see, but that he thought Natchez would consider himself bound to stay with Geronimo. I did all I could in a talk, and made arrangements to bring General Crook to meet him in the full of the March moon, at the San Bernardino Peak. I told him I could not be sure General Crook could come, but that I would take his message to him.

That evening several more women and children came in and said they were going back with us. We had now about twenty-five prisoners to take back. I never put them under guard at all, as they were all willing to go, and they were perfectly contented when not within the sound of Geronimo's voice. Geronimo certainly had an influence over them that controlled them when he was with them, but once away from him, they would do as they pleased. Now, for the first time, I could begin to see dissatisfaction in the renegade camp, and that was what I wanted to see.

At that camp on the Arras, where we jumped Geronimo, he could easily have given us a licking, or else a stand-off, had he made a fight, and all the Indians in the renegade camp thought that I had planned the fight to come off just as it did, and ran them down the draw among my best scouts.

It was true, I did send some of my best men with Shipp, but I did it because Shipp was young and inexperienced, and I thought he would need good men to take care of him, as I was sure we would have a hard fight. Of course, I never let on but that everything came out as I wanted it to.

Maus and Shipp knew different, but as they could not talk to either the scouts or the renegades, they could not give me away, and I took advantage of the wisdom I was supposed to have displayed. Then, too, the renegades all began to think more of me because I had headed off the scouts and would not let them kill any more women and children; and, taking it altogether, I was getting to be a great man in my own estimation!

In April 1886, General Nelson A. Miles replaced Crook, and the Apache war continued with Geronimo still on the loose, his warriors killing ranchers and Mexicans, kidnapping children, butchering cattle, and stealing horses.

Miles, who had dismissed all scouts including Tom and Al Sieber, ordered a selected group of troopers under Captain Leonard Wood, later colonel of Theodore Roosevelt's Rough Riders, then chief of staff, and H. L. Lawton to hunt down the Apache and bring them back to San Carlos. It was the old game of hare and hounds with the weary troopers returning empty-handed to the forts while Geronimo's warriors plundered at will as deep as central Arizona.

Miles realized he needed experienced scouts and asked Sieber and Horn to return. Sieber, crippled with rheumatism, refused, but Horn left his mine and returned to the army.

This time Lawton's men, guided by Horn, kept up a relentless pace, pressing the Indians deeper and deeper into the mountains so they could not stop to raid and steal fresh horses. At last Geronimo asked for a council.

Miles always insisted Geronimo surrendered to Lawton; Horn claims he persuaded the chief to talk to the army captain.

After the council with Miles, Geronimo's warriors stacked their arms and were loaded into boxcars to be imprisoned in Florida. It wouldn't be until 1908 when the remnants of the band were finally allowed to return to their beloved deserts and mountains.

The Apache war was over, there was no more need for scouts. Horn left San Carlos and returned to mining. In April 1887, he "joined some of the boys" in Arizona's Pleasant Valley "war" between cattlemen and rustling gangs. Later he became a Pinkerton detective and captured the notorious train robbers "Peg Leg" Watson and Joe McCoy. In his autobiography Horn described how he trailed the outlaws to their hideout.[4]

Geronimo and his warriors after their surrender following a council with Tom Horn. The famous chief is standing to the right of the horse. Chief Nana is mounted. *Courtesy National Archives*

Natches, left, and Geronimo after their surrender. During his meeting with General Crook, Geronimo complained that the general didn't "have a pleasant face." As he told Crook, "Why don't you smile at me? I am the same man. I have the same feet, legs and hands. Look and smile at me." But the grim-faced Crook told the old chief he didn't have any time for smiling but only wanted his surrender. *Courtesy National Archives*

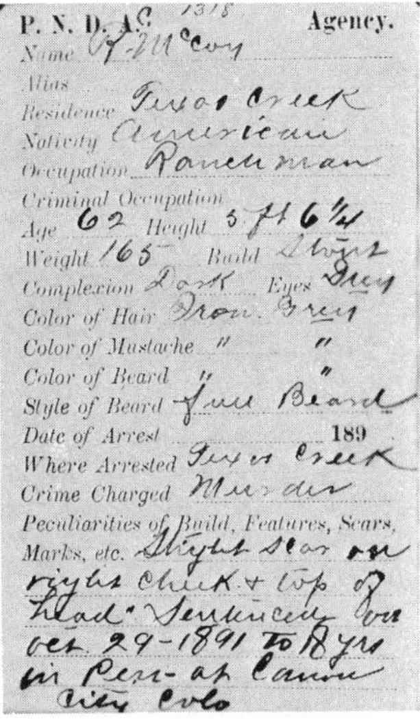

P. N. D. A. 1318 Agency.
Name R. McCoy
Alias
Residence Texas Creek
Nativity American
Occupation Ranchman
Criminal Occupation
Age 62 Height 5 ft 6¼
Weight 165 Build Stout
Complexion Dark Eyes Grey
Color of Hair Iron Grey
Color of Mustache " "
Color of Beard "
Style of Beard Full Beard
Date of Arrest 189
Where Arrested Texas Creek
Crime Charged Murder
Peculiarities of Build, Features, Scars, Marks, etc. Slight scar on right cheek & top of head. Sentenced Oct 29-1891 to 18 yrs in Pen at Canon City Colo

ichard (Dick) McCoy, leader of the McCoy gang of he Colorado train robbers, who was sent to prison or killing a stockman's detective. *Courtesy Pinkertons, Inc.*

P. N. D. A. 1319 Agency.
Name Joe McCoy
Alias " Jones
Residence Texas Creek
Nativity American
Occupation Cowboy & Laborer
Criminal Occupation
Age 25 Height 6 ft 2
Weight 195 Build Stout
Complexion fair Eyes Blue
Color of Hair light
Color of Mustache light
Color of Beard
Style of Beard Moustache
Date of Arrest Dec. 30 1891
Where Arrested Vernal Utah
Crime Charged Murder
Peculiarities of Build, Features, Scars, Marks, etc. index finger off at 1st joint 2nd finger off at 2nd joint Both on right hand. Broke jail at Canon City Jan 26 1890 is left handed

Joe McCoy, who held up the Denver & Rio Grande in Colorado. He was captured by Tom Horn, who trailed him across the foothills of the Rockies during a bitter cold Christmas week in 1890. *Courtesy Pinkertons, Inc.*

P. N. D. A. Chicago Agency.
Name Tom McCoy
Alias
Residence
Nativity
Occupation
Criminal Occupation robbery
Age 16 Height 5 ft 8 in.
Weight 135 Build
Complexion light Eyes gray
Color of Hair light
Color of Mustache
Color of Beard
Style of Beard
Date of Arrest Nov 13" 1891
Where Arrested
Crime charged robbery
Peculiarities of Build, Features, Scars, Marks, etc. smooth face, large teeth, thin lips, large mouth. arrested by Pinkerton Ofts & U.S. Mar. Brown.

Tom McCoy, captured by Tom Horn on the McCoy ranch near Cotopaxi, Colorado. The handsome sixteen-year-old cowboy was the horse holder during the Denver & Rio Grande train robbery. *Courtesy Pinkertons, Inc.*

Horn Captures "Peg Leg" Watson and Joe McCoy

In the winter I again went home and in the following spring I went to work on my mine. Worked along pretty steady on it for a year, and in 1890 we sold it to a party of New Yorkers. We got $8,000 for it.

We were negotiating for this sale, and at the same time the Pinkerton National Detective Agency at Denver, Colorado, was writing to me to get me to come to Denver and go to work for them. I thought it would be a good thing to do, and as soon as all the arrangements for the sale of the mine were made I came to Denver and was initiated into the mysteries of the Pinkerton institution.

My work for them was not the kind that exactly suited my disposition; too tame for me. There were a good many instructions and a good deal of talk given to the operative regarding the things to do and the things that had been done.

James McParland, the superintendent, asked me what I would do if I were put

A rare photograph of Tom Horn, hired gun for the cattle barons, in a train conductor's uniform that he probably used as a Pinkerton operative to uncover dishonest railroad employees. When Horn told James McParland, superintendent of the Denver Pinkerton office, that he disliked being a "spotter," McParland, with the approval of William Pinkerton, teamed him up with "Doc" Shores, the legendary Colorado man hunter. Together they broke up the McCoy gang of train robbers and killers. The man on the right has been identified as Harry Heeber. There is nothing known about him. *Courtesy Wyoming State Archives and Historical Department*

WEEKLY

Nevada State Journal.

SATURDAY, OCTOBER 10, 1891.

THE HORN CASE.

ho Defendant Makes a Statement—The Jury Finds Him Not Guilty.

The trial of Thomas H. Horn, indicted robbery was resumed in the District .rt yesterday before Judge Cheney. A etter written by Horn the night of the robbery and mailed the same night, containing his daily report, was offered in evidence. The prosecution objected to the introduction of the letter on the ground of irrevelancy. It was agreed by counsel that the testimony of Lee MaLotte, as given at the last trial, be considered as evidence in this trial. It was in Deputy Postmaster, and before 8 P. M. bear the post day and letters mailed later tha. bore the post mark of the following day. The letter was admitted as to its length and the fact that a letter had been written, but its contents were ruled out.

Thomas Thomas, the first witness called, said he was in Chase's saloon the night of the robbery, and said Horn came in and was cool and collected. That was about 11:30. Defendant was dressed in a brown coat. It was about 20 minutes before the robbery.

William A. Pinkerton, Superintendent of Pinkerton's National Detective Agency, was then called and testified as follows:

"I have resided in Chicago 40 years, and am one of the principals of the National Detective Agency. It is our business to detect criminals in all parts of the United States. I know the defendant and he has been in my employ several years. He was sent to Salem, Oregon, to locate a man who is supposed to be connected with the Lake Labish disaster, in the interest of the Southern Pacific Company. He was looking for a man by the name of McCabe. Horn was employed by us upon the credentials which he had. He has been a trusted employe of ours and while in our employ has been an honest and efficient employe."

In cross examination it was brought out that he was doing the work at the request of the Southern Pacific Company.

HORN'S STATEMENT.

Thomas H. Horn, the defendant, was then called and made the following statement:

"I was born in Missouri and am 31 years of age. I have worked at various occupations; I have worked on ranches and broke horses; have been a foreman on a cattle ranch; have been in the employ of the Government as an interpreter and scout and finally chief of scouts. Have spent most of my life in Arizona and Old Mexico. I worked for the Chiracaua Cattle Company, Ming & Jones, Bert Dunlop and at the San Carlos reservation, for the Government. As a scout I was under General Crook and afterward under General Miles. I was in the Apache war and was present at the time of and assisted in the capture of Geronimo. I acted as interpreter during the surrender of Geronimo. I had charge of 100 scouts. I went to Oregon the 3d of December last year and remained there until the 4th of April, 1891, when I received instructions to go to Truckee to look up this man McCabe, who was supposed to be connected with the Lake Labish disaster. While in Salem in order to get in with the men I was hunting, I commenced work by the day on a swamp ditch and worked right along with the men in order to gain their confidence. They were all ex-convicts. I slept with them and ate with them.

William A. Pinkerton, who has been attending the Horn trial, departed last night for San Francisco.

While working as an undercover Pinkerton operative on the frontier, Tom Horn was mistakenly arrested as a robber who had held up a Reno, Nevada, gambling hall. The Reno sheriff thought he had excellent evidence when he found a list of train schedules and the names of conductors, engineers, and brakemen along with $300—half the robbery loot—in Horn's pocket. Horn had been riding trains assigned to find crooked railroad employees. When a gambler identified Horn as one of the two robbers, he was put on trial. He was finally acquitted after army officers and William A. Pinkerton testified in his behalf. This is a rare copy of the *Weekly Nevada State Journal* reporting Horn's testimony. *The James D. Horan Civil War and Western Americana Collection*

on a train robbery case. I told him if I had a good man with me I could catch up to them.

Well, on the last night of August, that year, at about midnight, a train was robbed on the Denver & Rio Grande Railway, between Cotopaxi and Texas Creek. I was sent out there, and was told that C. W. Shores would be along in a day or so. He came on time and asked me how I was getting on. I told him I had struck the trail, but there were so many men scouring the country that I, myself, was being held up all the time; that I had been arrested twice in two days and taken in to Salida to be identified!

Eventually all the sheriffs' posses quit and then Mr. W. A. Pinkerton and Mr. McParland told Shores and me to go at 'em. We took up the trail where I had left it several days before and we never left it till we got the robbers.

They had crossed the Sangre de Cristo range, come down by the Villa Grove iron mines, and crossed back to the east side of the Sangre de Cristos at Mosca pass, then on down through the Huerfano Canon, out by Cucharas, thence down east of Trinidad. They had dropped into Clayton, N.M., and got into a shooting scrape there in a gin mill. They then turned east again toward the "Neutral Strip" and close to Beaver City, then across into the "Pan Handle" by a place in Texas called Ochiltree, the county seat of Ochiltree county. They then headed toward the Indian Territory, and crossed into it below Canadian City. They then swung in on the head of the Washita River in the Territory, and kept down this river for a long distance.

We finally saw that we were getting close to them, as we got in the neighborhood of Paul's Valley. At Washita station we located one of them in the house of a man by the name of Wolfe. The robber's name was Burt Curtis. Shores took this one and came on back to Denver, leaving me to get the other one if ever he came back to Wolfe's.

After several days of waiting on my part, he did come back, and as he came riding up to the house I stepped out and told him some one had come! He was "Peg Leg" Watson, and considered by every one in Colorado as a very desperate character. I had no trouble with him.

We had an idea that Joe McCoy, also, was in the robbery, but "Peg" said he was not, and gave me information enough so that I located him. He was wanted very badly by the sheriff of Fremont county, Colorado, for a murder scrape. He and his father had been tried previous to this for murder, had been found guilty and were remanded to jail to wait sentence, but before Joe was sentenced he had escaped. The old man McCoy got a new trial, and at the new trial was sentenced to eighteen years in the Canon City, Colorado, penitentiary.

When I captured my man, got to a telegraph station and wired Mr. McParland that I had the notorious "Peg," the superintendent wired back: "Good! Old man McCoy got eighteen years to-day!" This train had been robbed in order to get money to carry McCoy's case up to the Supreme Court, or rather to pay the attorneys (Macons & Son), who had carried the case up.

Later on I told Mr. McParland that I could locate Joe McCoy and he communicated with Stewart, the sheriff, who came to Denver and made arrangements for me to go with him and try to get McCoy.

We left Denver on Christmas eve and went direct to Rifle, from there to Meeker and on down White River. When we got to where McCoy had been we learned that he had gone to Ashley, in Utah, for the Christmas festivities. We pushed on over there, reaching the town late at night, and could not locate our man. Next morning I learned where he got his meals and as he went in to get his breakfast I followed him in and arrested him. He had a big Colt's pistol, but did not shoot me.

> We took him out by Fort Duchesne, Utah, and caught the D. & R. G. train at Price station.
>
> The judge under whom he had been tried had left the bench when McCoy finally was landed back in jail, and it would have required a new trial before he could be sentenced by another judge; he consented to plead guilty to involuntary manslaughter, and took six years in the Canon City pen. He was pardoned out in three years, I believe.
>
> Peg Leg Watson and Burt Curtis were tried in the United States court for robbing the United States mails on the highway, and were sentenced for life in the Detroit federal prison. In robbing the train they had first made the fireman break into the mail compartment of the compartment car. Then they saw their mistake, and did not even take the amount of a one-cent postage stamp, but went and made the fireman break into the rear compartment, where they found the express matter and took it. But the authorities proved that it was mail robbery and their sentence was life.
>
> While Pinkerton's is one of the greatest institutions of the kind in existence, I never did like the work, so I left them in 1894.
>
> I then came to Wyoming and went to work for the Swan Land and Cattle Company.

What turned Tom Horn from a loyal, zealous army scout, soldier, hard-working miner, cowboy, and tenacious detective into a cold-blooded killer for hire? The answer can be found in the man and his time. For years he had been hired by his country to hunt down and kill, if necessary, the Apache raiders.

The Apache, swift, silent, and ruthless, were the feared minority of the southwestern frontier. Horn grew up with the army's philosophy that good Indians were dead Indians and they had no right to the land sought by the white man.

After the Apache wars were over it was easy for Horn once again to join the major force, this time the powerful cattle barons, and wage war on another weak group of the frontier, the small rancher and sheepherder. He had a great deal of personal vanity and was proud of his skill with a gun and the fear he inspired.

"I'm an exterminatin' son-of-a-bitch," he once said proudly.

Horn became a hired gun for the large cattle owners some time after he had taken part in the Pleasant Valley range war. It was a period following Wyoming's Johnson County "invasion" when the barons, tired of seeing rustlers freed by sympathetic juries, turned to murder to protect their beef.

Horn was only one of a dozen stock detectives ranging the Wyoming territory; the others brought their defendants in to face the law but Tom left his victims on their land, on their doorsteps, or in their beds.

The big solitary man on horseback outlined against the sky or squatting over a lonely campfire became well known and feared. He was usually paid $300 to $600 a man and he satisifed his employers.

Rustlers, in the eyes of the cattle barons, did not always mean cow thieves; some were homesteaders who refused to leave the free range, had staked out water as part of their claim, and were stubbornly willing to fight it out.

Horn stalked them like the Apache he knew so well. One morning there would be a solitary shot and his victim's body would be found by his children, wife, or friends.[5]

Some frontier historians have Horn placing a small stone under the dead man's head as his trademark, but this appears to me to be a legend.

Horn worked for some of the wealthiest and most powerful cattlemen in Wyoming. Ostensibly, his job was breaking broncs and he would roam the countryside prowling the valleys and isolated canyons, searching for signs a rustler had used a running iron to change a brand.

While killing unarmed men and scaring others was lucrative, Horn yearned for the days of the Apache War when his enemies were as skilled as he was in tracking and killing. He also realized he was becoming a drifter on the high plains, moving from spread to spread, from one lonely campfire to another, with only transient friends and saloon admirers who crowded around him to hear his boasting tales and accept his drinks.

When the Spanish-American War broke out a restless Tom Horn was among the first to enlist. The army was almost a second home, he liked the officers, and men like Leonard Wood and Marshal Bucky O'Neill of Yavapai County, Arizona, whom he had served as a deputy, were joining an outfit called the Rough Riders; their leader was Teddy Roosevelt, who had once been a cowboy.

Horn joined a large packtrain being organized in Saint Louis. By the time the train reached Florida on the way to Cuba, he had been promoted to packmaster. The war was brief, Teddy Roosevelt stormed San Juan Hill to land in the White House, and Horn came down with fever without seeing any action.

Weak and still shaking from malaria, he arrived in New York to be discharged from the army as chief packer at $133 a month.[6]

He recuperated in the West, then returned to his old profession—a gun for hire.

In Brown's Hole, once Butch Cassidy's headquarters, Horn killed "Nigger Isam" Dart and Matt Rash, two suspected rustlers. He first tacked a note on Rash's door warning him to leave but Rash shrugged off the threat.

One July morning in 1900, Horn killed Rash as he was eating. In October he shot Dart as the black cowboy-rustler left his cabin in Brown's Hole. Jay Monaghan, Horn's biographer, quoted one coroner's juryman as saying he later found the spot where Horn had knelt and paced the distance to Dart's body; it was a hundred and ninety-six paces.[7]

Tom Horn hung up his rifle that winter but the cattle barons were satisfied. Running irons no longer glowed red in the campfires of the rustlers, and mavericks roamed free without being lassoed by the longest rope . . .

In the spring of 1901, Horn joined his old friend John Coble at the Coble ranch north of Laramie, Wyoming. Coble, son of a wealthy Pennsylvania family, had gone west rather than accept an appointment at the United States Naval Academy. He had established the Fontier Land & Cattle Company with Sir Horace Plunkett, a young Irish nobleman, only to be wiped out in the bitter winter of 1886-1887. Sir Horace returned to Ireland and a brilliant political career and Coble moved to Iron Mountain, Wyoming, where he established a horse ranch.

Coble first met Horn as a stock detective and they became friends. Coble, a romantic, undoubtedly viewed the killer as a living link to the fading frontier.

Horn played the role, entertaining Coble and his guests at the Cheyenne Club with tales of the days when he rode with the herds going up the Chisholm Trail and stalked the Apache with Al Sieber.

To repay Coble's kindness, Horn began to search out the rustlers who were preying on the Iron Mountain herds. In this way he first met the Millers, a homesteading family, and the strange little schoolteacher who boarded with them. Glendolene Myrtle Kimmell, a round-faced girl who some thought looked Oriental, had left a small town in Missouri not only to teach at the Iron Mountain School but also to satisfy a deep desire to see the Wild West with its gallant frontiersmen about whom she had read so much. The taciturn, stodgy Miller boys who only rode farm plugs had been a disappointment but Tom Horn fulfilled her dreams. As she later wrote, he was the true embodiment of the romantic man of the West, tall, lean, hawk-eyed with an air of danger about him.[8]

She was good for Horn's ego and he basked in her admiration. While casually paying her attention, Horn also learned of the feud between the Millers and their neighbor, Kels P. Nickell. Miller and Nickell had been in and out of court and once Nickell had tried to slash Coble with a knife.

When Nickell brought in sheep, the cattle country rose against him, but the fiercely stubborn Kentuckian defied his neighbors and stood guard over his flock with a shotgun.

On the morning of July 18, fourteen-year-old Willie Nickell went out to sad-

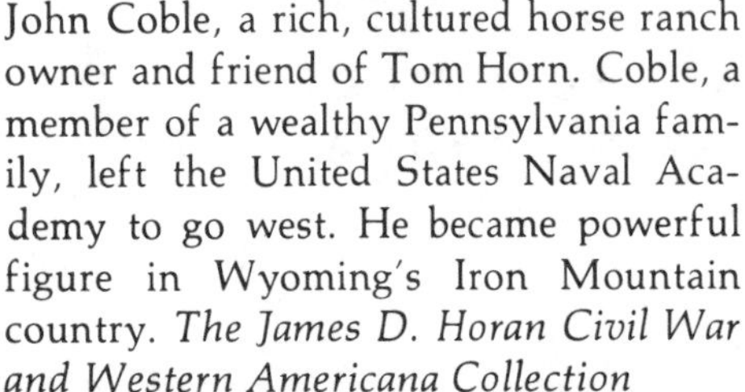

John Coble, a rich, cultured horse ranch owner and friend of Tom Horn. Coble, a member of a wealthy Pennsylvania family, left the United States Naval Academy to go west. He became powerful figure in Wyoming's Iron Mountain country. *The James D. Horan Civil War and Western Americana Collection*

Glendolene Kimmell, the schoolteacher who fell in love with Tom Horn. After his death she wrote: "Riding hard, drinking hard, fighting hard—so passed his days, until he was crushed between the grindstones of two civilizations." *The James D. Horan Civil War and Western Americana Collection*

dle up and stay overnight with his father at the sheep camp. His mother waved good-bye and went back into the house. Shortly after two shots rang out; apparently Mrs. Nickell did not hear them and remained in the house.

In the morning the two smaller Nickell boys found the body of their brother at the corral gate. Apparently he had been knocked from his saddle with one shot, then as he weakly tried to run toward the house he was shot a second time. The killer in stocking feet examined the body, then walked back to his hideout behind some rocks and rode away.

Some settlers who knew of Horn's reputation named him as the killer but he produced an alibi proving he was on a train between Laramie and Cheyenne on the day Willie was killed. Victor Miller was also a suspect but Miss Kimmell, the schoolteacher, testified at a coroner's jury he was at home when the shooting took place. The state matched the county's reward offer of $500 and reward posters appeared on fence posts and telegraph poles.

A few days later Willie's father was shot from ambush, the bullets shattering his arm; as he lay in the hospital he heard that masked men had clubbed some of his sheep to death. The cattle barons won their long fight against the erratic Nickell; he sadly sold his spread and moved to Cheyenne where he opened a steam laundry.

The sensational case gradually died away but Joe LeFors, the United States marshal in Cheyenne, doggedly continued to investigate the boy's murder. After he had interviewed the Millers, Miss Kimmell wrote a long letter to Horn —then on a spree in Denver—warning LeFors was asking questions about him.

Horn ignored the letter and continued to make his nightly tour of the saloons.

Horn who had not been in Denver for years now discovered the city was no longer a large cow camp where the cowboy with money was king. The night was lighted with electric signs, the wooden sidewalks were gone along with the old-fashioned stores and their false fronts. To the adoring Miss Kimmell, Tom Horn, in his high-heeled boots and sombrero, was a living legend; to Denver he was a living anachronism.

He was a powerful man, almost seven feet tall, straight as an arrow shaft, with broad shoulders and a slim waist. As many remembered, when Horn was sober he was a delightful companion who held the attention of a crowd with an endless storehouse of anecdotes and stories about the frontier. But drunk he was violent and unpredictable.

For many Horn was a link to the frontier that was fast becoming a romantic memory; when he entered a saloon he was quickly joined by admirers who were always ready to buy him a drink.

In one saloon he drunkenly tried to abuse a smaller man who was standing near him at the bar. Horn apparently never noticed the man's battered nose and the thick scar tissue over the eyes; he was "Young" Corbett, a noted prizefighter of his day. To the cheers of his entourage, Corbett skillfully and ruthlessly beat Horn into unconsciousness and left him with a fractured jaw.

While Horn's jaw mended LeFors was in Laramie, gathering information that on the day of the Nickell murder Horn had arrived in Laramie "on a steamy shaken horse" that obviously had been ridden hard and that Horn had left a bloodstained sweater at a cobbler's shop.

The marshal set a trap for Horn. On the pretext that a rancher-friend in Montana wanted a good stockman's detective, he got Tom in a boasting mood. Between chews of tobacco, the cattleman's hired killer told how he had been paid "twenty-one hundred dollars for killing three men and shooting five times at another." He also calmly told LeFors how he shot the Nickell boy at three hundred yards and called it "the dirtiest trick I have ever done . . . killing is my specialty . . . I look on it as a business . . ."

Behind the door of LeFors's office were Deputy Sheriff Leslie Snow and Charles Ohnhaus, the district court stenographer who took down in shorthand everything Horn told LeFors.

After Horn left, LeFors swore out a warrant for murder and Horn was arrested in the lobby of the Inter-Ocean Hotel.

Horn's trial in the fall of 1902 was one of the most sensational of its time. The West knew the big killer was not as important as the unspoken issue: wealthy, influential cattle barons against small, most times penniless homesteaders. It was the old century colliding with the new.

The cattle barons gave Horn the best counsel money could hire: John W. Lacey, general counsel for the Union Pacific and onetime Wyoming chief justice. The trial was held on the second floor of Cheyenne's old courthouse; every day the courtroom was jammed. Cattlemen and homesteaders came on horseback, in fringed carriages, and wagons loaded down with children, some who would boast years later to their grandchildren how they had seen Tom Horn, the range killer, during the days he had fought for his life in the small dusty courtroom. There were big city reporters from the East strutting about in derbies and celluloid collars; cowboys in tight Sunday suits and ties with tiny, greasy knots; self-conscious "witnesses" in their best suits; and farmers with mud-splattered boots and collarless shirts.

The highlight of the trial was the testimony of Joe LeFors and Tom Horn. The marshal detailed how he had set the trap for Horn, then read his "confession"; Horn denied he killed the boy and insisted LeFors had doctored the shorthand notes in his quest for the $1,000 reward.[9]

On the morning of October 23, 1902, the jury returned a verdict of guilty and Horn was sentenced to be hanged. He was returned to his cell while appeals took place. The Territory waited: Would Tom Horn betray his wealthy accomplices to save his life?

A plot to blow up the jail by Horn's cowboy friends was uncovered in December. In the saloons the story was repeated that Butch Cassidy was gathering his Wild Bunch riders to help in Tom Horn's escape. At the time Cassidy was in South America and most of his riders were dead or in jail. Five sticks of dynamite were found in the snow outside the wall of the jail and guards found a length of lead pipe hidden in the range killer's pants leg.

The winter passed, then in August as the city prepared for its annual Frontier Days, Horn made a desperate attempt to escape. His partner was Jim McCloud (also spelled Macleod), waiting trial for robbery.

The *Denver Post* gave a graphic account of Tom Horn's last break for freedom.[10]

Joe LeFors, Laramie County deputy sheriff, who trapped Tom Horn into confessing he had killed Willie Nickell, a fourteen-year-old sheepherder's son. *Courtesy History Department, University of Wyoming*

Tom Horn, in the sheriff's office of the Cheyenne County jail, with one of the many braided hackamores he had made while waiting to go on trial for the murder of fourteen-year-old Willie Nickell. *Courtesy Denver Post*

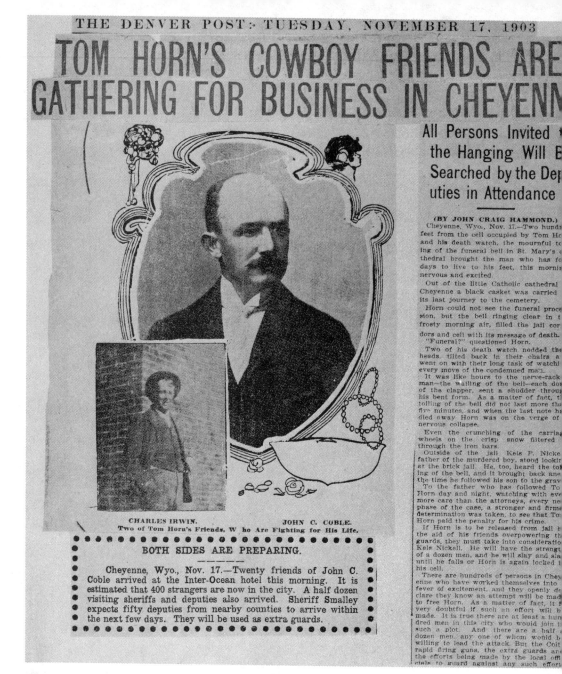

THE DENVER POST: TUESDAY, NOVEMBER 17, 1903

TOM HORN'S COWBOY FRIENDS ARE GATHERING FOR BUSINESS IN CHEYENN

All Persons Invited the Hanging Will B Searched by the Dep uties in Attendance

(BY JOHN CRAIG HAMMOND.)
Cheyenne, Wyo., Nov. 17.—Two hundr
feet from the cell occupied by Tom Ho
and his death watch, the mournful to
ing of the funeral bell in St. Mary's c
thedral brought the man who has fo
days to live to his feet, this mornin
nervous and excited.
Out of the little Catholic cathedral
Cheyenne a black casket was carried
its last journey to the cemetery.
Horn could not see the funeral proce
sion, but the bell ringing clear in t
frosty morning air, filled the jail cor
dors and cell with its message of death.
"Funeral?" questioned Horn.
Two of his death watch nodded the
heads, tilted back in their chairs a
went on with their long task of watchi
every move of the condemned man.
It was like hours to the nerve-rack
man—the wailing of the bell—each do
of the clapper, sent a shudder throu
his bent form. As a matter of fact, t
tolling of the bell did not last more th
five minutes, and when the last note h
died away Horn was on the verge of
nervous collapse.
Even the crunching of the carria
wheels on the crisp snow filtered
through the iron bars.
Outside of the jail Kels P. Nicke
father of the murdered boy, stood lookin
at the brick jail. He, too, heard the to
ing of the bell, and it brought back ane
the time he followed his son to the grav
To the father who has followed To
Horn day and night, watching with eve
more care than the attorneys, every ne
phase of the case, a stronger and firme
determination was taken, to see that To
Horn paid the penalty for his crime.
If Horn is to be released from jail b
the aid of his friends overpowering th
guards, they must take into consideratio
Kels Nickell. He will have the strengt
of a dozen men, and he will slay and sla
until he falls or Horn is again locked i
his cell.
There are hundreds of persons in Chey
enne who have worked themselves into
fever of excitement, and they openly de
clare they know an attempt will be mad
to free Horn. As a matter of fact, it i
very doubtful if such an effort will b
made. It is true there are at least a hun
dred men in this city who would join i
such a plot. And there are a half
dozen men, any one of whom would b
willing to lead the attack. But the Colt
rapid firing guns, the extra guards an
the efforts being made by the local offi
cials to guard against any such effort

CHARLES IRWIN. JOHN C. COBLE.
Two of Tom Horn's Friends, Who Are Fighting for His Life.

BOTH SIDES ARE PREPARING.

Cheyenne, Wyo., Nov. 17.—Twenty friends of John C. Coble arrived at the Inter-Ocean hotel this morning. It is estimated that 400 strangers are now in the city. A half dozen visiting sheriffs and deputies also arrived. Sheriff Smalley expects fifty deputies from nearby counties to arrive within the next few days. They will be used as extra guards.

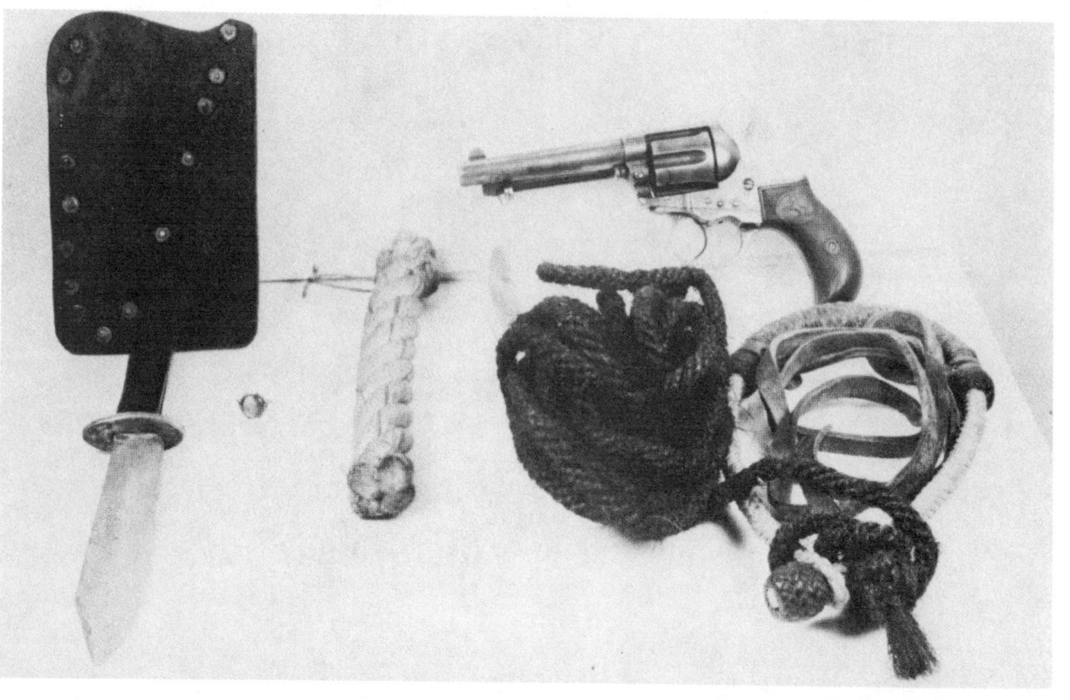

Weapons used by Tom Horn during his escape attempt. *University of Wyoming, Western History Department*

tand forth as a stone wall.

Talk with those who are not sufferin[g] [f]rom pent up excitement and they wil[l] [t]ell you that a stronger effort will b[e] [m]ade to let Horn take his own life. H[e] [h]as told his friends that he wants to d[o] [t]his if all other things fail. And they [h]ave failed, it would appear.

Under Sheriff Proctor declares there is [n]ot the slightest chance to give Horn a weapon or poison whereby he might kill [h]imself.

Death Watch a Secret.

Sheriff Smalley today declared that he would keep the names of the guards—the [d]eath watch—a secret until the day of the [e]xecution. The men have been picked with the greatest care. Their bravery is unquestioned and their honesty known. Still to keep all temptation out of their way, their names will be kept from the public.

Under Sheriff Proctor says he has no fear that the guards could be bribed, but they might meet with foul play or be threatened with death by some of Horn's friends if they did not join in the scheme to have him cheat the gallows.

The hour of the execution has been agreed upon, but the officials give it out that the drop will be sprung between the hours of 9 in the morning and 8 in the afternoon. No one is to know the exact time. It is expected that not more than thirty-five persons will be present. Six of these will be visiting sheriffs. Some eight newspaper men, the doctors, guards and six friends of Horn.

As an example of the great care being taken by the sheriff and his deputies is shown in the fact that each person will be searched before being permitted to enter the jail corridor.

Revolvers and knives will be taken from every person who bears an invitation. The guards on the scaffold, however, will still wear their huge revolvers.

Black Cap Arrives and All Arrangements for the Horn Finale Are Now Nearly Complete

Horn has decided upon the six friends he will ask to be present. He is guarding their names with great care and will not turn them over to the sheriff until the Thursday evening.

Today a little box was delivered at the sheriff's office. When it was opened it was found to contain the black cap, the last thing that will be added on the gallows before the trap goes bounding downward.

A Grewsome Sight.

It was a grewsome sight—this bit of black goods, cheap in material. Nearly a yard of common black dress goods was used in making the cap, which is more like a paper bag.

This was hardly stowed away in the sheriff's desk when a small boy came walking in with another box. It contained four long straps, two for the arms and two for the legs. The straps were made to order and under the direction of Under Sheriff Proctor. The buckles were so adjusted that they would slip into place without the slightest tugging. The straps were well oiled and made as flexible as possible. Mr. Proctor is trying to escape from having the least hitch in the scene upon the gallows.

COUNTY JAIL AT CHEYENNE.
Cross Shows Part of Building in Which Horn Is Confined.

The rope has been ordered and will arrive tomorrow. It has not been decided who will make the noose, but a number of persons are in the city who can make the peculiar knot that is to slip behind Horn's ear.

Maybe these are grewsome details, but they are not a marker for the stories being told on the street corners at all hours of the day and night. Not the slightest scrap of information is escaping the persons interested in the case.

Laramie county has not had a hanging for a number of years, and it was discovered that the some of the timbers used in the last scaffold were missing. An order was given for the lumber that will go to make the platform, while extra braces had to be ordered.

When Horn was arrested he was a powerful man—weighing 206 pounds. Today he weighs between 175 and 180 pounds. While this still makes him a large man, he is described as being a "skeleton to his former self."

Owing to his weight the gallows will be given extra tests. The bags of sand will be brought into play, some weighing more than 200 pounds. The rope will be tied around the bags and the trap sprung time and again.

To those who have witnessed a hanging one of the harrowing details has been the bang of the trapdoor as it flies downward and backward. Horn will have to listen to the thud of the sand bags and the crash of the trap a score of times before he steps on the gallows.

As Horn will be led from his cell on the march to his death, he will be met by his six friends. He will be given a chance to shake hands with them, and to say good-by.

One man at a time will pass by Horn and to them he will give his farewell messages. However, it is said that Horn will make a speech on the gallows. He will, it is claimed, call down vengeauce upon a number of persons. All hopes of his making a confession have been given up by a majority of persons. He has been asked to die game, and he has sent forth the word that "I will swing without peaching."

Horn has not asked for a minister or priest. In fact, he is a man without a religion. He refuses to talk about it, but as the time draws nearer it is expected by a few persons that he will ask to have a spiritual call on him.

Still he has never been a member of a church or has he taken any interest, even in his childhood days, in religion in any form. He is a man of the day, free from such thoughts.

A Score of Attempts.

While the public knows of the daring attempt Horn made to escape from jail. In fact, it has never been made public that he has made the attempt a score of times. There has not been a week gone by since Horn was arrested that something has not been found in his cell which he was trying to use to force his way out of jail.

Horn has a wonderful brain in many ways. He is constantly planning, thinking, acting. While his chances of an escape have been reduced a thousand fold, he is still at his old tricks.

Under Sheriff Proctor has an interesting collection of wires, bones, pieces of glass, caseknives, pieces of wood and wire that Horn has used in weeks past.

While it is not an elegant expression, the so-called "Shirt-Tail wireless telegraph system" shows that Horn is a man of brains. One day a few weeks ago Mr. Proctor found a ball of red string in Horn's cell. Incidentally he found a number of messages.

Horn was on the second tier of cells. He wanted to send a message to a prisoner who was on the first floor and on the other side of the jail. He tore a piece of his blanket about the size of a man's hand, rolled it into a ball, after placing his message inside, he stood at his cell door, gave the ball a snap with his middle finger and it fell to the first floor.

A prisoner managed to rake it in front of his door, and after placing it in just the right position gave it a snap with his finger and it went into the next cell. This was kept up until the little ball carrying the message was passed around the cell to the prisoner who was to be given his liberty the next day. The string was untied and Horn pulled it back for further use. When the string was found and taken away from him Horn did not give up. He wanted to send a second message, so he took his shirt and tore off the tails with great care. Then he made strips of the pieces until he had a long cord. He repeated the operation as above, using some three shirts in the operation. Horn has been on the constant lookout for

The *Denver Post*'s story of how Horn's cowboy friends were planning to free him. Wyoming's Governor Chatterton called in troops to prevent any attempt by Horn's friends to storm the jail. *The James D. Horan Civil War and Western Americana Collection*

TOM HORN MAKES ESCAPE FROM JAIL

Wyoming Murderer and a Companion Break Out, but Are Soon Recaptured

CHEYENNE, Aug. 9.—Tom Horn the condemned murderer of little Willie Nickell, and Jim McCloud, in custody for post-office robbery, escaped from the county jail at 8:40 o'clock this morning after overpowering Deputy Sheriff Proctor, but were recaptured after a brief but exciting chase. The ringing of firebells brought hundreds of armed citizens to the scene and it looked for a time as though a lynching would take place, but the escapes were hurriedly brought back to the jail and placed in their cells before the crowds could form themselves into a mob. The men got but two blocks away before they were retaken.

The plot which led to their escape was well planned. Horn and McCloud were the only prisoners confined on the upper floor of the jail. They occupied steel cells, so arranged that communication was comparatively easy. This morning McCloud complained to Deputy Proctor of being ill and requested some medicine and a glass of water. Upon returning with the articles asked for, he discovered that the men had left their cells, which were not locked, and had walked to the end of the corridor through which they were allowed to exercise. When Proctor opened the door to the corridor he was pounced upon by the two men and securely bound with a cord, which they had secured in some manner. Horn and McCloud demanded that he give them his keyes and although Proctor had them on his person he replied that they were locked up in the safe.

Proctor was then conducted to the safe and directed to open it. The order was obeyed, but on opening the safe Proctor snatched from inside a gun and turned on the men. They were too quick for him, however, and soon bore him down. In the brief struggle Proctor fired his revolver four times, slightly wounding McCloud. The shooting attracted the attention of Deputy Snow, who hastened to the scene, but was met at the doorway by McCloud, who had secured possession of a shogun in some manner. Snow retreated and Horn and McCloud escaped through a rear door of the jail, after binding the arms of Deputy Proctor.

McCloud secured the only horse in the sheriff's stable and mounted the animal and started toward the west. Horn ran in the opposite direction. About this time Sheriff Smalley arrived on the scene and started in pursuit of McCloud, firing his revolver without effect. After a short chase McCloud surrendered. When Horn left the jail yard the fact that he wore no hat and carried a revolver attracted the attention of O. M. Eldrich, who operates an amusement stand across the street. Eldrich gave chase, firing several shots at Horn, one of which grazed his neck. Horn, slightly wounded, turned and aimed his revolver at Eldrich, but the gun being of an automatic lock pattern, one with which Horn was unfamiliar, he was unable to discharge it, and realizing his helplessness Horn surrendered just as Eldrich was about to shoot again. When Eldrich approached Horn the latter showed fight, but was beaten into submission by his plucky pursuer.

By this time a number of officers and citizens had gathered at the spot, and Horn, bleeding from his wounds, was dragged back to the jail. Quiet prevails now and there is no probability of an attempt being made to lynch the jailbreakers.

After three futile attempts, Tom Horn finally escaped from jail. He managed to reach the street but was unable to work a new type of revolver he had taken from the sheriff and was captured by an armed merchant. Horn was returned to his cell as the jail's alarm bells were ringing. *The James D. Horan Civil War and Western Americana Collection*

Tom Horn Makes Escape from Jail

Tom Horn, the condemned murderer of little Willie Nickell, and Jim McCloud, in custody for postoffice robbery, escaped from the county jail at 8:40 A.M. this morning after overpowering Deputy Sheriff [Richard] Proctor, but was recaptured after a brief but exciting chase.

The ringing of firebells brought hundreds of armed citizens to the scene and it looked as though a lynching would take place but the escapees were hurriedly brought back to their cells before the crowds could form into a mob. The men got but two blocks away before they were recaptured.

The plot which led to their escape was well planned. Horn and McCloud were the only prisoners confined on the upper floor of the jail. They occupied steel cells so communication was comparatively easy.

This morning McCloud complained of being ill and requested Deputy Proctor to bring him some medicine and a glass of water. Upon returning he discovered the men had left their cells which were not locked and had walked to the end of the corridor where they were allowed to exercise.

When Proctor opened the door to the corridor he was pounced on by the two men and securely bound with cord which they had secured in some way. Horn and McCloud demanded that he give them the keys but although they were on his person Proctor told them they were locked up in the safe.

Proctor was then conducted to the safe and directed to open it. The order was obeyed but upon opening the safe Proctor snatched from inside a gun and turned on the two men. They were too quick for him however and bore him down.

In the brief struggle Proctor fired his gun four times slightly wounding McCloud. The shooting attracted the attention of Deputy [Leslie] Snow who hastened to the scene but was met at the doorway by McCloud who had secured possession of a shotgun in some manner.

Snow retreated and McCloud and Horn escaped through the rear door of the jail after binding the arms of Deputy Proctor.

McCloud secured the only horse in the sheriff's corral and started toward the west. Horn ran in the opposite direction. About this time Sheriff [James] Smalley arrived on the scene and started in pursuit of McCloud firing his revolver without effect. After a short chase McCloud surrendered. When Horn left the jail yard the fact that he wore no hat and carried a revolver attracted the attention of O. M. Eldrich who operates the amusement stand across the street. Eldrich gave chase, firing several shots at Horn, one grazing his neck.

Horn, slightly wounded, turned and aimed his revolver at Eldrich but the gun being an automatic lock pattern, one with which Horn was unfamiliar, he was unable to discharge it and realizing his helplessness Horn surrendered just as Eldrich was about to shoot him again.

When Eldrich approached Horn the latter showed fight but was beaten into submission by his plucky pursuer.

By this time a number of officers and citizens had gathered at this spot and Horn, bleeding from his wounds, was dragged back to jail. Quiet now prevails and there is no probability of an attempt being made to lynch the jail breakers.

Tom Horn was back in his cell but rumors had gangs of his cowboy friends gathering outside the city preparing to storm the Cheyenne County jail to free him. The city was tense, residents carried shotguns and six-shooters, and Kels Nickell, father of the boy Horn was convicted of killing, paced up and down

Laramie County Sheriff Edward Smalley whom Tom Horn tried to kill during his escape attempt. *The James D. Horan Civil War and Western Americana Collection*

in front of the jail, telling anyone who would listen, as he patted the stock of his shotgun:

"Let Horn make another break for it and I'll blow his head off . . . he's going to hang if I have to stay here for the rest of my life . . ."

Governor Fenimore Chatterton, who had received death threats, finally called out the militia, and armed soldiers patroled the streets while Gatling guns guarded the entrance to the jail. Deputies were housed in nearby St. Mary's Cathedral, in the barns at the rear of the jailhouse, and twenty-five or more, all armed with rifles, were stationed at every window of the courthouse.

Sheriff Smalley warned the public to keep away from the scene of the execution. He announced that witnesses to Horn's hanging would receive a strip of ribbon for their lapel but the color would remain secret.

As the *Denver Post* reported on November 18, "the town is filling up with strangers, every train is bringing in new arrivals."

In a press conference at the statehouse Governor Chatterton told reporters:

"I am not looking for trouble but it is best to be on the safe side. It will be impossible to rescue Horn and his friends should understand this. Any attempt will mean the slaughter of many persons."

An excellent account of those tense days was written by John Craig Hammond of the *Denver Post* who also discovered fascinating details of Horn's many escape attempts that had not been made public by the sheriff.[11]

Tom Horn's Friends Are Gathering for Business in Cheyenne

Two hundred feet from the cell occupied by Tom Horn and his death watch, the mournful tolling of the funeral bell in St. Mary's Cathedral brought the man who has four days to live to his feet this morning, nervous and excited.

Out of the little Catholic cathedral of Cheyenne, a black casket was carried on its last journey to the cemetery.

Horn could not see the funeral procession but the bell ringing clear in the frosty morning air filled the jail corridor and cells with its message of death.

"Funeral?" questioned Horn.

Two of his death watch nodded and then tilted their chairs and went on with the long task of watching every movement of the condemned man.

It was like hours to the nerve-wracked man; the wailing of the bell, each dong of the clapper sent a shudder through his bent form. As a matter of fact the tolling of the bell did not last five minutes but when it died away Horn was on the verge of nervous collapse.

Even the crunching of the carriage wheels on the crisp snow filtered in through the bars.

Outside the jail Kels P. Nickell, father of the murdered boy, stood looking at the brick jail. He too had heard the tolling of the bell and it brought back anew how he had followed his son to the grave.

To the father who has followed Tom Horn day and night, watching with more care than the attorneys every new phase of the case, a stronger and firmer determination was taken to see Tom Horn paid the penalty for his crime.

If Horn is released from jail through the overpowering of the guards by his friends, he will have to take in consideration Kels Nickell. He will have the strength of a dozen men and he will slay and slay until he falls or Tom Horn is again locked in his cell.

There are hundreds of persons in Cheyenne who have worked themselves into a fever of excitement and they openly declare they know an attempt will be made to free Horn. As a matter of fact it is doubtful if such an attempt will be made. It is true there are at least a hundred men in the city who would lead the attack. But the Colt-rapid firing guns, the extra guards and the efforts being made by the local officers against any such effort, stand as a stone wall.

Talk with those who are not suffering from such pent up excitement and they will tell you that a stronger effort will be made to let Horn take his own life. He has told friends he wants to do this if all others fail. And they have failed, it would appear.

Under Sheriff Proctor declared there is not the slightest chance to give Horn a weapon or poison to kill himself.

Sheriff Smalley today declared he will keep the names of the death watch a secret until the day of execution. The men have been picked with the greatest care. Their bravery cannot be questioned and their honesty known. Still, to keep all temptation out of their way, their names will be kept from the public.

Under Sheriff Proctor said that he has no fear that the guards could be bribed but they might meet with foul play or be threatened by friends of Horn if they did not join the scheme to let him cheat the gallows.

The hour of execution has been agreed upon but officials have let it out that the drop will be sprung between the hours of 9 in the morning and 3 in the afternoon. No one is to know the exact time. No more than thirty-five will be present. Six of these will be visiting sheriffs, some eight newspapermen, the doctors, guards and six friends of Horn.

An example of the great care being taken by the sheriff is shown in the fact that each person will be searched before being allowed to enter the jail corridor.

Revolvers and knives will be taken from every person who bears an invitation. The guards on the platform, however, will wear their huge revolvers.

Horn has decided upon the six friends he will ask to have present. He is guarding their names with care and will not turn them over to the sheriff until Thursday evening.

Today a little black box was delivered to the sheriff's office. When it was opened it was found to contain the little black cap, the last thing that will be added on the gallows before the trap goes bounding downward.

It was a gruesome sight, this bit of black goods, cheap in material. Nearly a yard of common black dress goods was used in making the cap which is more like a black paper bag.

This was barely stowed away in the sheriff's desk when a small boy came in with another box. It contained four long straps, two for the arms and two for the legs. The straps were made to order and under the direction of Deputy Sheriff Proctor. The buckles are so adjusted they will slip into place without tugging. The straps were well oiled and made as flexible as possible.

Mr. Proctor is trying to escape from having the least hitch in the scene upon the gallows.

The rope has been ordered and will arrive tomorrow. It has not been decided who will make the noose but a number of persons are in the city who can make the noose that will rest behind Horn's left ear.

Maybe these are gruesome details but they are not a marker for the stories being told on the street corners at all hours of the day and night. Not the slightest scrap of information is escaping those who are interested in the case. Laramie County has not had a hanging for a number of years and it was discovered that some of the timber used in the scaffold was missing. The order was given for the lumber to make the platform while extra braces also had to be ordered.

When Horn was arrested he was a powerful man, weighing 206 pounds. Today he weighs between 175 and 180 pounds. While this still makes him a large man he is described as being "a skeleton of his former self."

Owing to his weight the gallows will be given extra tests. The bags of sand will be brought into play, some of them weighing 200 pounds. The ropes will be tied around the bags and the trap will be sprung again and again.

To those who have witnessed a hanging, one of the harrowing details is the banging of the trap door as it flies downward and backward. Horn will have to listen to the thud of the sandbags and the crash of the trap many times before he steps on the gallows.

As Horn is led from his cell on the march to his death he will be met by his six friends. He will be given a chance to shake hands with them and to say goodbye.

One man at a time will pass by Horn and he will be able to give him his farewell message. However, it is said, that Horn will make a speech on the gallows. He will, it is claimed, call on vengeance upon a number of persons. All hopes of his having made a confession have been given up by a number of persons. He has been asked to die game and he has sent out word that "I will swing without peaching."

Horn has not asked for a minister or priest. In fact he is a man without a religion. He refuses to talk about it but it is expected by persons near him that he will call for a spiritual as the time draws nearer. Still he has never been a member of a church or has he had any interest in religion even in his childhood days. He is a man of the day, free from such thoughts.

While the public knows of the daring attempt Horn made to escape from jail, it has never been made public that he attempted to escape a score of times. There has not a week gone by since Horn was arrested that something wasn't found in his cell which he was trying to use to force his way out of the prison.

Horn has a wonderful brain in many ways. He is constantly planning, thinking, acting. While the chances of his escape have been reduced a thousand fold, he is still up to his old tricks.

Under Sheriff Proctor has an interesting collection of wires, bones, pieces of glass, case knives, pieces of wood and wire which Horn has used in the past weeks.

While it is not an elegant expression, the so-called "Shirt-tail Wireless Telegraph System" shows that Horn is a man of brains. Only a few weeks ago Mr. Proctor found a ball of red string in Horn's cell. Incidentally he found a number of messages.

Horn was on the second tier of cells. He wanted to send a message to a prisoner who was on the first floor and on the other side of the jail. He tore a piece of his blanket about the size of a man's hand, rolled it into a ball after he had placed his message inside. He stood at his cell door, gave the ball a snap of his fingers and it fell to the first floor.

A prisoner managed to rake it in front of his cell, and after placing it in just the right position, he gave it a snap with his finger and it went to the next cell. This was kept up until the ball with the message reached the cell of a prisoner who was to be given liberty the next day. The string was then untied and Horn pulled it back for further use.

When the string was found and taken away from him, Horn did not give up. He wanted to send a second message so he took his shirt and carefully tore off the tails. Then he made strips of these until he had a long cord. He repeated the operation as above using three shirts in the operation. Horn has been on the constant lookout for pieces of wire. Through the aid of prisoners who have the liberty of the corridor, he secured a half dozen different supplies.

A long stove pipe was suspended from the ceiling by some four feet of wire. Different men would climb on the cells, cut off a piece of wire and under the direction of Horn, tie up the pipe again. This has been kept up so often that the pipe is now only a few inches from the ceiling.

When this area of securing wire was stopped, Horn turned to the jail brooms. He was wise enough not to take off the outside wire but would part the broom cane and unwrap the wire. Mr. Proctor found half a dozen such pieces but it took him weeks to discover how Horn was getting the wire.

One day Horn was served with a soup bone. He managed to keep a piece of the bone about five inches long. With the utmost care he filed away at the bone for days and days until he had made a key to throw his cell bolt. He was busy at work when discovered and the bone key was taken away from him.

Just a thirty-second part of an inch and he would have fashioned a bone key to throw the bolt. He secured a feather duster one day and managed to cut off a piece of the wood between the feathers.

He used matches to burn away the wood until he had fashioned a key. The burnt end of his matches he used to write his messages. Horn also managed to collect a number of pieces of glass which he used to make a number of cell keys. He was skilled in bending wire into a score of shapes and was high on the way in making a key out of five pieces of wire when he was discovered.

These are but a few of the many schemes resorted by the clever prisoner. He managed to send out a number of messages but was detected and for some time past this avenue of sending messages to his friends has been cut off.

In the midst of the snowstorm which swept in from the north, last night a number of strange men came to Cheyenne. Who they are is not known at this time.

"I tell you thousands of people will come to Cheyenne for the hanging," said a local lawyer in the Inter-Ocean Hotel. "We will have a day second only to Frontier Day if the weather is anyway near fine."

The weather is to play a strong part in any attempt that may be made to "rush" the jail. If the weather is good then hundreds of persons will come and Horn's friends will mingle among the crowds. An effort is being made by the local police at this time to account for every stranger that comes to the city. The police declare they can pick out the average Westerner from the average traveler and it is the former who will be watched and in many instances will be asked to give an account of themselves. This has been done in a number of incidents during the past few days. A few persons have been warned to get out of town.

Tom Horn refused this morning to see the local preacher who came to talk to him about the hereafter. A man and a woman then called on him. They pleaded for half an hour and in the end Horn gave in.

Tonight at seven o'clock the three will be admitted to the jail and they will pray with Horn.

"It won't do any harm and not do much good for you to come," he said, "if it will make your happiness greater then come ahead, that is if Dick Proctor will let you."

Under Sheriff Proctor said he would be glad to have Horn consult with someone on the question of religion.

Ira D. Williams, his wife, Mrs. Mary Williams, and Sister Butler, all of Bay City, Michigan, have traveled a long way to pray with him.

"We hope to help this poor man," said Mr. Williams who has been spending the last few years saving souls.

"He is the very kind that can be saved," his wife added. "We will pray and talk to him for just one half hour tonight and again tomorrow if the sheriff will let us and Horn will listen. My husband, I pray, will be at his side when he goes to the other world."

Mr. and Mrs. Williams and Sister Butler said they will open a mission in Cheyenne if they can get Horn to his death a believer.

Horn's attorneys fought to the last hour to save him. The grief-stricken Miss Kimmell, who had gone back to Missouri, gave a last-minute affidavit in which she claimed she had overheard "on three different occasions" two men talk of how they had shot the boy.

The attorneys appeared before Governor Chatterton but after a hearing he ruled that the schoolteacher "was not telling the truth but seeking to shield Horn" and refused to postpone the execution.

He also revealed there was "a plan by which the train which took Horn to the penitentiary was to be wrecked and the prisoner freed. But that was contingent upon his securing a commutation of the sentence to life imprisonment. But I have given the matter the last consideration and the execution will take place on Friday without fail . . ."

On the morning of November 20, 1903, Horn, still "game," went to his death, scorning requests that he turn informer and name the wealthy cattle barons who paid him to murder the defenseless ranchers and rustlers.

The anonymous reporter for the *Chicago Record-Herald* wrote a terse but vivid account of the execution.[12]

FENIMORE CHATTERTON,
GOVERNOR.

THE STATE OF WYOMING.
EXECUTIVE DEPARTMENT,
CHEYENNE.

Miss Kimmell

Will you please let me take those letters again I read them so hurriedly yesterday I would like to see them again at my leisure.

The bearer is my deputy Secretary of State.

Yours truly,
F Chatterton.

To save Tom Horn, Glendolene Kimmell told Wyoming's Governor Chatterton she had "evidence which identified two other men as the killers of the Nickell boy." The governor dismissed the material and ordered the execution to continue. *The James D. Horan Civil War and Western Americana Collection*

Charles Irwin, a Wyoming rodeo rider and a close friend of Tom Horn. As the noose was put about his neck, Horn asked that Charles and his brother Frank sing the Baptist hymn "Life's Railway to Heaven." As he passed Horn, Charles asked, "Did you confess to the murder of Willie Nickell, Tom?" Horn replied, "No." Seconds later the trap was sprung. *The James D. Horan Civil War and Western Americana Collection*

The *Chicago Record-Herald's* story of the hanging of Tom Horn, who was "game to the last." Shortly before he went to the gallows, Horn gave his handwritten autobiography to horse rancher John C. Coble. In an earlier letter to Coble, he said he had "made an investment in writing material." Coble later denounced the "Colorado - Wyoming press" for their handling of the trial. *The James D. Horan Civil War and Western Americana Collection*

THE CHICAGO RECORD-HERALD, SATURDAY, NOVEMBER 21,

HORN HANGS ON TIME

Cowboy Friends Make No Attempt to Rescue Him From Gallows.

SHOWS NERVE TO THE LAST

Antonio Romano Is Executed at Geneva, Ill.—Mormon Murderer Shot to Death.

CHEYENNE, Wyo., Nov. 20.—Tom Horn, scout, Indian fighter and cattle detective, went smiling to-day to the gallows, where he expiated the murder of Willie Nickell, aged 14, who was shot and killed on July 18, 1901, at Iron Mountain. The trap dropped at 11:08, Horn's neck was broken and sixteen minutes later he was pronounced dead by the physicians.

With almost his last words, spoken to his intimate friend, Charles Irwin, a spectator at the execution, Horn denied that he had confessed to the murder for which he was

The condemned man was game to the last. Ten minutes before going to the gallows he lay on his cot smoking a cigar. After leaving his cell he was permitted to shake hands with Charles and Frank Irwin. Earlier in the day Horn had sent for his old employer, John C. Coble, manager of the Iron Mountain Cattle Company, and Coble was allowed to visit him in his cell.

After the spectators, about forty in number, had been admitted to the jail and Horn had come out of his cell, the execution was delayed while Rev. George H. Rafter prayed and Charles and Frank Irwin sang the cowboys' old railroad song, "Keep Your Hand Upon the Throttle and Your Eye Upon the Rail," bringing tears to the eyes of all the listeners except those of Horn himself.

HELPED ADJUST NOOSE.

At the conclusion of the song came an interview between Horn and Irwin. "Be game," said Irwin.

"You bet I will," replied Horn, who then assisted Under Sheriff Proctor and his assistant to adjust the straps, noose and black cap. His last words were spoken to County Clerk Joseph Cahill, who assisted him to mount the trap door. They were: "Ain't losing your nerve, are you, Joe?"

Soon after the trap fell the spectators passed out, each one shaking hands with Under Sheriff Proctor and congratulating him on the faultless execution. All had been searched for firearms before entering, and guards armed with rifles kept their eyes fixed on Horn's friends throughout the proceedings. Thousands of people were congregated in the vicinity of the jail, and the militia remained on guard until the execution was over and the crowd had dispersed. There was no disorder.

In a letter to John C. Coble, Horn details his movements in the Iron Mountain country at the time of the Nickell murder, and makes the sensational admission that two men tried to have him kill Willie Nickell, but he denies his alleged confession of the crime to Joseph Lefors, which led to his arrest. Rev. Ira D. Williams made affidavit this afternoon before County Clerk Cahill that Horn confessed

rank Irwin, who wept as he and his rother Charles sang a hymn at the equest of Tom Horn shortly before the unman died on the gallows. *The James). Horan Civil War and Western mericana Collection*

The cover of Tom Horn's autobiography, published by John C. Coble a year after the gunfighter's death. *The James D. Horan Civil War and Western Americana Collection*

Tom Horn, the hired gunfighter of the cattle barons, and one of the most controversial figures in the history of the Wild West. When he was executed, Horn had outlived his time; the frontier was gone and law and justice were no longer a gun on a man's hip. *The James D. Horan Civil War and Western Americana Collection*

Horn Hangs on Time

Tom Horn, scout, Indian fighter and cattle detective, went smiling today to the gallows where he expiated the murder of Willie Nickell, age fourteen, who was shot and killed July 18, 1901, at Iron Mountain.

The trap dropped at 11:08. Horn's neck was broken and sixteen minutes later he was pronounced dead by the physicians.

With almost his last words spoken to his intimate friend, Charles Irwin, a spectator at the execution, Horn denied he confessed to the murder for which he was to die. He made no speech on the scaffold.

The dead man was game to the last. Ten minutes before going to the gallows he lay on his cot smoking a cigar. After leaving his cell he was permitted to shake hands with Charles and Frank Irwin. Earlier in the day Horn had sent for his former employer, John C. Coble, manager of the Iron Mountain Cattle Company, and he was allowed to visit Horn in his cell.

After the spectators, numbering about forty, had been admitted to the jail and Horn was led out of his cell, the execution was delayed while Reverend George H. Rafter prayed and Charles and Frank Irwin sang the cowboys' old railroad song: "Keep Your Hand Upon the Throttle and Your Eye Upon The Rail", bringing tears to the eyes of all except those of Horn himself.

At the conclusion of the song came an interview between Horn and Irwin.

"Be game," said Irwin.

"You bet I will," replied Horn who then assisted Under Sheriff Richard Proctor adjust the straps, noose and black cap. His last words were to County Clerk Joseph Cahill who had assisted him to mount the trap door.

They were: "Ain't losing your nerve are you, Joe?"

Soon after the trap fell the spectators passed out, each one shaking hands with Under Sheriff Proctor and congratulating him on the flawless execution. All had been searched for firearms before entering and the guards armed with rifles kept their eyes fixed on Horn's friends throughout the proceedings.

Thousands of people were congregated in the vicinity of the jail and the militia remained on guard until the crowd dispersed. There was no disorder.

In a letter to John C. Coble, Horn details his movement in the Iron Mountain country at the time of the Nickell murder, and makes the sensational admission that two men tried to have him kill Willie Nickell but he denies his alleged confession to Joseph LeFors who made the arrest.

Horn's body was cut down and taken to the local undertaker. Kels Nickell met the corpse at the mortuary and pulled back the rubber poncho. He glanced at the dark blue face, nodded as if satisfied, then turned away.

John Coble paid for an elaborate coffin. Charles Horn accompanied the body of his brother to Boulder, Colorado, where more than two thousand followed the cortege to the cemetery.

The family kept a guard at the grave for some time to prevent ghouls "from digging up the corpse and selling it to showmen to put on exhibit."

In Cheyenne the story was circulated that Tom Horn was never executed but had been freed by the power of the cattle barons. Soon men were swearing they had seen outlined against the sky the arrow-straight figure headed for some lonely valley to ambush a troublesome nester or a rustler who had changed too many brands . . .

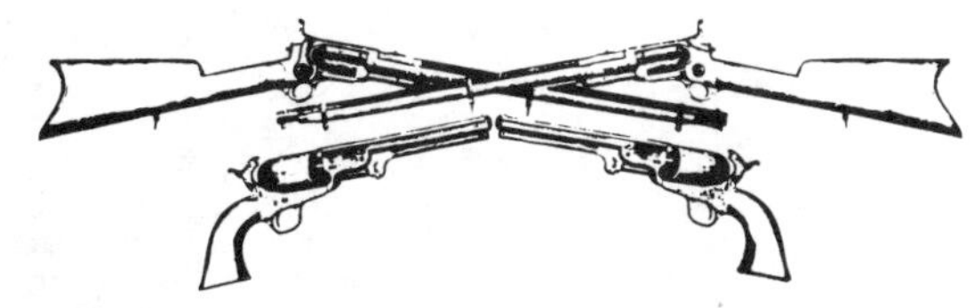

HARRY TRACY

ALMOST SEVENTY-FIVE YEARS AGO, HARRY TRACY, LEGendary outlaw of the Northwest, moved through the forest and small towns of Oregon and Washington with a sort of melancholy grandeur as he outwitted hundreds of possemen, sheriffs, marshals, bloodhounds and Indian trackers in what has been called the greatest manhunt in the nation's history.

He captured a steam launch to make a leisurely tour of Puget Sound, stole horses, mules, wagons, and walked hundreds of miles, at times joining the posses that were hunting him. He had tea with farmers' wives, thrilling them with stories of his adventures—they later described him as "gentlemanly"—and spent two days helping a farmer rebuild his barn, a delay that would cost him his life.

Like Billy the Kid, Tracy didn't flee when he had the chance but waited for his inevitable death. He could have escaped many times, back to Brown's Hole, Hole in the Wall, or across the border into Canada. A few times he dropped out of sight and the posses returned to their towns and villages. Then he reappeared, determined to play the role of a Robin Hood, any role, in fact, that would bring him the fame and notoriety he obviously cherished.

He was finally trapped in the sagebrush hills between Creston and Davenport, Washington. For hours his deadly rifle fire echoed across the treeless hills. After being severely wounded he killed himself. He left behind nine dead

Guard E. M. Carson, of Walla Walla, and his bloodhounds. Tracy continued to outsmart the hounds by walking up and down streams and changing boots, but when they finally picked up his scent and closed in, he killed them. *The James D. Horan Civil War and Western Americana Collection*

men and several critically wounded. During the two months he was the most wanted man in the West: Tracy robbed more than twenty homes, stores, saloons, captured a logging camp, and commandeered the large steam launch.

Tracy's story really begins on the bitterly cold afternoon of March 1, 1898, on a trail in Brown's Hole, a lonely valley with steep mountainous walls on the Green River, lying partly in Utah, Colorado, and Wyoming. A mountain storm had recently roared through the passes of the Uinta Mountains and now the sky was dull and leaden. A searing wind moved like an invisible broom across the snow crust and the rocks that looked like chunks of iron.[1]

Tracy, stocky, of medium height, and with deep-set blue gray eyes, crouched behind the rocks with Dave Lant and Patrick Louis "Swede" Johnson. Lant, twenty-seven, rustler and cowboy, had escaped from the Utah Penitentiary with Tracy the year before. Using stolen horses, they had made their way to Brown's Hole to join Butch Cassidy's gang of rustlers and train robbers. Blond-haired "Swede" Johnson, a Missourian and not Swedish, was a fugitive from a Utah murder charge. A few days before he had killed fifteen-year-old Willie Strang on the Red Creek Ranch owned by Valentine S. Hoy when the boy didn't move fast enough in getting his horse from the corral.

Johnson fled to the mountains; Tracy and Lant to avoid detection by the man hunters joined him. A posse led by Hoy, a vigorous foe of the rustling gangs in Brown's Hole, had taken up the chase.

Tracy, Johnson, and Lant with a packhorse crossed the valley into Colorado. Near Vermillion Creek they learned a posse was nearby hunting rustlers so they headed toward Douglas Mountains. Hoy and his posse caught up with them on a steep trail leading from Ladore Canyon.

When Hoy walked to their hideout, Tracy ordered him to retreat.

"We don't want you, Tracy," the rancher shouted above the wind. "It's Johnson we want . . . this is not your fight . . ."

"Come any closer, Hoy, and I'll kill you," Tracy warned.

When Hoy kept coming toward them, Tracy killed him with a single shot through the heart.

The posse retreated to the south of the canyon where they found Jack Bennett, a friend of Tracy, bringing supplies to the three fugitives. When the raging man hunters couldn't find a cottonwood they used a corral bar to hang him.

Lawmen from Utah, Wyoming, and Colorado moving toward Brown's Hole found a campfire where the outlaws had killed their horses for food and made boots from the hide. Following the bloody tracks, the posses finally surrounded the trio in a valley near Lookout Mountain.

In the freezing cold morning Sheriff William Preece of Vernal ordered the trio to throw out their guns and surrender.

"Come in and get me," Tracy taunted.

"Have it your way, Tracy," Preece replied. "It gets pretty cold around here without blankets . . ."

The hours went by. Behind the rocks Lant and Johnson, blue with cold, begged Tracy to surrender but he refused.

Finally, as another posse prepared to move in, Johnson, hands raised, came stumbling through the snow crying, "Don't shoot . . . I give up." Lant soon joined him. Preece called out several times for Tracy to surrender but the outlaw only replied: "Come in and get me . . ."

The temperature continued to drop until Tracy, so numbed by the cold he was no longer able to hold a rifle, finally called out "I'm coming in!" Still defiant and cursing Lant and Johnson as cowards, he crawled from behind the rocks and surrendered.

The tristate posses agreed that Johnson would be turned over to Wyoming for the Willie Strang murder, while Colorado Sheriff Charles Neimann would take Lant and Tracy in custody for the Hoy killing.

Johnson was placed in the Green River jail to avoid a lynch mob forming in Rock Springs while Neimann took Tracy and Lant to the Hahn's Peak, Colorado, jail, using a little known trail when he heard Cassidy's Wild Bunch riders were preparing to free the two outlaws.

On March 6, J. S. Hoy wrote a bitter letter to the *Denver News* condemning the lawlessness of Brown's Hole and Hole in the Wall, which had brought about his brother's death. He suggested that instead of sending in the militia to clean out the gangs as had been proposed, that a select group of ranchers in both sections be deputized:

"One or two men on the trail of a criminal will succeed where 100 men will be sure to fail. They must be hunted down like wild animals, once on their trail stay on it, camp on it until the scoundrels are run down, and there are men who will do it, men just as brave, as cunning and as determined as the outlaws themselves . . ."[2]

When they read the letter, Cassidy, Harvey Logan, and the other Wild Bunch riders were so indignant they rode over the Colorado line and looted one of Hoy's large cattle camps; what they didn't steal they burned.

On March 24, Tracy and Lant slugged Sheriff Neimann into unconsciousness and escaped. The lawman followed the pair to Steamboat Springs and took a stage, sure he would meet up with the fugitives. Six miles out of Steamboat, Tracy and Lant hailed the stage. They got in only to be covered by Neimann.

"Welcome home, Tracy," the sheriff said grimly, "your breakfast is waiting."

As the *Denver News* reported, "Both outlaws were disgusted at anyone from Hahn's Peak being aboard at such an early hour."

It seemed no jail could hold Tracy. A few months later he broke out of the Aspen, Colorado, jail after whittling a gun out of soap and covering it with tinfoil.

But Lant had enough of outlawry. He and Tracy parted, Lant enlisting in the army and serving with distinction in the Philippines and Tracy moving to Oregon.

In Portland, Tracy lived among the dance-hall girls and the gambling houses. He dressed mostly in blue suits and sported a thick reddish moustache. He was careful in his drinking habits and rarely became intoxicated.

Women were strangely drawn to him. Perhaps behind the easy smile and courtly manners of this man in conservative blue, they sensed something unrevealed, mysterious. Among the rough loggers, pimps, gamblers, horse thieves, bank robbers, and all the rest of the human flotsam thrown up by the rapidly developing Northwest, his manners were incongruous. With a well-turned phrase he could make the tawdriest dance-hall girl feel like a princess.

He was a born leader and men quickly found themselves under the spell of his personality. He was always welcome at the faro tables and the bars, and soon became a familiar figure in the honky tonks.

"I'm Tracy," he would quietly introduce himself.[3]

In 1899 Tracy met Dave Merrill, a small-time gambler, in a saloon. Both men stared at each other, then turned to the mirror; they looked enough alike to be twins. That night Merrill took Tracy home. His sister, Rose, a pretty buxom girl with hair the color of new honey and a flashing smile, won the outlaw's heart.

Tracy began a furious courtship. Within a month he married Rose and they settled down in a small cottage near the Willamette River. There were added responsibilities and Tracy formed a partnership in crime with his brother-in-law. A few months after the marriage ceremony, Portland was rocked by a series of daring daylight robberies of stores and banks. The bandits wore false faces and soon were dubbed the "False Face Bandits."

Money poured in and the outlaw family lived high. But Merrill began bragging in the saloons. One day a stool pigeon whispered into the ear of Ben Weiner, a Portland detective, and Merrill was picked up. He quickly confessed.

"We'll put in a good word for you if you tell us where Tracy is," the detective promised.

"All right but if he finds out he'll kill me," said the frightened Merrill.

The same day a small posse surrounded the little white cottage. The front door was crashed in and the police officers swarmed through the house. There was a cry outside.

"There he is."

Tracy had leaped from the rear window and was running through the trees. Under police rifle fire he kept twisting from side to side, heading for the railroad not far from the cottage. As he reached the tracks a train chugged by, slowing for a curve. He jumped aboard, then gun in hand he raced through the cars to the cab.

"Jump," he ordered the startled engineer. The trainman took one look at the cold eyes and jumped. Tracy grabbed the throttle. The train began to pick up speed. Suddenly there was a piercing hiss and the train jerked to a halt, the big wheels grinding on the rails. In the rear car a conductor had pulled the emergency air cord.

Waving his revolver Tracy leaped from the cab. Shots rang out. One creased his head, knocking him unconscious.

"Well, we got him," one of the man hunters said, as he quickly slipped handcuffs on the unconscious man.

That, it appeared, was only one man's opinion . . .

A few weeks after their capture Tracy was sentenced to twenty years and Merrill to thirteen in the Oregon State Penitentiary. They donned the old-fashioned convict's cotton suit of jacket and trousers with broad red stripes and took their places in the stove foundry. From the minute the iron gates clanged behind him, Tracy was eyeing the walls and the outer barricades. Escape—the word drummed in his mind.[4] In May 1902, convict Harry Wright, whose term was soon to expire, was brought into the plan. After Wright was released he sent word back to Tracy through the prison grapevine: Guns would be delivered.

Tracy smuggled out this promise: "Get the guns and you'll have $5,000 within a year."

Dave Merrill, Tracy's partner. They first met in a Portland saloon, staring at each other in a mirror behind the bar. "My God, we could be twins!" Tracy observed. Tracy, who married Merrill's sister, killed his brother-in-law in a forest "duel." *The James D. Horan Civil War and Western Americana Collection*

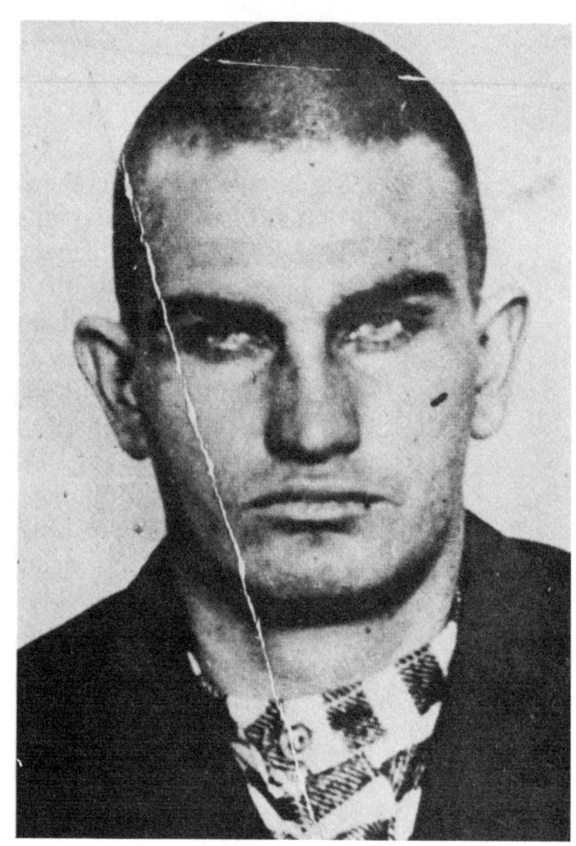

Harry Tracy when he entered the Oregon State penitentiary. Tracy was arrested with his brother-in-law David Merrill after they had terrorized Portland in a series of daring daylight holdups. *The James D. Horan Civil War and Western Americana Collection*

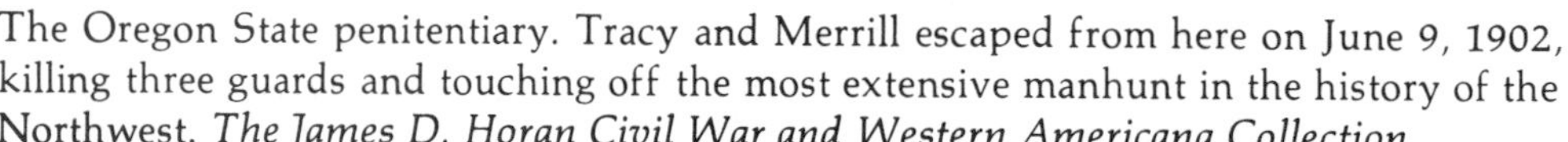

The Oregon State penitentiary. Tracy and Merrill escaped from here on June 9, 1902, killing three guards and touching off the most extensive manhunt in the history of the Northwest. *The James D. Horan Civil War and Western Americana Collection*

Wright stole a horse and buggy near Salem and sold the outfit to a Portland livery stable. With the money he bought two shotguns, ammunition, and a seaman's rope ladder. On a night in the first week of June, Wright crept up to the prison walls and flung over the guns and the ladder wrapped in a tarpaulin.

A mysterious "Mr. X," whose name was never disclosed, picked up the bundle and hid the weapons in a pattern case in the foundry and marked the lid with a chalked symbol. On the morning of June 9, 1902, at about 8:30 A.M., guards Frank Girard and Frank B. Ferrell escorted the lockstepping file of prisoners across the court prison yard into the foundry.

Ferrell barked as usual, "Line up."

The sullen men formed an uneven line. Ferrell rattled off the names.

"Ingram . . . Smith . . . Powers . . ."

Tracy nudged Merrill. They both eyed the chalk mark on the wooden lid. Tracy nodded. The count off was finished. Girard opened his mouth to give the order to march, when Tracy leaped to the box, flung open the lid, grabbed one of the rifles, and jerked it to his shoulder. The blast filled the small room.

Ferrell, his throat torn, died instantly. Tracy turned the gun on Girard, who pushed it aside. Tracy aimed again but Frank Ingram, a lifer, knocked up the weapon, crying: "Don't kill him, Tracy, he's the best man we got!"

In the struggle Tracy shot and critically wounded Ingram.

Girard and another guard, John Stapleton, fled down the center aisle of the building while Tracy and Merrill rushed out of the rear door of the shop. From behind a pile of boxes Tracy began picking off the guards on the east wall. B. F. Tiffany and Duncan Ross, slightly wounded, fell to the ground. While Tracy kept firing, Merrill ran across the yard with the ladder and hooked it onto the wall. When they reached the top, Tracy killed S. R. T. Jones, the guard at the northwest corner.

Under the intense rifle fire of guards led by Deputy Warden Dilley, Tracy calmly pulled up the ladder and attached it to the outside wall. On the ground they picked up the wounded guards, Tiffany and Ross, and, using them as shields, retreated to a bridge about forty yards from the wall. When they reached Mill Creek, Tracy killed Tiffany. In the burst of gunfire Ross fell and played dead. Minutes later the two convicts had vanished in the thick brush that lined the banks of the creek.

Behind them the prison was in an uproar; sirens were wailing and the milling, shouting convict population appeared ready to storm the penitentiary gates. But finally the guards, using their gun butts and firing shots overhead, herded the convicts back into their cells.

Law officers throughout the entire state were alerted and the sheriff of nearby Salem ordered every available man within fifty miles who owned a gun to report. By noon more than a hundred men gathered in the streets outside Salem's courthouse while the fresh June afternoon was shattered by the banshee wailing of the prison sirens.[5]

The greatest manhunt in America's criminal history had begun.

One of the armed posses that hunted Tracy across the Northwest wilderness. He constantly outsmarted them, one time even joining a group of lawmen. Tracy told wives of farmers he feared newspapermen more than the posses. "They're everywhere," he complained. *The James D. Horan Civil War and Western Americana Collection*

Tracy and Merrill stayed in the brush all that day and late that same night passed through Salem. On the outskirts they held up a farmer, J. W. Roberts, and forced him to give them clothing. A nearby barn supplied them with horses. They rode until daybreak, moving cautiously along the roads. At 9 A.M. the next morning, June 10, they forced D. C. S. White and Edward Dupuis of Gervais, ten miles from Salem, to surrender their buggy.

Tracy, as always, was polite. "I'm Tracy," he said to the two men. "We have to take your buggy—we need it more than you do."

As they set off, Tracy called out a cheery "Good morning, gentlemen" to the two men in the road.

A short time later the outlaw partners were riding through the main streets of Gervais with Tracy nodding to the flustered ladies, who wondered who was that smiling stranger in baggy clothes . . .

The county was alive with possemen. Bloodhounds had been sent from the Washington Penitentiary and their baying echoed across the quiet countryside.

Tracy ordered the buggy abandoned and he and Merrill headed north for the state of Washington via Portland. On the morning of June 11, they were trapped in the woods near Gervais where a hundred heavily armed men strung out in a line, cut off the roads, and guarded the Southern Pacific tracks. In the late afternoon Company F of the Oregon State National Guard joined the possemen by the order of the governor. It was dark by this time and the order was given to remain on the alert all night and move forward at daybreak.

In the deep woods Tracy made his decision.

"We can get past them," he told Merrill. "If we are spotted we'll shoot our way out. There's so many they'll be hitting each other."

In the early hours of the morning Tracy and Merrill, crawling through the brush like Comanche on a horse stealing raid, passed the lines. They could see pacing guards outlined by the campfires but were never challenged.

They next appeared, bearded and hungry, at the Akers farm. After his usual "I'm Tracy" introduction, Tracy excused their appearance. He ordered breakfast and, as they sat in the kitchen, assured the frightened woman:

"Don't worry, ma'am, ladies are always safe with me."

He left a few bills on the table and after praising Mrs. Akers's cooking, said good-bye.[6]

Mr. Akers was soon shouting the news into the telephone and the Clackamas County posse took up the chase with fifty men.

The hunt went on for five days. The governor of the state declared a state of emergency and the rewards soared to $7,000.

The *New York World* in a page one dispatch from its anonymous correspondent who accompanied the man hunters declared:

"The territory is in a state of terror. The order to shoot to kill has been given."

On June 14 the pair forced another farmer's wife to cook them a meal. They stole two horses that same day and galloped along the countryside to the Columbia River. On the bank was a small boat. After searching along the river's edge they came on a rancher living in a lonely cabin.

"Who owns the boat, old-timer?" Tracy asked.

The rancher replied, "Mr. Holtgrieve."

"Can you run it?" the outlaw inquired.

The old man shook his head. "Nope—never set foot in that thing."

Tracy said quietly, "Know who I am?"

The old man nodded. "I reckon you are those two fellows who broke out of Salem."

"Right the first time, old man," Tracy said with a grin. "Now get us some food and we'll go and see this man."[7]

An hour later Charles Holtgrieve, the frightened owner of the boat, was rowing them across the Columbia. A high wind came up and for a moment it appeared that the craft would capsize. Tracy sat in the stern of the boat, his rifle across his knee, as Holtgrieve later recalled, "laughing and shouting out jokes in a jovial mood."

Once Merrill twitted Tracy about refusing to let him kill one of the local sheriffs.

Turning to Holtgrieve, Merrill said jokingly, "I had him in my sights and Tracy wouldn't let me kill him."

The blue-eyed man replied: "Why kill a man when you don't have to, Dave? I never have yet and never will. Only Ferrell [the dead guard]—and he had it coming to him."

On the Washington side, Tracy bade Holtgrieve good-bye and apologized for the long pull back across the river.

A farmer by the name of Peedy was their next victim. His money and horse were taken and again Tracy was profuse with his apologies.

"When we're finished with the horse," he told Peedy, "I'll pin your name on the saddle with a bill. Somebody will return it to you."

The next day the horse was returned with a five-dollar bill.

In Clark County, near Vancouver, Washington, Tracy and Merrill were cor-

Captain A. J. Clark's big gasoline launch, the N. & S., which Tracy captured and used to tour Puget Sound. At one point he wanted to prove his marksmanship by shooting the guards off the walls of McNeills' Island federal prison, but Clark and his crew dissuaded him, pointing out they might be killed in a return of fire. During the trip, lasting several hours, Tracy described to Clark how he had killed Merrill in a duel. *The James D. Horan Civil War and Western Americana Collection*

nered by a posse. This time the curly-haired outlaw brought the battle to the enemy, blasting his way through the lines with rifle fire.

They next appeared at a farmhouse north of Castle Rock on the Cowlitz River. While a farm woman cooked their meal, Tracy sat by a kitchen window and read a newspaper.

"Say, there's our pictures, Dave!" he exclaimed. Then he added: "There's a good likeness but I didn't have the moustache when that picture was taken."

He read on. His face never changed. No one would have guessed that he was reading the story given out by the police of how Merrill had traded him for a lighter jail sentence.

As always Tracy left some money and apologies for their appearances. For days the posses saw nothing of them. Then on the morning of July 2, Tracy appeared alone. As the sun was breaking through a thick fog hanging over South Bay, Olympia, he walked up to the office of an oyster company to begin one of the strangest episodes in the manhunt, Tracy's harrowing cruise of Puget Sound.

W. N. Carter, a Chicago writer, retraced the route of the manhunt, interviewing Tracy's victims, lawmen, and newspapermen who had been with the posses. At Olympia the men who had taken Tracy on his tour of the Sound described the eerie trip and how the outlaw told them of his "duel" with Merrill.[8]

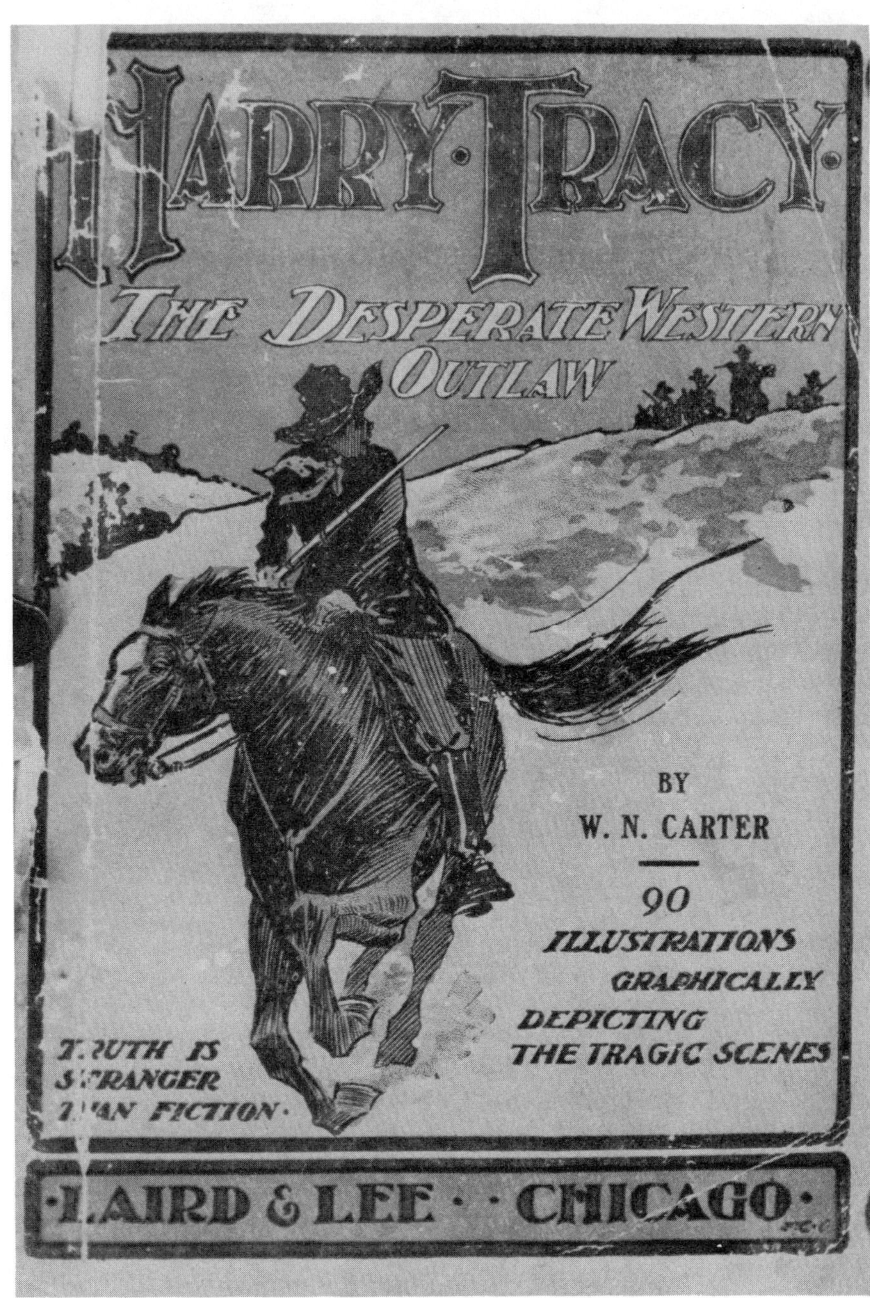

The cover of W. N. Carter's biography of Tracy, published in 1902. Carter retraced the route taken by Tracy and the posses, and interviewed lawmen, prison officials, farmers, and ranchers captured by Tracy and Captain Clark of the launch commandeered by the outlaw. *The James D. Horan Civil War and Western Americana Collection*

Admiral Tracy on Puget Sound

After passing through Olympia at 1:30 Wednesday morning, Tracy headed for South Bay, breaking a leg of his horse on the way. He stole another animal and arrived at the headquarters of the Capital City Oyster Co., on South Bay, at 5 a.m.

He walked into the shanty of the Company and took possession, although Horatio Alling and William Adair, his cook, were inside. Tracy disclosed his identity and ordered the men to prepare breakfast for him. While the meal was on the stove, John Munro and Frank Scott, employees of the Oyster Company, entered the building, and they were ranged along the wall while Tracy ate his breakfast.

In the Bay, near the shanty, was the big gasoline launch N. & S., in charge of the owner, Captain A. J. Clark and his son. Tracy demanded, Clark and the son should come before him and they, too, were placed under the all-seeing eye of the 30-30 rifle of the murderer. With all of the men in the neighborhood under his orders, Tracy informed Captain Clark that he wanted to ride on Puget Sound in the launch. Clark replied that it required four men to operate the boat, which is one of the largest on the Sound and has a capacity of fuel which permits of a 1,000-mile run without replenishing the tanks. The Captain was told he might take as many men as he wished.

Tracy then informed the men that he had killed Merrill. "I shot him in the back," he said, "because he intended to shoot me. The day before the quarrel we found a newspaper which contained an account of our escape and the pursuit. That account gave Merrill equal credit with myself for the deeds which I alone committed, as the papers have done right along. The fact of the case is that he did not have the nerve of a rabbit. He always wanted to sneak through the country, keeping under cover, and preferred to go hungry rather than show himself for the purpose of getting food.

"That is not my style. No man can take me alone. And if I had a proper traveling companion, a man of nerve, I couldn't be taken by a regiment of deputies. If I am shot it will be from behind. And with another man to guard the opposite direction, a man of some nerve, who knew how to handle a gun, we could go wherever we wanted to and not be compelled to keep under cover a portion of the time as I am in traveling alone.

"But Merrill was n.g. He was never anything but an impediment to me, and I am glad he is out of the way. I never could trust him on guard except in places where there was no danger, anyway, and then he was so frightened that at times he would wake me up needlessly in the fear that we were being surrounded.

"So when I got the paper and saw that the reporters and the people thought he had some nerve, it made me hot. I thought at first I would shake him and travel alone, but before we decided to separate, I taunted him with his cowardice and he got huffy. Then we agreed to fight a duel. This was in the woods in Lewis County, not far from Chehalis.

"We agreed to start together from a line and walk ten steps each, in opposite directions, and then turn simultaneously and begin to fire. From his haggling in arranging the terms, I was convinced that he intended to turn before he had taken the ten steps, and I was determined not to let him get the drop on me. So when I had taken eight steps, I turned around and took a shot at him. I hit him in the back. The first shot did not finish him and I shot again. I then concealed the body in the brush and proceeded on my way.

"Merrill got what he deserved. He fell into the pit which he had dug for me. He intended to turn and shoot me in the back; then he would have sneaked out of the country through the big timber and would not have been heard of for months. I would not only have been dead, but would never have been found, because he would have been afraid to tell where my body was."

Tracy told of driving through one town in a buggy in daylight, and of traveling part of the way on the train. He was plainly suffering from loss of sleep, and talked like a crazy man. He said he would have no compunction in killing to effect his escape; that he was never so cool as when fighting, and that he gloried in it.

The convict's boastful talk and conceited air, together with his ever-watchful eyes glittering like daggers, and with his deadly rifle ever ready to do murder—kept his audience as under a charm. Mortal fear filled their hearts, but it was not unmixed with an absorbing interest in the desperado's singular character nor unrelieved by a quiet amusement at the audacity of the man and the humor of the situation.

After satisfying the inner man, the central figure of this dramatic scene ordered

Munro to tie Alling and Adair, and then he marched the others in Indian file down the beach to the launch, and assisted in preparing the craft for the voyage, all the while holding his rifle in readiness for action. He announced to his captives that he had 200 rounds of ammunition with him, and that he wished to go to Seattle.

He then sent Munro back to the house to get some clothes and a pair of shoes, saying that he wished to disguise himself. At the time Tracy was wearing shoes he had obtained from a cripple. One had a sole several inches thick, while the other had a thin one.

Munro took a coat and vest belonging to Alling, and also the cook's trousers and shoes. While at the shanty, Munro released his friends, who were lying upon a bed which Tracy had been caused to be brought down from upstairs for their convenience. When he returned to the boat, it was 9 o'clock a.m., and the new commander started at once on the famous trip up the beautiful Puget Sound toward Seattle.

When passing McNeil Island, where the United States penitentiary is located, Tracy ordered Captain Clark to hug in close to the shore, swearing that he would kill any guard he might see upon the beach. The men, however, dissuaded him from such action.

Later, Tracy remembered that Munro had returned to the shanty for clothing, and asked if he had released Alling and Adair at that time. Munro confessed that he had, and Tracy feared that some revenue cutter might try to capture the launch if the released prisoners had given the alarm. He coolly but firmly declared, if a revenue boat appeared, he would immediately blow out Munro's brains.

When passing the entrance of Tacoma harbor, he expressed an ardent desire to kill the captain of the tug "Sea Foam," because the tug persisted in heading toward the launch.

Captain Clark wanted to cover the distance as soon as possible, but Tracy mildly expostulated, saying he was in no hurry to reach Seattle before darkness set in. As a result of the high speed at which the launch was traveling, the engine became overheated, and had to be stopped twice.

Tracy entertained his fellow passengers with blood-curdling tales of his life, and invited them to a frugal lunch with him shortly after the noon hour. He proved a jolly companion on the long trip, joking with the men and teasing young Clark about his red hair. He talked wildly of bloody crimes he had committed in the past, and said that he would not hesitate to kill anyone if it was necessary in order to secure his own safety. He never let his rifle leave his hands during the voyage.

The all-day trip was a tiresome one, but the convict stood it through dogged determination and the shanghaied crew from necessity.

The launch passed the entrance to the Seattle harbor about 6 o'clock, in broad daylight, and went on to Meadow Point, two miles north of Ballard, a Seattle suburb.

Captain Clark, in relating the famous adventure, said:

"I had been at work for the Capital City Oyster Company, my launch being under charter to that concern to carry oysters from one bed to another. I entered the Company's building about half past seven in the morning and I found a man with a gun there, backed into the door leading to the stairs. I supposed the boys were playing some prank and paid no further attention to him or to the other men, but proceeded to eat breakfast. I noticed that the men were unusually and strangely quiet, but this did not cause me to look around or to ask any questions, my thoughts being on other matters.

"When through breakfast I happened to put my hand in my pocket, and then for the first time after I came into the room, the stranger spoke:

" 'Take your hand out of your pocket, Captain. You have a gun there. It is no use for you to draw it.'

" 'Who are you?' I demanded, turning around.

" 'Tracy,' he replied, as coolly and simply, as if I had asked him what day of the week it was.

"I cannot well describe the feelings or thoughts that crowded my brain and nerves at the hearing of that name, but I remember that my first inclination to take him for a joker was instantly dispelled by the fire in his eyes and the dejected, hang-dog attitudes of my fellow-captives. Then there was a moment of indignant rebellion in my heart, accompanied by a silent determination not to submit to his dictation, but it was clear that for the present we had to humor him, watching for our chance to overpower him—and thus it remained to the end.

"It was far from being a pleasant trip. The weather was fine enough. The sunlit waves danced in the stiff breeze, the air was bracing; the mountains, promontories and deep bays of beautiful Puget Sound stood out in all their glory; our launch was plowing at full speed through the waters as clear as crystal—a scene inspiring man to energetic activity, and an observer might have believed us bound on some great imperative mission, while we were a set of puppets, not daring to move, lest our suspicious commander mistake our intention and pull the trigger. It was nerve-wracking torture, and we were in the company of Tracy from 9 o'clock in the morning until 6:30 in the evening. All day he displayed the most daring recklessness regarding the taking of human life, and all day he exercised the most exacting vigilance to prevent any one of us from getting the drop on him in any manner, or from discussing the matter among ourselves for the purpose of forming a plan for simultaneous action. We were all unarmed.

"On just one occasion during the day did there seem to be for a single moment an opportunity to take him at a disadvantage. This was, when off McNeil Island he leaned over the side of the launch to take a shot at a seal. That was the only time during the day he actually fired off his rifle, though he was constantly pointing it at men and objects, including us. The seal was on the surface of the water, some 200 yards from the boat, and in a spirit of bravado he raised his rifle and fired at it. He missed the seal, for the waves were tossing the boat fiercely, but the ball struck in the water immediately beyond the animal, showing a first-class shot.

"When he raised his rifle to take aim, the chance for which I had been watching, seemed to present itself for a moment, and I made a move toward him, thinking to push him overboard while his back was turned. But at that instant he rose slightly, as though he had abandoned the idea of shooting, and in order to elude any suspicion on his part as to my intentions, I turned my face away as if to look after the boat. As I did so he fired, and before I could turn my attention to his action again, he had turned around and reloaded his rifle from the magazine chamber.

"The launch passed the entrance to the Seattle Harbor between 5 and 6 o'clock, while it was still broad daylight. Tracy sat in the boat, and coolly commented on the appearance of the city from the water. We reached Meadow Point about 6:30 and dropped anchor. We remained there for about an hour, when dusk began to set in, and the convict said he was ready to go ashore.

"Before going, he made Scott tie and bind the others. My son has a sore wrist, and Tracy noticed it as Scott was obeying his orders. The other men were tied with their hands behind their backs, a thin rope being wound tightly around their wrists, and then attached to their feet. The boy, however, on account of his sore wrist, was bound by the elbows.

"Tracy insisted that Scott should go ashore with him. He seemed to have taken a liking to this man. The two landed about two and one-half miles north of Ballard and walked slowly into the town.

" 'I'll send you a lot of money to make up for kidnapping you and the launch, Captain Clark,' said Tracy, as he went over the side, 'for I'll have a lot of dough pretty soon now. And I won't forget you other fellows. You have acted pretty decent by me. Well, so long.'

"Tracy had 200 rounds of ammunition, and his now famous 30-30 rifle. He bemoaned the fact that he had not a six-shooter. 'But I will soon fix that,' he remarked to Scott. 'I'm going to search for a policeman first, and get his gun before I do any real business here.' "

After he had freed Scott, Tracy next appeared in the tiny town of Bothell. Carter described the brief but savage battle the fugitive fought with a posse.[9]

The Battle of Bothell

After Scott's departure the movements of Tracy were lost for a few hours. He probably sought some barn or clump of bushes and slept during the night. At about 5:30 the next morning he was seen on the railroad track, walking in the direction of Bothell, a suburb of Seattle.

On the alarm being given by the launch crew, posses of deputy sheriffs and policemen were immediately formed, and the hunt for the outlaw began at once.

Nothing was seen, however, of Tracy until about three o'clock in the afternoon when one of the posses, composed of Deputy-Sheriff Raymond, Deputy-Sheriff Jack Williams, Deputy-Sheriff L. J. Nelson, Karl Anderson and Louie B. Sefrit, newspaper men, was ambushed by Tracy at Bothell, where a short but fierce battle was fought.

The men, it seems, had walked down the railroad track toward Woodinville, where they met a man whom they mistook for the criminal and held him up. Then they went on down the track towards Seattle, until they were a quarter of a mile west of Wayne. They met Deputy-Sheriff Brewer and reported back to Bothell. They heard that Tracy had been seen near Wayne. They doubled back on their tracks from Bothell, and entered a gulch on the west side of Wayne. Here the party decided to make a search, as it was an ideal hiding-place.

Sefrit noticed a path running down to a cabin near the railroad track. It bore the fresh imprint of a man's foot.

"This is our place," said Raymond, and stepped forward to lead the deputies to the cabin. It was then about 3:14 p.m., and the rain was falling almost in torrents.

Nelson and Brewer were on the east side of the hut, Sefrit and Anderson on the west.

The men marched toward the little building, with their rifles and revolvers ready for action.

Suddenly from a stump about thirty feet away, Tracy's face and neck shot into view, and at the same moment he flung his 30-30 Winchester rifle into position across the stump. The report came almost simultaneously with his appearance.

He had fired point blank at Anderson, the bullet grazing his face. Anderson

> tumbled headlong into a ditch, partly stunned. The cold water into which he fell revived him, however, and he was on his feet in an instant.
>
> As he rose, Tracy again fired twice, and Raymond, who had just crouched to shoot, reeled backward against Anderson and dropped to the ground, stone dead.
>
> As Raymond staggered back, Sefrit fired at Tracy, and the convict turned his attention to him. Sefrit dropped quickly to the ground and fired again at the convict. Tracy twice shot savagely in quick succession at his assailant, wounding him, but not seriously.
>
> Anderson, in the meantime, was plunging through the brush to flank the convict. He met Nelson and Brewer, but before they could get a shot at the desperado, they heard him fire three times in rapid succession and then they saw, with horror and consternation, Deputy Williams crawl out of the brush on his hands and knees into the opening around the cabin, with blood apparently streaming from every part of his body. He was shot three times under the heart, and even as he appeared to view he lurched to one side unconscious.
>
> As Williams collapsed, the villain disappeared. The whole battle had lasted but two or three minutes.
>
> Raymond lay dead, still clutching his revolver. Williams held his gun firmly grasped in his hand.
>
> For the first time since he escaped from the Salem penitentiary, the outlaw had come face to face with his pursuers and with deadly results. Another earnest and concerted effort to capture or kill the murderous bandit had been defeated by his watchfulness, marksmanship and vicious energy. Two good men, in full enjoyment of health and vigorous manhood a few minutes before, were lying on the rain-soaked ground in the semi-darkness of the woods, while the desperado himself was unhurt. The news was bound to add new terror to his name.
>
> The smoke from the battle had not lifted from the scene before the survivors were working over the dead and wounded. Anderson carried Williams up the railroad track to a place where Brewer and Raymond had tied a horse and rig. He took the wounded man to the hotel at Bothell, from where he was sent to the hospital, and finally recovered after a long siege of illness. Raymond's body was taken to Seattle by train.

A half mile outside Bothell, Tracy, posing as a deputy, stole a horse and buggy, then forced Louis Anderson, a farmer, to be his packhorse. The outlaw and his prisoner, who later reported he was "treated with a great deal of courtesy," moved through the forests, dodging the numerous posses and companies of national guardsmen as they made their way toward Seattle.

Tracy's nemesis by this time was King County Sheriff Edward Cudihee, a soft-spoken lawman who had sworn to run the killer to his death. The sheriff, plotting the progress of Tracy and his human packhorse from hunters, ranchers, and farmers who had been forced to feed the pair, led a posse to the home of Mrs. R. H. Van Horn in Woodland Park, on the outskirts of Seattle. Tracy had selected the house "because of its cosy appearance."

During his stay Mrs. Van Horn described Tracy as "speaking almost incessantly, giving the impression of a man possessed of some education, considerable intelligence and a great deal of courtesy." As he was eating the meal prepared by Mrs. Van Horn, Sheriff Cudihee's posse surrounded the house. Late that night Tracy, between Johnson and a member of the Van Horn family, walked outside.

A deputy foolishly joined them. "Have you seen Tracy?" he asked.

"No," Johnson and the other man called out.

As the deputy turned, he caught the glint of moonlight on Tracy's rifle.

"Drop that, Tracy!" he shouted, as another deputy joined him.

Tracy fired twice, both men died on their feet. He backed into the woods, his rifle fire driving back Cudihee and the others who tried to cut him off. Within minutes, pushing Anderson before him, he disappeared. Appropriately they slept that night in a graveyard.

The next day, July 4, Tracy and Anderson watched the fireworks from the outskirts of Seattle, then moved on to capture the ranch of August Fisher, near Maple Leaf, northwest of Green Lake, not far from Pontiac. After Mrs. Fisher gave him breakfast, Tracy refused to take Fisher's "Sunday suit" but selected his son's workshoes.

"These cursed man hunters are after me all the time," he explained, "and I have to throw them off the track. I'm not afraid of the men—I can stand them off all right—but I don't like the dogs a little bit."

Before he left, Tracy in his strange way, pointed to the Fisher baby.

"I can't tie you people up," he said, "someone has to take care of that baby. One thing I want you to do, give me your solemn promise you will not contact anyone for forty-eight hours and let them know I was here."

The Fishers quickly agreed; Tracy praised Mrs. Fisher's cooking, apologized to their son for taking his shoes, then left. The terrorized family who feared Tracy might be hiding nearby waited until the following day to notify Sheriff Cudihee.

Tracy and Anderson meanwhile moved on to Renton, Washington, where they joined two teen-agers, May Baker and Charles Gerrells, who were picking salmonberries. Miss Baker, who became a celebrated heroine of the manhunt, refused to be intimidated by the reigning terror of the West and calmly continued to pick berries.

Miss Baker and Gerrells later reconstructed the scene for Carter.

A Bandit's Gallantry

The story of Tracy's visit to the Gerrells home reads like one of Alexander Dumas' romances. Nothing that Jesse James or the Dalton brothers or Jim Cummings ever did in the way of daring and audacity could equal the calmness of the famous outlaw while in the house.

For five hours he played the gallant to the three women who were in his company. The last hour or two the cottage was surrounded by armed guards, but the outlaw showed no sign of apprehension or uneasiness.

To May Baker, a Seattle girl of the age of eighteen, he was especially attentive, and the picture of Tracy that she will doubtless carry with her through life is that of a gallant, tender-hearted man, a brilliant conversationalist, a merry "josher," a man with decided respect for womanhood, but above all a man of iron nerve.

After loafing around Renton all Monday night, Tracy, with Anderson in tow, started up the tracks. The pair journeyed slowly. They sat down and rested in the dense brush beside the track a few rods on the Renton side of the Gerrells home. They remained there for some time, until Miss Baker and Mrs. McKinney, who were picking blackberries in that vicinity, passed them.

May Baker, the eighteen-year-old Seattle heroine of the Tracy manhunt. She was picking berries when Tracy appeared and escorted her to a farmhouse near Renton, Washington. After spending the afternoon with her and other farm women, Tracy shaved and offered to steal "the best buggy around" to drive her back home. He left as a posse moved in, promising to return and help her pick berries. As always, Tracy easily slipped through the lines of the frustrated man hunters. *The James D. Horan Civil War and Western Americana Collection*

Tracy watched them for a long time. Once they were so close that he could almost have touched them with his hand. They passed on up the track from Renton toward the house.

Tracy ventured nearer the track. Just then Charles Gerrells, an eighteen-year-old boy, came up the track. It was then 11:30 in the morning.

"Hey," cried Tracy, "stop a moment, my boy."

He stepped from the bushes and walked up to the lad.

"Well, I guess you have heard of me," remarked the convict. He smiled pleasantly as he spoke. The two women were a few yards away.

"That's Tracy," said Mrs. McKinney, jestingly, when the murderer spoke the first time.

"No," said Miss Baker, "I don't know who you are."

"Well, I'm Tracy," replied the outlaw.

His words created consternation among the trio.

"Now, don't be afraid," said Tracy; "I won't hurt you."

"Well, Mr. Tracy," began Mrs. McKinney, recovering from the shock, "I'm glad to see you."

"I would never have known you by your picture," exclaimed Miss Baker.

"Ah, now, you are jollying me," said the slayer of half a dozen men. "But don't be afraid. I never harmed a woman in my life," and as he spoke, he took off his hat respectfully to the two women before him. When he heard that young Gerrells' home was a few rods up the track, he informed the party that all would have to go there. Before they reached the house, Tracy sent the boy ahead to warn the mother of the approach.

"Tell her," said Tracy, earnestly, "that I bring harm to none of hers."

They entered the house and Tracy took off his hat to Mrs. Gerrells.

"Excuse me, lady," he said, "for entering your home, but you have nothing to fear."

He went in by the front door as he spoke, and sat down on a trunk at the side of the room. Inside of five minutes he had quelled all fear among his listeners with the exception of Mrs. Gerrells, who was somewhat nervous throughout his visit. With the one exception he convinced them that he meant no harm.

As he sat on the trunk, his unwilling companions were able for the first time to observe him closely. He looked fresh and strong. Aside from his eyes, his face was serene and pleasant. The eyes, however, were an unnaturally dark hue. He had an uncomfortable habit of rolling them when he made a threat. Mentally, the ladies say, he was one of the keenest men they ever met. He was dressed in a black suit and wore a black felt hat. His trousers were considerably too short, a matter of much merriment to himself. He had neither tie nor collar, but had jewelry to spare.

One of Mrs. McKinney's children began to cry when Tracy entered the house, and Mrs. Gerrels looked terrified. The outlaw called the child to him.

"Now, now, little girl," he said, passing his hand around her shoulder and stroking her hair, "don't cry. I wouldn't let any one harm an innocent little creature like you."

When the guards collected around the house afterward, the child crept to Tracy's side for protection.

One of the watches mentioned previously as given to the boy to sell was a gold hunting-case timepiece; the other a silver open-case watch.

"I want two 45-Colts with six-inch barrels," said Tracy, "and two boxes of cartridges. Now, if you give me away, kid, you may have cause to regret it."

"I am kind of scared, Mr. Tracy," said the boy, as he left, "but I will help you."

"If he betrays me," said Tracy to Mrs. Gerrells, "I will kill your two other children." Besides Charles, the Gerrells have two other boys, Cyrus and Harvey. Mrs. Gerrells looked frightened and tears came into her eyes.

"That was only a bluff," said the outlaw. "Mother, you have nothing to fear from me. I have a mother—and she was a good mother to me. She is reading the papers every day to see if I am caught. When I last heard from her she was in Indiana. God knows where she is now. I wouldn't care about all this scrape I am in, if it were not for her sake. God knows, lady, I wouldn't harm a hair on your head, let alone these innocent little children."

The three women declared positively that as Tracy spoke of his mother, the tears stood in his eyes and for the first time the bravado in his manner left him.

A silence followed Tracy's words. To relieve the tension, Miss Baker said, after a pause of a few minutes:

"Mr. Tracy, why do you wear a mustache?"

"Why?" retorted Tracy. "Why do you ask?"

"Because I don't like to see a man with a mustache," said the young woman.

"Have you got a razor around here?" exclaimed Tracy, quick as a flash. From that moment until his departure, the murderer and the three women were engaged in amusing repartee most of the time.

After Tracy had sat on the trunk for a while, he put his rifle in one corner of the room. He asked the women to excuse him for a second and, going to the kitchen, washed himself. As the murderer was thus engaged, he noticed Anderson, and immediately led him to the back porch.

"Sit there until I tell you to move," said the convict.

"I put the Swede on the back porch," said the outlaw, as he returned from making his toilet, "so that if any of those deputies come around anxious to shoot they can practice on him."

Mrs. Gerrells began preparing a meal and Tracy helped her. He cut the kindling, carried water from the spring and made himself generally useful. When he went out for the water, the special train from Renton with the deputies on board came rushing past. Tracy had just time to duck into the bushes and he waited until the train passed before emerging from cover.

The cars stopped about a mile up the track and then returned to a quarter of a mile below the Gerrells residence. Deputies left the train at each place and apparently cut off Tracy's escape. The outlaw watched the train return from the front window.

"They had a red-haired reporter when they went up the track," he said to Miss Baker, who was standing beside him. "I can always spot the newspaper men. When I am running from the posse if I happen to look around there is always a reporter about a mile in advance of the rest, with a camera under one arm and a big bunch of notepaper under the other. I am fleeing from the interviewers, you know," he continued, laughing heartily. "I am sorry, but I can't waste the time."

"What's your address," Tracy asked Miss Baker. She refused to tell him.

"Tell me and I will go down-town to-night and rob a jewelry store for you," he said. "Is there anything you would especially like?" He then joked Miss Baker about a ring she had on her left hand; she retorted and the fun was fast and furious when they all sat down to dinner. Tracy went to the rear porch and led Anderson in. The two men sat on one side of the table and the women on the other. The children sat at the ends.

Tracy made himself generally useful again. He ate very little but was assiduous in his attention to the women and children.

"This is just like home," he declared. "You don't know how much I am enjoying your society."

"You spoiled our berry-picking expedition," complained Miss Baker.

"Well," said Tracy, "we'll all go berry-picking in a little while if you like. I'll help you."

"But we will be late in getting back home to Seattle," objected Mrs. McKinney.

"That's all right," said Tracy, gallantly, "I will steal the best buggy in the whole neighborhood and drive you home, if you will only say the word."

After much good-natured chaff between Tracy and Miss Baker and Mrs. McKinney, the outlaw picked up an old paper and read of the Underwood case.

"Now, there is a man who, in my opinion, is one of the biggest cowards in the state," he remarked. "To go and kill a little innocent baby! Why, hanging is too good for Underwood. He should be shown no mercy. Some of the papers say that Tracy is a coward, but they don't know me. I kill men. I never harmed a woman or a child in my life."

"But you shot Merrill in the back," said Miss Baker.

"That is unjust," exclaimed the murderer. "The papers have the wrong story. When the newspaper men come around to interview you about my visit, tell them for me that I killed Merrill without treachery. He was a mean-spirited sort of a man. When we quarreled and decided to fight, I was willing to be square. I always fight square. But I knew him and as we walked away ten paces from each other I watched him over my shoulder. At the eighth step he turned to fire. I jumped around and let him have it. As he reeled and fell I shot him again in the back. Then I walked up to his prostrate body and shot him in the head."

"But you should not have killed Breece."

"I had to," said Tracy. "The newspapers have got the wrong story about that fight. I told Breece to fling down his gun. In a second we were locked in each other's arms. We struggled for barely a moment, when I raised my revolver and shot him. The men with us then started to run."

By this time the house was well surrounded by guards. Tracy, however, showed no nervousness. His rifle still rested in the corner of the dining-room. He kept his revolver by him.

"We can wait here until it is dark," remarked Tracy, as they rose from the table, "then we will walk down the track together. I will go with you as far as Renton. It will be a nice moonlight walk and especially if one is in good company," with a bow to Miss Baker.

"Well, I don't know," she replied. "It won't be very pleasant if deputies are shooting at us."

"But I will be safe," said Tracy, jestingly. "The ladies will have to form a cordon around me. You would do that for me, wouldn't you?"

"Oh, sure," said Miss Baker; "we would like to get killed for you—I don't think."

Tracy then spoke about his crude efforts at making bread and asked Mrs. Gerrells a number of questions about the proper methods. She explained things to him.

"Why don't you take your wife in Portland along with you?" said Mrs. McKinney, "she could do the cooking."

"The girl whom the police are watching in Portland," said the murderer, with impressive earnestness, "is not my wife. She is the sister of Dave Merrill. Her family were not treating her right, and I took pity on her. I couldn't stand by and see a woman get the rough end of life. I cared for her. She was sick. I sent her money so that she could get proper attention. She never got the money until I found out that it was being held back. Then I had to send it through a third person. No man could stand aside and see a woman badly treated. I know I couldn't, and I don't suppose I would stand very high among most people. That's all there is to that story."

"By the way," he continued, a few moments later, "I liked the graham bread we had at dinner. I wish I knew how to make it."

"Oh, dear," said Miss Baker. "I feel tired of staying in the house all day and doing nothing. Can't we go out?"

"You bet not," said Tracy. "Do you dance?"

"Yes," said Miss Baker, "I like to dance—sometimes."

"Does any one here play?" questioned the murderer.

"But why do you ask?" exclaimed Mrs. McKinney.

"Why I thought we might have a little music and Miss Baker and myself could take a turn or two around the room," said Tracy with great sangfroid.

At that moment every outlet of escape seemed blocked. The posse was scattered on all sides of the house. Tracy never lost his nerve. A man approached the door and knocked loudly. Tracy took Miss Baker and Mrs. McKinney into the kitchen with him. Mrs. Gerrells was left to answer the caller. It was a Renton butcher.

"Is Tracy in here?" he asked the lady, refused to take "no" for an answer and walked into the house. He went as far as the door into the kitchen, which was half open. Tracy retreated through the back door. He stood with it half open. Tracy's revolver was pointed straight at Miss Baker's heart. Anderson sat dejectedly in a chair on the porch behind the convict.

It was a moment of terrible suspense. Miss Baker's life hung in the balance, depending on the nerve and adroitness of each member of the group in not betraying Tracy by word or gesture, or even a quiver of the lip.

"Is Tracy in here, then?" the butcher asked.

"What would Tracy be doing here?" asked Miss Baker, scornfully. The woman's quick wit certainly fully controlled her actions in this trying moment, because she succeeded in convincing the caller that she was speaking the truth while as a matter of fact the bandit was within one or two feet of her. The man went away baffled.

The general gaiety of the conversation had been interrupted. The party in the house talked for some time regarding the posse until somehow the question of drink came up.

"Liquor," said Tracy, "is a dangerous thing. It should be avoided. I am glad to say I have never been drunk. A man like myself dare not touch the stuff. It dulls the brain. It's almost a curse to humanity."

"What nationality are you?" he asked Mrs. McKinney, in an effort to make conversation general.

"I am Scotch-Irish," she said.

"Why, so am I," exclaimed Tracy, cordially. "And you?" turning to Miss Baker.

"I'm of English descent," she answered. "I was born in Texas."

"I knew you were a Southern girl," said Tracy, admiringly. "I knew it by your speech and because you are so plucky."

Tracy by this time—the hour was about 5 p.m.—began to think of leaving the house.

"I wish my trousers were not so short," he remarked pleasantly. "I think I will go out and hold up one of the deputies. Do you see any one upon the track whose trousers would fit me?"

He watched his pursuers for some time and then irrelevantly remarked: "You have beastly weather on Puget Sound. Why, it has rained all the time nearly since I landed here. I think this is an unhealthy country."

One of the boys grinned.

"No, I meant unhealthy in its ordinary sense," laughed Tracy.

"Well, of course, that was understood," said Miss Baker.

"I think I will go to Seattle to-night," he continued. "I would like to see Clancy's place. Do you know just where it is?"

"Of course, we don't," said Mrs. McKinney, resentfully. Tracy apologized at once.

"The people are all out for the reward," continued Tracy, watching the men gathering on the bank. "They are all after the $5000."

"No, it's $8250 now," said Miss Baker. "They have increased it."

The murderer frowned.

"That's the way," he said. "They don't want to catch me so I can be punished. They are all after the money."

"A banker has offered $1000," remarked one of the women.

"Do you know his name?" demanded Tracy. They replied in the negative. He rolled his eyes.

"I'll find out," he said.

"Here's a little memento," said the outlaw a few minutes later, handing Miss Baker a lady's gold watch, "a compensation for spoiling your berry-picking expedition."

He then removed a gold watch chain, which he was wearing around his neck, and presented it to Mrs. McKinney.

"I am sorry I haven't anything to give you, Mrs. Gerrells," said Tracy, "but some day I'll have money, and then I'll send you some."

Tracy then left the house and forded the river, but returned in five or six minutes and told Mrs. Gerrells to take Anderson to the chicken coop. He then sent her for some straps, bound his companion to a post, and then looked once more into the house from the back door. "Well, good-bye," he said. "It was just like home."

He walked down to the river bank and plunged into a field on the west side of the house. It was filled with shrubs and ferns shoulder high. He crept along the ground to about the middle of the field and then rose to his feet with his rifle in his hands, facing the house. Several saw him from the railroad track, but supposed that he was one of the deputies. His daring stratagem was successful and sufficient. Then he crouched down again, crawled another short stretch, repeated the same tactics, and then disappeared in the tall underbrush.

The bloodhounds were baying from the woods near by, but he never showed the least hesitation. Two newspaper men noticed his figure amongst the bushes on the river bank and said:

"There is a fool of a deputy exposing himself."

The manhunt continued for weeks. Anderson, Tracy's human packhorse, May Baker, the Gerrells, and Mrs. McKinney had told their stories, which were featured on the front pages of many of the nation's largest newspapers. A few weeks later, bloodhounds picked up Tracy's trail in King County but he threw them off by walking along small streams.

He was spotted in eastern Washington and it was believed that he was attempting to reach the outlaw high command post of Hole in the Wall valley. Unknown to Tracy, the Wild Bunch had been scattered and the lost leader, Butch Cassidy, was on his way to South America to introduce American outlawry to the pampas. While Tracy was prowling the north woods, Cassidy, Harry Longbaugh, the Sundance Kid, and Etta Place were taking in the sights of New York City before sailing for Argentina.[11]

Once during that week in eastern Washington Tracy called a sheriff from a farm country store, which he held up for food and, after the usual "I'm Tracy" introduction, told the law officer:

"I just wanted you to know I'm still around." The sheriff sputtered and Tracy said soothingly: "Oh, don't get mad, after all at least you talked with the man you're after. Goodbye."

But in eastern Washington there were more telephone wires and Tracy's route could be traced more easily and the man hunters gathered more swiftly. Tracy was pressed hard. He appeared at a logging camp and virtually captured it when he ate. Then this incredible man leisurely entertained the rough tough men with stories of the manhunt. Although they outnumbered the outlaw, the loggers made no move to capture or kill him. It was, as the *World*'s correspondent pointed out, "another example of the strange dominance with which Tracy hypnotized people."

The following week he came upon A. B. Shurer who was hunting deer and ordered him to throw up his hands. Shurer hesitated and Tracy fired a shot that grazed the hunter's cheek.

"I'm Tracy. I don't want to hurt anybody but those who get in my way—but when I say put up your hands—put them up."

Shurer hastily complied and Tracy gestured to the cooking pot over the fire. "That smells good, let's eat."

After the meal Tracy looked up at the sky. "I guess it's going to rain," he said. "Well goodnight and thanks for the food."[12]

Then on July 15 the body of Merrill was found five miles from Chehalis, just where Tracy had said he killed his convict-partner.

Tracy was spotted again and again—as he headed east toward Spokane, crossing the Columbia River. Once he was spotted by a posse and wounded but disappeared in a thick swamp and threw off the bloodhounds. How long this man of iron stayed there is not known but it must have been a horrible ordeal: the shotgun wound glowing like a red coal, the swarms of mosquitoes, and the continual plodding through the reeds and scummy water.

He was seen again by a woman walking along a road and although he was lean and hungry as a wolf he still maintained his courtly manners and told the woman "the pellets in his back hurt a great deal."

One day in the last week of July after he had not been seen for a week, Tracy came down out of the Cascades and the shelter of the forests. Still insisting "I respect all womanhood," he took over a cabin at Ellsworth and had the settler's wife prepare him a meal. He thanked her and left. He next appeared at a farmhouse near Wenatchee, riding a horse and leading another.

As the summer dragged on he became a wraithlike figure in the dry country

SUNDAY MORNING, JULY 13, 1902.

AMERICA'S FIRST AND ONLY MUSOLINO!

MAN WHO HELD UP ITALY HAS A WESTERN DOUBLE.

ARMY AND NAVY FAIL TO CATCH THE DESPERADO.

Tracy Has Eluded a Pack of Hounds

And the Encircling Sheriff's Posse.

Disappeared as If By Subtlest Magic

Every Time He Has Been in Reach.

Unknown Pals Have Aided Flight,

While Farmers Are Impressed By Him

And Forced To Do His Bidding at Points of Stilettos and Guns.

During the summer and fall of 1902, Harry Tracy was page-one news across the nation, in Canada, and Europe. Here are a number of headlines, one comparing him with an Italian desperado. *The James D. Horan Civil War and Western Americana Collection*

of the coulee. Man hunters were now everywhere and Indian trackers were talking seriously of preparing a silver bullet for this man who seemingly could not be killed.

Tracy kept moving through the sagebrush country using back roads and hiding out in the valleys and coulees. On the afternoon of August 3, George Goldfinch, a young rancher, met Tracy on a road ten miles south of Creston.

"I'm Tracy," the bandit said, then ordered Goldfinch to take him to the nearby Eddy brothers ranch.

"You go ahead," he ordered casually, "and tell them I'm coming."

Tracy, still mounted and leading a packhorse, leisurely rode to the ranch and introduced himself to the Eddy brothers.

The ranchers later described those last days to Carter.[13]

The Death of Harry Tracy

"When Tracy came to the ranch Sunday evening," said L. B. Eddy, in telling of the unwelcome visit of the desperado, "accompanied by young Goldfinch, he subjugated and enslaved us in his own inimitable style. First I had to unsaddle and feed his horse. The other two boys had to go with him or rather before him. In nearly every case when he took us around in a bunch, he would say:

"I guess I had better go behind."

"He wanted me to trade horses with him, and asked me what kind of animals I had. When I told him a 3-year-old colt and a 14-year-old mare he didn't care to trade, but decided to wait at the ranch until his own horses were rested.

"The convict said they had traveled a long distance and were tired, adding, 'I believe in taking good care of my horses, because I depend on them for my escape.' He fed them regularly and was very good to them. The animals were kept in a little shed and one was always saddled, ready for a quick flight, if it should become necessary.

"After we fed the horses that evening, he wanted a revolver pouch, and in order to get one he went to my saddle and cut off one side. He said he would rather work at that in the house, so he took us all in with him.

"Tracy always carried his rifle or revolvers. He said he had two revolvers, but I never saw but one.

"For convenience, he cut the front of his shirt open just at the top of the band of his trousers, and then put the gun through that hole. That kept it concealed. He then made a cartridge belt, saying he might have to use it a great deal while passing through this country. After the work was completed, he cleaned up his rifle. He took the peep sight from my brother's rifle and put it on his. After his gun was ready he said he would test the sights. He paced off 60 yards, and shot at a knot in a pine board. The knot was not larger than a 5-cent piece, and he hit it as near the center as possible.

"On returning to the house he handed me the gun and asked if I ever saw such a smooth stock. Of course, all the loads were out of it, and Tracy knew that I could not do him any harm. He was always good-natured, and did not seem to worry. While in the house during the daytime, he would sit in the corner of the kitchen near the window with his back to the wall. From this position he could look in nearly every direction, and could watch us. He would not sleep in the house at night, preferring the haystack, evidently believing himself safer there from a night attack. He made my brother sleep with him, while I slept in the house.

Eugene (Gene) Eddy, one of the owners of the Eddy ranch, in a photograph taken in 1901 when he was twenty-eight. Tracy made his last stand at the ranch. After being wounded in the leg, he committed suicide. *Courtesy Robert E. Eddy, Cashmere, Washington*

Lucius (Lou) Eddy, who with his brother Gene owned the Eddy ranch where Harry Tracy was trapped and killed himself. Tracy stopped off at the ranch for a few days and helped the brothers build a barn. He told them he was on his way back to Hole-in-the-Wall, stronghold of the Wild Bunch, "where I will be a thief among thieves." *Courtesy Robert E. Eddy, Cashmere, Washington*

A rare photograph of the posse that traded shots with Harry Tracy on that hot August day he was trapped on the Eddy ranch. Tracy was hidden behind a rock with only a small part of his leg showing. One of these sharpshooters wounded him in the leg. Unable to stop the flow of blood, he killed himself. This photograph was taken shortly after his body was discovered. *Courtesy Robert E. Eddy, Cashmere, Washington*

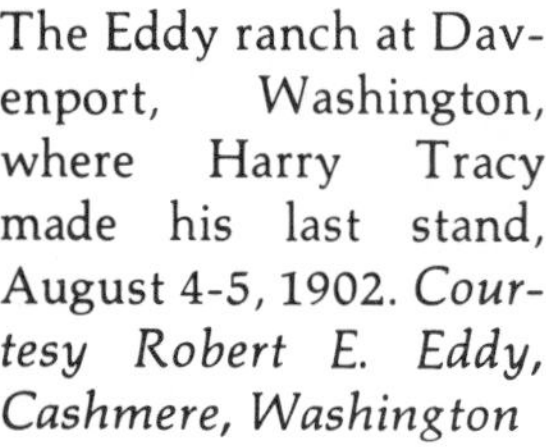

The Eddy ranch at Davenport, Washington, where Harry Tracy made his last stand, August 4-5, 1902. *Courtesy Robert E. Eddy, Cashmere, Washington*

"We were not uneasy while he was around, for we felt if we did what he told us, he would not harm us. We woke up at 5 o'clock Tuesday morning, and our visitor helped to prepare breakfast. The longer he was with us, the more he trusted us. Young Goldfinch was released Monday morning, but not until Tracy had instructed him repeatedly that if he told, he (Tracy) would kill my brother and me. He took a bath and a shave while he was here, but his rifle was standing against the wall near him while he was at that job, nor did he take his shirt off this time, but rolled it back when bathing. He did not intend that we should take him unawares.

Young Goldfinsh did not shake off the fear instilled into him by the outlaw's threats until the next morning, when he hastened, all excitement, to the town of Creston, where he wired the information to Sheriff Gardiner of Davenport. Section Boss J. J. Morrison overheard the youth dictating the message to the operator, and at once consulted with several of his town friends, who had the reputation of being good grouse hunters.

Had it not been for Goldfinch, the outlaw would probably be still alive; therefore the young man should certainly be rewarded in some way.

The result of the conference was the secret formation of a party of five, consisting of Morrison, Constable C. A. Straub, Dr. E. C. Lanter, Attorney Maurice Smith and Frank Lillengren, who, fully armed, proceeded by team to the Eddy ranch on Lake Creek. They left at 2 o'clock Tuesday afternoon, Aug. 5, and a quick drive of eleven miles brought them close to the farm, where the outlaw, in fancied security, was recruiting his travel-worn horses. It was then about 4 o'clock in the afternoon.

It was not thought at all probable by the Creston party that Tracy was still at the Eddy farm, but they started there at once in order that they might get some clew of the direction in which he went. When they came near to the ranch, they separated and approached the house from different directions, so as to be sure that their man had gone before they exposed themselves.

While two of the men were going up to the back of the building, they saw that Eddy was down in the field, half a mile from the house, busily mowing.

"Surely, he cannot be there or he would make them all stay near him so they could not give the alarm," remarked one.

"Better be careful, though," said another. "He may be there, after all."

They decided that the best thing to do was to go down and have a talk with Eddy, and started towards him. They began a friendly conversation, and the farmer did not offer to tell of the presence of the outlaw until they pressed him closely with questions.

"Haven't you a visitor?" they asked.

"I had Tracy here for a while, but he is gone now."

"When did he leave?"

"This morning."

"Do you know which way he went?" was asked. The farmer not giving a ready and satisfactory answer and showing unusual uneasiness, the men at once suspected that there was something wrong, and told him so.

Just then Tracy stepped out of the blacksmith shop with Eddy's brother. The two men had been repairing a barn door and had gone to the shop to get a pair of hinges.

"There he is now," said Eddy, "talking to my brother; but if he knew that I was telling you, he would murder me before he could be killed. He allows one of us to work and makes the other one stay with him. He helps us with the work and wants us to pass him off as our hired man. He carries his gun concealed and never offers harm to any one unless he thinks they are going to injure him. But I will have to drive on or he will be out here in a very short time and demand the reason for stopping."

The man-hunters, suppressing their excitement at the sudden revelation, proceeded to a small hill where they could watch every movement without exposing themselves fully to view.

Eddy drove to the house and Tracy came out of the barn and began to assist his host in unhitching the horses. In an instant the keen eye of the fugitive detected the men who were destined to end his murderous career, but his composure never left him.

"Do you know who those men are, up there?" he asked, turning sharply to Eddy.

"No," replied the farmer; "never saw them before."

Although the outlaw took in the situation at once, he betrayed no excitement. He finished unhitching the horses, knowing, of course, that the men could not see plainly enough from that distance to be able to risk a shot. He then started to lead the horses into the barn, using them and Eddy as shields, but when he was a few feet from the door, let go of the rope and rushed through the door.

A moment later he reappeared with his rifle in his hand, and wearing a black hat, which he had exchanged for a cap he wore. The outlaw then started on a swift run down a gulch to a rock 150 yards distant.

This proved another fatal mistake, born of too much contempt for the marksmanship of his pursuers. He might have remained at the barn with the Eddys as shields, and escaped at night in the friendly darkness. But he preferred a different method of warfare, and would take no chances of being surrounded in a barn.

The men on the hill fired at him, and Tracy, without stopping, returned their fire with such accuracy as to cause them to seek shelter behind a rock.

The fleeing outlaw had gone but a short distance, when two others of the posse rose up from behind a rock, situated at a different angle to his route from the place where his first assailants kept up a steady firing, and shouted:

"Hands up!"

The only answer was another remarkably accurate, but ineffectual shot, which the outlaw delivered from the hip without slackening his pace.

Tracy reached the boulder without receiving a scratch, and for a while conducted a lively duel with his pursuers. Every time one of the posse showed his head from behind the barricade, the outlaw's rifle rang out and a bullet chipped the rock. Here again, he might have remained until night in comparative safety, but in this position he was at a decided disadvantage because he was compelled to shoot "at the sun" in his duel with the man-hunters, and the fierce glare on his rifle barrel prevented accurate aim. It was this alone that barred the famous outlaw from adding to the long list of his unfortunate victims.

Tracy was quick to perceive this, and, in his endeavor to gain a more commanding position, the fatal end came. Leaving the shelter of the boulder he ran swiftly toward another rock located in a barley field, fully exposed to the fierce fire of the men who had bravely volunteered to kill or capture the terror of the Puget Sound country.

Just as he reached the field he fell, a rifle ball having broken his leg. For seventy-five yards he dragged himself through the barley after receiving the wound, seemingly in the direction of the shed where the horses were hitched, one of them saddled, ready for any emergency.

Once he stopped and sent back a defiant shot that threw dust from the rock into the eyes of one of the pursuers.

The moving grain showed his course through the field, and a steady fire from the hunters followed him.

An artery had been severed and he was bleeding copiously, evidently near the shadow of death.

Once again he stopped, and taking a small strap from his person, buckled it around his leg tightly, in an effort to staunch the flow of blood.

Another bullet struck him in the thigh. But still he crawled on, his clothing torn by the rough ground, and his wounds leaving behind a trail of blood.

He stopped again, and threw aside his ammunition bag. He was growing weak; death was surely hovering over that summer scene; but he still clung to his dear old Winchester—his only friend.

He crawled on, stopping frequently to rest and to look back in the direction whence a volley of shots still came occasionally.

What his thoughts were during those last moments must be left to the imagination of the reader.

Perhaps he thought of his mother, whom he said he was going to see.

Perhaps he cursed the men who had hounded him to his death.

Undoubtedly he tried to take another last shot, but his strength failed him and his eye was fast becoming dim.

He was dying.

He probably thought himself only fainting from loss of blood.

The defiant spirit of the hunted man was still unconquered. He was still determined never to be taken alive.

His hands sought the revolver hidden in his bosom—the precious weapon brought to him from Tacoma by Farmer Johnson—and he placed the muzzle against his temple.

His strength was so far gone that he had to use his thumb to pull the trigger.

It was half an hour after he had stumbled and fallen, that a muffled report came from the barley field, and the man-hunters replied with another savage volley.

But justice had been cheated; the outlaw had departed from this world by his own weapon.

It was half past five o'clock.

Although their victim was sleeping the sleep of the dead, his executioners, not aware of their success, and deceived again and again by the waving of the grain in the evening breeze, kept firing occasional volleys in the direction where they supposed Tracy to be.

A sheriff came, and standing on the hillside, fired into the barley field at random.

All night the men watched anxiously at a safe distance, fearing that the shrewdest and most cold-blooded desperado ever known in criminal history would outgeneral them and escape again.

With the first rays of the morning sun, the men on guard began to approach the field. They advanced cautiously to the rock where the outlaw had made his last desperate struggle for life, and picking up the trail, followed it to the spot where he probably received the fatal shot.

From that time on it was very distinct—marked by grain crushed down, and a trail of clotted blood.

Still they approached warily, each man with his rifle ready to fire. They came to the place where he had turned to send back his last leaden message. The earth clods were crushed and saturated with blood.

A little further on he evidently had stopped to buckle the leather compress around his shattered leg.

The grain was trampled down in a circle, and a pool of clotted blood had not yet dried up.

They came to the discarded ammunition-bag, and a few feet further on saw a white shirt which shone through the waving grain.

Slowly and noiselessly they approached, ready to fire on the slightest move from the prostrate form.

A crow flew across the field, cawing loudly, and the men stopped, looking at each other in a startled manner.

They approached closer, but the form did not move; and they knew, from the flies buzzing around the silent and bloody head, that he was dead.

There lay the body in a pool of blood, with the face turned up to the morning sky.

The left hand, with the thumb upon the trigger, grasped the revolver with which he had shot himself.

The right still caressed the famous 30-30 Winchester that lay on the ground beside him.

A hole in the head over the left eye revealed the meaning of that muffled shot they had heard the afternoon before.

The bullet wounds in the leg indicated the cause of his despondency and suicide.

The body was covered with blood from head to foot.

A bloody handkerchief, which he had evidently tried to push into one of his wounds, lay close by.

The muscles of the wounded leg were bruised and contorted by the fierce pressure of the tightly-drawn strap.

They stood looking at the dead outlaw in silence for fully a minute, and then with a great shout of exultation sprang forward and disarmed the corpse.

Even in death the rigid hands refused to surrender the weapons without an effort on the part of the victors.

The body was stiff and cold.

Both bones of the right leg, below the knee, were broken, and a bullet had pierced the right thigh.

The top of the head was shattered by the bullet fired by the bandit's own hand.

After the first shout of exultation, the men relapsed into silence again and spoke only in suppressed tones of awe.

The outlaw was dead, but the hypnotic influence of his presence seemed to cling to him still.

The body was dressed in a pair of blue overalls, a white shirt, badly torn from dragging himself along the ground, a black hat and a heavy pair of shoes. His socks were of an inferior quality, and his only underclothing was an undershirt, soiled from long usage. He was without coat or vest. There was not an ounce of superfluous flesh on his body, and he was in the pink of condition. His face, though covered with blood, was exactly the one pictured so many times during the exciting days—the eyes wide apart, and with a sullen, determined look; a broad forehead, sloping back from the tips of his eyebrows; a wide, projecting chin, and lips firmly set even in death.

Beside the Winchester and the revolver found in his hand, there was another pistol inside of his trousers. A search of his pockets revealed only a jack-knife and a brass compass with a broken glass. His buckskin ammunition-bag contained 150 rifle cartridges, and there were two boxes of pistol cartridges on the ground beside the bag. The Winchester contained nine shots, and had evidently been emptied once at his pursuers and reloaded, after which a single shot had been fired.

The body of the dead outlaw, together with his arms, horses and other effects, were taken to Davenport, the county seat of Lincoln County, where an inquest was held in the afternoon.

News that the corpse of the famous outlaw was being brought to town, set the people of Davenport in a wild ferment of excitement. By the time the procession reached the morgue, the streets were crowded with shouting crowds clamoring for a view of the body and a relic to carry away.

They got both, and in a short time there was nothing left but the naked body. Some one secured the clotted, blood-stained handkerchief, found by the dead man's side, and even that was divided into bits. Another got the bloody strap, with which the dying bandit had tried to check the flowing of his life-blood. His trousers were cut into strips, and still again divided. Many locks of hair were clipped off, and in places his head was left bald. His cartridges and ammunition-bag were divided among the posse and others.

His slayers kept the two pistols found on him, and the famous 30-30 rifle went to the Governor of Oregon. The horses and accoutrements were taken possession of by the sheriff, to be returned to the owners.

A short time later Sheriff Cudihee appeared at Stone's Funeral Home in Davenport. For a long moment the exhausted lawman, whom Tracy had feared and hated, looked down at the battered body of the man he had sworn to capture or kill.

"Gentlemen, you have done well," he quietly told the members of the posse who crowded into the room. "I would have given $500 to have been one of your party."

He walked away, turned for one last look at the body on the wooden stretcher, then left.

After a brief inquest, the corpse, attired in a cheap dark suit and shirt, was placed in a sealed zinc coffin and taken back to the Salem penitentiary. Crowds of relic hunters at Seattle and Portland, "where the cars were changed," whittled splinters from the outside pine box "and jested at Tracy's speedy return to prison."

On August 9, two months after his escape, Tracy's body was delivered to the warden. The coffin was opened, the remains formally identified, acid was poured on the face to prevent "body snatchers who might be tempted to steal the body for exhibition," then Tracy was taken to the prison cemetery.

A rare photograph of the body of Harry Tracy in the wheat field of the Eddy ranch. This photograph was taken shortly after dawn on August 5, 1902, when the posse sprayed the field with rifle fire, then slowly advanced to discover Tracy had killed himself. Note the six-shooter in his right hand, the rifle, and poke of shells. The photograph was taken by E. H. Paige, a photographer who accompanied the man hunters. *Courtesy Robert E. Eddy, Cashmere, Washington*

A rare photograph of the horse Tracy used during the manhunt, led by a member of the posse that trapped him. In the classic cowboy tradition, Tracy, when he took over a ranch or farmhouse, first ordered his horse fed, watered, and groomed before he ate. *Courtesy The Wenatchee* (Washington) *World*

There was no priest, no hymns, no prayers, only a team of convicts who filled in the unmarked grave. Then suddenly the prison gong shattered the stillness, the signal for the convicts to surrender their shovels and march back to their cells.

On September 9, 1902, the state of Oregon paid $1,500 to the members of the posse that trapped Tracy on the Eddy ranch; Sheriff Cudihee did not receive a share. By this time ballads about the manhunt were being sold in Seattle and Portland and poems, detailing his life, appeared in newspapers. He was usually compared to Robin Hood, "the outlaw bold . . ."

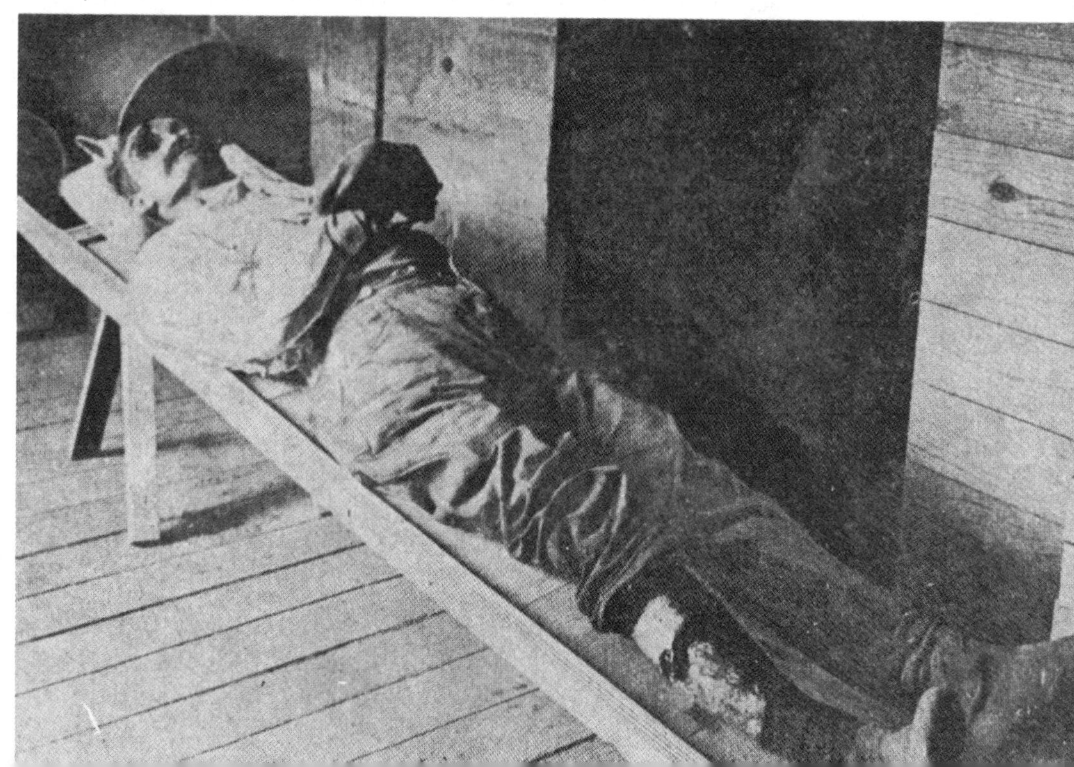

The body of Harry Tracy in Stone's Funeral Parlor, Davenport, August 5, 1902, before crowds of souvenir seekers stripped the corpse naked and left the head almost bald. The gunfighter's bloody handkerchief was torn into bits and divided. His famous 30-30 rifle was presented to the governor of Oregon. When the body was removed by train to the Salem penitentiary graveyard, relic hunters cut splinters from the rough pine coffin. On August 9, almost two months after Tracy scaled the walls, his body was buried, "no priest, no hymn, no prayer." *The James D. Horan Civil War and Western Americana Collection*

NOTES

BILLY THE KID

I consider these three collections in the National Archives to be of the utmost importance to the history of the Lincoln County War and Billy the Kid:

1. *Department of Justice:* "In the Matter of the Examination of the Causes and Circumstances of the death of John Tunstall, British Subject—Testimony. Frank Warner Angel, Special Agent. Mail and Files Division." Hereafter cited as Angel.
Department of Interior Appointment Papers: "Letters and Final Report to Secretary of the Interior Concerning an Investigation of New Mexico Governor S. B. Axtell, Territory of New Mexico, 1850-1907." Hereafter cited as Report.
National Archives: "Court of Inquiry of Lt. Col. N. A. M. Dudley, 9th Cavalry, Fort Stanton, March 1879." Navy and Old Army Branch, Military Archives Division. Hereafter cited as Dudley. Letters and papers of Carl Schurz, Secretary of the Interior, Library of Congress.
The material is voluminous. There are about 300 pages in Angel's file of his investigation and about 1,500 pages in the Dudley inquiry. The material, all eyewitness accounts, gives a flavor of the cast of characters including the Kid, Dudley, McSween, etc., and those who surround them. However, anyone writing about Billy the Kid must pay tribute to those who have dug long and deep into his life: Philip J. Rasch, R. N. Mullin, the late Maurice G. Fulton, W. A. Keleher, W. E. Koop, Jeff C. Dykes, John Curtis, George Fitzpatrick, F. Stanley.
2. Marshall Ashmun (Ash) Upson, was born in Wolcott, Connecticut, November 23, 1828, the son of Samuel Wheeler Upton and Sally Maria Stevens Upson, and died in Uvalde, Texas, October 6, 1894. According to *Las Vegas Gazette,* March 3, 1877, he was also a printer. It is unfortunate he never wrote his memoirs. Upson was known and trusted by both the outlaws and lawmen and knew more of what was going on in Lincoln County than most men.

The man, who the *Gazette* said "is known as Ash to everyone in the Territory," lived a hard drinking, rollicking life of a tramp newspaperman on the post-Civil War frontier, sometimes postmaster and storekeeper. Pat Garrett, the man he immortalized, buried him.

3. There is one thing missing in the documentary reconstruction of the Kid's life—his birth certificate. I hunted for it in the files of the New York City Health Department, the State Department of Health in Albany, and the City Municipal Archives in the early 1950s; then again in 1968 when I sought and found the birth certificate of Charles Schreyvogel, the frontier artist. The late Sylvester Vigilante, of the New York Public Library's History Room and the New-York Historical Society, joined me when a reader sent on information from a frontier newspaper (*Grant County Herald*, August 3, 1878) that Billy's name was W. H. McCarty. Still no luck. However, other official documents—his mother's marriage certificate, her land claims, Antrim's statements in the pension records, etc.—establish beyond any doubt that Billy the Kid's name was Henry McCarty and he was born in New York City. See also "Dim Trails: The Pursuit of the McCarty Family" by Philip J. Rasch and R. N. Mullin, New Mexico *Folklore Record*, p. 641, vol. VIII, 1953-1954.

4. The land claim filed by Billy's mother is in the General Archives Division, National Archives. It consists of four documents: Receiver's Receipt, Final Certificate, Applicant's Affidavit, and Applicant's Proof (signed by Antrim). See also "Billy the Kid: The Trial of a Kansas Legend" by W. E. Koop, Kansas City Posse of Westerners, 1965.

5. William H. Antrim's "Declaration for Invalid Pension," Old Navy and Army Branch Records, National Archives, sketches the background from his family's Bible, his brief military background, the various towns where he resided, his marriage to Catherine McCarty, and his two stepsons. He notes: "We had no children. My wife had two boys, one died in the Eighties (Billy) and the other (Joe) I have not heard from in 14 years." Of his wife's former marriage he stated: "She was married to McCarty, date not noen [sic] died in New York City, date not noen [sic]. "Billy's brother, Joe, a gambler, died in Denver in 1930.

6. Mrs. McCarty's land claim and Antrim's affidavit lists the improvements they made to the house and land.

7. Antrim's pension application states Billy's mother died of tuberculosis. The brief obituary in the *Silver City Mining Life*, September 19, 1874, gives cause of death as "an affection of the lungs."

8. *Tragic Days of Billy the Kid* by Frazier Hunt, New York, 1956, p. 70. This is one of the best written books on the outlaw but sadly lacks an index, sources, notes, bibliography, and illustrations. This is puzzling since Hunt's publishers boasted he did his research in New Mexico under the guidance of the late Colonel Maurice G. Fulton, a dedicated Billy the Kid scholar, and had access to much unpublished material.

9. R. N. Mullin had an interview with Truesdell. See "The Twenty-One Men He Put Bullets Through," by Philip J. Rasch, New Mexico *Folklore Record*, pp. 8-14, vol. IX, 1954-1955.

10. "Billy the Kid's Friend Tells for the First Time of Thrilling Incidents," *Arizona Daily Citizen*, March 28, 1931.

11. Billy probably was engaged in rustling after he fled from Camp Grant. Thomas Ceuse in his *Apache Days and After*, Caldwell, Idaho, 1941, tells how Captain Adna R. Chaffee removed the agent of the San Carlos Reservation because he had purchased two thousand head of cattle from "that damn little outlaw they call Billy the Kid." This was not Chaffee's first brush with a celebrated western desperado; one of his scouts in the Geronimo campaign was Tom Horn.

12. Wilbur Coe in his *Ranch on the Ruidoso*, New York, 1968, pp. 16-17, tells of the first meeting between the Coe brothers and Billy the Kid, hereafter cited as Ruidoso. George Coe in his autobiography, written with Nan Hillary Harrison, *Frontier Fighter*, Albuquerque, 1934, also tells how he met Billy, pp. 33-41. George Coe's book gives a hint of how closemouthed Billy was about his real identity. Although the Coe brothers were friends of the outlaw, they gave his name as William E. Bonney and repeated the usual folklore tales of his hatred for Antrim, his stepfather, how he stabbed to death a blacksmith who had made "slurring remarks" about his mother, etc.

13. John Simpson Chisum, one of the most powerful ranchers in the Southwest, was born in Madison County, Tennessee, April 15, 1824, and died in Eureka Springs, Arkansas, December 20, 1884. He started in 1867 with herds he had driven to New Mexico from Paris, Texas. Within

a few years he had established his enormous spread in the Pecos River country, supplying Indian agencies with beef by government contracts.

14. Brewer, born in Vermont in 1852, spent his formative years on a farm in Dayton Township, Wisconsin. He left home when he was about eighteen and settled on the Rio Feliz. See *Violence in Lincoln County* by William A. Keleher, Albuquerque, 1957, hereafter cited as Keleher. Keleher credits R. N. Mullin with the notes on Brewer.

15. Ruidoso, p. 17.

16. McSween's story of the insurance policy, his trip to the New York City home office of the insurance company, and an accounting of his expenses are included in his affidavit to Frank Warner Angel.

17. Angel.

18. Ibid.

19. The signed statements of Billy the Kid, John Middleton, Samuel R. Perry, and John Wallace Olinger are included in Angel's file.

20. Ruidoso, p. 25.

21. Angel.

22. *The Las Vegas Gazette,* March 16, 1878; Keleher, pp. 97-100.

23. Angel. See also Ruidoso, pp. 31-33; "Blazer's Mill" by A. N. Blazer, *New Mexico,* January 1938, pp. 20, 48-49.

24. Angel.

25. Governor Axtell's proclamation is included in Angel's report.

26. A number of writers have had difficulty with O'Folliard's name. Eugene Cunningham in his *Triggernometry,* Caldwell, Idaho, 1952, spells it "Tom O'Phalliard."

27. Dudley, for all his excellent record in the field, should have been retired from command long before his entrance into the Lincoln County War. There is little doubt he was protected by his Washington political connections. My account of the battle is based on eyewitness testimony taken in the Dudley court inquiry.

28. The *Las Vegas Gazette,* from June 1 to the end of July 1878, described the rising tensions in and around Lincoln. On June 1 the editor advised its readers to "keep your temper . . . don't be drawn into this whirlpool of violent words and still more violent deeds . . ." On June 22 the paper warned that "both parties are in the field and the collision is imminent . . ." The *Grant County Herald,* August 3, reporting the battle, said McSween was killed immediately after Bob Beckworth had been shot. "He cried out, 'Oh, my God' and fell dead," after the sheriff's posse, shouting "Revenge Bob Beckworth," fired a volley.

The violence and killings drove out many settlers and ranchers, according to the county newspapers. The *Gazette* reported six wagons of "emigrants" from Lincoln County, who refused to take sides, had left, "driven out by the lawless element," and one rancher "had moved every hoof of cattle he had to the Panhandle . . ."

When Frank Warner Angel was revealed to be a Washington agent, the *Gazette* gave him a hostile reception. On September 14, 1878, the paper described him as a "satrap of Carl Schurz, sent out on the European plan; with a wave of his hand, like Bismarck, and instructions that if anyone presumed to differ with you, refer them to me." After a meeting with Governor Axtell, the *Gazette* wrote that "the young fledgling went off in a huffy" and recommended the governor's removal.

29. Angel to Axtell, August 13, 1878, also Angel to Schurz, August 24, 1878, National Archives.

30. Axtell to Angel, Santa Fe, August 12, 1878, National Archives.

31. Report, "In the Matter of the Investigation of the Charges Against S. B. Axtell, Governor of New Mexico, Final Report of Frank Warner Angel, Confidential Agent."

32. Report, Angel to Schurz, September 6, 1878.

33. The violence in Lincoln County was not Wallace's only problem. The Comanche and Apache under Victorio, one of the ablest of the chiefs, were on the warpath. Wallace asked Washington for more troops but an idiotic secretary of war, Alexander Ramsey, told Schurz that Wallace's fears "are greatly exaggerated." Ramsey said the Comanche were "more than a thousand miles from the Guadalupe Mountains in New Mexico." Wallace bitterly replied: "The people in Alabama will be astonished to hear they have an addition to their population." See *Lew*

Wallace: An Autobiography, vol. II, pp. 916-919. Before the Indians were subdued, 400 men, women, and children had been killed, among them Judge McComas and his family, close friends of Wallace.

34. Chapman originally came from Burlington, Iowa. He had lost his arm as a young boy. After his death his father, in a revealing letter, wrote that his one-armed son "spurned the idea that he could not accomplish with one hand, anything the others could do with two." Wallace wrote to Schurz in July 1880, describing Leonard as a former resident of Missouri who had come to New Mexico for chronic asthma, "a good lawyer, a true Republican, an enemy of the old 'ring' [Santa Fe Ring] and a most respectable gentleman in every way."

35. Angel.

36. An eyewitness account of the Chapman murder was sent in the form of an anonymous letter to *Las Cruces Thirty Four*, February 19, 1879.

37. The letters of Billy the Kid to Governor Lew Wallace are in the Lew Wallace Collection, William Henry Smith Library, Indiana Historical Society, Indianapolis, Indiana, hereafter cited as Wallace Collection. Permission to use the letters has been granted by William N. Wallace.

38. In his letter Wallace wrote Schurz that Billy was "held in tender regard" by the local citizens.

39. Report, Wallace to Schurz, March 31, 1879.

40. An examination of that day's rulings from the bench gives a good example of how the Kid was betrayed by Wallace; 200 indictments had been returned by the grand jury, nearly all were dropped under the governor's amnesty and defendants released. Arson indictments lodged against Colonel Dudley and Sheriff Peppin for burning McSween's home were granted a change of venue to Dona Ana County—Rynerson's home base—and later dismissed. Of all the indictments, the one against Billy the Kid was not dropped because Rynerson refused to give his consent. See the *Grant County Herald*, May 10, 1879, and the *Mesilla Independent*, May 3, 1879.

41. The *Las Vegas Gazette*, February 2, 1880. The killing had taken place January 10, 1880.

42. Rudabaugh, also spelled Rudebaugh, had been captured in January 1878 by Bat Masterson after robbing a train at Kinsley, Kansas.

43. For an excellent account of Garrett's life, see *Pat Garrett: The Story of a Western Lawman*, by Leon C. Metz, Norman, Oklahoma, 1974. Curiously the author does not mention Frank Warner Angel, his investigation of the Lincoln County War, and Governor Axtell's conduct.

44. Wallace Collection.

45. The capture of the Kid and his riders was considered important enough for the *Gazette* to issue a midnight extra, Sunday, December 27, 1880.

46. Ibid., December 28. The interviews took place in the jail and at the depot.

47. "The Old Regime in the South West: The Reign of the Revolver in New Mexico" by Albert E. Hyde, *Century Magazine*, March 1902.

48. Wallace Collection. The governor couldn't leave New Mexico fast enough. In his autobiography he included a letter to his wife, Susan, December 4, 1879, complaining about the number of citizens who visited the governor's palace and interrupted his finishing *Ben Hur*. Apparently, the New Mexico citizens didn't get too much service from Wallace. At the peak of the Lincoln County War he wrote his wife that he was writing "from 10 A.M. to 10 P.M." and complaining about "all sorts of interruptions" from citizens who were begging for protection from lawlessness, rustling, and Indian attacks. In addition to finishing his novel, Wallace told Susan that he was trying "to sell some mines."

On March 9, 1881, Wallace wrote his son Henry that he held office in New Mexico until "I accomplished what I wanted—the acquirement of what I consider as good mining property as there is in the Territory."

Susan Wallace was also unhappy about her life-style on the frontier. She complained to her husband on May 11, 1879, that "this way of living does not suit me." Billy the Kid, she wrote, "has a gang of admirers and followers and they dash up to a ballroom, shoot out the candles and gallop away and nobody [is] hurt." See *Wallace*, vol. II, pp. 920-924.

There is little doubt from Wallace's letters that he was completely absorbed by his novel during the time he was serving as New Mexico's chief executive; the life and times of Christ were all that mattered to him. He wrote one friend he had spent so much time in one room working late at night on the death of Christ that he called it "the Crucifixion Room."

As a writer Wallace overlooked one of the great dramas of his time taking place around him on the New Mexico frontier: Billy the Kid, the charismatic orphan boy who was even a legend in the time Wallace held office; the life and death struggle of the Apache and Comanche; the settlers who stubbornly held on to their blood-drenched land; the dying days of the cattle barons such as John Chisum; the incredible siege of Lincoln; etc. As evidence that these colorful times failed to make an impact on Wallace's imagination is his autobiography—his term in office as territorial governor and his relationship with Billy the Kid are mentioned only briefly.

49. *Lincoln County Leader,* January 15, 1890.

50. Poe, a Kentuckian, was born near Maysville, Mason County, October 17, 1850. He became a buffalo hunter in the 1870s and is reputed to have been part of a group that killed 20,000. After serving as sheriff of Fort Griffin in 1877 he became a stockman's detective, employed by the Canadian River Cattle Association. He came to New Mexico in the spring of 1881. Poe, a stolid, taciturn man, never demonstrated any extraordinary skill as a gunfighter but he was a good administrator and his personal courage was never questioned. He died in Roswell, New Mexico, in 1927.

51. "Billy the Kid," *Wide World Magazine,* London, November or December 1919. The article is by western historian E. A. Brininstool but happily the author only briefly sketched the Kid's career, then allowed Poe to tell his story of what happened that night.

Leon C. Metz in his Garrett biography states, based on information given to him by the son of Tip McKinney, that Pete Maxwell, incensed by the attention Billy was giving his pretty sister Paulita, had sent word to Poe in White Oaks that Billy was hiding out in Sumner. I don't accept this version. Deluvina, who loved the Kid, would have known if Maxwell's "trusted vaquero" had ridden off to White Oaks and would have alerted Billy. Also the story of the grateful drifter is just too imaginative a lie to have been invented by the taciturn Poe.

In an interview in June, 1927, with J. Evetts Haley, the western historian, which is now in the archives of the Panhandle-Plains Historical Museum, Canyon, Texas, Deluvina denied she had been summoned after Billy had been killed—a story many writers have picked up. Garrett, she said, "wanted someone to call me if the Kid was dead but no one came . . . the story is that I went in there [the room] with a candle to see if Billy was dead but I did not do that. Pete [Maxwell] took a candle and held it in the window and Pat stood back in the dark where he could see in the room. When they saw he was dead they went in. I did not see Billy the night he was killed but saw him the following morning . . . most of the native people [Mexicans] who lived there [Fort Sumner] went to his funeral."

Billy, she said, "could whirl his gun about his finger and shoot. A boy from Vegas tried to act like him but shot himself and died . . ."

WILD BILL HICKOK

1. "Wild Bill" by Colonel George Ward Nichols, *Harper's New Monthly Magazine,* vol. XXXIV, February 1867. This is one of the most outrageous fabrications in frontier literature—and there were many. I believe Nichols wrote it exactly as told to him by Hickok. What is difficult to understand is how it took sixty years to uncover the real story. First editions of *Heroes of the Plains* by James William Buel, Saint Louis, 1882, are very scarce. Buel, who helped create the myth of Buffalo Bill and Wild Bill, claimed Hickok's widow, Agnes Lake Thatcher, gave him her husband's "diary." Her son-in-law denied Hickok ever kept a diary. It is hard to believe that in between drinking, gambling, whoring, and gunfighting, Hickok would keep a day-by-day account of his life. I found the first mention of the Rock Creek Affair, in the July 25, 1861, issue of the *Nebraska Advertiser,* which had a garbled account of the killings.

2. Connelley, perhaps out of jealousy, attempted to dismiss George W. Hansen's excellent research and presentation, which exploded the Hickok-McCanles myth in the *Nebraska History Magazine.* Connelley's book is horribly written and includes such myths as Calamity Jane capturing Jack McCall, Hickok's killer, with a meat cleaver in a butcher shop. This work cannot be compared to his earlier *Quantrill and the Border Wars,* published in 1909. Connelley's book on Hickok was edited by his daughter, Edith Connelley Clift, and published three years after his death.

3. *An Investigation into the Wild Bill-McCanles Affair* by George W. Hansen, *Nebraska History Magazine*, April-June 1927.

An example of Connelley's pique over Hansen's research was his article on the Rock Creek affair in the Kansas Historical Collection, 1926-1928 (pp. 2-27) in which he tried to minimize Hansen's "preposterous account" and correct "these misrepresentations" because he claimed the gunfighter was "one of the greatest" of his state's heroes. Without citing any sources, Connelley went on to picture McCanles as a brutal, ruthless man, a thief and an associate of the murderous border ruffians of Palmetto, surely an outrageous statement. As he triumphantly pointed out, "this was the man who never did any questionable thing according to a publication of the Nebraska Historical Society." In his "Examination of the Statement of George W. Hansen," Connelley tried to dismiss the Nebraska article but in my opinion he only proved that Hansen and Monroe McCanles had at last destroyed a fraudulent tale that had too long been the basis for an American myth.

4. Charles Dawson in his *Pioneer Tales of the Oregon Trail,* Topeka, 1912, has McCanles armed with a shotgun. It seems more logical to me that the three men were unarmed as Hansen states. McCanles, proud of his ability to physically subdue any man, would have scorned carrying arms and certainly not a deadly shotgun to face the cowardly Wellman and the young stock tender. The presence of his twelve-year-old son is a strong indication that McCanles went to the station not to seek a fight but only to collect his money.

5. The daguerreotype is at present in the California State Library but without Stein's note. It was picked up in 1921 or 1922 in Oakland, California, by Harry C. Peterson curator of Sutter's Fort Historical Museum of Sacramento, who restored the image by cyanide. Peterson gave a copy to Arthur Chapman along with the note for his book, *The Pony Express,* New York, 1932, pp. 173-174. Stein's note is a good example of how early the Hickok legend had been established. By the time it reached Stein in California, Wild Bill had fought off seven men single-handedly. Stein, an executive of the company who could be held accountable for the three killings, apparently was only too eager to accept Nichols's fabrication.

6. Hickok's assignment as a scout at five dollars a day allowed for a horse and equipment, *Department of Missouri,* vol. 269, p. 254, *Special Orders Number 89, District of Southwest Missouri,* 1864.

7. *Weekly Patriot* (Springfield, Missouri), July 27, 1865, p. 3, col. 1, has a card game as the motivation for the shooting. Both Richard O'Connor, *Wild Bill Hickok,* New York, 1856, hereafter cited as O'Connor, and Joseph G. Rosa, *They Called Him Wild Bill,* hereafter cited as Rosa, bring in that weary legend of the allegedly beautiful Susanna Moore as the reason for the gunfight. I believe there is a strong possibility she never existed. O'Connor, pp. 84-89; Rosa, pp. 73-81.

8. *Fort Wallace and Its Relation to the Frontier* by Mrs. Frank C. Montgomery, collections of the Kansas State Historical Society, 1926-1928, pp. 189-283.

9. The *Weekly Missouri Democrat,* April 16, 1867.

10. In the mid-1950s, 1960s, and 1970s, I asked the newspaper research staff of the Chicago Public Library to find the much quoted interview with Lydia, Hickok's sister, in which she tells how he stoically endured an operation on his leg at home. The story supposedly appeared in the *Chicago Daily Record,* December 26, 1896. The library's staff reported they could not find the interview during that period. They also surveyed the *Chicago Daily News* and *Inter-Ocean* without success.

11. O'Connor, pp. 125-126. O'Connor's books on Masterson and Hickok sadly lack illustrations, notes, or an index. There is no source for this story.

12. The unreliable Buel is the source for the Wilson story. In 1951 I found Wilson's torrid love letters to Rose O'Neal Greenhow, the Civil War's glamorous spy, in the national archives but was unable to locate anyting that connected Hickok to Wilson. Until some document is uncovered, Buel's story must be suspect.

13. Custer's *My Life on the Plains,* New York, 1874, pp. 33-34. Also in *Galaxy* magazine, 1872. The magazine was Custer's particular favorite; in 1876 it carried Custer's Civil War memoirs.

14. Mrs. Custer's *Following the Guidon,* New York, 1890, pp. 160-161.

15. Undated article from the *St. Louis Republican,* quoted by O'Connor, pp. 134-135. C. J.

Bascomb in charge of the "water services" of the Union Pacific for many years claimed Hickok shot and killed two men who taunted him about the Nichols article in *Harper's.* Bascomb described one as "Estes," who may have been the son of Wilson Estes, owner of a Leavenworth foundry. He said that Hays was the frontier's "new headquarters for wickedness" when Hickok became sheriff. My clipping, "Wild Bill Days," is undated but it may be the article that appeared in the *Kansas City Star,* June 13, 1915. Bascomb's manuscript is in the Kansas State Historical Society.

16. One wonders at the total amount of whiskey consumed by the Indian Fighting Army. In my clipping Bascomb tells an eyewitness story of Sheridan making a "tour" by engine and coach of the water towers between Ellsworth and Hays. Sheridan and ten officers consumed five gallons of whiskey with Sheridan advising his juniors to "use a tin cup, and they can't tell how much you take." On the return trip the whiskey gave out six miles west of Hays. Bascomb was shocked at the tongue-lashing Sheridan gave one of his captains for not having an ample supply. "Dammit, Captain, didn't you know *I* was going?" he roared.

17. The *Abilene Chronicle,* November 3, 1870; *Junction City Union,* November 4, 12, 19, 1870.

18. See the chapters on Hardin and Thompson.

19. My information on Agnes Lake Thatcher comes from the lengthy obituary in the *Jersey City Evening Journal,* August 23, 1907. Hereafter cited as Thatcher. There is a reference in the obituary to an interview with her by a *Journal* reporter but Bruce Brandt of Jersey City's library research staff searched the newspaper's files on the library but reported it apparently had not been published.

20. *Outdoor Life,* vol. XVII, no. 6, June 1906 (letter to the editor).

21. National Archives, *Records of the Social and Economic Records Division,* Group 75. See also Rosa, pp. 163-169.

22. The best biography of Buffalo Bill is the *Life of the Honorable William Frederick Cody, Known as Buffalo Bill,* by Don Russell, Norman, Oklahoma, 1960.

Correspondence between Colonel Sidney Barnett and the commissioner of Indian affairs regarding the appearance of Pawnee Indians at the show in which Hickok was the star at Niagara Falls is in the National Archives, Records Division, Group 75. The file includes a telegram from Barnett to the Indian Bureau stating "arrangements" had been made by Major North to take part in the "Niagara Falls Buffalo hunt" on June 20, 1872; a letter from Barnett's attorneys, Griffith & Porter, Niagara Falls, to F. A. Walker, Indian commissioner, Washington, D.C., July 3, 1872, in which Barnett pleads with Washington to let the Pawnee participate in the hunt "because Mr. B., as a young man does not want to begin life with any suspicion of humbug" and the Indian Bureau's "firm refusal."

Hickok appeared in two productions with Buffalo Bill and Texas Jack, *Scouts of the Plains* and *Buffalo Bill, King of the Bordermen.* In addition to Hickok's improvising and demanding whiskey instead of tea, he also had an "effeminate voice," according to Hiram Robbins, manager of the show. See Rosa, pp. 161-171.

23. *Missouri Democrat* (Saint Louis), March 15, 1873.

24. Joseph G. Rosa in his Hickok biography makes the startling charge that Mari Sandoz, the well-known frontier historian, fictionalized certain sources. Anyone who knew the late Miss Sandoz's countless boxes of index cards listing numerous sources for any book she was writing will find this accusation hard to believe.

Mr. Rosa makes his accusation based on Miss Sandoz's reference to Hickok receiving an eye examination from the army surgeon at Camp Carlin near Cheyenne. After failing to find the date of the examination, he wrote to Miss Sandoz who replied, pointing out that Hickok's failing eyesight was no longer questioned by frontier historians and that she had seen the evidence in 1937 in the old army medical records then stored on Virginia Avenue, Washington, before they were transferred to the National Archives.

Mr. Rosa then asked the writer Earle F. Forrest "for assistance" and he "took the matter to the highest level." Why Mr. Rosa decided to have someone intercede for him at the National Archives is puzzling, since everyone applying for information at the Archives is treated with the same courtesy and diligence.

However, the records were not found. On this basis, Mr. Rosa writes:

"It is unfortunate that for reasons unknown to herself, Miss Sandoz was not adverse to causing confusion by producing references to historical characters that eventually turned out to be fictitious."

Apparently Mr. Rosa overlooked the possibility that records stored in Washington more than a quarter of a century ago could have been lost, misplaced, or misfiled, especially when they had been transferred from one building to another. As Forrest's "highest level" friend wrote him: "it [medical record] disappeared before the Archives obtained possession." He also pointed out: "There is an indication that such a record existed at one time in some warehouse in Washington."

In the winter of 1954, when I was putting together the first issue of the *New York Westerners Brand Book* with Peter Decker, the well-known rare book and western Americana dealer, Miss Sandoz offered to write an article on Hickok.

She had examined Frank J. Wilstach's own copy of his book, *Wild Bill Hickok, The Prince of the Pistoleers,* in which the author had made marginal notes and had assembled a group of letters, notes, and photographs.

Miss Sandoz wrote that Wilstach's notes on the frontispiece of his book calling attention to the dullness of Hickok's left eye, "reminded me of an entry in the documents and handwritten records called the Medical History of Camp Carlin, Wyoming, War Records, National Archives, Washington, D.C. The post surgeon at Carlin recorded a call from Hickok. He had come to him in preference to a civilian doctor because it must not be known how nearly blind he was; he had too many enemies who would shoot him down if they knew how little he could see. The doctor examined Bill's eyes and diagnosed the case as advanced glaucoma, with total blindness in both eyes only a matter of a short time.

"It was with this verdict and this coming darkness on his mind that James Butler Hickok went to Deadwood in 1876" (*New York Westerners Brand Book,* vol. 1, no. 1, New York, Winter 1954, p. 8).

Mr. Rosa twice describes Miss Sandoz's book, *The Buffalo Hunters,* as a "novel." The book, of course, is nonfiction. At one point he suggests that "recollections of old timers are often suspect" but some of his sources indicate he relied on just that. In his reconstruction of the Hickok-McCanles affair at Rock Creek, he dismisses the documents uncovered by Hansen as "interesting . . . they do not throw any new light on the affair." In my opinion, shared by many others, Hansen's research was a major milestone in the life of Hickok.

25. *Omaha Daily Bee,* Friday, March 31, 1876, p. 2, cols. 3 and 4.

26. This account of the Hickok killing by McCall is based on eyewitness testimony in the McCall murder trial, published in the *Yankton-Press Dakotaian,* Tuesday, December 5, and Thursday, December 7, 1876.

27. *The Black Hills: Or the Last Hunting Grounds of the Dakotahs,* Saint Louis, 1899. The reporter for the Chicago *Inter-Ocean,* August 17, 1876, wrote that Hickok was buried in an elaborate coffin with silver ornaments but Doc Peirce, the Deadwood barber who prepared the body for burial, said he was buried in a rough coffin. Hickok, he said, had "bled out quickly and appeared to be a wax figure. . . . Wild Bill was the prettiest corpse I have ever seen . . ." *Wild Bill Hickok, The Prince of the Pistoleers,* by Frank Wilstach, New York, 1926, pp. 284-285; Chicago *Inter-Ocean,* August 17, 1876; *Deadwood Pioneer Times,* August 22, 1925; O'Connor, pp. 258-265; Rosa, p. 299.

28. *Yankton Press and Dakotaian,* December 5, 1876.

29. Ibid., March 1, 1884, p. 4.

BEN THOMPSON

1. Curiously, Ben Thompson, with all the drama in his life, has never been a popular folklore hero. The rather pudgy man in top hat with cane and diamond ring, the most popular picture of Thompson, certainly does not make him appear as one of the most dangerous gunfighters on the western frontier. Then again those homicidal drunken rages that sent him into the night firing wildly at streetlamps hint at paranoia. Once again frontier newspapers and the biography to which he contributed a great deal of information are the primary sources: *Life and Adventures*

of Ben Thompson, the Famous Texan, by William Walton, published by the author, Edwards and Church, news dealers, 1884. Hereafter cited as Thompson. Walton was a close friend of Thompson. An account of the duel can be found in the *Austin Daily Statesman,* March 13, 1884. Hereafter cited as *Statesman.* The most trustworthy contemporary biography of Thompson is *Ben Thompson: Man with a Gun,* by the late Floyd Benjamin Streeter, that wonderful historian of the Kansas cow towns. Hereafter cited as Streeter.

2. *Statesman,* Thompson, pp. 13-16.

3. Thompson tells in his own words the killings over the game and his war experiences, Thompson, p. 22-70.

4. Thompson, p. 80.

5. Thompson, pp. 83-88.

6. Thompson does not mention his meeting with John Wesley Hardin in Abilene.

7. *Triggernometry,* by Eugene Cunningham, Caldwell, Idaho, 1941, p. 249, quoting Brown Pascal, an old-time Texas cowboy, recalling the day he came into Abilene and caught his first glimpse of Hickok.

8. *Life of John Wesley Hardin,* written by himself, Seguin, Texas, 1896, p. 50.

9. Walton quotes at length Bud Cotton's version of the gunfight in which Hickok killed Coe Thompson, pp. 127-134.

10. It took place Friday, August 15, not August 18 as it appears in Stuart Lake's biography of Wyatt Earp. The erroneous date has been picked up many times. See also Streeter, pp. 94-102.

11. There is no payment of money to Thompson listed among the archives of the Union Contract Company and Rio Grande Extension Company, an affiliate of the Rio Grande Railroad, or the files of the Santa Fe. Thompson's long and detailed obituary in the *San Antonio Express,* March 13, 1884, states he received "a bonus of $2,300 and several diamonds." Walton asserts the gunfighter refused a bribe of $25,000 to surrender the roundhouse. The award of diamonds appears in several newspaper accounts of Thompson's life.

12. "Famous Gunfighters of the Western Frontier," by Bat Masterson, *Human Life,* vol. IV, January 1907.

13. Typewritten copy of an undated article on Thompson in the *New York Sun,* James D. Horan Civil War and Western Americana Collection.

14. Thompson, endorsed by the *Austin Daily Statesman,* was defeated the first time by Edward Creary, a popular former city marshal; the vote: 1174 for Creary, 744 for Thompson. The second time Creary ran for sheriff and Ben was elected, 1,173 to his rival's 933. During his term there was not one murder, assault with intent to kill, or burglary.

15. The *San Antonio Express,* from July 12, 1882, to January 1883, contains stories of the shooting, the coroner's inquest, Thompson's indictment, arraignment, trial, and acquittal. See also Streeter, pp. 179-186.

16. "Captain Lucy Explodes the Ben Thompson Myth: A True Story," *The Austin America,* March 14, 1927, p. 8; Streeter, pp. 152-154.

17. *Albany Echo,* February 8, 1884.

18. "The Unsolved Murder of Ben Thompson," by Paul Adams, *Southwestern Historical Quarterly,* January 1945, pp. 327-329; *Austin Daily Statesman,* March 13-16, 1884; *San Antonio Express,* March 13-15, 1884; *Galveston Daily News* (San Antonio Dateline), March 12, 1884; the *Daily Express,* Thursday morning, March 13, 1884, carried a full account of the coroner's inquest. See Thompson, pp. 196-227.

19. The *Austin Daily Statesman,* March 16, 1884.

20. *Glamorous Days* by Frank H. Bushick, San Antonio, 1934.

JOHN WESLEY HARDIN

1. John Wesley Hardin to Jane Bowen Hardin, June 24, 1888. John Wesley Hardin Collection, Southwest Texas State University Library, San Marcos, hereafter cited as Letters. The collection was given to the university by E. D. Spellman of Burnett, Texas. Mr. Spellman's wife was the daughter of Molly (Mollie) Hardin Billings, Hardin's granddaughter. The collection consists of over 300 letters written by Hardin to his wife, daughters, son, relatives, and friends, mostly

when he was in Huntsville prison from 1877 to 1894. There are also letters from his legal clients when he had a law office in Gonzales.

See *Selected Correspondence of John Wesley Hardin, from Capture to Parole, Thesis, Presented to the Graduate Council of Southwest Texas State University in Partial Fulfillment of the Requirement for the Degree of Master of Art,* By James L. Sievers, New Braunfels, Texas, November 15, 1972. Hereafter cited as Sievers. Also, *A Chronological Calendar of the Letters in the John Wesley Hardin Collection in the Southwest Texas State University Library, San Marcos, Texas* by Boyd H. Grimes, December 7, 1941. The Barker Texas History Center, The University of Texas, Austin, has photocopy coverage of the collection.

2. Lewis Nordyke, *Frontier Killer Champ, Frontier Times,* Spring 1958, p. 5, also Hardin's autobiography, *The Life of John Wesley Hardin, from the Original Manuscript Written by Himself,* Seguin, Texas, published by Smith & Moore, 1896, hereafter cited as Hardin.

I don't see how Ramon Adams, editor of *Six-Guns and Saddle Leather,* can possibly describe Hardin as an "illiterate." Hardin was not only a practicing lawyer when he emerged from Huntsville but had been a student in both his father's school in Sumpter and in another private academy with his brother Joe. His early letters to his wife while he was on the dodge were many times ungrammatical with misspelled words, certainly not unusual for the times or for a reckless young killer constantly on the move to avoid capture. In view of the extant evidence, certainly Hardin cannot be classified as "illiterate," Hardin, p. 4.

3. Sievers.

4. Hardin, p. 5.

5. Hardin, pp. 9-10. See also *John Wesley Hardin, Texas Gunman,* by Lewis Nordyke, 1954. Hereafter cited as Nordyke. For a description of Texas under Union rule, see *Texas, The Lone Star State* by Rupert N. Richardson, New York, 1943; *Handbook of Texas* (2 vols.) by Walter Prescott Webb, Austin, 1952.

6. Hardin, p. 11.

7. Hardin, p. 12.

8. Hardin, p. 14. Nordyke also covers the shooting of Simp Dixon.

9. See *The Texas Rangers: A Century of Frontier Defense* by Walter Prescott Webb, Austin, 1965, for a description of Governor Davis's state police and an excellent history of the Rangers. Hardin hated the state police. In a letter to Jane he boasted: "Before my majority I had vanquished E. J. Davis's police from the Red River to the Rio Grande, from Matamoris to Sabine Pass." (Hardin to Jane, June 24, 1888.)

10. Hardin, pp. 20-21.

11. Jane was a long-suffering, patient wife, enduring the deadly escapades of her wild, young husband, which she hoped—and probably prayed—he would abandon. Yet, from their letters there is little doubt they deeply loved each other, star-crossed lovers, as they might have been. As Hardin once wrote to Jane: "It seems the strong arm of Man is against us . . ."

12. Wild Bill's biographers scoff at the idea of a teen-ager outsmarting the renowned marshal but there is an air of authenticity about this iron-nerved young killer that makes me believe his story. See *Triggernometry* by Eugene Cunningham, Caldwell, Idaho, 1941, pp. 46-47; *They Called Him Wild Bill* by Joseph G. Rosa, Norman, Oklahoma, 1974-1975, pp. 185-189. For Hardin's version, see Hardin, p. 44.

13. Hardin briefly mentions Sublette's escape in a letter to Jane in 1884. His version is in Hardin, pp. 48-50.

14. There is some confusion about the details of the Trinity City shooting. Some sources place Manning Clements and Jane at the scene but Hardin, pp. 60-61, names a friend, Dave Harrel, as the one who assisted him in leaving the hotel and does not have Jane leaving Gonzales.

15. An excellent account of the feud can be found in the *Texas Vendetta or the Sutton-Taylor Feud* by Victor M. Rose, New York, 1880.

16. Mollie M. Goldbold, *Comanche and the Hardin Gang,* Southwestern Historical Quarterly, LXVIII, July 1963; Sievers. For material on the feud, see *Memoirs of Daniel Fore (Jim) Chisholm and the Chisholm Trail* by Louis and Fullen Astrip, Boonville, Arkansas, 1949; *The Sutton-Taylor Feud* by Jack Hays Day, San Antonio, n.d.; *Famous Texas Feuds* by Claud Leroy Douglas, Dallas, 1936; *Indianola Scrapbook,* George French (ed.), Victoria, Texas, 1936, hereafter cited as *Scrapbook.*

17. *Frontier Justice* by Wayne Gard, Norman, Oklahoma, 1949, pp. 43-44; Hardin, pp. 81-82; *Scrapbook*, pp. 85-91; Hardin, pp. 76-77.
18. This is Hardin's version of the incident as incorporated in his petition to Governor Hogg for a pardon, Letters, January 1, 1894. Gard, pp. 227-228, Hardin, pp. 78-84.
19. In a letter to Jane, July 14, 1889, Hardin described Webb as a "would-be assassin who tried to hide himself behind the law to murder for filthy glory. This act of self-defense made me become an unwilling fugitive not from justice but injustice in the form of mob rule."
20. Letters, Hardin, to Jane, Decatur, Alabama, August 25, 1877.
21. Sievers describes the collection as being in three large boxes that also contain photographs of Hardin, his wife, and relatives. The photocopy of the collection covers ten volumes.
22. Letters. Hardin to Jane, August 7, 1877.
23. Ibid. Hardin to Jane, December 5, 1877.
24. Ibid. Hardin to Jane, May 18, 1877.
25. Ibid. Hardin to Jane, June 11, 1878.
26. Ibid. Hardin to Jane, December 28, 1878.
27. Ibid. Hardin to Jane, January 6, 1884.
28. Ibid. Hardin to McCulloch, August 26, 1885.
29. Ibid. Hardin to John Wesley Hardin, Jr., March 7, 1886.
30. Ibid. Hardin to Jane, November 2, 1890.
31. Ibid. Hardin to Molly, August 21, 1892.
32. Letters. The excerpt from Jane's last letter was quoted by Hardin in a letter to his cousin, Buck Cobb, November 6, 1892. Ironically this was the day Jane died.
33. Sievers quotes an editorial from *La Opinion del Pueblo*, October 13, 1894, which thanks Hardin for helping the Mexican-Americans of Gonzales.
34. Grimes in his calendar of Hardin's letters lists letters from Hardin's clients. Some gave him horses, wagons, and produce to pay for his legal services.
35. Ibid.
36. The *El Paso Daily Herald*, August 30, 1895, included an interview with Selman who told the reporter that Hardin met him in the Acme Saloon and called him a " 'cowardly --- of a -----.' I said, 'Hardin, there is no man on earth who can talk to me like that about my children without fighting, you ---.' Hardin said, 'I'll meet you smoking and make you pull like a wolf around the corner.' "

For all his self-proclaimed bravery, the autopsy showed that Selman shot Hardin in the back of the head while he was playing dice at the bar. Testimony of F. F. Patterson at the coroner's inquest confirmed this.

37. The *El Paso Times*, April 5, 1896. Scarborough claimed that Selman called him out into an alley adjacent to the saloon where they had been drinking. After a brief argument, Selman, as quoted by Scarborough, said: "I think I'm going to kill you." Scarborough then drew his six-shooter and fired. Not satisfied with the first shot, he sent two more into Selman's body as the dying man sagged to his knees.

KID CURRY AND THE LOGANS OF MONTANA

1. For years, fascinated by this chilling man and his brothers, I have sought out all the frontier newspaper references I could find, old ranchers who knew them, court documents, early magazine articles, etc. In my opinion Harvey Logan—Kid Curry—was the most dangerous man in America's Wild West. Harry Tracy, Ben Thompson and John Wesley Hardin, are in his company but they did not possess his complete indifference for death or violence. According to files of the National Criminal Identification Bureau (taken over by the Federal Bureau of Investigation), that mild-looking man with the melancholy dark eyes had the longest criminal record ever known in the United States (circa 1910). At the turn of the century one expert estimated it had cost the Union Pacific Railroad a million dollars in rewards, manpower, etc., to capture him. By 1900 the rewards for Curry, dead or alive, totaled forty thousand dollars.
2. Letter from an "Old Timer," who had read *Desperate Men* in 1949.

3. Given to me by Lowell Spence in 1948, shortly before he died in Chicago.
4. *Harlem* (Montana) *Enterprise*, June 5, 1900.
5. Montana News Association insert, Montana Historical Society.
6. An excellent account of Landusky and his fight with Harvey Logan is told by John Ritch in the *Great Falls* (Montana) *Tribune*, January 20, 1935. Ritch was in Landusky at the time and knew the Logans. Hereafter cited as Ritch.
7. Ritch. Charlie Siringo, the cowboy detective disclosed in his autobiography that Elfie Landusky had a son she named Harvey. In 1958 Elfie, better known as Elsie, returned to the Little Rockies for a brief visit. She was described as an alert white-haired lady of seventy-eight.
8. Ritch tells the story of how Landusky abused Harvey Logan as do several other frontiersmen in their memoirs.
9. Ibid.
10. *Fort Benton River Press*, February 3, 4, 5, 1896. Those who knew Johnny Curry have pictured him as a swaggering young bully, always eager to use his fists or a gun. There were times when his intended victims were not impressed with his gunfighter's role. On July 20, 1892, he "pummeled" a German prospector. The miner returned armed and they fought a duel with Winchesters. Curry's arm was shattered and he was taken to Fort Benton. The *Fort Benton River Press* reported the wounds were so severe his right arm was amputated. No other newspaper, particularly those who reported the Winters-Curry shooting, described Curry as having one arm.
11. Ritch.
12. *Harlem Enterprise*, January 17, 1900.
13. *Desperate Men*, New York (revised), 1960, pp. 208-209. Hereafter cited as *Men*. *The Outlaw Trail*, by Charles Kelly, New York (revised), 1959, p. 116. Hereafter cited as *Trail*.
14. Undated clipping, "Kid Curry Robs Train," an interview with Robert J. Harvey, "son of Squire Harvey of Concord," The James D. Horan Civil War and Western Americana Collection.
15. *Men*, p. 213; *Trail*, pp. 111, 120.
16. *Men*, pp. 294-296; *Trail*, pp. 282-286.
17. *Fort Benton River Press*, July 26, 27, 29, 30, 1901.
18. *Harlem Enterprise*, June 5, 1900.
19. Ibid.
20. Ibid.
21. *Harlem Enterprise*, March 4, 1900.
22. *Men*, pp. 259-262; *Harlem Enterprise*, January 17, 24, March 14, June 5, 1900; *Glendale* (Dawson County, Montana) *Review*, March 8, 1900.
23. Ibid.
24. Catherine Cross is a mystery figure in the story of Logan's period in Knoxville. She appears to have been a daily visitor to the jail—along with other women—but there are no newspaper photographs or physical description of her, unlike Annie Rogers and Fanny Porter whose pictures and background I have found. Considering the jail's incredible loose security, and her own "infatuation" with Kid Curry, she could have been his messenger or courier. Curiously, when she was murdered, although the police admitted she had been close to the outlaw, had been a frequent visitor, and had planned to leave the city with him, there was no further investigation of what role she could have played in the celebrated, bizarre escape. Despite the obvious official corruption, there was no federal grand jury probe, the government seemed content with suing the sheriff in civil court. Three years after Curry's escape, a "compromise" was agreed upon between Sheriff Fox's lawyers and the government representative in which Fox was to pay $3,000 and court costs!
25. The shooting of the two Knoxville policemen, the hunt for Logan, and his arrest are taken from the files of the *Knoxville Journal and Tribune* and the *Knoxville Sentinel*, December 14, 1901-January 15, 1902.
26. The *Knoxville Sentinel*, Monday, December 23, 1901, "Many Callers."
27. The *Knoxville Journal and Tribune*, November 1-30, 1902. The article, "Strong Chain of Evidence Forged Link By Link," in the November 20 issue is an excellent description of the government's case. See also "Guns and Gunmen" by Stacy W. Osgood in the *Westerner's Brand*

Book, Chicago Corral, March 1961; *Desperate Men* by James D. Horan (revised), New York, 1962, pp. 304-310; the *Chicago Sunday Chronicle*, "Bandit Is Convicted," November 30, 1902.

28. Copy of Logan's appeal in the United States Circuit Court of Appeals, "Harvey Logan alias—Harvey Curry, Kid Curry, Bob Jones, Tom Jones, Bob Nevilles, Robert Nelson, R. J. Whalen and Charles Johnson vs. the United States in Error." Docket No. 1187. The James D. Horan Civil War and Western American Collection.

29. The *Knoxville Sentinel*, Saturday, June 27, 1903. The *Sentinel*'s coverage of the escape was excellent. When Logan casually made his way out of the prison's exit and down the street on the sheriff's mare he waved to a little girl playing outside her house. Some years ago that little girl, as a grandmother, wrote to me, vividly recalling the moment when she exchanged waves with Logan.

In 1930, in a series of three articles on Kid Curry, W. P. Chandler, reporter for the *Knoxville Sentinel* who covered the outlaw in jail and when he was on trial, claimed the Kid described for him how the Wild Bunch riders had their famous picture taken in Fort Worth.

"We agreed to be mugged in our new clothes when we rented an apartment and were living in style. One day one of us saw a Pinkerton detective on the street and in thirty minutes the apartment was empty."

The Kid said the old Negro woman in charge of the apartment didn't know where they went "but found the picture for the Pinkerton men."

Chandler, who was a Knoxville city official at the time of the interview, said Kid Curry had given him the love letters written by Annie Rogers. However, he insisted the "ladies' man" of the Wild Bunch was Ben Kilpatrick, "the Tall Texan."

The Kid said he brought "Deaf Charley" Hanks into the Bunch, "because he was a good man to handle the outside of the train and was an expert pistol shot. "Hanks," he said, "came well recommended."

30. Tap Duncan's brothers were Richard, hanged at Eagle Pass, Texas, for the murder of a woman and her two children during a robbery, and Bygo, a rancher near Knickerbocker, Texas, San Saba County. Tap Duncan married a sister of "Black Jack" Ketchum, executed at Clayton, New Mexico, for the Colorado & Southern Railroad holdup. The Duncans lived about sixty-five miles from Sheffield, Pecos County, where the Kilpatricks had their ranch. Ben Kilpatrick was the "Tall Texan" of the Wild Bunch. Both the Kilpatrick and Duncan ranches were long known to railroad detectives as hideouts for the Wild Bunch riders. Shortly before the robbery George Kilpatrick and Jack Sheffield, a notorious Texas outlaw and rustler, joined a third man said to have been Harvey Logan. Riding good horses loaded down with provisions, "they left for a destination unknown," as one frontier newspaper put it.

I have the report of R. Brunazzi, special agent for the Rio Grande and Globe Express Company, who attended the removal of the body and autopsy. Brunazzi said Doctors Clark and McAllister insisted there was no wound scar on the left wrist. This was the pivotal identification point. The physicians also said in their report, quoted by Brunazzi, that the dead man had old buckshot wounds and a "peculiar" wound scar on the end of his nose. Later the sheriff of Brady, Texas, discussed the wound had been made by Deputy Sheriff Joe Arkey who had struck Duncan with his gun several years before. The buckshot wounds, the law officer declared, had been made when Duncan was shot from his horse during a running gun battle. However, the dead man had the same measurements and dark complexion as Logan. Lowell Spence agreed the right wrist scar was absent but pointed out the body was decomposed.

31. One fact bears out Spence; Logan was never seen again after the aborted train robbery and suicide.

At first Logan was believed to have been with Butch Cassidy, Harry Longbaugh, the "Sundance Kid," and Etta Place in the Argentine Republic. But Frank Dimaio, the detective who trailed the trio to Buenos Aires, told me that was impossible. In a series of interviews I had with Dimaio shortly after the end of World War II, he told me he had met with Dr. Newberry, a dentist in Buenos Aires and leader of the group of American businessmen in the city and the president of the London River Platte Bank in Buenos Aires where Cassidy and Longbaugh had deposited their money—all loot from the Union Pacific robberies. They identified only three bandits from the photographs. Dimaio showed them: Cassidy, the Sundance Kid, and Etta Place.

TOM HORN

1. The morning Horn was to be executed he said good-bye to his close friend, rancher John C. Coble. After they had shaken hands, Horn thrust a package into his hands and said: "You've been askin' for it, here it is."

The package contained Horn's autobiography, written in pencil. Hereafter cited as Horn. The book is surprisingly well written and presents a vivid account of his early life and the part he played in the Apache campaign. Horn, of course, was anything but candid about the role he played as a gun for hire for the cattle barons. The book ends with the capture of Geronimo. True to his code he took his secrets to the grave. See also *The Last of the Badmen* by Jay Monaghan, New York, 1946, an excellent Horn biography. Hereafter cited as Monoghan.

2. Horn, pp. 42-45.

3. Horn, pp. 218-231; Monaghan, pp. 90-91. The army never officially gave Horn credit due him. Some writers have insisted he only had a small role and some question if he had been really there. I have found in the *Journal of the U.S. Cavalry Association,* vol. V, December 1892, an article on Crawford's death by Lieutenant W. E. Shipp, Tenth Cavalry, who was an eyewitness. Shipp praises Horn for his bravery under fire, even when he received what Shipp described as "an ugly wound." First Lieutenant M. P. Maus, who received the congressional medal of honor for his bravery in the Apache campaign, later wrote in *Personal Recollections of General Miles,* p. 471: "I can not commend too highly Mr. Horn, my chief of scouts. His gallant services deserve a reward which he has never received."

4. Horn, pp. 259-263. *The Pinkertons: The Detective Dynasty that Made History* by James D. Horan, New York, 1967, pp. 380-383.

5. *The Outlaw Trail* (revised), by Charles Kelly, New York, 1959, pp. 224-233.

6. Monaghan, pp. 161-168.

7. *The Laramie Daily Boomerang,* July 12, 1900, has an account of the Rash killing.

8. "Sweetheart," *The Cincinnati Enquirer,* Sunday, November 1, 1903.

9. *The Cheyenne Daily Leader,* other Wyoming newspapers, and some in neighboring states published large sections of the daily testimony. *The Saga of Tom Horn* by Dean Krakel, Laramie, Wyoming, 1954, includes a great deal of testimony and appeals.

10. *Denver Post,* August 10, 1903.

11. Ibid., December 19, 1903.

12. "Horn Hangs on Time," *Chicago Record-Herald,* no date, but probably November 20, 21, or 22, 1903.

HARRY TRACY

1. The *Denver Post,* "Tracy Led the Hole-in-the-Wall Gang," June 10, 1902. *The Outlaw Trail,* by Charles Kelly, New York (revised), 1959, pp. 189-206. *Desperate Men* by James D. Horan, New York, 1949, pp. 260-269. Hereafter cited as *Men. Harry Tracy The Desperate Western Outlaw,* by W. N. Carter, Chicago, 1902. Hereafter cited as Carter.

Shortly after the end of World War II, I began to gather material in Washington and Oregon on the manhunt for Tracy. However, in the quarter of a century since *Desperate Men* appeared, many readers—a great many who have since died—sent me eyewitness accounts of Tracy and the hunt for him, photographs, copies of officials documents, etc. During this period I also collected a file of day-by-day newspaper accounts that begins when Tracy and Merrill broke out of prison, killed the guards, and vanished into the forest, and ends with interviews of the possemen who trapped the fugitive in the wheat field and later found his body. Included among my correspondents was Robert E. Eddy, member of the family on whose ranch Tracy made his last stand.

2. The *Denver Post,* March 11, 1898, The *Denver Evening News,* February 17, reportedly contained a vivid account of how "Harvey Ray" (Harvey Logan or Kid Curry) and the Wild Bunch riders made a wide sweep of all the cattle herds in their path, "driving everything before them into Hole-in-the-Wall," but the *News* was only printed November 23, 1926—November 5, 1928. The *Rocky Mountain News* of the same date has no such story, which has been picked up by many writers from Kelly's book.

3. "Tracy's Trail of Death and Crime in His Wild Flight," *Chicago Inter-Ocean,* July 10-11, 1903. The paper assigned a staff member to write an article on Tracy's background and life as an outlaw. The reporter traced the killer's beginnings to Boston where the police there told him they had been afraid to arrest Tracy, "singlehanded." After a senseless, vicious beating of a man and woman in a brothel, he fled West, killed Hoy, and eventually ended up in Portland.

See also *The Hunt for Harry Tracy* by James D. Horan, *True Magazine,* and *I Shot It Out with Harry Tracy* by former federal agent Maurice Smith as told to Hollis B. Fultz, *Frontpage,* April and May 1938; correspondence with the author and Stuart Whitehouse, Seattle, December 16, 1949.

4. The *Morning Oregonian,* June 10, 1902, "The Wake of Death," is an excellent account of the prison escape. It also contains a solid background article based on interviews with detectives Ford, Cordano, and Weiner, who had trailed and captured Tracy, then terrorizing the Northwest. Weiner told of the time when Tracy brought the Wild West into Portland by holding up a trolley car and robbing the passengers.

5. The *New York World,* July 27, 1902; Carter, pp. 68-74. My yellowing, brittle file of *World* clippings reveals the newspaper sent a special correspondent to the Northwest. The accurate stories are detailed and accompanied by woodcuts, halftones, and sketches. The general newspaper coverage of the manhunt was excellent, probably because the correspondents accompanied the posses instead of gathering their information from spurious handouts at some rear headquarters. One reporter was in a gun battle with the killer. Tracy complained of the newspapermen's energy. As he told one family (*New York World,* July 10): "Look out there! that's always the way it is—reporters with photographers a mile ahead of the posses! I'm fleeing from them—not the man hunters!"

6. Carter, p. 75.

7. Carter, pp. 111-124; *Men,* p. 263-265; the *Chicago Sunday Chronicle,* July 13, 1902; undated clipping, probably *Chicago Enquirer,* July 13, 1902. For the discovery of Merrill's body, see the *New York Herald,* July 16, 1902; *Chicago Tribune,* July 16, 1902.

8. Carter, pp. 119-123.

9. Ibid., pp. 142-158.

10. Ibid., pp. 176-195.

11. *Men,* pp. 302-303.

12. The *New York World,* undated, James D. Horan Civil War and Western Americana Collection.

13. Carter, pp. 255-279. Robert E. Eddy, to the author, January 12, 1960; Jack Level, to the author, December 1950. Mr. Level told of the frenzied scramble for "Tracy souvenirs" as the body was brought to Stone's Funeral Home in Davenport, Washington, by the posse. The *Inter-Ocean,* Friday morning, August 8, 1902, described how the crowd "ripped the clothes from the corpses . . . until nothing was left but the body itself . . . someone picked up the blood-stained handkerchief which Tracy used to try and keep from bleeding to death . . ."

Additional sources that may be consulted include: *Tacoma Evening News,* June 16, 1902, describing Tracy and Merrill's "Invasion" of Washington; a general article on the manhunt, *Seattle Post-Intelligencer, Northwest Today,* Sunday, January 23, 1972; an article on the discovery of a copy of Carter's book, still one of the most reliable sources on the manhunt, the *Seattle Times,* Sunday, May 31, 1970; "The End of Harry Tracy," a feature article, Wednesday, October 10, 1972, Wenatchee, Washington, *World;* "I Touched Harry Tracy's Corpse," by Charles M. Anderson, M.D., who recalled how the body of the outlaw was brought into Davenport, the *Pacific Northwesterner,* Fall 1973; *Illustrated History of the Big Bend Country,* 1904; *History of the City of Spokane and Spokane County,* vol. 1, and files of the *Spokane Review,* July to December 1902.

BIBLIOGRAPHY

ABBOTT, E. C., and SMITH, HELENE HUNTINGTON. *We Pointed Them North: Recollections of a Cow Puncher.* New York, 1939.
ADAMS, RAMON F. *Six-Guns and Saddle Leather.* Norman, Oklahoma, 1969.
AIKMAN, DUNCAN. *Calamity Jane and the Lady Wildcats.* New York, 1927.
APPLEMAN, ROY E. *Charles Siringo: Cowboy Detective.* Washington, D.C., 1968.
ARNOLD, OREN. *Thunder in the Southwest: Echoes from the Wild Frontier.* Norman, Oklahoma, 1937.
ATHEARN, ROBERT G. *William Tecumseh Sherman and the Settlement of the West.* Norman, Oklahoma, 1956.
BAKER, Pearl. *The Wild Bunch at Robber's Roost.* Los Angeles, California, 1965.
BENNETT, ESTELLINE. *Old Deadwood Days.* New York, 1928.
BIRNEY, HOFFMAN. *Vigilantes.* New York, 1929.
BOTKIN, B. A. (ed.) *Folk-Say: A Regional Miscellany.* Norman, Oklahoma, 1930.
———. *A Treasury of American Folklore.* New York, 1944.
———. *A Treasury of Western Folklore.* New York, 1944.
BOURKE, FRANCIS. *Great American Train Robberies.* New York, 1909.
BRADLEY, R. T. *Outlaw of the Border.* Cincinnati, Ohio, 1882.
BREAKENRIDGE, WILLIAM M. *Helldorado.* New York, Boston, 1928.
BRIGGS, HAROLD EDWARD. *Frontier of the Old Northwest.* New York, London, 1940.
BUEL, J. W. *The Border Outlaws.* Saint Louis, Missouri, 1881.
———. *Heroes of the Plains.* Saint Louis, Missouri, 1882.
———. (ed. by J. Brussel). *The True Story of Wild Bill Hickok.* New York, 1946.
BURCH, JOHN C. *Charles W. Quantrill.* Vega, Texas, 1923.

BURKE, MARTHA JANE (CANNARY). *Life and Adventures of Calamity Jane by Herself.* 1896.

BURKEY, REVEREND BLAINE. *Wild Bill Hickok, The Law in Hays City.* Hays, Kansas, 1973, 1975.

BURNS, WALTER NOBEL. *The Robin Hood of Eldorado.* New York, 1932.

———. *The Saga of Billy the Kid.* New York, 1926.

———. *Tombstone, An Illiad of the Southwest.* New York, 1927.

BURT, MAXWELL STRUTHERS, *Power River: Let'er Buck.* New York, Toronto, 1938.

Calamity Jane: White Horse Eagle Wir Indianer, as told to Edgar von Schmidt-Pauli, Verlag für Kultur-Politik. Berlin, 1927. (*We Indians,* translated from the German by Christopher Rede Turner. London, 1931.)

CAMPBELL, MALCOLM. *Malcolm Campbell, Sheriff.* Casper, Wyoming, 1932.

CARTER, H. N. *Harry Tracy: The Desperate Western Outlaw.* Chicago, 1902.

CASEY, ROBERT J. *The Black Hills and Their Incredible Characters.* New York, 1950.

———. *The Texas Border and Some Borderliners.* New York, 1950.

Cody, William F. *Life of the Honorable Frederick Cody, Known as Buffalo Bill, The Famous Hunter, Scout and Guide, an Autobiography.* Hartford, 1879.

COE, GEORGE W. (with Nan Hillary Harrison). *Frontier Fighter.* Albuquerque, 1934.

COLLIDGE, DANE. *Fighting Men of the West.* New York, 1932.

CONNELLEY, WILLIAM ELSEY. *Quantrill and the Border Wars.* Cedar Rapids, Iowa, 1909.

———. *Wild Bill and His Era.* New York, 1933.

COURSEY, OSCAR WILLIAM. *Beautiful Black Hills.* Mitchell, South Dakota, 1926.

CROY, HOMER. *He Hanged Them High.* New York, 1962.

CULLEY, JOHN HENRY. *Cattle, Horses and the Western Range.* Los Angeles, 1944.

CUNNINGHAM, EUGENE. *Triggernometry.* New York, 1934.

DAVIS, CLYDE BRIAN. *The Arkansas.* New York, 1940.

DOUGLAS, C. I. *Famous Texas Feuds.* Dallas, Texas, 1936.

DUFFUS, R. L. *The Sante Fe Trail.* New York, 1930.

DYKES, JEFF. *Billy the Kid: The Bibliography of a Legend.* Albuquerque, 1952.

EDWARDS, J. B. *Early Days in Abilene.* Abilene, 1940.

EISLE, WILBERT E. *Wild Bill Hickok.* Denver, 1931.

FARBER, JAMES. *Texas with Guns.* San Antonio, 1950.

FERGUSSON, ERNA. *Murder and Mystery in New Mexico.* Albuquerque, 1948.

FORREST, EARLE R. *Arizona's Dark and Bloody Ground.* Caldwell, Idaho, 1952.

FREEMAN, LEWIS RANSOME. *Down the Yellowstone.* New York, 1922.

FRENCH, WILLIAM JOHN. *Some Recollections of a Western Ranchman.* New Mexico, 1883-1890, London, 1927.

FULTON, MAURICE GARLAND (ed.). *Pat F. Garrett's Authentic Life of Billy the Kid.* New York, 1927.

GANZHORN, JACK. *I've Killed Men.* New York, 1959.

GARD, WAYNE. *The Chisholm Trail.* Norman, Oklahoma, 1954.

———. *Frontier Justice.* Norman, Oklahoma, 1949.

GARDNER, RAYMOND HATFIELD, with MONTOE, B. H. *The Old Wild West.* San Antonio, 1944.

GLASSCOCK, CARL BURGESS. *Bandits and the Southern Pacific.* New York, 1929.

GOODMAN, SERGEANT THOMAS (ed.). *Captain Harry A. Houston.* Des Moines, Iowa, 1868.

HALEY, J. EVETTS. *Charlie Goodnight: Cowman and Plainsman.* Norman, Oklahoma, 1949.

———. *Jeff Milton: Good Man with a Gun.* Norman, Oklahoma, 1948.

HANDRON, J. W. *The Story of Billy the Kid.* Sante Fe, New Mexico, 1948.

HARDIN, JOHN WESLEY. *The Life of John Wesley Hardin.* Seguin, Texas, 1896.

HARMAN, S. W. *Hell on the Border.* Fort Smith, Arkansas, 1898.

HARRINGTON, FRED HARVEY. *Hanging Judge.* Caldwell, Idaho, 1951.

HENDRICKS, GEORGE D. *The Last of the Bad Men of the West.* San Antonio, 1942.

HODGE, FREDERICK WEBB (ed.). *Handbook of the American Indians North of Mexico.* Washington, D. C., 1897.

HOLLOWAY, CARROLL C. *Texas Gun Lore.* San Antonio, 1951.

HORAN, JAMES D. *Desperate Men.* New York, 1949 (revised), 1961, 1974.

———. *Desperate Women.* New York, 1952.

———. *The Great American West.* New York, 1959 (revised), 1962.

———. *The Pictorial History of the Wild West* (with Paul Sann).New York, 1956.

———. *The Wild Bunch.* New York, 1958, 1970.
HORN, TOM. *Life of Tom Horn by Himself.* Denver, 1904.
HOUGH, EMERSON. *The Story of the Outlaw.* New York, 1907.
HUGHES, DAN LE LARA. *South from Tombstone.* New York, 1938.
HUNGERFORD, EDWARD. *Wells Fargo: Advancing the American Frontier.* New York, 1949.
HUNT, FRAZIER. *The Tragic Days of Billy the Kid.* New York, 1956.
JACKSON, JOSEPH HENRY. *Bad Company.* New York, 1939.
———. *Tintypes in Gold.* New York, 1939.
JENNEWEIN, LEONARD J. *Black Hills Book Trails.* Mitchell, South Dakota, 1962.
———. *Calamity Jane of the Western Trails.* Huron, South Dakota, 1953.
KELEHER, WILLIAM A. *Violence in Lincoln County, 1869-1881.* Albuquerque, 1957.
KELLY, CHARLES. *The Outlaw Trail.* New York, 1939, 1959.
KOOP, W. E. *Billy the Kid: Trail of a Legend.* Kansas City, 1965.
KRAKEL, DEAN. *The Saga of Tom Horn.* Laramie, Wyoming, 1954.
LANGFORD, N. P. *Vigilante Days and Ways* (2 vols.). New York and Saint Paul, 1893.
LEFORS, JOE. *Wyoming Peace Officer.* Laramie, Wyoming, 1953.
MCCOY, JOSEPH. *Historic Sketches of the Cattle Trade of the West and Southwest.* Kansas City, Missouri, 1874.
MCDANIEL, RUEL. *Vinegaroon.* Kingsport, Tennessee, 1939.
MCKEE, IRVING. *Ben Hur Wallace.* Berkeley, California, 1947.
MCNEAL, THOMAS ALLEN. *When Kansas Was Young.* New York, 1922.
MCREYNOLDS, ROBERT. *Thirty Years on the Frontier,* Colorado Springs, 1906.
METZ, LEON C. *Pat Garrett.* Norman Oklahoma, 1974.
MONAGHAN, JAY. *Civil War on the Western Border (1854-1865).* Boston, 1955.
———. *Last of the Bad Men.* Indianapolis, Indiana, 1946.
NOYES, ALVA JOSIAH. *In the Land of the Chinook.* Helena, Montana, 1917.
O'CONNOR, RICHARD. *Bat Masterson.* New York, 1957.
———. *Wild Bill Hickok.* New York, 1959.
O'NEIL, JAMES B. *They Die But Once.* New York, 1936.
OTERO, MIGUEL ANTONIO. *My Life on the Frontier* (2 vols). New York, 1935, Albuquerque, 1939.
———. *The Real Billy the Kid.* New York, 1936.
PANNELL, WALTER. *Civil War on The Range.* Los Angeles, 1943.
POE, JOHN W. *The Death of Billy the Kid.* Boston, 1933.
POE, SOPHIE A. *Buckboard Days.* Caldwell, Idaho, 1936.
RAINE, WILLIAM MACLEOD. *.45 Caliber Law, The Way of Life on the Frontier.* Evanston, Illinois, 1941.
———. *Guns of the Frontier.* Boston, 1940.
———, and WILL C. BARNES. *Cattle.* New York, 1930.
———. *Famous Sheriffs and Western Outlaws.* New York, 1939.
RAYMOND, DORA NEILL. *Captain Lee Hall of Texas.* Norman, Oklahoma, 1940.
RIDINGS, SAM P. *The Chisholm Trail.* Guthrie, Oklahoma, 1936.
RIPLEY, THOMAS. *They Die with Their Boots On.* New York, 1936.
RISTER, CARL COKE. *The Southeastern Frontier: 1865-1881.* Cleveland, 1926.
ROSA, JOSEPH G. *The Gunfighter: Man or Myth.* Norman, Oklahoma, 1969.
———. *They Called Him Wild Bill: The Life and Adventures of James Butler Hickok.* Norman, Oklahoma, 1964, 1974.
ROSE, VICTOR M. *The Texas Vendetta or the Sutton-Taylor Feud.* New York, 1880.
RUSSELL, DON. *The Lives and Legends of Buffalo Bill.* Norman, Oklahoma, 1960.
SABIN, EDWARD LEGRAND. *Wild Men of the West.* New York, 1929.
SANDOZ, MARI. *The Buffalo Hunters.* New York, 1954.
SANLAND, JOHN MILTON. *Life of Pat Garrett.* El Paso, Texas, 1908.
SHIRLEY, GLENN. *Toughest of Them All.* Albuquerque, 1953.
SIRINGO, CHARLES. *A Cowboy Detective.* Chicago, 1912.
———. *The History of Billy the Kid.* Sante Fe, 1920.
———. *A Lone Star Cowboy.* Sante Fe, New Mexico, 1919.
———. *Riata and Spurs.* Boston and New York, 1927.

SONNICHESEN, C. L. *I'll Die Before I Run.* New York, 1951.
SPRAGUE, MARSHALL. *Money Mountain. The Story of Cripple Creek Gold.* Boston, 1953.
SPRING, AGNES WRIGHT. *Cheyenne and Black Hills Stage and Express Routes.* Glendale, California, 1949.
———. *Colorado Charley: Wild Bill's Pard.* Boulder, Colorado, 1953.
STANLEY, F. (pseud. of Stanley Crocchiola). *Dave Rudabaugh: Border Ruffian.* Denver, 1961.
———. *Desperadoes of New Mexico.* Denver, 1953.
———. *Fort Union.* 1953.
———. *The Las Vegas Story (New Mexico).* Denver, 1951.
———. *Socorro: The Oasis.* Denver, 1950.
STECKMESSER, KENT LADD. *The Western Hero in History and Legend.* Norman, Oklahoma, 1965.
STREETER, FLOYD BENJAMIN. *Ben Thompson: Man with a Gun.* New York, 1957.
———. *Prairie Towns and Cowtowns.* Boston, 1936.
SULLIVAN, JOHN W. *Twelve Years in the Saddle for Law and Order on the Frontier of Texas.* Austin, Texas, 1909.
SUTTON, FRED ELLSWORTH (as written down by A. B. MacDonald). *Hands Up!* Indianapolis, Indiana, 1927.
TALLENT, ANNIE D. *The Black Hills: Or the Last Hunting Grounds of the Dakotahs.* Saint Louis, Missouri, 1899.
THORP, JACK (with Neil McCullough). *Partners of the Wind.* Caldwell, Idaho, 1945.
———. *Spirit Gun of the West: The Story of Doc W. F. Carver.* Glendale, California, 1957.
Tilghman, Zoe A. *Spotlight: Bat Masterson and Wyatt Earp as U.S. Deputy Marshals.* Oklahoma City, Oklahoma, 1960.
VESTAL, STANLEY. *The Old Sante Fe Trail.* New York, 1952.
———. *Queen of the Cowtowns: Dodge City, 1872-1880.* New York, 1952.
WALKER, TACETTA B. *Stories of Early Life in Wyoming.* Casper, Wyoming, 1936.
WALLACE, LEW. *An Autobiography.* (2 vols.) New York, 1906.
WALTON, WILLIAM H. *Life and Adventures of Ben Thompson.* Austin, Texas, 1884.
WARNER, MATT, as told to MURRAY EDWIN KIND. *The Last of the Bandit Riders.* Caldwell, Idaho, 1940.
WEBB, WALTER PRESCOTT. *The Great Frontier.* Boston, 1952.
———. *The Great Plains.* Boston, 1931.
———. *The Texas Rangers.* Boston, 1935.
WRIGHT, ROBERT MARR. *Dodge City: The Cowboy Capital.* Wichita, Kansas, 1913.

PERIODICALS

ADAMS, PAUL. "The Unsolved Murder of Ben Thompson." *The Southwestern Historical Quarterly,* XLVIII, January 1945.
AIKMAN, DUNCAN. "Deadwood, the Dreadful." *American Mercury,* November 1927.
BALL, EVE. "Billy Strikes the Pecos." *New Mexico Folklore Magazine,* 1949-1950, Albuquerque, New Mexico, 1950.
"Billy the Kid, Newly Found Documents in the Office of the Secretary of State, New Mexico, in Sante Fe, 1947." *New Mexico Historical Review,* vol. 23, 1948. (James H. Purdy, Historian, State Records Center and Archives, Sante Fe, informed me that when the department went into operation in 1960 staff members searched for these records but were unsuccessful. However, photostats of some were obtained from other sources.)
BLAZER, A. N. "Blazer's Mill." *New Mexico Magazine,* Sante Fe, New Mexico, January 1938.
BLEWITT, ANDREW. "Calamity Jane." *The English Westerners Brand Book,* vol. 2, no. 2 (January 1963).
BROOME, BERTAM. "The Kid's Tomorrow." *New Mexico Magazine,* Sante Fe, New Mexico, July 193-?.
"The Case of James Butler Hickok, alias 'Wild Bill.' " *Westerners Brand Book,* Chicago, vol. III, nos. 2-3, April-May 1946.
CHAPMAN, ARTHUR. "Getting the Drop and Living." *New York Herald Tribune Magazine,* January 3, 1932.

Connelley, William Elsey. "Wild Bill Hickok—James Butler Hickok: David McCanles at Rock Creek." *Kansas State Historical Collections*, XVII, 1926-1928.

Corle, Edwin. "Billy the Kid in Arizona." *Arizona Highways*, XXX, February 1954.

Cunningham, Eugene. "The Kid Still Rides." *New Mexico Magazine*, Sante Fe, New Mexico, March 1936.

Currie, Barton W. "American Bandits: Lone or Otherwise." *Harper's Weekly*, September 12, 1909.

Curtis, John B. "A Footnote to Frontier History." *New Mexico Magazine*, Sante Fe, New Mexico, XXVL, May 1953.

Cushman, George L. "Abilene, First of the Kansas Cowtowns." Kansas State Historical Society *Quarterly*, vol. LX, no. 3, August 1940.

Dick, Everett. "The Long Drive: The Origin of the Cow Country." *Collections of the Kansas State Historical Society*, 1926-1928, XVII.

Fitzpatrick, George. "Biscuits and an Obituary." *New Mexico Folklore Record*, 1949-1950, Albuquerque, New Mexico, 1950.

Fulton, Maurice. "Billy the Kid in Life and Books." *New Mexico Folklore Record*, Albuquerque, New Mexico, IV, 1949-1950.

Godbold, Mollie M. "Comanche and the Hardin Gang." *Southwestern Historical Quarterly*, July 1963.

Hansen, George W. "The True Story of Wild Bill-McCanles Affray in Jefferson County, Nebraska, July 12, 1861." *Nebraska History Magazine*, vol. 1, no. 2, April-June 1927.

Henshall, John A. "Tales of the Early California Bandits." *Overland Weekly*, second series, vol. 53, 1909.

Holbrook, Stuart. "Calamity Jane." *American Mercury*, vol. 64, February 1947.

Johnson, Dorothy. "Kid Curry, Durable Desperado." *Montana Magazine*, April 1952.

Keleher, William A. "In 'Re' Billy the Kid." *New Mexico Folklore Record*, 1949-1950, Albuquerque, New Mexico, 1950.

Lord, John. "Picturesque Road Agents of the Early Days." *Overland Monthly*, second series, vol. 70, November 1917, San Francisco.

Lundstrom, John B. "George Armstrong Custer: The Making of a Myth." *Lore*, Summer 1973, vol. 23, Milwaukee, Wisconsin.

McCarty, Lee. "Billy the Kid's Funeral." *True West*, November-December 1960.

Masterson, William Barclay. "Famous Gunfighters of the Western Frontier." *Human Life*, vol. 4, Boston, February 1907.

Michelson, Charles. "Stage Coach Robbers of the West." *Munsey's Magazine*, vol. 25, July 1901.

Montgomery, Mrs. Francis C. "Fort Wallace and Its Relation to the Frontier." *Collections of the Kansas State Historical Society*, 1926-1928, vols. X, XVII.

Nichols, Colonel George Ward. "Wild Bill." *Harper's New Monthly Magazine*, vol. XXXIV, no. CCI, February 1867.

Nolan, Frederick W. "A Sidelight on the Tunstall Murder." *New Mexico Magazine*, Sante Fe, New Mexico, July 1956.

Nolan, Warren, and White, Owen P. "The Bad Man from Missouri." *Colliers*, January 14, 1928.

Patterson, W. "Calamity Jane." *Wide World Magazine*, vol. II, August 1903.

Rasch, Philip, Jr. "The Twenty-One Men He Put Bullets Through." *New Mexico Folklore*, IX, Albuquerque, New Mexico, 1954.

———, and Mullin, R. N. "Dim Trails: The Pursuit of the McCarty Family." *New Mexico Folklore Record*, Albuquerque, New Mexico, 1954.

———. "Jesse James in New Mexico Folklore." *The New York Westerners Brand Book*, 1957.

———. "New Light on the Legend of Billy the Kid." *New Mexico Magazine*, Sante Fe, New Mexico, XXXL, May 1953.

Rice, Wallace. "Dedication of the Memorial to James Butler Hickok, Wild Bill." *Journal of the Illinois State Historical Society*, vol. 23, 1930.

Russell, C. M. "Some Incidents of Western Life." *Scribner's Magazine*, vol. XXXVII, no. 2, February 1902.

Ryder, David Warren. "Stage Coach Days." *Sunset*, vol. 59, San Francisco, September 1927.

SMITH, WILBUR. "The Amigo of Billy the Kid." *New Mexico Magazine*, April 1933, Sante Fe, New Mexico.

THOMPSON, GEORGE G. "Bat Masterson: The Dodge City Years." *Fort Hays Kansas State College Studies*, No. 6, Topeka, 1943.

TUNSTALL, JOHN H. "A Document of the Lincoln County War: John H. Tunstall's Letter to His Parents." Foreword by William A. Keleher. *New Mexico Folklore Record*, vol. X, 1955-1956, Albuquerque, New Mexico.

WHITE, ROSE P. "Full May A Flower—" *New Mexico Folklore Record*, 1949-1950, Albuquerque, New Mexico.

MANUSCRIPTS, JOURNALS, LETTERS, TAPE RECORDINGS, OFFICIAL DOCUMENTS

ANGEL, FRANK WARNER. Affidavits Collected as Special Agent of the Department of Justice, Department of Justice, File No. 4-8-3, Special Section: Final Report and Letters to Carl Schurz, Secretary of the Interior; Report and Extensive Exhibits, Interior Department, Appointment Papers, Territory of New Mexico.

ANTRIM, WILLIAM HENRY HARRISON. Pension Records and Affidavits, Military Service Records, National Archives.

BOLDS, GEORGE. (Taped) Reminiscences as a Frontier Deputy under Wyatt Earp, Bat Masterson, Bill Tilghman and Participant in the County Seat Wars of Kansas. Letters, newspaper clippings, etc. The James D. Horan Civil War and Western Americana Collection.

BONNEY, WILLIAM H. (Billy the Kid). Letters to His Excellency, General Lew Wallace, Governor of the Territory of New Mexico, Wallace Papers, Indiana Historical Society (William Henry Smith Memorial Library); Coroner's Inquest, Death Warrant for William H. Bonney, State Records Center and Archives, Sante Fe, New Mexico.

BRUNAZZI, R. Result of the Examination of the Body of Cowboy "Tap" Duncan Said to Be That of Harvey Logan. The James D. Horan Civil War and Western Americana Collection.

Captured Confederate Correspondence, Department of State Records, National Archives.

CATRON, THOMAS B. Papers of University of New Mexico Library, Albuquerque, New Mexico.

DUDLEY, NATHAN A. M., Lieutenant Colonel. Court of Inquiry, Old Army Records, National Archives.

EAST, CHARLES, Memoirs of Old Arizona. Arizona Historical Society, Tucson.

EDDY, ROBERT E. Reminiscences of the Hunt for Harry Tracy and Photographs. The James D. Horan Civil War and Western Americana Collection.

HARDIN, JOHN WESLEY. Chronological Calendar of the Letters in the John Wesley Hardin Collection in the Southwest Texas State University Library, San Marcos, Texas, by Boyd H. Grimes, December 7, 1971.

———. Letters of John Wesley Hardin Collection, Southwest Texas State University Library, San Marcos, Texas.

———. Selected Correspondence, from Capture to Parole, Thesis, presented to the Graduate Council of Southwest Texas State University in Partial Fulfillment of the Requirements for the Degree of Masters of Art, by James L. Sievers, New Braunfels, Texas, November 15, 1972.

HAYES, RUTHERFORD, President. Presidential Proclamation, October 7, 1879, Violence in New Mexico, Lincoln County. Diplomatic Branch, National Archives.

HICKOK, JAMES BUTLER (Wild Bill). The Complaint Warrant, Bond, Nine Subpoenas, Bill of Cost, Allowances of the Bill of Cost, The Commission Record No. 1 (all in connection with the killings at Rock Creek), Nebraska State Historical Society; Letters and Telegrams between Colonel Sydney Barnett and the Indian Department, National Archives; Wedding Certificate of Hickok and Agnes Lake Thatcher (copy), Connecticut State Library; Hickok's appointment as a scout, Department of Missouri, vol. 269, p. 254, Special Orders No. 89, District of Southwest, Missouri, 1864, National Archives.

HOLMES, H. A. Reminiscences of Ben Kilpatrick (The Tall Texan) and His Brothers. The James D. Horan Civil War and Western Americana Collection.

McCarty, Catherine (mother of Billy the Kid). Land Entry Records; Receiver's Certificate, Final Certificate, Applicant's Affidavit, Applicant's Proof-Statement (of William Henry Harrison Antrim), National Archives; Marriage Certificate, State Records Center and Archives, Santa Fe, New Mexico.

Maus, Lieutenant Marion. Report in Annual Report, Secretary of War, 1886.

Rice, Mike. Reminiscences of Early Tombstone. Arizona Historical Society.

Schurz, Carl. Secretary of the Interior, Letters of Library of Congress.

Siringo, Charles. Letters Relating to Billy the Kid, John Wesley Hardin and Other Gunfighters of the Wild West. The James D. Horan Civil War and Western Americana Collection.

Spence, Lowell. Hunting Harvey Logan. The James D. Horan Civil War and Western Americana Collection.

Thompson, Ben. Inventory of His Estate. Probate Division, Travis County, Texas.

Wallace, Lew. Collection, Indiana Historical Society Library, William Henry Smith Memorial.

Newspapers consulted are listed by name and date in the text and footnotes.

INDEX

Angel, Frank Warner, assigned by Secretary of the Interior Carl Schurz to investigate Tunstall murder and official corruption, 23; gets affidavits of A. McSween, Billy the Kid, John Middleton, Samuel Perry, John Wallace Olinger, 23-28; Antonio Martinez's charge, 40; Billy the Kid's description to Angel of Lincoln Battle, 44; sends "interrogatories" to Governor Axtell, 45; final report, 46; meets Rynerson in New York City, 47; description of reports, affidavits, etc., 287; hostile reception, 289
Antrim, William Henry Harrison, 10-14, 288
Appel, Dr. D. M., 38
Armstrong, Captain John, 173
Axtell, Samuel Beach, 23, 39, 41, 45-49

Baker, Frank, 39
Barnett, Colonel Sidney, 110-11, 293
Beckwith, Robert, 42
Bell, J. W., 70
Bennett, Jack, 257
Billy the Kid. *See* McCarty, Henry
Blazer's Mill, Battle of, 40
Bonney, William E. (Billy the Kid). *See* McCarty, Henry
Bothell, Battle of, 269
Bowdre, Charles, 40, 44, 80
Bowen, Brown, 173, 174, 176, 178
Bowen, Neal, 176, 178, 182
Brady, Sheriff William, 22, 24, 25, 39, 58
Brewer, Richard, 24, 28, 39, 289
Brink, J. W. (Dock), 82, 86-90
Brown, Hendry (Henry), 50
Buel, J. W., 84, 95, 292
Bullion, Laura, 205
Bull's Head Saloon, Abilene, 131, 132
Bushick, Frank H., 154

Cahill, F. P., 16, 17
Campbell, Bill, 52-53, 56, 58
Cassidy, Butch, 199, 203, 258, 299
Catron, Tom, 18, 21, 46, 47, 60
Chaffee, Captain Adam R., 222, 223
Chapman, Houston, 50, 52, 53, 56, 290
Chatterton, Governor Fenimore, 247
Chavez (Chaves), Martin, 41, 42
Chisum, John Simpson, 17, 24, 41, 288
Clark, Captain A. J., 265, 266, 267, 269
Clements, Gip, 165-67, 168, 169
Clements, Manning, 156, 158, 160, 165, 166, 167 168, 170, 171, 172, 178, 179, 184
Coble, John, 239, 240, 299-300
Cody, William F. (Buffalo Bill), 97, 110-11, 293
Coe, Frank, 18, 37, 38, 41, 288
Coe, George, 17, 288
Coe, Phil, 104, 129, 134, 135, 159, 167

Connelley, William Elsey, 85-86, 93, 291
Copeland, John, 41, 46
Cotton, Bud, 134, 135
Coy, Jacob S., 149, 150, 151, 154
Crawford, Captain Emmett, 223, 227, 228, 232
Cripple Creek, Colorado, 195, 202, 203
Crook, General George, 223
Cross, Catherine, 188, 205, 218, 298
Cudihee, Sheriff Edward, 285, 286
Currie, Flat Nose George, 195, 198, 199
Curry, Bob (Lee), 190, 195-96, 203
Custer, Mrs. Elizabeth R., 103
Custer, Brevet Major George A., 97, 102-3

Dart, Isham, 239
Davis, Governor Edmund J., 158, 169, 171, 296
Davis, Maud, 188, 203
Dawson, Charles, 85, 90-92, 292
Deane, Sheriff William, 198
Deluvina (Maxwell), 73, 80
de Tours, Emile, 124
Dixon, Simp, 158
Dixon, Tom, 158, 170, 171, 172, 173, 182
Dolan, Jimmy, 17, 18, 21, 22, 24, 25, 26, 27, 35, 37, 39, 41, 46, 50, 52, 53, 54, 58
Dudley, Colonel Nathan Augustus Monroe, 42, 43, 50, 52, 56, 58, 287, 289
Duncan, Tap, 218-20, 299

Ealy, Dr. Taylor E., 38, 44
Eddy brothers, 279-85
Evans, Jessie (Jesse), 18, 19, 22, 24, 25, 26, 27, 28, 35, 52, 56

Fisher, John King, 4, 148-51, 154
Forsyth, Colonel George A., 222
Free, Mickey, 222
Fritz, Colonel Emil, 18, 19, 21, 23, 25, 40

Garrett, Pat, 49, 59, 60-64, 66-70, 72, 74-80, 288
Gauss, Godfrey (George), 22, 36, 70, 72-73
Geronimo, 223, 229, 230, 232
Gerrells, Charles, 271-77
Gildea, Gus, 16, 17
Gill, A., 194, 199, 202
Girard, Frank, 261
Goldfinch, George, 279
Gordon, James, 82, 84, 88, 89, 90
Grant, Joe, 59
Greathouse, Jim, 59, 60-62, 64
Great Northern, Montana, Train Robbery, 199, 213

Hanks, Camilla (Deaf Charley), 199, 205
Hansen, George W., 86-92
Hardin, James C. (Preacher), 155, 157, 159
Hardin, Jane Bowen, 160, 169, 170, 174-83, 296, 297
Hardin, John Wesley, birth of, 155; early years, 156-57; kills Union patrol, 158; meets Ben Thompson, 159; courts Jane Bowen, 160; confrontation with Wild Bill Hickok, 160-69; marriage to Jane Bowen, 169; joins Sutton-Taylor feud, 170-71; kills Deputy Sheriff Charles Webb, 171-72; flees to Alabama, 173; letters to Jane, 174-83; refuses to save Brown Bowen, 178; leads prison escape, 178; death of Jane, 182; opens a law office and marries Callie Lewis, 184; killed by John Selman, 186; letter describing Webb shooting, 297
Hardin, John Wesley, Jr., 170, 179
Hardin, Joseph, 172, 173, 182
Hardin, Molly (Mollie), 170, 179, 180, 183, 295
Harris, Jack, 144
Harris, Jake, 191
Hayes, President Rutherford, 22, 47, 49, 51
Hickok, James Butler (Wild Bill), birth of, 81; dubbed "Duck Bill," 84; role in Rock Creek gunfight, 86-94; earns nickname, 96; Civil War service, 96; kills Dave Tutt, 97; serves under Custer, 97; interviewed by Henry M. Stanley, 99-101; fight in Chicago saloon, 101-2; sheriff of Hays City, 103-4; marshal of Abilene, 104; meets Agnes Lake Thatcher, 104-5; marksmanship, 108-9; takes part in Niagara "buffalo hunt," 110-11; advises editor he is not dead, 111-13; eyesight fades, 115; in Deadwood, 115-16; shot by Jack McCall, 117-18
Holtgrieve, Charles, 263
Horn, Tom, birth of, 222; meets Al Sieber and Mickey Free, 222; tells how Captain Crawford was killed, 227-33; tells how he captured "Peg Leg" Watson and Joe McCoy, 235-38; works as hired gun for cattle barons and meets John Coble, 239-40; meets Glendolene Kimmell, 240; kills Willie Nickell, 241; arrested by Joe LeFors 242; escapes from jail, 246; his cowboy friends "gather for business," 247-51; his execution, 252-54; bravery discussed, 300
Hoy, J. S., 258
Hoy, Valentine S., 257, 258

Johnson, Patrick Louis "Swede," 257, 258

Kane, Robert A., 108-9
Kilpatrick, Ben (the Tall Texan), 199, 205
Kimmell, Glendolene Myrtle, 240, 251
Kinney, John 41-44, 50

Landusky, Elfie (Elsie), 192
Landusky, Montana, 189, 191
Landusky, Powell (Pike), 191, 192, 194
Lant, Dave, 257, 258
Lee, Mrs. Hiram, 190, 202
LeFors, Joe, 241, 242
Leonard, Ira E. 50, 54, 56
Lincoln, Battle of, 41-44
Logan, Harvey (Kid Curry), Lowell Spence's description, 189-90; birth of, 190; early years in the Little Rockies country, 190-91; feud with Pike Landusky, 192; kills Landusky, 194; holds up Overland Flyer, 196-98; robs Butte County

bank, 198-99; holds up train at Wagner, Montana, 199; kills Jim Winters, 199-202; tours the South, 203; charms Catherine Cross, 205; shoots policemen in Knoxville, 208-9; becomes a celebrity in jail, 210-13; convicted of train robbery, 214-15; escapes from Knoxville jail, 215-17; killed by posse, 218; body identified as Harvey Logan, Kid Curry, 219-20; record of, 297; account of Landusky fight, 298; describes group Wild Bunch picture, 299
Logan, Johnny (Curry), 190, 194-95, 298
Logan, Lonny, 193, 194, 196, 202-3
Longbaugh, Harry (the Sundance Kid), 199, 203, 277, 299

McCall, Jack 116-22
McCanles, David 82, 87-95
McCanles, William Monroe, 82, 87-92
McCarty, Catherine, 10, 11, 12, 13, 14
McCarty, Henry (Billy the Kid), legends of, 10-11; birth of, 10; in Wichita, 12; in Silver City, 13; kills first man, 16; meets Coes, 17, 18, 19, 20; hired by Tunstall, 21; meets McSween, 21; defends Tunstall ranch, 22, 26; statement to Frank Warner Angel, 28-35; tells Coes of Tunstall's death, 37-38; ready to kill Riley, 38; held by Sheriff Brady, 39; ambushes Brady, 39; charged with killing Roberts, 40; takes part in the Battle of Lincoln, 41-44; gives Frank Warner Angel his affidavit, 45; learns of Wallace appointment, 49; meets Pat Garrett, 49; witnesses Chapman's murder, 52-53; letters to Wallace, meets Wallace, 54-56; escapes from jail, 56-57; testifies in Dudley inquiry, 58; kills Joe Grant, 59; denies to Wallace he is a horse thief, 61; captured at Stinking Springs, 62-64; *Las Vegas Gazette* interview 64-65; faces the mob, 67-68; escapes from Lincoln jail, 70-73; killed by Garrett, 74-79; buried at Fort Sumner, 87
McCloud, Jim, 246
McCoy, Joe, 237
McCulloch, Ben, 176, 179
McKinney, Thomas L. (Tip), 74
McSween, Alexander A., 19, 21, 22, 23, 24, 25, 26, 38, 40, 41-44
McSween, Susan, 43-44, 50
Mann, Carl, 120-21
Mann, Jim, 174
Marsh, "Dad," 191
Masterson, Bat, 123, 142
Mathews, Bill, 22, 26
Maximilian, Emperor (Ferdinand Maximilian Joseph), 125-28
Mejia, General Tomas, 125-28
Merrill, Dave, 258, 259, 262, 263, 266
Merrill, Rose, 259
Middleton, John, 29, 44, 50
Miles, General Nelson A., 233
Miller, Gus and Victor, 240
Milton, Jeff, 185, 186
Morton, Billy, 39
Murphy, L. G., 18, 21, 22, 23, 24, 25

Nana, 231
Neimann, Sheriff Charles, 258
Nichols, Colonel George Ward, 81-82, 92, 96, 291
Nickell, Kels P., 240, 241, 246, 248

O'Folliard, Tom, 41, 44, 50, 52, 56, 58, 59, 60-63, 288
Olinger, John Wallace, 37
Olinger, Robert (Bob), 70-73
Omohundro, John B. (Texas Jack), 110-11, 293

Patron, J. B., 24, 25
Peppin, Sheriff George, 40, 41-44, 50
Perry, Samuel R., 35-37
Pickett, Tom, 59, 60-64
Pinkertons, 202, 203, 219, 233, 237, 238
Place, Etta, 203, 277, 299
Plunkett, Sir Horace, 239
Poe, John, 74-80, 291
Porter, Fanny, 188, 210
Proctor, Richard, 248, 249, 250, 251
Purington, Colonel George A., 42

Riley, Jimmy, 18, 21, 24, 38, 46, 50
Roberts (Shotgun, Buckshot) Andrew L., 28, 40
Rock Creek Station, Battle of, 86-90
Rogers, Annie, 188, 203
Rudabaugh (Rudebaugh), Dave, 59, 60-66, 68
Rynerson, Colonel William L., 40, 46-47, 56-57, 58

Scarborough, U.S. Marshal George, 186, 297
Schefflin, Ed, 222
Schurz, Carl, 22, 45-49, 56
Scurlock, Josiah (Doc), 44, 58
Selman, John, 186, 297
Shields, D. P., 25, 26
Shull, Sarah, 85-86, 94
Sieber, Al, 222, 223, 233
Slaughter, Gabriel (Gabe), 171
Spence, Lowell, 189, 219
Stein, Nat C., 95
Strang, Willie, 257, 258
Sutton-Taylor feud, 170, 171

Teagarden, William, 180
Thatcher, Agnes Lake, 104-5, 115, 293
Thompson, Ben, birth of, 123; duel with Emile de Tours, 124; Civil War service, 124; with Maximilian, 125-29; in Abilene, 129-34; Battle of Ellsworth, 135-41; his role in the "railroad war," 141-42; Bat Masterson's opinion, 142; Thompson's interview with the *New York Sun*, 142; city marshal of Austin, 142-43; kills Jack Harris, 144; exploits in Austin, 145; death of, 148-51; estate of, 152-53; postmortem and funeral, 154
Thompson, Billy, 125, 129, 135-40, 143

Thornhill, Jim, 191, 194, 202
Tracy, Harry, fights off tristate posse, 256-57; escapes from Aspen, Colorado, jail, 258; meets David Merrill, 259; escapes from Oregon State Penitentiary, 259-60; crawls through posse lines at Gervais, 262; steals a rowboat, 263; sees photograph in a newspaper, 264; tours Puget Sound, 265-69; tells how he killed Merrill, 268; in Battle of Bothell, 269, 270; takes over Van Horn home, 270; meets Miss Baker, 271-77; his death on the Eddy Ranch, 279-85; burial, 285-86; early years, 300; fear of newspapermen, 301
Truesdell, Chauncey I., 13, 16
Tunstall, John, 18, 22, 23, 24, 25, 26, 28-37, 38, 39, 287
Tutt, Dave, 97

Upton, Marshal Ashmun (Ash), 10, 39, 287, 288

Van Horn, Mrs. R. H., 270

Waite, Fred, 27, 39, 40, 44, 50
Wallace, Lew, 47-49, 50-56, 58, 71, 289-91
Walton, William M., 125, 295
Watson, "Peg Leg," 237
Webb, Deputy Sheriff Charles, 171-72, 182, 297
Wellman, Horace, 82, 86-95
Whitney, Chauncey B., 135-40
Wilcox (Wyoming) robbery, 196, 199, 203
Wild Bunch, 199, 203, 258
Wilson, Billy, 59, 60-65
Wilson, J. B., 26, 39, 46
Wilstach, Frank J., 85, 294
Windenmann, Bob, 22, 28
Winters, James M., 194, 195, 199, 202
Woods, Thomas, 84, 86-90